Can Germany Be Saved?

Can Germany Be Saved?

The Malaise of the World's First Welfare State

Hans-Werner Sinn

The MIT Press
Cambridge, Massachusetts
London, England

For information on quantity discounts, email special_sales@mitpress.mit.edu.

Set in Syntax and Times Roman by SNP Best-set Typesetter Ltd., Hong Kong. Printed and bound in Spain.

Library of Congress Cataloging-in-Publication Data

Sinn, Hans-Werner.
[Ist Deutschland noch zu retten? English]
Can Germany be saved? : the malaise of the world's first welfare state / by Hans-Werner Sinn.
    p. cm.
"Contains extensive updates and added material"—Per publisher on electronic galley.
Includes bibliographical references.
ISBN 978-0-262-19558-4 (hardcover : alk. paper)
1. Germany—Economic conditions—1990– 2. Labor laws and legislation—Germany. 3. Labor market—Germany. 4. Foreign trade and employment—Germany. 5. Competition, Unfair—Germany. I. Title.
HC286.8.S56213   2007
330.943—dc22
                                                  2007000556

10 9 8 7 6 5 4 3 2 1

Physical Processing   Order Type: **NTAS**

Sel ID/Seq No:

151241

/169

540603

Cust/Add: **170280000/02**	**LSSC**	**SIERRA COLLEGE LIBRARY**

Cust PO No.   **07-08**   Cust Ord Date: **21-Apr-2008**

BBS Order No: **C922965**   Ln: **43**   Del: **1**   BBS Ord Date: **21-Apr-2008**

0262195585-28621135   Sales Qty: **1**   #Vols: **001**

(9780262195584)

<u>Can Germany be saved?</u>

Subtitle: **the malaise of the world's first welfare state**   Stmt of Resp: **Hans-Werner Sinn.**

HARDBACK   Pub Year: **2007**   Vol No.: _____   Edition:

Sinn, Hans-Werner.   Ser. Title:

MIT Press

Acc Mat:

Profiled   **PromptCat Barcode US   Mylar Dust Jacket (Clot**
Tech   **Barcode Label Applicati Spine Label Protector U;**
Services: **Barcode Label Protector Spine Label PromptCat**
             Base Charge Processing

Fund: Location:

Stock Category: Department:

Class #:   Cutter: Collection:

Order Line Notes:

Notes to Vendor:

Blackwell Book Services

for Gerlinde, Annette, Philipp, and Rüdiger

Contents

Preface

What ever happened to Germany? Europe's biggest and the world's third-biggest economy, the world's first welfare state, is in a state of despair. Dubbed an "economic miracle" after World War II, the country seems to have been abandoned by fortune and now seems to lack the wherewithal to encourage its return. From 1995 to 2005, Europe was the world's slowest-growing continent, and, next to Italy, Germany was the slowest-growing country in Europe. Once a locomotive, it was the laggard of the continent, if not of the world. In recent years, Germany has had the lowest net investment share of all developed countries next to Japan, bankruptcies have climbed to alarming records, capital has been fleeing to cheaper locations in Eastern Europe and Asia, the extent of unemployment has become ever more menacing, and yet the world's poor continue to arrive at its doorstep. Although Germany will remain Europe's biggest economy for many years to come due to its sheer population size, one European neighbor after another is overtaking Germany in per capita income. Germany has become the sick man of Europe, unable to keep abreast with Austria, Denmark, Ireland, Finland, Great Britain, or the Netherlands. The Wirtschaftswunder, the much-admired German economic miracle of the postwar period, seems to have moved on to other places. No miracle has been sighted in Germany for years now.

As the German economy threatens to erupt, the population continues to dance on the volcano. In tourism Germany remains the world champion, and its cruise ships plough the oceans more defiantly than ever. The pension system is defended, although not enough children are being born to finance it in the future and no real policy changes are being made to address this fact. The population is shrinking faster than that of any other developed country. Young couples have traded in baby carriages for second cars. Everyone wants to be in love and dreams of happiness, but there are no babies in these dreams. It is simply unquestionably accepted that pensions come from the government, just as electricity comes out of the wall socket.

Smart politicians know better than to awaken voters from their dream of a fairytale world provided for by an inexhaustible welfare state. Those who are stupid or honest enough to do so stand no chance of political survival. Gerhard Schröder, who took a step in this direction with his Agenda 2010, was immediately punished. He is no longer chairman of his party and no longer chancellor. With his Agenda 2010, Schröder made the first move away from expanding the welfare state further toward a more market-oriented approach since the 1950s, When they saw that more market orientation meant fewer transfer incomes, the Germans quickly lost their appetite for reforms. Many voters moved away from the Social Democrats to the Linkspartei (Left Party), a new party that includes the frustrated former finance minister Oskar Lafontaine and former communists from East Germany. And even the new chancellor, Angela Merkel, who nearly lost the election because her campaign program was too market-oriented, seems to have forgotten her goals. She quickly understood that success can be more easily claimed if a "rich people's tax" is introduced and if pensions and public health insurance are cross-financed with general taxes so as to please the median voter. Now that she is an elected official, not a candidate, she has become more timid, and there are no signs that she is planning to implement the kind of changes that Germany's current economic situation requires.

Of course, Germany's economic problems cannot be solely blamed on recent administrations. Previous administrations bear even greater responsibility for the current mess. The social-liberal coalition of the 1970s got the ball rolling by raising the public debt, and the government of Helmut Kohl mishandled the economic unification of the country with absurd promises and unrealistic policy programs. Present-day politicians are not to blame for the scale of the problem. However, they must be faulted for their abysmal failure to rectify past mistakes.

Germany needs a radical cultural and economic revolution—a revolution as courageous as the one that occurred in Great Britain under Margaret Thatcher, though not identical to it. After 50 years of progressive entanglement, Germany is ripe for this. Who knows, maybe Angela Merkel has a streak of Maggie in her.

Germany's institutions must be transformed, uncomfortable questions must be asked, and radical rethinking must start. Can the power of the unions continue to be tolerated? Why is the welfare state permitted to pay such generous benefits for idleness? How long can the languishing economy of Eastern Germany be endured, and at what stage will it be simply too expensive to finance a West German standard of living there? Can the ratio of debt to gross domestic product continue to rise? Must the government tax away two-thirds of even a low-earning worker's returns to additional effort? Why is Germany's population ageing so quickly, and can anything be done about this? Should the childless receive a full government pension? Are immigrants a burden, or a blessing? Are the Germans prepared for competition from Poles, Czechs, Slovaks, and Hungarians, whose countries joined the European Union in 2004? Where is the new Europe headed, and what tricks does the European Union have up its sleeve? These questions demand honest answers, and then Germany needs courageous economic and social reforms with which to buy back its future.

The necessary reforms will be painful, and it will take years before these produce any notable results. This explains why German politicians, forever with an eye on the next election, have balked at undertaking reforms with the requisite rigor.

If the pragmatism of politicians is lamentable, it is at least understandable. What is less comprehensible is the failure of many German intellectuals to recognize a B-grade movie when they see one. Preoccupied with the intricacies of Goethe, Kant, Grass, and Habermas, they neglect the most basic laws of economics. They rest their faith in the primacy of politics, behaving as if optimal economic conditions can be willed into existence, with or without the market.

Democracy in the television age eschews the deep debate of real issues for superficial discussions of flavors of the day. On talk shows, eloquence wins over expert knowledge, and he or she who masters the economics of sound bites wins the favor of acolytes and audiences alike. Serious analysis that gets to the bottom of problems does not see the light of day as stations vie for ratings. The country is on the brink of decline, and still nothing is more important than the outcome of a soccer game, an image of a stout Angela Merkel taking a bath in the sea, or the sex life of Boris Becker.

I never saw as many German flags in my life as during the World Cup soccer championship hosted by Germany in 2006, except in the summer of 1990, when Americans celebrated German unification even more enthusiastically than the West Germans did. While older Germans did not participate in the soccer jubilations of 2006, for the first time since World War II a generation of young Germans showed an innocent, unencumbered affection for national symbols, enthusiastically supporting their young and dynamic team. The nation is being reborn as a soccer team. As much as I endorse this shift in orientation, given Germany's problematic past, I wish that some of that enthusiasm and sense of coherence could also revitalize the German economy.

Unfortunately, as long as lobbies and political parties pursue their special interests, it will be impossible to find common ground. Unions and employers still fight over minuscule wage increases. The political mainstream is paralyzed by the rise of the Linkspartei. Each group balks at advancing radical market-oriented reform proposals for fear of being demonized by its political adversaries. The Social Democrats do not dare to continue Schröder's reform path, because they are afraid of losing voters to the new party. The Christian Democrats stay put, because they fear losing votes to the Social Democrats should they sympathize with Thatcherite ideas.

Time passes and no progress is made. Meanwhile, Germany's star continues to sink. The worldwide boom from which Germany is currently profiting gives the illusion that Germany's economy is afloat, but in fact the boom is merely extending Germany's tenuous paralysis as reforms are delayed even further.

Germany may still have a future as one of the world's top economic powers. But this will require a concerted effort to overhaul its welfare state and its economic system (that is, the laws and institutional rules that define the scope of the economic decisions made by firms and private households). The reforms debated in Germany these days are not nearly enough. Nothing short of a new order, in which old taboos are discarded and powerful interest groups are shown the door, will suffice. It is possible that this reconstruction will not occur until Eastern Germany's economy has fallen apart altogether. But there is no time. If Germany wants to secure its economic future, it has to act now. The figures and facts are on the table. All that remains is to do something to set them right.

This is an abbreviated and edited English version of the eleventh edition of my book *Ist Deutschland noch zu retten?* My intent in the German edition was to help stimulate a discussion among the broader German public of the economic issues facing their country.

Sadly, however, Germany's problems are not unique: They are characteristic, albeit on a lower scale, of many other European Union countries. In dealing with its pension system, Germany faces demographic and economic problems that Spain, Italy, and the Netherlands will also be confronting in the coming decades. In fact, the whole Western world, including the United States and Japan, faces similar problems. And the labor-market problems resulting from the increasing difficulties of the welfare state to cope with international low-wage competition by the formerly communist countries are not limited to Germany either. France, in particular, exhibits many of Germany's symptoms and threatens to be the next to succumb to the disease that I describe in this book. The French riots of 2005 and the mass demonstrations against a minimal adjustment of labor-tenure clauses show how badly distorted the French labor market is and how little the French public understands how the market economy works.

In this English-language edition, it is my hope that studying the German example will also lend insight into the problems facing these other countries, particularly those in Europe. The European welfare state was built after the German model that Chancellor Bismarck introduced in the 1880s. It has come under threat and needs to be overhauled to be able to cope with the forces of globalization and demographic change. Using the German example, I try in this book to explain how this could be reasonably done while respecting Europe's social values and preferences. Whether German politics will follow my recommendations remains to be seen. In any case, some solutions will have to be found, for the historical end of the traditional European welfare state has come, and once again the German solutions may define the direction in which the whole continent will have to move.

My objective in this book is to inform the reader about the state of the German economy, about how a well-functioning market economy operates, and about obvious defects of a welfare state of the German type. But I will try to avoid making prophecies. I am neither a guru nor an evangelist. I am an economist and, as such, I can only describe institutional conditions that, on the basis of past experience and the insights from economic theory, would generate a healthier economy. I do not want to take my readers to a new dream world; I want to wake them up to reality. Successful policy decisions require facts and sound economic explanations. I want the economic arguments to be heard, and I hope that hearing them will enable the reader to separate the wheat from the chaff in the public debate. Only broad public support for tough economic reform will derail the demagogues and the dreamers who now monopolize public discussions. I want a better Europe for my three children—a continent that will give them a future.

I revised the book in Wassenaar, where the polder model, which paved the way for a recovery of the economy of the Netherlands, was initiated in 1982. The Netherlands Institute for Advanced Studies (NIAS), where I am kindly hosted, provides the right *spiritus loci*. Final revisions were made in Munich and in Italy after the annual CESifo Summer Institute in Venice, whose proud republic fell into an irreversible decline.

Acknowledgments

This book is the result of many years of intensive examination of a complex economic reality. I want to thank all those with whom I was able to discuss the topics addressed in this book. I am especially indebted to my colleagues in the Scientific Advisory Council at the Ministry of Economics, to the members of the German Council of Economic Experts, to the members of the European Economic Advisory Group at CESifo, and to the staff and my colleagues at the Ifo Institute for Economic Research and the University of Munich.

I remember warmly the lively discussions with the audiences at my public and university presentations and with the participants of many public panel discussions, including a sizable number of debates broadcast on German TV. The TV debates and my newspaper articles induced hundreds of people to write me letters and emails, all of which I tried to answer. This exchange sharpened my eyes for signs of where non-economists had difficulty understanding my arguments, and it pointed me toward problems that I had previously neglected. Over the years, the public debates in which I was involved (some of which I had initiated) have helped me to better understand the problems about which I was writing, and occasionally to develop new ideas about essential economic mechanisms that had been overlooked in the literature. Communicating with the public is a true challenge for an economist who comes from the ivory tower and who usually develops his ideas with mathematical tools, addressing his colleagues who also dwell in that tower. I beg my scientific colleagues to forgive the style made necessary by the attempt to reach the public, and I hope that they will nevertheless accept this book as a serious attempt to contribute to economic history and scholarly policy debate.

For concrete assistance on this book I am especially indebted to Robert Koll, who organized the gathering of data and was my sparring partner in all questions of content; to Martin Werding, who contributed a lot of information on the welfare system; to Meinhard Knoche and Wernhard Möschel, who explained the legal details of the Industrial Constitution Law and Collective

Bargaining Law; to Peter Sörensen, who informed me about the Danish reforms; to Reinhard Hild, from whom I learned about the outsourcing and offshoring trends; to Sascha Becker and Peter Jäckel, who initiated me into the secrets of German direct investment statistics; to Gebhard Flaig, who constructed a forecast of long-term economic growth and unemployment; to Rüdiger Parsche, who advised me on matters of taxation; to Uwe Christian Täger and the late Rainer Fehn, who briefed me on the exodus of small and medium-size firms; to Wolfgang Ochel and Frank Westermann, with whom I discussed questions of the European social union and the East German states; and to Ludger Wößmann, who explained the details of the PISA study to me. I thank Herbert Hofmann, Robert Fenge, Wolfgang Nierhaus, and Volker Rußig for answering various special questions, and I thank a large number of people in various public offices and institutes who provided statistical information. I accepted much, though not all, of the advice I was given. I alone am responsible for any remaining errors.

Important support in all technical aspects was given by Elsita Walter, who created all the graphs, and by Wolfgang Meister, who procured the latest data. Barbara Hebele helped in various stages, including proofreading.

This book is based on Heidi Sherman's translation of an early edition of my German book *Ist Deutschland noch zu retten?* (Econ, 2003). She did a very good job. However, the book is not a straight translation. After the initial translation it underwent a long evolution, and it now differs from the original book in many places. The time elapsed made it necessary to update the figures and react to political debates, and the international nature of the English-language version's audience required me to provide more background information in some places and less detail in others. In the meantime, I also learned about new facts and thought up new arguments.

I thank Heidi Sherman, Raji Jayaraman, and Julio Saavedra for careful editing jobs. I am grateful to Elizabeth Murry, then at The MIT Press, for reading the whole book and making many suggestions for improving its style and content. The questions she asked forced me to once again revise a manuscript that had already undergone nine revisions for eleven German-language editions plus a substantial revision on the occasion of preparing the English-language version. I also thank Paul Bethge for carefully editing the final manuscript and for making further useful suggestions.

I am grateful to the Netherlands Institute of Advanced Studies in Wassenaar, where I wrote the English-language version in April, May, and June of 2006, for providing the hospitality and quiet atmosphere that I needed to work undisturbed.

I dedicate this book to my family—in particular, my grandchildren and great-grandchildren, should I be blessed to have them.

Can Germany Be Saved?

1 The First Shall Be Last

From the Land of the Economic Miracle to the Sick Man of Europe

After World War II, Germans enjoyed a number of remarkable achievements. Two lost world wars had failed to kill their dynamism. Cities were rebuilt from beds of rubble left in the wake of firebombs, and with much vigor a re-industrialization of the country was pushed forward. Eventually, a solid democracy with a rich economy that now is the biggest pillar of the European Union was created.

The task was particularly difficult, as Germany was divided after the war. About one-third of its territory was given to Poland, and 11 million ethnic Germans were expelled to the West. The remainder of the territory stayed German, but was divided into West and East Germany. A few years later, West Germany became the Bundesrepublik Deutschland (Federal Republic of Germany, here abbreviated FRG) and East Germany became the Deutsche Demokratische Republik (German Democratic Republic, here abbreviated GDR). One-fifth of the population stayed in the East and came under communist rule, while four-fifths lived in the West and were able to enjoy the benefits of a free-market economy. Berlin, the former capital, was divided too, with West Berlin remaining an allied enclave until reunification in 1990.

The eastern part of Germany never really prospered under communist rule, and it has continued to face severe economic problems, even after reunification. But West Germany flourished, establishing a strong export industry and raising the living standard of the masses. The combination of high-level engineering and (in the early years) low wages made West Germany a serious contender on world markets and a great beneficiary of globalization.

At the same time, well-oiled public institutions combined with an excellent legal system provided the framework within which the young West German population was able to effectively channel its energy. The Allies' bombing raids in response to Hitler's aggression destroyed nearly all of Germany's cities (not just Dresden), killing a sizeable fraction of the civilian population and shattering most of the country's cultural treasures. Yet the war did not wipe out knowledge in the minds of survivors. Germans knew the rules of the market economy—the written and unwritten laws of productive cooperation in a specialized economy that, in the mysterious ways of the invisible hand, make sure that millions of people interact sensibly. And they obeyed these rules with great discipline.

In the direct aftermath of World War II, many Germans flirted with social- ist ideas. Even the early economic and political program of the Christian Democrats (Ahlen 1974) showed a significant socialist influence. But when Ludwig Erhard (Germany's first postwar economics minister) and his "Administration for Business" succeeded in pointing the way, and when the end of rationing soon showed results, there was no holding back. The economic miracle had begun that would define West Germany for much of the second half of the twentieth century.

The West German economy grew by leaps and bounds, and before long there were jobs for everyone. From 1950 to 1960 real gross national income (GNI) increased by 114 percent, and in the following decade it grew by a further 54 percent.[1] In the 1960s the two parts of Germany had almost no unemployment, and in 1970 about 150,000 people were jobless—less than one-thirtieth the present number. West Germany enjoyed an economic boom that hardly anybody had deemed possible at the end of World War II, and for which it was both envied and admired.

Of course, West Germany actually rose from the ashes. East Germany sang of resurrection in its national anthem, but in practice resurrection remained elusive. The communist government failed to unleash the country's produc- tive forces and came nowhere near providing its citizens a standard of living comparable to that enjoyed by their former compatriots. In the early 1970s, East German cities were still full of rubble, and food packages from West German relatives remained in high demand to supplement the meager social- ist menu. The only things the GDR really excelled in were doctoring produc- tion and erecting billboards to hide the ruins. Eventually even the "heroes of labor" had enough of this nonsense and demanded the West German standard of living, which they saw on television every day. In November 1989, they remembered Ronald Reagan's advice to Mikhail Gorbachev and tore that wall down.

The seeds of a long recession that has yet to be resolved, however, were being planted even as the West German economic boom reached its peak in the early 1970s, before the first oil crisis. It was during this period that people really began to squabble over the spoils of the postwar economic boom and the Social Democrats wanted to "crash test" the economy by increasing the tax burden to finance their social dreams. At the time of the social-liberal coalition under chancellors Willy Brandt and Helmut Schmidt, which lasted from 1969 to 1982, the welfare state was significantly extended in order to let everyone share in the fruits of a still-prosperous economy. Unemployment compensation and social assistance were raised, working time was reduced, and early-retirement options were created. The education system was expanded, the average age of entry into the labor force was increased, university fees were abolished, and a generous student stipend system was introduced. Municipalities received voluminous federal grants to expand the consumptive infrastructure including the building of public swimming pools, sports facilities, and conference halls. The pension insurance system was expanded by granting pension eligibility to the self-employed in exchange for almost purely symbolic contributions on their parts, and so on. Under the social-liberal coalition, the ratio of government spending to GDP, which had stood at 39 percent in 1970, rose to nearly 50 percent by 1980. (See chapter 6.) The subsequent government of Christian Democrat Helmut Kohl, which took office in 1982, made some attempts to limit government spending. However, in order to win the elections it also had to bow to the social-democratic mood of the time and allowed its agile labor minister, Norbert Blüm, to further expand the early-retirement options. It was not until German reunification that West Germany policy of social democracy ended because then the available funds were needed for the East Germans, who also wanted to partake of the West German welfare state's benefits.

Parallel to the social expansion, wage rates rose. Encouraged by the economy's stellar performance, the unions kept raising their wage demands. Each year witnessed large wage increases, and firms' wage costs climbed faster than their competitors' wage costs in most other industrialized countries. Thus, the real hourly wages of manufacturing sector employees increased by 60 percent from 1970 to 1980 and by another 35 percent from 1980 to 2000.[2] Real hourly wages rose by 117 percent from 1970 to 2000. Wages at the lower end of the salary scale rose even more than the average, because unions tried to gradually level wages by their policy of lump sum instead of proportional wage increases. As a result, West Germany had the highest hourly wage costs of manufacturing workers in the whole world for 20 years, from the early 1980s to the beginning of this decade.

The explosion of wage costs inevitably undermined the international competitiveness of German manufacturing workers. Faced with new low-wage competitors from within and outside Europe, labor-intensive German firms found it doubly hard to keep up. It was a strange role reversal for German companies which had thrived on their low-wage advantage in the 1950s. While most of the exposure to the new competitive forces resulted from exogenous developments ranging from the rise of Japan and the participation of Asian Tigers (including Indonesia, Singapore, and Thailand) to the fall of the Iron Curtain, some competition has been self-imposed. Since the European Union (EU) created an integrated market for goods and services, Germany has lost its former advantage of having a larger domestic consumer market than most of its competitors. With the advent of the euro (1999–2002), which extended the German monetary system to the entire eurozone, German firms also lost their advantage of having lower capital costs. And since the EU's "eastern enlargement" of 2004, German firms have been facing low-wage competition from eastern EU countries where wages are as low as one-eighth the West German level. As a consequence, Germany's attractiveness as an investment location has deteriorated dramatically, and investors have been looking for profits elsewhere in the world.

West Germany's share of net domestic product (NDP) used for private investment averaged 18.8 percent in the 1960s. Although lower in the following two decades, it still amounted to 12.9 percent on average in the 1970s and 7.9 percent in the 1980s. Even in unified Germany it averaged 8.7 percent in the 1990s. In the period 2001–2005, however, it averaged a paltry 2.8 percent.[3] As figure 1.1 reveals, in 2005 the net investment share of NDP— 2.69 percent—was the second-lowest among all OECD countries, next to Japan (which faces similar difficulties).

In 2005, German savings aggregated over all sectors amounted to 145 billion euros (180 billion dollars), but of this amount only 50 billion euros were invested at home.[4] The lion's share of savings—95 billion euros (118 billion dollars) was invested abroad. Thus, in net terms, Germans invested nearly twice as much abroad as at home—mostly in the form of portfolio investment, but also as direct investment. This is hardly paralleled in other Western countries. Weighted by the respective ownership shares, by 2004 Germany's foreign direct investment had created about 4.6 million jobs abroad, of which about 675,000 were located in the new eastern EU countries.[5] The jobs created abroad by financial capital exports certainly have a much higher dimension, but no statistics are available that would allow assessment of that number. The rapid growth of international outsourcing and off-

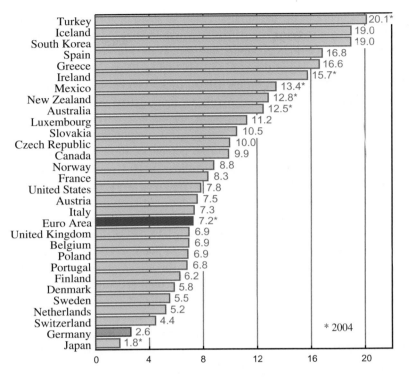

Figure 1.1
Net investment share (percent) in net domestic product, 2005. Sources: OECD database, National Accounts, volume I, main aggregates, 2006, release 03; Ifo Institute calculations.

shoring activities has kept Germany's manufacturers on track. Germany itself, however, is no longer the place where businessmen believe they will be able to make money by investing money and creating new jobs.

The extremely fast increase of manufacturing wages that began in the 1970s and continued in the 1980s caused firms to look for escape routes. German companies evaded high labor costs not only by investing abroad, but also by leaving the economy's labor-intensive sectors and by resorting to a wide range of labor-saving strategies, including mechanized production and the use of industrial robots. Only some of the dismissed workers have been able to find jobs in the rapidly expanding export sectors. An increasing fraction of the workers who lost their jobs have stayed unemployed. Although these structural changes have raised firm productivity and made Germany the world's second-largest exporter, these adjustments have lowered the economy's aggregate productivity as the unemployed have a productivity of zero.

As a consequence of the declining investment share in net national product and excessive flight reactions, there has been a dramatic slowdown of growth. Whereas the West German economy had grown by 114 percent in the first decade after the founding of the FRG in 1949 and by 54 percent in the second decade, it grew by 31 percent in the 1970s, by 23 percent in the 1980s, and by only 17 percent in the 1990s.[6] While to some extent this was a natural outcome for the end of a catch-up period, the adverse developments of the labor market show that it also had a pathological component.

From 150,000 unemployed in 1970 (0.6 percent of the labor force), West German unemployment increased to 3.4 million or 10.1 percent by 2005, to which another 1.4 million East German unemployed workers must be added for a total of 4.8 million unemployed. This does not even include the hidden unemployed who, by way of early-retirement and partial-retirement schemes, training, job-creation measures. and similar tricks, were removed from the unemployment statistics but account for at least another 1.2 million people.[7] Neither does it include the silent reserve of discouraged potential employees who have given up searching for a job, which could account for another 0.7 million.[8] The overall number of German unemployed is about 6.7 million. While the official German unemployment rate was 11.7 percent in 2005, the effective rate corresponding to the 6.7 million unemployed was 16.1 percent. The cost of open and hidden unemployment has gone out of bounds in Germany. In 2005, the overall cost was a good 100 billion euros or 125 billion dollars a year, not counting the huge administrative costs entailed in delivering unemployment benefits.[9]

Figure 1.2 shows that Germany is one of the few countries without a "natural" rate of unemployment, to use a theoretical economic term that indicates a stable rate of unemployment resulting from the usual frictions in the labor market. Since 1970, unemployment in West Germany has increased along a nearly linear trend with ten-year cycles. Over one five-year period unemployment increases and over the next five years it declines, but it never declines as much as its previous increase. Whenever the unemployment rate declines, the ruling coalition invariably congratulates itself on having brought about a trend reversal. The celebrations are always misplaced. On the last such occasion, the Schröder administration took credit for an economic recovery that had already started well before the 1998 election which had propelled them to power.

Today, Germany finds itself in the middle of its fourth decade of cyclical unemployment growth. The first cycle lasted from 1970 to 1980, the second from 1980 to 1991, and the third from 1991 to 2001. Unemployment increased until 2005 but now may decline over the next few years thanks to the

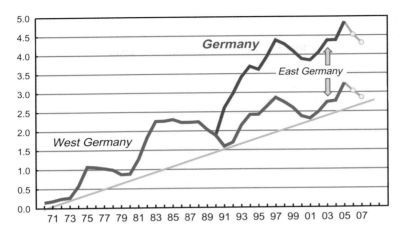

Figure 1.2
Unemployment (millions) in West Germany (including West Berlin) and East Germany (including East Berlin), 1970–2007. Sources: Bundesagentur für Arbeit; from 2001 regional differentiation of Berlin; IFO Institute calculations; 2006 and 2007 forecast of Institutes, Joint Analysis, autumn 2006.

worldwide economic upturn.[10] Unfortunately, however, there are no signs yet of a lasting trend reversal, because the blend of internal institutional problems and international low-wage competition that gives rise to Germany's structural problems is unlikely to change in the foreseeable future. When the current decade is over, the next wave of rising unemployment may begin.

However, the increasing unemployment trend, which has lasted for 35 years, cannot continue any longer. It seems very unlikely that the FRG could survive it for a further 35 years. Unemployment would then be as high as in the early 1930s, a situation that had, as is well known, devastating political consequences. Thus the trend will have to be broken by courageous reforms of the kind that will be discussed in this book.

Germany's labor-market problems were aggravated by the reunification process, which was not as smooth as politicians had predicted. Neither the often-proclaimed self-sustained upswing nor the blooming meadows that Helmut Kohl said would spring up after "three, four, five years" have materialized. Since the expiration of the Regional Development Law (Fördergebietsgesetz), which had initially caused a short-lived boom due to enormous government subsidies, the gap between East and West Germany's economic performance has widened every year. East German industry has yet to recover from a privatization process that managed to destroy three-fourths of all manufacturing jobs. In East Germany the share of privately employed wage and salary earners who work in the manufacturing sector is only about two-thirds that of West Germany, a divergence similar to that between the chronically sick Italian Mezzogiorno (the southern part of the country) and the rest of Italy (including the industrial economy centered in the north).[11] Although relative to the West an excessively large share of East German wage and salary earners are government employees, this region's employment declined from 9.8 million before the fall of the Berlin Wall to 6.1 million in 2005.

The East German economy has been financially dependent on West Germany since reunification, and it will not be able to stand alone in the foreseeable future. One-third of the euros that are being spent in East Germany on goods and services were not earned there but were provided by others as loans or gifts, primarily in the form of social transfers financed out of West German taxes and social security contributions. There probably has never been so large a region or country as dependent, in relative terms, on external support. The growing interest-payment burden borne by the German state is due in large part to the additional debt incurred to compensate for the largely avoidable mistakes committed during the reunification process. National and international firms that invest their funds in Germany know that they will be asked one day to help finance the unresolved problems of German reunification, which is one of the reasons why Germany's investment rate is so low.

Germany was once Europe's growth engine, but since the mid 1990s it has brought up the rear on the European growth train. As figure 1.3 shows, while the German economy expanded by 14.5 percent in the period 1995–2005, the total output of the EU-15 (that is, the pre-enlargement EU countries) output rose by 24.2 percent. Indeed, Germany competes with Italy for the questionable title of having had the lowest growth rate of all EU countries during that period, be these located in Eastern or Western Europe.[12] Even outside the EU, there are no countries in Western Europe that grew more slowly. Germany and Italy are the sick men of Europe.

The Rise, Decline, and Resurrection of Britain: Lessons for Germany

The economic growth of countries moves in cycles. Nations take turns being on top, but it can take generations to go from one state of affairs to another. There are very short business cycles that change the degree of capacity utilization in about a two-year rhythm, and there are cycles with ten-year intervals like those shown in figure 1.1. The truly long structural cycles that take place over several decades are, however, the most important; it is these longer periods that change the relative economic position of individuals countries in a lasting and meaningful way. Germany and Britain are excellent examples of these historical ups and downs.

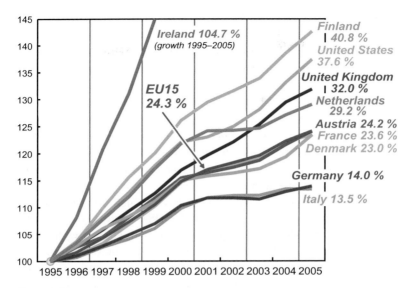

Figure 1.3
Gross domestic product in selected countries in 1995 prices (1995 = 100). Sources: Eurostat; U.S. Bureau of Economic Analysis; Ifo Institute calculations, November 2006.

The first half of the nineteenth century belonged to Britain, where the industrial revolution began. Then Germany caught up. After its victory over France in 1871, Prussia reestablished the German empire, which (as the "Holy Roman Empire of German Nation") had been destroyed by Napoleon in 1806, in a reduced form without Austria, and prepared the ground for unparalleled economic and scientific prosperity.[13] Germany became a tough competitor to the British industry and enjoyed much more rapid growth in industrial production than Britain did. However, it never did quite catch up. In 1870, Germany's national income per capita had stood at 57 percent of that of the United Kingdom (which at that time included Ireland), and by 1914 it had risen to almost 80 percent.[14] As Germany's population was 44 percent larger than Britain's, this of course did not mean that the German economy was smaller.[15] In fact, the data cited imply that aggregate national income was 14 percent higher in Germany than in Britain.

After its defeat in World War I, Germany had a hard time recovering under the Weimar government. In 1938, German per capita income was still only about 80 percent of the British value, as it had been before World War I.[16]

The relative situation changed again after World War II. Although culturally and scientifically Germany has never managed to recover from the two world wars, it surprised everyone by the pace of its economic growth after 1945, especially relative to Britain. Britain could justifiably bask in the glory of having won the war, but economically it stagnated. Victory led to complacence, and structural economic reforms were put on the back burner. Only the Labour Party carried out extensive social and economic reforms, including the nationalization of British industry. If these were structural reforms, they went into the wrong direction by hampering British competitiveness. Extremely high taxes on "unearned" capital income and the comprehensive protection against dismissal enjoyed by British workers made the economy extremely inflexible. As a result, Britain grew modestly and had increasing difficulty keeping up with the rest of Europe.

This sluggish British growth enabled Germany to catch up more quickly than it might otherwise have been able to do. By 1960 the two countries had roughly the same per capita income, and by the mid 1960s Germany surpassed Britain. Britain had become the sick man of Europe. The sun seemed to have finally set on the British Empire. Intoxicated its economic miracle, Germany surged forward so rapidly that by 1978 it enjoyed a per capita income double that of the United Kingdom, valued at current market prices and exchange rates.

The shock this stagnation called forth in the British people was deep-seated. In 1979, Britain's economic woes catapulted Margaret Thatcher, the Conservative Party leader, to the office of Prime Minister, which she held until 1990. During this time, Britain underwent an economic revolution by moving toward privatization and free-market values.

Margaret Thatcher turned the entire economic system upside down by using extensive legal reforms to give more weight to the principles of a market economy and the idea of assuming responsibility for oneself.[17] She did not shy away from conflict, picking quarrels with powerful interest groups, most notably the unions. With the Employment Acts of 1980, 1982, and 1984, Thatcher limited strike measures that adversely affected third parties, and she abolished the widespread company commitment declaration for recognizing unions. She weeded out closed-shop practices with which the unions had tried to keep non-union employees out of public and private companies, and she instituted more democratic participation within unions in order to get rid of Mafia-type union governance. Thatcher privatized state-owned companies with a high concentration of unionized workers. She favored the introduction of wages in the form of profit sharing, and she supported self-employment and entrepreneurship. Above all, Thatcher pushed economic deregulation by, among other things, freeing the labor market from unnecessary rules and regulations. She reduced the top personal income tax rate from 60 percent to 40 percent. The share of the public sector in GDP declined by nearly 4 percentage points during her administration. Thatcher reduced the role of the state pension system by promoting the change from the public pay-as-you-go system to a privately funded system. She reduced social benefits across the board, curtailing housing allowances and cutting social assistance. But she also created a new system of helping the poor by establishing welfare-to-work schemes. She privatized the state-owned monopolies and opened their markets to competition. This stimulated a wave of privatization all over Europe. In Germany, this meant deregulation of the power and telecommunications sector, leading to substantial price reductions from which German consumers continue to benefit.

Of course, Margaret Thatcher's social reforms were not beyond reproach. The stereotypical German social activist still shudders at the thought that her radical reforms may one day be implemented in Germany. It is true that Margaret Thatcher's reforms left many behind. Any tourist in London could surmise from the number of homeless sleeping in doorways that her policies may not have helped alleviate poverty. And having to endure Britain's public transport system makes it amply clear that privatization is not always a good thing, at least not the British brand of railway privatization.

Yet on the whole Thatcherism was a huge success for Britain. The Iron Lady steered her country back on the right track, exceeding all expectations and silencing her critics. Although the complete economic benefits of her structural reforms did not show up until after she had been ousted, these have endured. Thatcher's bold reforms made John Major and Tony Blair's lives easier, as they will the lives of future British prime ministers.

Britain's unemployment rate, at its peak higher than even Germany's is today, rose consistently during the first half of Thatcher's tenure. Thereafter, it declined steadily, falling below the German level in 1997. In 2002, when German unemployment was at a dizzying 7.8 percent, unemployment in the United Kingdom was down to 5.2 percent.[18] Of course, such data should be interpreted with caution. There is good reason to believe that the British unemployment data underestimate the true level of unemployment because many displaced workers moved from unemployment compensation to health-related benefits and were then no longer accounted for in the unemployment statistics.[19] However, the German unemployment data do not show the true level of unemployment either. In Germany, many unemployed are technically hidden in early-retirement schemes or in the generous system of social aid.

Arguably, the success of Margaret Thatcher's policies is best seen in the data on Britain's economic growth. As figure 1.3 shows, between 1995 and 2005 the United Kingdom's output growth exceeded Germany's by 18 percentage points and that of the entire EU by 7.7 percentage points. During the slump of 2001–2003, as the world economy stumbled after the attack on the World Trade Center, the British economy grew by an average 2.2 percent per annum, while the German economy practically stagnated with an average growth of only 0.4 percent. And when the world economy convincingly recovered in 2004 and 2005, the British growth rate averaged 2.6 percent, while the German rate was only 1.1 percent.

This performance gap exemplifies the German problem. Germany is as affected by the global business cycle as the next country. But there is something fundamentally wrong with its long-run growth. The country's dynamism is gone. In 2005 its trend growth rate was little more than 1 percent per year— one of the lowest rates in Europe. This is not just a business-cycle problem that can be resolved using short-term stimulation. It demands major structural reforms.

France, Austria, the Netherlands, and Others Also Overtake Germany

During the 2002 federal election campaign, Franz Müntefering, then party secretary and later chairman of the Social Democrats, Germany's traditional party of social reform, attributed Germany's relatively poor recent growth performance to the tremendous lead it had held over other countries for many years. The further behind you are, the faster you have to grow in order to catch up with the leader, and Germany, he explained, is already where the other European nations aspire to be.

This is a cute theory, but not all cute theories are accurate. The truth is that Germany is being overtaken by one neighboring country after another not only in terms of growth, but also in absolute terms with respect to output per capita. Today, Germany is in the same situation in which Britain found itself toward the end of the 1960s. Not only has Germany's output growth slowed; its level of output is lower than those of many other countries.

Figure 1.4 shows nominal per capita national incomes in absolute terms from 1960 to 2005 according to national statistics. The lines are determined by the evolution of real output, the national price level, and exchange rates. Therefore, these do not necessarily correspond to the real improvement of the respective economies. The comparison between different countries is nonetheless revealing, as it reflects the relative global market value of their national products. Over long periods of time, countries can only be compared reasonably at current prices and exchange rates.[20]

The line for Germany in figure 1.4 shows the evolution of per capita gross national income (GNI) of the Federal Republic of Germany (that is, West

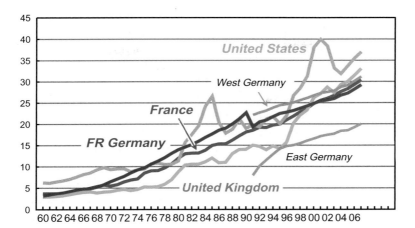

Figure 1.4
France and the United Kingdom in the passing lane: Per capita gross national income in thousands of euros at current prices and exchange rates. West and East Germany: Gross domestic product. Here West Germany includes West Berlin and East Germany includes East Berlin. Regional differentiation of Berlin: Ifo estimates. Sources: OECD, National Accounts, 2006; Arbeitskreis Volkswirtschaftliche Gesamtrechnungen der Länder, August 2006; Deutsche Bundesbank, 2006; Ifo Institute calculations.

Germany until 1990 and West and East Germany thereafter).[21] One can see that German national income dips at the time of reunification. This reflects the numerical effect of integrating East Germany into the Federal Republic: the low output of East Germany reduced the average of the entire country. But even afterwards the pace continues to be slower than before. Other countries are drawing ever nearer, and some have already overtaken Germany.

In comparison to Germany, Britain's growth is particularly remarkable. The country's stagnation in the 1970s, before the election of Margaret Thatcher in 1979, is clearly discernible. One can see that the relative distance between the British and German curves was largest around 1978, when the British per capita income was only half that of the German. These were the circumstances that brought Margaret Thatcher to power. After she took office, things turned around. Britain enjoyed a growth surge that started in the 1980s, accelerated further in the 1990s and ended up with the United Kingdom overtaking Germany in per capita terms in 2000. It is true that unadjusted UK growth since the mid 1990s partly reflects the appreciation of the pound sterling. However, figure 1.3 is adjusted for exchange-rate and inflation effects, and, as it clearly shows, the British economy has continued to grow rapidly even in real terms, despite the fact that the pound's sustained appreciation has been making British products more expensive to foreign buyers. Given that the current surge in Britain's real income is so great, its per capita income cannot be pushed below Germany's in the next few years unless the pound depreciates relative to the euro.

The fact is that according to official statistics (that is, if national income is valued at current market prices and exchange rates) the United Kingdom has already surpassed Germany in per capita income. Again it must be emphasized that, as the British population is much smaller than Germany's, this does not mean that the British economy as such is bigger than the German one. In 2005, Germany's gross national income exceeded that of the UK (including Northern Ireland) by 23 percent. However, it does reveal that the overall output per capita as evaluated by markets is higher in the UK than in Germany. This baffles Germans, who typically have a poor image of British business, especially after the failed BMW-Rover deal, and have an inflated image of their own economic power. This self-image reflects past achievements rather than the present state of affairs. It ignores the British successes with information and communication technologies. It also ignores Britain's success in the services area: boosted by the rapidly growing market for financial services. London and its surrounding metropolitan area is today the richest region of Europe. German reunification is not the only reason for Britain's superior performance. In per capita income, Britain is slightly ahead even of West Germany alone.

Germany's deficiencies are even more striking if the country is compared with the United States. Figure 1.4 shows a volatile curve for the United States because the exchange rate between the dollar and the deutschmark or the euro, respectively, has changed substantially in the last few decades. Nevertheless, in 2005, American gross national income per capita was 23.4 percent above the German level despite the dollar's exceptionally weak value against the euro.

Germany's poor showing is not limited to a comparison with Britain and the United States. France, too, has just surpassed Germany in per capita terms, despite all its domestic problems. As the exchange rate between Germany and France was constant long before the introduction of the euro, exchange-rate effects cannot be used to explain this fact. Like Britain, France used to have a somewhat lower per capita income than Germany. Until 1969 it was roughly on par with Germany, but during 1970s and the 1980s it was unable to match Germany's growth. By 1990, France's per capita income was only about 80 percent of Germany's.

Things changed in the 1990s, when Germany slumped and France continued to grow at the EU average. France overtook Germany in 2002. This is another reversal of fortune that has escaped the notice of Germans, whose image of the French economy trails reality by decades. France is no longer the country of the rattling, rusty little Renault. It has become a high-tech country, excelling in particular in nuclear technology, aerospace, and genetic engineering. Even in the automotive industry, Germany's remaining treasure, France is gaining on Germany's market share in Europe.

Germany and Denmark were neck and neck until German reunification, after which Denmark raced ahead. By 2005, Denmark's per capita income exceeded Germany's by about 37.4 percent. As figure 1.5 shows, this surely had something to do with the numerical averaging between East and West Germany. Yet the radical 1993 reforms with which Denmark cleaned up its labor market deserve credit. Much will have to happen before Germany can hope to follow the Danish example.

The Netherlands and Austria also lagged behind Germany for a long time, but they moved ahead in 1999. Gone are the times when Germany looked with pity at the mountain inhabitants to the south and the plain dwellers to the northwest.

The Netherlands had a serious growth crisis in the late 1970s and early 1980s. This crisis was gradually overcome by a policy of wage moderation initiated by the 1982 Wassenaar Agreement and implemented in the 1980s and the 1990s. Year by year, the Dutch economy regained its competitiveness, and in the 1990s high growth rates were achieved. The Netherlands' lag behind Germany shrank gradually and then turned into a lead.

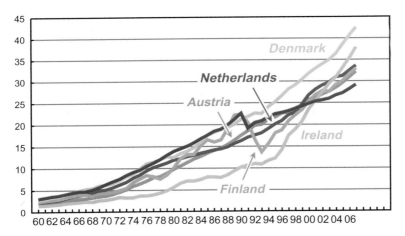

Figure 1.5
Per capita gross national income (thousands of euros, at current prices and exchange rate) in the "small tigers" of the European Union. Sources: OECD, National Accounts, 2006; Deutsche Bundesbank, 2006; Ifo Institute calculations.

Austria's development is also impressive. In 1970, Austria's national output was only 59 percent of West Germany's. Austro-Socialism strangled the country, and Austria was afraid to undermine its neutrality pact with the Soviet Union by moving in the direction of free-market economics. Bruno Kreisky had the country fully in his grip with his SPÖ (Austrian Social Democratic Party). Then began the détente. Mikhail Gorbachev granted more freedoms, and Austria slowly dared to open up, most visibly by joining the European Union in 1995. All of this boosted growth and finally resulted in Austria's surpassing a Germany weakened by reunification. It is now the Austrians who look down from their mountaintops with pity on their fellow German-speakers.

Ireland's growth has been nothing short of miraculous. In the 1960s Ireland belonged in the European poorhouse with a per capita output less than 50 percent that of Germany. A combination of factors gave rise to its now having by far the highest growth rate in Europe. These include EU accession in 1973, which brought new trade options and the funds for rebuilding and extending its infrastructure, and a low-tax policy characterized by a corporate income tax rate of only 10 percent, consciously designed to attract internationally mobile capital. Added to this was an extremely market-friendly economic policy, modeled on that of the United States, which minimized business regulation and cut back on the welfare state. At only 32 percent, Ireland has one of the lowest public-sector shares in Europe[22], and, thanks to its low social security contributions and weak labor unions, it has only about 70 percent of West German labor costs. During the 1990s, Ireland achieved an average annual real rate of growth of 6.5 percent. Even in the lull year of 2002, when the German economy stopped growing altogether, the Irish added another real 3.3 percent. In terms of per capita national income, Ireland has moved far ahead of the European average and Germany as well. According to international comparable data for 2005, Ireland's per capita gross national income exceeded Germany's by 23.4 percent, with no slowdown of the growth trend in sight.

Ireland's economic boom is evident when one travels in the country. There is construction everywhere, there is hardly any unemployment, and the country is gripped by a spirit of optimism. To be sure, there is considerable income inequality. Economic dynamism has its price in that wages typically are low and lag behind productivity gains. But wages are pulled up with the general growth of the economy. Today Irish wages are much higher in real terms than they were before the economic takeoff, and the day may come when they will exceed German wages. Ireland's housing stock and infrastructure do not yet meet German standards. However, they reflect past rather than present levels of economic activity. It is only a matter of time until Ireland's increasing wealth will be visible.

It is sometimes claimed that the official Irish economic statistics are inflated by tax fugitives from all over the world shifting their profits to Ireland. The claim is that if these profits are excluded from the Irish data it will be clear that Ireland has not yet overtaken Germany. This is incorrect. Figure 1.4 refers to gross national income, not gross domestic product per capita. Only the latter contains profit incomes that accrue to foreigners. In 2004, Ireland's gross domestic product was 17 percent higher than its gross national income, whereas Germany's GDP and GNI diverged by only 0.02 percent. The Irish curve would shift to yet a higher level if the graph were comparing data on gross domestic product rather than data on gross national income. Figure 1.5 does show the lower of the two values, i.e. the national income earned by the Irish themselves. It is, of course, true that this income was able to grow so rapidly because, among other things, the huge capital inflows attracted by low taxes and labor costs raised Irish wages and rents via indirect effects. But this is exactly what makes a high-quality location high-quality. East Germany could take a page from Ireland's example.

It does not stop there. The growing list of European countries with better economic performance than Germany includes such unlikely candidates as Finland. And this cannot just be blamed on exchange-rate shenanigans, since the Finnish currency is suspected to have joined the euro area at an undervalued rather than an overvalued exchange rate.

Finland is no longer just a small country on the Russian border, fondly remembered for saunas, lakes, forests, and a nearly bankrupt television manufacturer called Nokia. Though the country suffered a serious economic crisis after the collapse of the Soviet Union, it recovered, boosted by EU accession in 1995, and it has achieved solid economic growth. Finland, too, has surpassed Germany in GNI per capita since 2001, and by 2000 Nokia—now reconfigured as a telecommunications leader—was the company with the highest market capitalization in Europe.

Intellectual and Scientific Decline in the Land of Goethe

Long before its relative economic decline, Germany suffered a decline in its cultural position. Even in areas where the land of the poets and thinkers believes itself to be ahead of the rest, things are no longer as they were.

German culture produced many early contributors to modern civilization, including Martin Luther, Johannes Gutenberg, Nicolaus Copernicus,[23] Johannes Kepler, Immanuel Kant, Arthur Schopenhauer, Gottfried Wilhelm

Leibniz, Carl Friedrich Gauss, Wolfgang von Goethe, Friedrich von Schiller, Johann Sebastian Bach, Wolfgang Amadeus Mozart, and Georg Friedrich Händel. However, the real breakthrough of German culture came in the late nineteenth century.

From the second half of the nineteenth century up until World War II, Germany was responsible for a disproportionately large number of important scientific and cultural ideas that had impact around the world. The German judicial system was exported to a number of other countries and with it the institutions that are characteristic of modern industrial society. The German social security system, the first in the world, was also copied by many countries and became the foundation of the European-type social market economy. Even communism and socialism sprang from the German political debate.

Most remarkable was Germany's academic leadership. The educational system established by Wilhelm von Humboldt was exemplary, and German universities were home to the world's academic elite. Between 1901 and 1933, 10 of 31 Nobel prizes in physics, 14 of 28 Nobel prizes in chemistry, 6 out of 27 Nobel prizes in medicine, and 5 of 31 Nobel prizes in literature went to Germany.[24] No other country had collected more prizes in any of these disciplines.

At the same time, Germany was responsible for a substantial share of inventions. The natural sciences were the unchallenged domain of the Germans, and even today a sizeable portion of the technological knowledge that created modern industrial society and its standard of living is based on German inventions and research findings. The range of technical inventions includes the telephone (Johann Philipp Reis, 1861), the dynamo motor (Werner Siemens, 1866),[25] the motorcycle (Gottlieb Daimler, 1885), the automobile (Karl Benz, 1885), the four-stroke engine (Nikolaus August Otto, 1876), the diesel engine (Rudolf Diesel, 1892), the jet airplane (Hans-Joachim-Pabst von Ohain, 1939), the liquid-fueled rocket (Wernher von Braun, 1926),[26] the binary and programmable computer (Konrad Zuse, 1941), and the first programming language (Zuse, 1945). Nuclear physics and its central theoretical findings were developed primarily in Germany, as was modern organic chemistry. The German dominance of the natural sciences was so omnipresent until well into the 1930s that for some time German served as the international scientific language. Foreign scientists published their findings in German, and in the United States some scientific periodicals were issued in German.

Indeed, Germany had substantial influence on the development of the sciences in the United States. Starting with Johns Hopkins University in Baltimore, American universities offered graduate programs patterned on

German ones, and the German "Wissenschaftsgeist" (scientific spirit) and the "freedom of research and teaching" became prominent attitudes at American universities. The motto of Stanford University is "Die Luft der Freiheit weht," meaning "The wind of freedom blows."[27]

A century has passed since Germany's intellectual golden age, and nothing is as it once was. Was it the poisoning of the intellectual spirit by the Nazis? Was it the loss of scientists and research time during the war and the subsequent reconstruction period? Was it the extermination and expulsion of the Jews, who had made great contributions to German culture? Was it the success of Churchill's attempt to bomb the country back to the Middle Ages? Was it the loss of pride, tradition, and self-esteem after two devastating military defeats? Was it the implication of social-democratic politics that emphasized consumption by the masses rather than the achievements of the country's cultural elites in order to counter the promises of the East German communists? No one can give simple answers to these questions. However, the facts are undeniable.

Since the end of World War II, German scientists have been striving for a place as equals in the international scientific community, but they are confronted with formidable domestic obstacles. No longer the "worldly dukes" they were in the days of the Kaiser-Wilhelm-Gesellschaft, German researchers—now administrators of an egalitarian science operation—have lost the esteem of German society. Aspiring young German scientists emigrate to the United States, as they did in the 1930s. Only a few "star disciplines," including physics and chemistry, have managed to retain leading researchers. Most German contributions hardly make a dent in the international scene. Even the star disciplines are not what they once were. Between 1970 and 2005, Germany earned only 3 of 36 Nobel prizes in physics, 2 of 36 Nobel prizes in chemistry, and 3 of 36 Nobel prizes in medicine.[28]

The pathetic state of the German school system fits this picture of a decline in excellence. According to the PISA report of the OECD,[29] in practically all tests, but especially in language proficiency and mathematics, the performance of 15-year-old German students is just about at the OECD average. Figure 1.6 shows only the results for mathematics, as this discipline provides a more objective comparison across countries than, for example, language proficiency (in which Germany did equally poorly). It is not surprising that the German school system cannot compete with the rigidly run school systems of Japan and Korea. But it is remarkable that Germany lags so far behind Finland, Switzerland, France, and Sweden.

It is true that the OECD report may not reflect the full picture. It ignores the specific performance of the German vocational school system, which is

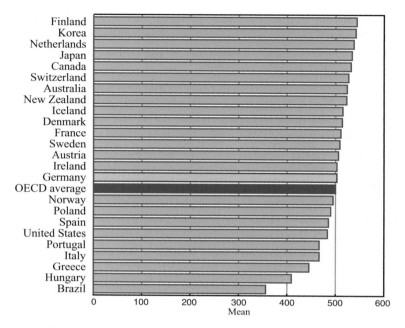

Figure 1.6
Educational proficiency in mathematics. Source: OECD, first results from PISA 2003 study, 2004, p. 356, table 2.5c.

rightfully held in great esteem. For that, the 15-year-olds who were tested were too young. The study also does not take account of the fact that in Germany pupils start school at a later age than in other countries and that in Germany many children repeat one or even two grades if their performance is below par. Still, by and large the study cannot be criticized. It starkly demonstrates that Germans are drawing on past glory and not living in the present. They remain under the delusion of belonging to the country of great poets and thinkers while in reality, at least with regard to education, they are merely average.

This present situation is incompatible with a prosperous future, which entails revamping the German educational system. The range of such measures includes lengthening the school day (today children go to school only from 8 A.M. to 1 P.M.), improving preschool education, administering centralized examinations, offering higher pay for teachers to attract better ones, quality control and better incentives in the schools, and introducing more competition among universities.

It is hard to tell whether the educational weakness is one of the reasons for Germany's present economic crisis. As will be discussed in chapter 4, it may be contributing to the high unemployment in the low-wage sector. In any case, the educational weakness and the economic crisis are the combined result of politicians' misguided focus over the past 30 years on developing the German welfare state. Whether driven by the need to compete with the socialist system of the GDR or by the student revolts of 1968, the welfare state gobbled up funds that could have been invested in education, and this has hurt the labor market by creating comfortable alternatives to gainful employment and educational effort. To date, the economy seems to have weathered the effects of poor education. So far, Germany has been able to draw on a pool of highly skilled workers and first-class engineers. This is why Germany still leads the European pack with regard to patent registrations. Measures taken today to improve the education system would pay off for the labor market from 2020 on, when the better-educated students would enter the work force. Unfortunately, it does appear that any such measures will be adopted in the foreseeable future.

The Maastricht Treaty: One That Hurts Another Hurts Oneself

In this comparative international context, it is worrisome to watch the evolution of the German public finances. Government debt, which ballooned as a result of the error of financing German reunification by issuing bonds rather than by increasing taxes, has risen enormously in recent years. Between 1990 and 2005, it went from 539 billion euros to 1.52 trillion. The debt increase was so huge that before the introduction of the euro Germany even missed the Maastricht Treaty target to keep government debt below 60 percent of gross domestic product.

The problems are now further exacerbated by the economic conditions in Germany. When the economy is not doing well, tax revenues decline, and the welfare state quickly becomes more expensive because the rising unemployment must be financed by the government. The most convenient strategy for the finance minister is to balance the revenue shortfall by borrowing even more—that is, by increasing the budget deficit. Moreover, when the economy stagnates, it is not possible to keep the debt/GDP ratio under control by expanding the denominator of this ratio in line with its numerator. In 2005, Germany's debt/GDP ratio had reached 68 percent.

It is true that excessive borrowing is blocked in principle by the European Stability and Growth Pact that limits the deficit to 3 percent of gross domestic product. Germany no longer seems to take the pact seriously, however. It violated the pact during the period 2002–2005 with deficit ratios well above the ceiling. The violations caused the EU to start formal proceedings against Germany, as called for in the pact.

This fiscal deficit spending is of special interest insofar as it was Germany that insisted on the Stability and Growth Pact in the first place, even against the will of other EU countries. In the 1991 Maastricht Treaty, the EU countries had agreed on a new currency without laying down a timetable. Germany was hesitant to abolish its deutsche mark, even though the new monetary system was based very much on its own, with an independent central bank and an internal structure similar to that of the Bundesbank. However, in the end it was willing do so on condition that the euro-area countries would permanently honor the 3 percent deficit ceiling that originally had been agreed only for the period preceding the introduction of the new currency. It further demanded effective penalties in case that the ceiling was exceeded. The other countries, which wanted to get rid of the deutsche mark and the dictate of the Bundesbank, were not happy about this proposal, but had to accept it. Germany's conditions were accepted in the Stability and Growth Pact of 1996. It was, therefore, with a good bit of hidden Schadenfreude that they registered Germany's formal violation of the deficit criterion. One that hurts another hurts oneself.

The Germans had overestimated the strength of their economy in a period of worldwide slump, and they had underestimated the costs of their generous welfare system.

The German government hesitantly reacted to its violation of the Stability and Growth Pact. Instead of cutting expenditures, it proposed some measures to broaden the tax base in 2002. These measures did not suffice, however, to provide a safe margin to the deficit ceiling. Thus, in 2003 a budget deficit of about 4.0 percent materialized, and in 2004 and 2005 deficits of 3.7 percent and 3.3 percent resulted.

The EU's Ecofin Council has been hesitant to enforce the pact against Germany. Germany allied itself with France, which also violated the pact, and implicitly also with the potential violators Italy and Portugal, and succeeded in convincing the Council not to take action. Small wonder: the Ecofin Council is the assembly of the European finance ministers. The ministers, who were their own judges and jury, easily agreed not to penalize one another and to postpone the proceedings. The decision of the Ecofin Council was not in conformance with the law, however. The European Commission brought suit before the European Court and won. The deficit proceedings against Germany had to be continued.

The German government's hope for mercy was in vain. Fearing the fines foreseen in the treaty, the new German government under Angela Merkel eventually announced a three-percentage-point increase in the value-added tax. Combined with the slight upswing in the wake of the booming world economy, this is enough to keep the deficit way below 3 percent of GDP in 2007.

Nevertheless, the credibility of the European financial system has been severely undermined by Germany's negligence. At the first opportunity for its application, the Stability and Growth Pact was challenged. Such a policy threatens not only the reputation of Germany, but also the stability of the young currency that was to be safeguarded.

It must be admitted that the Stability and Growth Pact could have been better designed. During a boom, when the finance ministers have lots of money, the debt and deficit ceilings could be tighter, and during a slump they could be looser. The rules do not induce the countries to practice spending discipline in good times to be able to ease up during bad times in order to stimulate economic activity. That is why the European Economic Advisory Group at CESifo proposed to change the pact in a way that would permit a country, during prosperous periods, to save more and reduce the debt level in order to create the desired greater flexibility for periods of downturns.[30] A country that succeeds in lowering its debt level below 55 percent of its gross domestic product may then temporarily run deficits of more than 3 percent of GDP. But that proposal has not been adopted, and it would not have helped Germany, whose debt level already far exceeded 60 percent of GDP.

History's Guinea Pig

Germany, once the economic powerhouse of Europe, is unable to keep pace with its neighbors and unable to satisfy the increasing demands of its citizens. Two devastating wars did not destroy the country's dynamism, but the peaceful development since World War II has been doing just that.

Germany is because it is being strangled by the very welfare state that the prosperous and peaceful episodes in its history have produced. Aspiring to be model neighbors to their European partners, German voters, politicians, union leaders, and employer representatives have tried to fulfill the dream of the just and everlasting welfare state, but in doing so they have overburdened their own economy. For good will to succeed, one cannot violate basic economic laws. But this is what the Germans have been doing.

The country has been caught in a vicious circle since the expansion of the welfare state accelerated in the 1970s while the economic growth rate simultaneously began to decline. For three decades the government has tried both to raise the country's social standards and to cushion the consequences of a weakening economy by increasing public transfer payments to the unemployed. But this has made things worse and has increased the need for further costly welfare state actions. Germany is suffering from economic overstretch.

Germany's share of public social expenditure in GDP exceeds 30 percent. An astonishing 41 percent of its adult population lives on social transfers from the government, including public pensions. Taxes, contributions, and public borrowing finance these expenditures. The marginal employer and employee tax and contribution rate on the value added produced by an average industrial worker is nearly two-thirds. Black-market activities flourish under these conditions, but the legitimate economy is struggling to survive. Chapter 6 will go into the details.

The German disease is a disease of the welfare state, which, despite being the cornerstone of the German model, has incurred immense fiscal costs and has destroyed economic incentives.

Germany invented the welfare state. In the 1880s, Chancellor Otto von Bismarck introduced public health insurance, public disability insurance, and the public pension system to appease the disgruntled masses and help reconcile them to the capitalist market system. He succeeded in preventing the revolution that his compatriot Karl Marx had predicted and that later was to take place in Russia.

Bismarck's welfare state became the model for Europe. One European country after another copied his reforms in the first half of the twentieth century, stabilizing and modernizing their societies. Even outside Europe, the model earned friends among the industrialized countries. There were only few exceptions—among them the United States, which did not follow the German road.

The threat of revolution and a communist victory over capitalism not only shaped German social politics at the time of Bismarck, it continued to do so until the collapse of the Iron Curtain in 1989. German governments had always been frightened by Lenin's claim that their country was to be the main battlefield for the communist revolution, and once the Soviet Union succeeded in establishing a communist state on German soil after World War II, West Germany tried to convince its workers of the superiority of its system by offering them an ever-expanding welfare state. And it succeeded. The main reason for the collapse of communism was the visible superiority of the living standard of the West German working classes over that of their countrymen in the East. They also wanted bananas. The GDR had not been able to afford to import bananas, and bananas were the most sought-after items that the East

Germans bought in the West after they set their feet on western ground when the wall came down.

As the birthplace of socialism, Germany retains a peculiar mental kinship to socialist ideas. As the country that developed the welfare state earlier and more rigorously than other countries, it now suffers more intensely from its repercussions than have other countries. So how Germany confronts and solves this current difficulty can set a model for other countries that must grapple with these same issues, especially as welfare systems confront a historic demographic transition that will take place later in this century.

The problem of the welfare state is not only that it absorbs resources and imposes a high burden on the private market economy. It also creates distortions in the labor market, a theme which is developed in chapter 4. By offering generous replacement incomes to the unemployed, the German government was trying to make joblessness tolerable, but ended up making it too attractive, establishing high wage demands that the private sector has been increasingly unable to meet. While German firms have been facing growing competition from low-wage suppliers all over the world, the German welfare state established itself as a second competitor in the labor market. Double competition in the product and labor markets has been squeezing out more and more private jobs in Germany and has caused the rising unemployment from which the country is suffering.

The wage competition set up by the government has been a particular problem in the East German regions (Länder) that were integrated into the Federal Republic. These regions, which had been shattered by socialist mismanagement and were operating with only 7 percent of West Germany's productivity, would have needed a long period of low wages to be able to compete with the productive West German economy. However, as will be discussed in chapters 3 and 5, neither the West German system of wage bargaining nor the West German welfare state—both of which were implemented in the East overnight—allowed this to happen. As the economies of the new Länder had to compete with replacement incomes, which were adjusted to the country with the highest wages in the world, the disaster was pre-ordained. Obviously, many people preferred receiving their money from the state to working for competitive wages, especially when there was little difference between the amounts paid for working and not working.

The replacement incomes also distorted German migration patterns, a topic that is analyzed in chapter 8. Unemployment benefits kept wages high and attracted more than the efficient number of migrants. Moreover, by making wages rigid, they prevented the creation of additional jobs for the immigrants. The result was an indirect immigration into unemployment. New immigrants took the jobs, and the existing employees took the easy chair that the welfare state was offering them.

The repercussions of the welfare state are not limited to the labor market. As will be argued in chapter 7, even Germany's demographic problems, more severe than those of any other industrialized country, might be attributed to it. Today, Germany has the lowest birth rate relative to its population among all developed countries. It is aging exceptionally fast, and the pension crisis, which most OECD countries will face within 30 years when the Baby Boomers will claim their pensions, is particularly severe in Germany.

The reason for this crisis could be Germany's leading role in establishing a pay-as-you-go-pension system. When Bismarck introduced this system in 1889, he effectively nationalized the contributions that the working generation was able to make to their parents, cutting the link between the decision to have children and the economic well-being in old age that traditionally had been a strong fertility motive. Under the influence of the pension system, Germans learned earlier than others that a decent life in old age was possible without having children, and thus they decided to reduce the number of children they had. Gradually, generation by generation, they changed their lifestyles and family plans according to the new economic environment that had resulted from Bismarck's reforms. However, the pension system itself cannot survive without children being born to replace the people currently supporting the system. Germans will therefore have to learn the hard way that their pension system has just nourished illusions of old-age security.

Things cannot go on like this. A welfare state cannot be constructed in the naive way Germany has tried. This book will clarify why, and what has to be done to overcome the deficiencies. It is neither necessary nor wise to abolish the welfare state altogether. To do so would mean throwing the baby out with the bathwater. There is an important role for a welfare state: it evens out people's chances in life, and it serves as career insurance against sheer bad luck. However, a well-constructed welfare state would not offer full-coverage social security and would avoid the distortions from which Germany is suffering by setting other conditions under which people are eligible for state support.

In some sense, Germany is the guinea pig of history. Other countries, in particular the newly emerging countries of Asia, can learn from its experience in order to avoid some obvious mistakes. Sadly, today Germany provides something of a case study of what not to do in designing a prosperous future. But who knows, perhaps a new Germany will one day emerge and provide an example of courageous social reforms necessary to rectify history's missteps.

The challenges Germany faces are shared by most other Western societies, if currently to a smaller extent. Low-wage competition by the Asian and former communist countries is a problem for all of them, and all have to find socially acceptable and economically feasible ways to maintain full employment. Likewise, all Western countries have to find ways to handle mass immigration of the poor, and all need to find answers to the reduction of birth rates and the obvious implications for their pension systems. While this book discusses these and many more problems in the German context, it is written in the hope that the solutions it offers will be of use for Western societies in general.

to a former classmate who now helps produce Hohner harmonicas in China, in the hope that he will convince the Chinese to trade their harmonicas for German tourist services

2 How German Workers Lost Their Competitive Edge

The Globalization Shock: China, India, the United States, and Many Others

Many of Germany's economic problems over the last 30 years have been home-brewed. These self-inflicted injuries could not, however, have led to the crisis experienced in recent years if German business had not been faced with dramatic changes in international competition. These changes must be understood before outlining the reforms necessary restore Germany's competitiveness (to be more precise, the competitiveness of German workers).

Germans wonder why their economy has been doing so poorly of late. They cannot understand what has gone wrong. After all, West Germany is still basically the same as it was at the time of reunification when the country's economy was bustling. That is exactly the point. The country is the same, but the world has changed. External challenges have come together and demand a fitting response, as the historian Arnold Toynbee once claimed.[1] Nations that find such a response can turn these challenges into success and become stronger. Nations that do not react perish. Globalization including the rise of China and India, the European common market, the euro, EU eastern enlargement (the expansion of the EU by the accession of eight Eastern European countries in 2004), and, last but not least, German reunification have changed the environment in which German firms are operating. If Germany fails to respond to these challenges swiftly, it is bound to have continuing problems.

It is not the case that Germany has an adequate response laying in wait up and is simply, as Chancellor Angela Merkel once claimed, having trouble implementing it. Rather, there is fundamental failure to understand the causes of Germany's difficulties. Hardly anyone in Germany, either a politician or an ordinary citizen, is willing to acknowledge that German workers have lost their competitive edge—that they are no longer better, just a lot more expensive than workers from other countries. While Germany is at the OECD average in terms of educational performance, it definitely leads the pack in terms of wage costs. There is a serious disconnect between the price and quality of German labor. As a consequence, the German economy continues to fall behind as unemployment surges ahead.

At the same time, German exports are booming and many German firms are doing quite well. Germany is still runner up in world exports, after the United States. This is somewhat puzzling, and it warrants explanation. Part of the reason why German exporting firms have managed to stay competitive is because they offer quality products and have found ways to circumvent high German wage costs. They are mechanizing their production processes and keeping their labor costs under control through offshoring and outsourcing. The irony is that many German firms do many things very well and are extremely successful exporters, but the country's domestic environment, in particular its labor market institutions and its social system, is not conducive to true economic success in a global economy. We will revisit this issue throughout the book.

This chapter discusses the changes in Germany's competitive environment brought about by Asia, the European Union and Eastern Europe, and it deals extensively with the German economy's domestic reactions to huge cross-country wage differences. The analysis of this German reaction can be extended to many other Western European countries with rigid labor markets and generous welfare systems.

Who are the competitors threatening Germany? In the 1960s and the 1970s it was Japan that moved in on German business, but today Japan is only a paper tiger struggling to remain competitive. From 1990 to 2004 it underwent a major economic crisis, with rising unemployment, exploding public debt and one of the lowest growth rates among the industrialized countries. The real tigers are the newly industrializing countries of Southeast and East Asia, including South Korea, Malaysia, Singapore, Taiwan, Thailand, and Vietnam. South Korea is successful in shipbuilding, in automobiles and consumer electronics; Malaysia is strong in electronics and in non-ferrous metals; Singapore puts its trust in information and communication technology; Taiwan holds a top position in the production of computer chips; Thailand produces cheap textiles, leather articles and clothing, and so does Vietnam which, in addition, is a significant exporter of crude oil. In recent years, these countries have substantially improved their products and process technologies and are now making goods attractive enough to be serious global players.

The big advantage of the Asian Tiger countries lies in their wage rates, which are only a tiny fraction of German wages. At the same time, Asia's productivity is catching up faster than its wages, further improving their competitiveness. The Asian Tigers have an extremely industrious population which is eager to learn and adapts readily to even the most complicated production processes. Like Germany, they have old cultures and proud intellectual traditions.

It is no wonder then that today many German firms prefer to import products from Asia or produce them there themselves. Among the buyers of these products are Karstadt, Quelle, and Metro (the German counterparts of Sears, Wal-Mart, and Kmart). The cheap textiles and clothing they offer come mostly from Vietnam, Malaysia and Indonesia. Practically all big German manufacturers in all sectors have directly invested in Asia. One immediately recognizable name is Siemens, which has numerous plants in Indonesia, Japan, Malaysia, South Korea, and other countries. Foremost among the range of products Siemens produces there are those related to information and communication technology, automotive parts, lighting, and medical technology. Another example is DaimlerChrysler, which has a wide network of production and assembly plants in Japan, Thailand, and Indonesia.

If these Southeast Asian countries are, by now, major players in the global market place, even they promise to be dwarfed by the rise of China and India, which together constitute 38 percent of the world population. China, in particular, has developed rapidly over the past 15 years, after having largely detached itself from its ideological involvement with Marxism-Leninism in favor of a more market-oriented economy. If the official statistics are to be believed, China's real gross national product grew by 286 percent from 1990 to 2004[2]—an average of 10 percent per annum. And China is not only producing for domestic consumption; it is growing so rapidly because of its integration into East Asian trade. To date, Chinese growth has been generated primarily by the coastal regions that use the China Sea as their trade route. China's banana-shaped 1,400-mile coast is the fastest-growing region in the world.

German industries have had a Chinese presence for some time now. Volkswagen built two big joint venture production plants in Shanghai and Changchun that also assemble Audi models. In 2003, BMW initiated a joint venture with the Chinese producer Brilliance. DaimlerChrysler, already present with a Chrysler Jeep assembly, is also planning additional Chinese ventures for producing commercial vehicles. Siemens built the Transrapid, a magnetic levitation train for the rail connection between the airport and downtown Shanghai.

Siemens has 45,000 employees in Asia, many of whom are located in India, which is thickly blanketed with Siemens subsidiaries. India has followed China and has started a big development surge. Bangalore, in the South Indian province of Karnataka, is home to the world's second-largest software-development center (second only to California's Silicon Valley). Every major software producer has a presence there. Bangalore is a name to be remembered by Europeans and Americans, because their business will have to meet the challenge of the new business centers there.

Germany has not only Asia but also the United States to worry about as a competitor. The United States grew at an amazing pace during the 1990s. On the one hand, this growth was based on the "new economy," including the computer and software industry, and its direct and indirect effects on the rest of the economy. On the other hand, it resulted from political efforts to develop the low-wage sector under President Clinton. Although the United States is a high-tech country, its low wages for simple labor relative to Germany have made it a preferred location for labor-intensive production of lower-tech products. Many German firms have undertaken huge direct investments in the United States in order to serve the market directly from the lower-cost American plants rather than from expensive German locations.

According to an estimate of the German Chamber of Industry and Commerce, German manufacturing firms recently relocated 45,000 jobs abroad per annum. The total number of jobs created by German firms abroad was about 4.6 million by the end of 2004 if weighted by the German ownership shares in the companies involved. Foreign direct investors had created only 2.2 million jobs in Germany.[3] In 2005, German inbound direct investment was 26 billion euros, while outbound investment was 37 billion euros.

Inbound and outbound investment differ substantially. While outbound investment typically involves transfers of knowledge and the starting up of new plants, inbound investment often takes the form of acquiring German firms.

As was shown in chapter 1, direct investment is only a small part of total international investment, which primarily flows via the banking system. In 2005, Germany's net capital export, comprising financial and direct investment in both directions, amounted to 95 billion euros (4 percent of its gross national income), while internal German net investment amounted to only 50 billion euros.

And the flight of firms seems to be increasing. According to a May 2003 survey by the German Chamber of Industry and Commerce, nearly one-fourth of industrial firms were planning to relocate at least part of their production to foreign countries in the following 3 years.[4] This was up from one-fifth in 2000.

Among the motives for relocation, high domestic labor costs received top mention (at 45 percent), followed by the level of taxes and fiscal charges (at 38 percent). Lesser reasons were exchange-rate risks and the German bureaucracy, at 7 percent and 5 percent respectively.

The extent of relocation intentions varies from industry to industry. In the clothing industry, 47 percent of the firms planned to move parts of their production abroad within the next three years, in electrical engineering the corresponding proportion was 40 percent, in textiles 33 percent, in radio, television, and information technology 32 percent, and in mechanical engineering 28 percent. Nonmetallic mineral products, publishing, and printing are industries that by and large had no immediate plans to relocate; here only 10 percent of the surveyed firms intended to move abroad.

The Flight of the SMEs to Eastern Europe

Of course, it easier for larger companies than for small firms to move production abroad, as meeting the substantial start-up costs as well as the fixed costs of management in a foreign legal and cultural environment will be less of a hurdle for a large business. Increasingly, however, German small and medium-size enterprises (SMEs) are also setting their sights abroad, and this is Germany's true challenge. Germany's historic economic strength lays not in its internationally recognized large corporations, but in its high-performance SMEs. Most Germans work for SMEs, and together they generate the bulk of the nation's gross domestic product. Although there is no general consensus regarding the cutoff for being classified as an SME, if this is drawn at 500 employees, then close to 80 percent of all people employed in the private sector work for SMEs, accounting for about half of private gross domestic product.[5]

Many SMEs command large world market shares in their respective market segments, despite their relatively small size. These firms are, in some sense, Germany's unsung economic heroes. How many people—German or otherwise—know that Trumpf is the world leader in laser-based metalworking machines, or that Krones holds the international technological lead in beverage-filling equipment, or that Heraeus is the name to reckon with in vacuum technology? If they are middleweight title holders, with fewer than 5,000 employees, then the light weights and feather weights are even more impressive. Aesculap is number one or two in surgical instruments, with 2,300 employees. With 1,000 employees, the machinery producer Grenzebach is the global champion in cutting, loading, and stacking installations for producing flat glass and machinery for making building boards. With 480 employees, Hill & Müller is the market leader in cold-rolled strip steel. With 75 employees, Hensold is the market leader in binoculars and telescopic sights. No less than 90 percent of the movies a reader in any country may have seen in recent years were shot with cameras produced by Arri, a Munich company with fewer than 800 employees. This is only a small sample from a list of about 450 largely unknown and unheralded world champions that form the backbone of German industry. And there are a further 500 or so firms that operate in the very top range of their niche markets.

Germany undoubtedly is world champion in niche products. It is through the sale of these specialized products, known primarily to insiders and belonging primarily to the intermediate product sector that Germans earn the bulk of their foreign exchange. Without the exports of the SMEs, Germany would not have the money to buy American computers, Korean stereo systems, or holiday trips to Mallorca. In this context, an exodus of SMEs would have catastrophic consequences.

Whether the SMEs will be staying put is an open question. On the one hand, many SMEs are going out of business altogether. The recent record number of bankruptcies has already been mentioned. Among those who have survived, however, an alarming number are relocating production abroad. This does not get a lot of press, since these firms do not have widely recognized names and since the departure of each individual firm does not affect a large number of workers. But the aggregate effect amounts to a trend of surprising proportions.

As many as 59 percent of the SMEs with fewer than 5,000 employees, surveyed by the employers associations' Cologne Institute for Business Research, have already established plants in other EU countries, and 57 percent of these have set up shop outside the old EU countries. Two-thirds of even the smaller firms, with up to 500 employees, are now engaged abroad.[6]

The former Eastern Bloc countries that joined the EU in 2004 or have signed accession treaties are an especially attractive destination for SMEs. In contrast to locating in East Asia, the logistical costs involved in these countries are bearable for SMEs; in these geographical neighbors, German SMEs see a fighting chance for meeting the challenge of intensifying international competition.

About 675,000 of the 4.6 million jobs that German firms maintained abroad in 2004 were based in the new eastern EU countries. This is only a little less than the number of jobs created by German companies in the United States during the last few decades (746,000).[7]

Soon after the 1989 collapse of the Iron Curtain, German firms founded tens of thousands of subsidiaries in Eastern Europe, thereby establishing themselves as the major direct investors in the region. These subsidiaries have steadily expanded in the wake of political stabilization, EU membership and huge differences in wage costs. Today, Germany is by far the largest direct investor in Eastern Europe, bigger than the United States, France and Britain put together.[8] The level of investment by German firms is now responsible for a substantial part of the output of the East European countries. Hungary, which welcomed German investors early on, tops the list. The Hungarian government claims that up to 40 percent of Hungarian manufacturing output in 2003 was generated by German firms.[9]

The list of little-known SMEs that have moved substantial activities to Eastern Europe is long and grows monthly. To mention just a few examples, Behr produces air conditioners in the Czech Republic, Hako Holding builds cleaning machines in Poland, Edscha manufactures car parts in the Czech and Slovak Republics, Hugo Kern and Liebers produce car springs in the Czech Republic and Estonia, and Leoni manufactures cable sets in the Slovak Republic and Hungary. The incentive to relocate is especially large in the labor-intensive textiles and clothing industry. Steilmann Fashions and Gerry Weber produce most of their women's clothing in Romania. The sporty Frankenwälder clothes are produced in Romania and Bulgaria, and the elegant clothes of Hammer Fashion are sewn in the Czech Republic and Hungary.

German SMEs have spearheaded capitalist development in Eastern Europe, and have enjoyed fat profits in the process. This has not gone unnoticed by international investors. Private equity funds in particular have become increasingly interested in the acquisition of German companies that are seen as providing clues to profitable engagement in Eastern Europe. The reason is simple. It is typically difficult to control direct investment in Eastern Europe from the United States or Great Britain, as immature legal institutions and geographic distance often constitute insurmountable obstacles. Acquiring German SMEs is one solution. With their technological knowledge and their geographical and cultural proximity, they are the ideal vehicles by which American equity capital can be transported to Eastern Europe to earn high rates of return. Sometimes, the investors were not primarily interested in the German production sites, but wanted to acquire the brand name, the engineering skills and the production know-how. After establishing control over the acquired firms, they scaled down the production in Germany and opened up plants in other countries with lower production costs. Many German politicians see this trend as an alarming development. In the 2005 election campaign, Social Democratic Party Leader Franz Müntefering, currently Germany's vice-chancellor, went so far as to compare the private equity investors with locusts that raid the harvest and then vanish from sight. Müntefering was motivated by the fate of Grohe, a world leader in metal bathroom fittings that was bought up by BC Partners, Texas Pacific Group, and CSFB Private Equity (an affiliate of Credit Suisse First Boston). They had planned to shift substantial parts of Grohe's production to other countries, but after the public outcry caused by Müntefering's intervention, the company decided to close only one of its plants. While Müntefering drastically overstated the case and overlooked the fact that private equity companies provide German SMEs with urgently needed venture capital, he did express a fear about globalization and open capital markets that is widely held in Germany.

Of course, most German SMEs continue to center most of their activities in Germany. However, the enormous acceleration in relocating SMEs in recent years, coupled with an extremely low level of domestic investment and huge financial outflows, bodes poorly for employment prospects in Germany. And in the current economic environment, Germany simply cannot afford to view these developments with indifference.

A Bazaar Economy

In the face of intense international competition, thousands of German firms are moving ever-larger parts of the value-added chain to low-wage countries. Many firms are eager to benefit from low-cost production abroad, but are unwilling to inform German consumers about where these goods were primarily manufactured. They continue to offer their wares under the traditional German brand names. Consumers continue to believe that they are buying German-made products when very often only the final assembly of prefabricated intermediate imports and the distribution is done in Germany, and German jobs connected with the product are primarily located behind the sales counter. The products are shipped to Germany from Asia or Eastern Europe, sometimes already with a German brand label attached. The money earned on production is made abroad while Germany, for its part, slowly converges to a bazaar economy that specializes on engineering, design, final assembly and trade.[10] The domestic value added per unit of production value, the so-called production depth, is declining year by year.

Not even the automobile industry, the showpiece of German industry, has been immune to misleading branding. The brand name is all important, and it does not matter where the car or the parts are produced. Not a single Audi motor is now produced in Germany. The entire production process for the engines has already been relocated to Györ in Hungary, which created a duty-free zone especially for Audi in anticipation of EU accession. In addition to its Polo, VW produces its Touareg in Bratislava in the Slovak Republic. Porsche nominally assembles its Cayenne in Leipzig, but in fact only the engine is actually installed there. The cars that leave the factory gates do not look much different from the ones that enter the factory through the back door, having been shipped in from Volkswagen's plant in Bratislava. According to a study by Dudenhöffer, barely 33 percent of that car's production cost continues to be German.[11] Even for a BMW, 73 percent of the production value is generated by suppliers, about half of whom are located abroad. And the suppliers located in Germany have large parts of their output produced in foreign plants. Yet each of these firms claim to produce "German" cars.

This is the trend of the time. The French automobile industry would not have been able to recover had they not been able to integrate Japanese engines and German high-tech equipment such as anti-lock brake controls, fuel injection, and GPS systems, and it is doubtful whether Toyota would be as competitive as it is without its wide net of intermediate parts producers spread over East Asia. However, it seems that the German manufacturers have driven this trend to a particularly high degree of perfection.

In a sense, Germany has always been a bazaar economy. Its SMEs offer the world a fabulously rich variety of high quality manufacturing products, typically intermediate products bought by other firms rather than by final consumers. The width of the intermediate product range offered is hardly matched by another country. Having 450 world market leaders and another 500 champion league companies is impressive. It is also impressive that 15 of the 20 biggest trade fairs of all kinds, their size measured by indoor exhibition space, take place in Germany. They include Bauma & Mining in Munich, CeBIT in Hanover, Automechanika in Frankfurt, interpack in Düsseldorf, and IIAA in Frankfurt, but not such important fairs as the Frankfurt Book Fair or the Cologne Photokina, which do not rank in the top twenty.[12]

What is new, however, is that the country now seems to specialize more and more in bazaar activities. In earlier times, the German bazaar sold goods that were produced on its own backyard workbenches. Nowadays, these workbenches are increasingly shifted abroad, predominantly to in the new Eastern European EU member states whose labor force, on average, works for one-eighth of the German industrial wage.

The relocation of value added by the manufacturing industry has two manifestations: offshoring and outsourcing. Offshoring, as mentioned earlier, is the relocation of parts of the firm to its own foreign subsidiary. Outsourcing is the relocation of production processes to suppliers who may be located at home or abroad. Offshoring includes the spectacular examples cited above. Due to the increased use of Internet tenders, outsourcing to foreign countries has also greatly accelerated of late. More and more parts that go into German manufacturing products are supplied by low-price suppliers that are located elsewhere in the world. The production depth—that is, the firms' own share of value added in the final products on shop shelves—is continuously shrinking.

Of course, this picture of Germany as a bazaar economy is only a caricature. It is not true that most German producers are only assembly firms that order the necessary parts via the Internet somewhere in the world and then put them together like model airplanes. Nor is it true that German manufacturers will in the future only supply the world with goods which have been produced exclusively in Germany's Eastern European hinterland. Reality, however, may be catching up with this caricature faster than most believe possible.

The speed of this development can be seen in figure 2.1, which presents index curves for important characteristics of manufacturing production, based

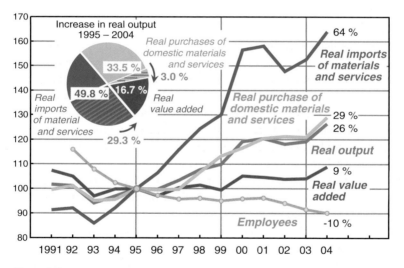

Figure 2.1
The bazaar economy: Components of the change in German manufacturing output from 1991 to 2004, with 1995 as the base year. Shaded areas show the extent to which reduction of production depth may be traced to a more than proportional increase of materials and services purchased from other domestic and foreign sectors. Sources: R. Hild, "Produktion, Wertschöpfung und Beschäftigung im verarbeitenden Gewerbe," *Ifo Schnelldienst* 57, no. 7, 2004, pp. 19–27; input-output tables: Statistisches Bundesamt, Fachserie 18, Reihe 2; national accounts: Statistisches Bundesamt, Fachserie 18, Reihe 1.1, Statistisches Bundesamt, Fachserie 18, Reihe 1.2; foreign trade: Statistisches Bundesamt, Fachserie 7, Reihe1; price indices for imports and exports: Statistisches Bundesamt, Fachserie 17, Reihe 8; price indices for industrial products: Statistisches Bundesamt, Fachserie 17, Reihe 2; Ifo Institute calculations.

on data from 1995. Especially notable are the curves representing real output and real value added. Real output is the inflation adjusted total value of the manufacturing goods produced in one year, and real value added is that part of this value that was produced in the manufacturing sector itself. Value added corresponds to the primary income and taxes earned in the manufacturing industry—that is, essentially the sum of gross profits, interest paid, gross wages and salaries, social security contributions, and indirect taxes. What is not included are intermediate inputs supplied from elsewhere. Because of the intermediate inputs, the value of the final output is always greater than the value added. Both numbers would grow at the same rate if the share of intermediate inputs remained constant over time—that is, if the industrial production depth did not change. But that is not the case, as figure 2.1 shows.

Since the mid 1990s the curves have diverged dramatically. Whereas the manufacturing sector's real output rose by 26 percent from 1995 to 2004, a bit faster than the growth of European gross domestic product (see figure 1.2), the manufacturing sector's real value added increased by only 9 percent. To a considerable extent the increase in German manufacturing production can apparently be traced to an increase in intermediate inputs from other areas. No wonder then that employment in manufacturing declined by 10 percent in the period under consideration.

Where have the intermediate products come from? Two obvious locations are other domestic sectors and foreign sectors. Not much appears to have changed in the former: The output of domestic sectors delivering goods and services to the manufacturing sector rose by 29 percent, only a bit faster than output itself. There has, however, been a lot of action in imported intermediate goods, shown in the uppermost curve in figure 2.1. From 1995 to 2004, the intermediate imports of the manufacturing sector rose by 64 percent in real terms; seven times the rate of value added and 2.5 times that of production. Although imports declined temporarily in 2002 for cyclical reasons, the trend is truly dramatic. It reflects the flight of German manufacturers to Eastern Europe and elsewhere, as was described earlier.[13]

Another way to demonstrate this point is to set the increase in the manufacturing sector's real output during the period considered equal to 100 percent and then decompose this increase in terms of value added. This is shown by the pie chart in figure 2.1. Obviously, the German manufacturing sector itself contributed only 16.7 percent to its output increase. Additional intermediate inputs from other domestic sectors accounted for 33.5 percent, and additional intermediate inputs from abroad accounted for 49.8 percent.[14] The contribution by domestic sectors outside manufacturing is not particularly remarkable: It results primarily from the fact that these sectors contributed their normal share to manufacturing output. Remarkably, however, 49.8 percent of the additional output of the manufacturing sector resulted from an increase in intermediate inputs produced abroad, which is 29.3 percentage points more than the share expected on the basis of 1995 data.

The shaded parts of the pie chart show what fractions of the components of the increase in value added in manufacturing since 1995 have been displaced by other domestic sectors and foreign countries. Had all three components of manufacturing output—i.e. own value added of the manufacturing sector, intermediate inputs supplied by other domestic sectors, and intermediate inputs from abroad—changed in fixed proportion, the share of the manufacturing sector's own value added in the increase of its output would have amounted to 49 percent. That this share is actually only 16.7 percent results from the displacement effects that together amount to 32.3 percentage points. The above-mentioned 29.3 percentage points were crowded out by imported intermediate goods, and 3 percentage points were crowded out by additional purchases of domestic intermediate goods. This can also be expressed by saying that ten-elevenths (29.3/32.3) of the reduction in production depth of the German manufacturing sector from 1995 to 2004 resulted from offshoring and international outsourcing and the remaining one-eleventh (3/32.3) from outsourcing to other domestic sectors.

Why the Bazaar Effect Is Too Strong

The public is usually more alarmed by outsourcing and offshoring activities than are economists. Economists tend to argue that the relocation of manufacturing production abroad is a natural development that generates the classical textbook-type gains from specialization and trade. Economists see it as a sign of an improved international division of labor that increases welfare in all countries, and argue that in view of the increased international low-wage competition in intermediate manufacturing goods it is wise for Germany to specialize in those exporting sectors where it has a comparative advantage or to develop the internal sectors that are not subject to international competition. Thus the service, construction and high-tech sectors could expand at the expense of simple manufacturing work. How convenient that the Chinese and the Poles are willing to do those unappealing industrial jobs for Germans, enabling them to put the former manufacturing workers to better uses! These former workers can wait on tables, build new houses, or, even better, sit at computers and do things that generate higher value added and incomes than would have been possible in manufacturing. This is supposed to make both the Chinese and the Germans happy. They all enjoy gains from trade and specialization.

Although not false in principle, this assessment does not do justice to the actual situation. It is true that manufacturing employment has declined substantially in recent years. Actually, there is no other OECD country where it declined as quickly as in Germany since the collapse of the Iron Curtain.[15] But if the observed development were indeed such a healthy restructuring process, there should have been a sufficient number of additional jobs created in the rest of the economy. Unfortunately, these have not materialized. During the period 1995–2005, the total number of full-time-equivalent (FTE) jobs in the German manufacturing sector declined by 1.21 million, but in the entire rest of the economy there were no additional jobs in net terms. In fact, even there, FTE employment declined by 150,000, adding to a total of 1.36 million FTE job losses.[16]

Where did the displaced manufacturing workers go? There is only one answer: They went from a state of employment to the welfare state. That was the improvement in the division of labor à l'Allemande. The blue-collar industrial jobs went away, but the displaced workers have not gone to the service or construction sectors, and they do not sit in front of a computer screen in a high-tech company. They lay back and relax at home, enjoying their unemployment or early-retirement benefits. If they do sit in front of a screen, then chances are it is a TV screen.

This rather disturbing state of affairs calls into question the textbook view of the gains from trade and specialization. In principle, outsourcing and offshoring are useful developments for Germany. However, the pace of this development is accelerated by institutional deficiencies in the German labor market. As will be shown in chapters 3 and 4, German wages are extremely rigid because of the power of unions and because of the wage-replacement incomes paid by the welfare state. The maintenance of domestic wages above the market clearing level results in excessive outsourcing and offshoring in manufacturing, and too few jobs are created in other parts of the economy to compensate for these losses. The result is reflected in the rapid decline in aggregate employment.

At some level, the comparison between the status quo in Germany and the first-best economic solution (where with flexible wages the economy reacts efficiently to the changing world environment) may be unfair. The fact of the matter is that there exist institutional constraints on wage flexibility. Thus, an alternative angle would be to take a second-best view, taking Germany's wage structures as given.

Certainly, if one assumes that German wages and the institutional causes of their rigidity are carved in stone, relocation of value added abroad may be welcomed insofar as many German manufacturers would otherwise have to file for bankruptcy in the face of international competition. This would result in even higher job loss than is currently the case. Viewed in this light, the public blame put on those firms that relocate their jobs abroad is misplaced. Not only is it morally unjustified; it overlooks that in the present global economic circumstances this is a strategy to preserve jobs that otherwise would have been lost. If anyone is to blame, it is the politicians who remain resistant to institutional and economic change.

The public should be grateful that EU eastern enlargement has given German firms the possibility to outsource and offshore parts of their production chains to low-wage countries. Just in the nick of time, the companies have found a way to fend off competition from the Chinese and the Asian Tigers in their product markets. By averaging German and Eastern European wage costs, not only they but also some of their German workers remain competitive. And in some cases, as with the Porsche Cayenne, it may even be possible to generate at least a few additional jobs in Germany. Without industry in Bratislava, there would be no industry in Leipzig.

These considerations are also important for an evaluation of the bazaar effect. The development toward a bazaar economy is, in principle, compatible with a best reaction of the economy. A perfect market economy with flexible wages should, if confronted with low-wage-location alternatives, offshore and outsource some of the labor-intensive upstream parts of the production chain and shift the released factors of production to more capital-intensive sectors that are more immune to international low-wage competition. However, Germany is not a perfect market economy. Due to rigid high wages and the resulting unemployment, the actual pace of the development is too fast relative to the first-best outcome. The current pace of outsourcing and offshoring may be optimal only in a second-best sense, when the rigidity as such is taken as given. It can be interpreted as a strategy of damage avoidance.

However, that there is damage can hardly be disputed. Germany's enormous increase in unemployment (figure 2.2) and its poor growth performance (figure 2.3) speak for themselves. A country whose growth rate is the second-lowest in Europe, which builds up more and more unemployment, and which is gradually being surpassed in national income by one country after another is doing something wrong. In recent years, Germany has been unable to react flexibly to the forces of globalization and unable to take advantage of these forces. Historians may one day wonder why the dangers were not recognized and counteracted in time.

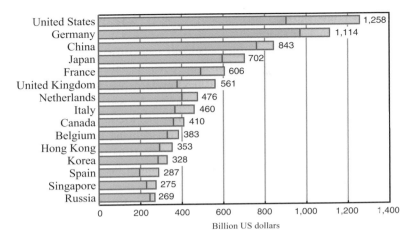

Figure 2.2
Merchandise export (blue) and export of commercial services (orange) by the fifteen leading exporters in 2005. Source: WTO World Trade Report, 2006.

The Export Puzzle

There are other opinions about Germany's ability to realize gains from trade and an improvement in the division of labor than the one presented here. Some economists, particularly left-leaning ones, assert that the country cannot be in such bad shape because, after all, it is the world's export champion.[17] And politicians are happy to repeat this benign argument. In every other speech, former chancellor Schröder praised German export championship, and his rival, Oskar Lafontaine, founder of the Linkspartei, continues to do the same. The presumption is that a country that is the world's export champion can hardly suffer from dwindling competitiveness. Wages cannot possibly be too high or too rigid, for if they were, exports would be lower. The warnings of the 253 German economics professors who publicly declared[18] on June 29, 2005 that Germany must find ways to liberalize its labor markets and reduce wage costs are dismissed as neo-liberal nonsense.

Do the left-leaning economists have a point here? How can a country be a growth laggard and experience ever-increasing unemployment if, at the same time, it manages to beat all other countries in world markets?

Economists on the left maintain that Germany is competitive but lacks domestic demand because wages are too low. Higher wages, they claim, would boost the domestic economy in addition to the export sector, so that Germany could return to full employment and growth. This argument, routinely presented on TV talk shows, enjoys great popularity in Germany because it requires no real change or sacrifice.

Apart from the fact that higher wages would not increase aggregate demand (as will be explained below), this solution is unconvincing because Germany's problems go far beyond the short-run business-cycle explanation, for which Keynesian demand arguments may be appropriate. As a result of the debt financing of reunification expenses, Germany has had the largest Keynesian deficit spending program in history. If Keynesian demand policies helped, Germany really should have been Europe's most dynamic region over the period 1995–2005 instead of its laggard. The solution of the puzzle must lie elsewhere.

Before we try to solve the puzzle, it is instructive to examine the extent to which Germany actually is the world's export champion.

First, it is true that Germany has the highest nominal commodity export volume in the world. In commodity exports, Germany tops the United States, China, and Japan—a remarkable achievement indeed. However, Germany is the champion only in exports of commodities, excluding services (such as tourism, computer software, and financial services). In total exports, the United States is the world's unchallenged champion. In 2005, American exports amounted to 1,258 billion dollars (1,011 billion euros) at current exchange rates, while German exports stood at 1,114 billion dollars (895 billion euros), followed by China's at 843 billion dollars (678 billion euros). Figure 2.2 shows the relevant numbers with and without services.

Second, the evolution of the world share of German exports is heavily influenced by exchange-rate movements, which often mask real economic changes. Exchange-rate shifts result in opposite and deferred price and quantity reactions of exports. In the short run, the price reaction always dominates; in the long run, it is the quantity effect that dominates. Consider, for example, the appreciation of the euro from an average of US$ 0.90 in 2001 to US$1.24 in 2005. This will surely have a negative effect on export quantities. However, the quantity reaction takes place with a delay and may not yet have unfolded completely. In the short run, the dominant effect is a mere revaluation of German exports if measured in dollar terms. In and of itself, the currency revaluation increased the dollar value of German exports by 39 percent, given the export quantities.

Third, the volume of German exports increasingly involves goods that, in large part, were produced abroad. Audi cars, which are exported from the German town of Ingolstadt to the United States, are included in German export data at full value, although their engines and other components are supplied from Győr in Hungary and other foreign locations. Similarly, 100 percent of the Porsche Cayenne, shipped from Leipzig to Paris, is counted as a German export, but most of the Cayenne is produced outside Germany. The international success of Audi and Porsche reflects the companies' competitiveness to the extent that their automobiles bear valuable trademarks that stand for excellent engineering and elegant design, but it does not necessarily reflect the competitiveness of German jobs. Recall that during the period 1995–2005 no fewer than 1.21 million full-time-equivalent jobs were lost in German manufacturing, while no other jobs were created in the rest of the economy in net terms.

A bazaar economy can post wonderful export statistics, but these do not necessarily demonstrate the underlying strength of its domestic manufacturing sector—sometimes the opposite. Hong Kong, for example, is a mature bazaar economy that functions as a crossroads. In 2003, the city had an export volume equal to 166 percent of its own gross domestic product. But nobody would deduce from this number that Hong Kong is an important manufacturing location or that Hong Kong's industrial workers are particularly competitive on the global stage. If anything, the export volume tells something about the competitiveness of a country as a place of transfer—a bazaar.

After the German publication of this book and the ensuing public debate, the German statistical office did a special investigation into the import content of German exports for a limited number of years to clarify the issue.[19] The results show that the imported value-added content of German exports had increased from 27 percent to 39 percent in the period 1991–2002. Moreover, it follows from the data provided by the office that at the margin the real import content of German exports was 53 percent.[20] That is, of each additional real euro a German exporter earned on exports, he needed 53 cents to buy the intermediate imports necessary to produce these exports. This number provides some corroboration that, as figure 2.1 shows, 49.8 percent of the increase in real manufacturing output from 1995 to 2004 can be attributed to additional imports of intermediate products. (Note that manufacturing output is not identical to exports and that the time periods considered are not fully identical. Thus a slight difference in these numbers is not implausible.)

The sharp increase in the import content of German exports implies that exports grow faster than the domestic value added contained in those exports. In fact, the information provided by the statistical office implies that the elasticity of real exports with regard to real value added contained in exports was 1.3 in the period 1991–2002.[21] Thus, adjusting for inflation, a one percent increase in domestic value added contained in exports resulted in a 1.3 percent increase in the export volume.

The three qualifications made above should be borne in mind in interpreting the export statistics. Nevertheless, it certainly remains true that the value-added content of German exports—that is, the income earned in the export sector, is growing faster than GDP or any other measure of aggregate income. While the value-added content per unit of exports declines, the quantity of exports increases so rapidly that the decline in the value-added content per unit of exports is more than compensated. Germans earn a growing share of their incomes in the export industry even though an increasing fraction of their exports are being produced outside Germany.

Critics have cited the increase in export-induced value added as evidence that Germany enjoys new gains from international trade and is a winner of globalization.[22] But this conclusion is too hasty. Gains from trade are gains from an improvement in the division of labor. Whether such gains have actually occurred cannot easily be inferred from trade statistics. Rather, a proper judgment requires a look at the labor market data. It is the labor market where a better division of labor should become visible. Unfortunately, however, the increase in unemployment clearly speaks against a favorable assessment that Germany ultimately is able to augment its gains from trade.

Trade statistics themselves cannot be interpreted in the way the critics suggest because there is such a thing as a pathological export boom in terms of value added, i.e., an excessive increase in the sum of all factor incomes earned in the export industry. This excessive increase may result from an artificially maintained wage differential with regard to international trading partners that does not follow from the law of supply and demand, but rather from institutional constraints such as the actions of unions and repercussions of the wage competition posed by the welfare state.[23] To explain why this is the case, suppose that a country like Germany—that is, a country rich in material and human capital, with high wages for unskilled labor—opens up trade with another region or country that is poor in capital but rich in unskilled labor (say, the Asian Tigers, where wages are low). Let the term "capital" include both material and human capital, and let "labor" as well as the "wage" refer to unskilled labor. Suppose for a moment that Germany has flexible wages. It will then react like a well-functioning market economy and specialize in capital-intensive production. The labor-intensive industries will shrink, releasing their factors of production, and the capital-intensive sectors will grow, absorbing these factors. When all the released capital is reemployed in the capital-intensive sectors and the technologies of the sectors do not change, some of the jobs will, by definition, be lost. Therefore wages will fall. The fall in wages induces two reactions. For one thing, both sectors will switch to less capital-intensive production processes. More importantly, the switch from the labor-intensive to the capital-intensive sectors itself slows down. With lower wages, a brake is put on this switch that allows for a fine-tuning of the structural change. Because of the wage reduction, more activities in the labor-intensive sectors can survive, in which case fewer workers and less capital move to the capital-intensive export sectors, and less value added is generated there, than would otherwise have been the case. Both reactions combined would prevent any unemployment, implying that a flexible Germany would efficiently exploit the new trade options.

But Germany does not have flexible wages. If German wages cannot fall, no sector will change its capital intensity, and, in particular, the sector shift will not slow down. The brake for fine-tuning the structural change is blocked. As a result, the economy moves too far in the direction of the capital-intensive export sector. There is overspecialization, overcapitalization in both sectors, and unemployment. Value added in exports is too high and value added in the aggregate is too low, due to the idleness of some of the work force. There is a pathological export boom.

The rigidity of wages explains why Germany can be the world champion in merchandise exports and a growth laggard with mass unemployment at the same time. Germany's wages for unskilled workers are determined not by supply and demand but by strong unions and the repercussions of the welfare state. The next two chapters will investigate this in detail.

The bazaar effect does not play a particular role in this explanation, but it reinforces the export boom, making export quantities grow faster than value added. As upstream activities in production chains tend to be more labor intensive than downstream activities, the bazaar effect in itself is a particular example of specialization in more capital-intensive sectors. A Germany with flexible wages that reacts efficiently to the forces of globalization would also exhibit the bazaar effect to some extent. The effect would be limited, however, because declining wages would again slow down the specialization in bazaar activities. In contrast, when wages are rigid and the sector shift brake is not operative, the sector shift becomes a landslide instead of a more controlled adjustment. There is excessive vertical specialization on downstream activities—that is, on those parts of the production chains that are close to customers. This is what justifies the pejorative undertone in the term "bazaar effect." Thus, not only is there too much value added in exports, there is also too much export volume relative to this value added. There is a pathological export boom in a double sense.

In summary: To a considerable extent, Germany reacts to the forces of international low-wage competition as is predicted by the economic theory of foreign trade. Labor-intensive sectors (e.g. textiles and leather production) shrink, while capital-intensive sectors (e.g. automobiles, chemistry, toolmaking) expand. The country specializes in activities where it has a comparative advantage. However, because of the rigidity of its wages for its workers, it lacks the brake on sector shift that would limit and fine-tune the specialization on capital-intensive export sectors. There is a landslide sector shift toward export industries with excessive destruction of the domestic sectors. And as the sector shift also entails cutting off and shifting abroad the upstream parts of the production chains, the export volume even increases more than value added generated in exports. This is the solution to the German puzzle. The sluggish growth, the increase in unemployment, the weakness of the domestic sector, the rapidly declining production depth and the world vice-championship in exports all have the same sad explanation.

And the Export Surplus?

Economists on the left also point to Germany's huge current-account surplus as evidence of its competitiveness. In 2005, the current-account surplus amounted to 95 billion euros (118 billion dollars).[24] This, they maintain, proves that the country is enjoying gains from trade and is integrating well into the changing world economy.[25]

Unfortunately, this argument is also flawed for the simple reason that the current-account surplus measures Germany's capital exports. There is no difference between saying that Germany has a surplus in its current account or that it is a net exporter of capital. The surplus of goods and services relative to foreign countries implies an increase in Germany's stock of foreign currencies. As this stock bears no interest, the Germans use it for other purposes. Logically, if they do not want to keep it, they can either use it to buy foreign assets or give it away to foreigners without return. The former is called "capital exports," the latter "international transfers." The capital exports include the purchase of foreign stocks, bonds, firms or real estate that Germans buy abroad. The international transfers include, for example, federal contributions to the EU budget, guest worker remittances to their families or development aid. Subtracting the international transfers from the export surplus thus yields capital exports, but by definition this is the current-account surplus.

A current-account surplus caused by competitive forces may imply capital exports as a residual, but capital exports may also move the current account. No matter which is the case, the two items are always identical.

Although Germany ran current-account deficits in the 1990s, it has run a surplus since 2001. The deficits were likely caused by the costs incurred for reconstructing East Germany, and the surplus was at least in part caused by capital flight from Germany.[26] The assets acquired abroad include, not least, the many companies and subsidiaries established there by German firms. And these include the supplemental loans granted to those firms for their involvement abroad, as well as loans that German banks extended to foreigners to finance profitable investment abroad. With regard to Eastern Europe, this relationship is obvious. Eastern European countries have very large current-account deficits because they attract international capital for the reconstruction of their economies by offering low wages and high returns on capital. These deficits are matched by the current-account surpluses of the capital-exporting countries, including Germany.

A country like Germany characterized by capital flight and minimal domestic net investment must have a current-account surplus. As was mentioned in chapter 1, in 2005, aggregate German savings amounted to 145 billion euros.[27] Net investment, however, was only 50 billion euros. (See figure 1.1.) The difference—95 billion euros, or 5.9 of NDP—showed up as capital exports and a current-account surplus.

The surplus may originate from direct exports of machinery produced in Germany and shipped abroad. More often, though, it is generated indirectly when, as a consequence of exports of financial capital, capital goods purchases are relocated from the home country to foreign countries. The relocation makes goods cheaper at home and more expensive abroad, and, as a consequence, trade flows are redirected from the home country to foreign countries implying more exports of goods and services. The capital-exporting country achieves a current-account surplus because its goods become cheaper. Its rate of inflation declines or its currency depreciates. In contrast, a country that imports capital will see its goods become more expensive via inflation or appreciation and will have a deficit in its current account. This is worth keeping in mind when interpreting the data.

Today, Germany is definitely in a situation in which its goods are becoming cheaper compared to other euro-area countries. The country is experiencing a so-called real depreciation, because with a common currency an open depreciation is no longer possible in the euro area. While a nominal depreciation requires a reduction in the foreign exchange value of a country's currency, a real depreciation takes place by way of having a lower inflation than other countries. During the first five years after European Monetary Union Germany's inflation rate amounted to 1.3 percent, while the average of the euro-area countries was 2.0 percent. Temporarily, there were even fears that Germany might experience deflation.

It is therefore likely that the German current-account surplus reflects capital flight. Because of high wage rates compared to other locations in Eastern

Europe and elsewhere, financial and real capital is finding more profitable investment opportunities abroad.

To some extent this capital flight may be efficient. It makes sense for rich countries such as Germany to invest some of their savings in poor countries with low wages, because higher private and social returns to capital can be generated there than at home. However, if the domestic wages that drive this process result from labor market rigidities rather than from competitive forces, the country's reaction is not efficient. Its capital exports are too large, and so is its current-account surplus.

In fact, as wages are rigid, the production technology (capital/labor ratio) remains fixed and the current-account surplus measures the dislocation of jobs abroad. Thus the surplus in part reflects German workers' competitive problems rather than a particular competitive strength of the German economy, as maintained by the left-leaning economists.

Here, the pathological component of the current-account surplus bears a striking similarity to the pathological export boom. The international low-wage competition that arose in Asia and in the formerly communist European countries rendered many labor-intensive firms in Germany unprofitable. These firms released their capital by closing down or failing to reinvest in their depreciating capital stock. As was explained in the preceding section, the process went too far because German wages did not fall despite the low-wage competition from abroad, causing unemployment. Some of the freed capital moved to the capital-intensive sectors of the economy that needed only a small number of expensive workers. This shift caused the pathological export boom. However, some capital also moved abroad creating the current-account surplus. Both the high exports and the high current-account surplus resulted in part from Germany's rigid wage structures.

For these reasons, neither the high export volume as such nor the high export surplus says anything about the competitiveness of German workers. The competitiveness of German workers can only be truly discerned in one number and that is the unemployment rate itself. When it rises, their competitiveness has deteriorated, and when it falls, it has improved. Right now, almost five million Germans are unemployed. Five million Germans are no longer competitive. That is the bitter truth.

Three Simultaneous Shocks: The EU Internal Market, the Euro, and EU Enlargement

Many European countries face similar challenges to those faced by Germany, but most of them seem to be coping much better. Germany, once Europe's economic leader, is now its laggard and is being surpassed by one country after another in terms of per capita income. Until the 1980s, West Germany was the big player in the EU. Its economy was by far the largest, its per capita income ranked in Europe's top group, and its combination of prosperity and social protection was envied and admired in both the East and the West. Abutting the Iron Curtain, its economic power and the high living standard of its workers were a permanent threat to Communists, as these attributes clearly demonstrated the inferiority of their system and contributed to the growing opposition of the people in the East. Germany's large industrial network of firms was dense and extremely productive, and the increasing number of unemployed as well as substantial transfers to the EU could, it seemed, easily be financed from the government budget. The deutschmark had become the world's second-biggest transactions currency after the dollar and was widely used in Eastern Europe and elsewhere. Germany was the place of stability and prosperity whose benefits many others wanted to share. Why has the situation changed so dramatically, why has Germany fallen behind, why does it have so much more difficulty coping with globalization than other European countries?

One unique reason is surely the reunification process in the early 1990s, which imposed a large burden on Germany. Another reason is Germany's institutional rigidities, including the rigidity of the labor market and, in particular, the wrong incentives created by its social system. These rigidities prevent the country from responding appropriately to external challenges such as globalization and international low-wage competition, and, indeed, this is the main theme of this book. However, the challenges themselves may have been more difficult for Germany than for other countries.

There are three main challenges which affect Germany differently than other EU countries: the creation of the European internal market, the introduction of the euro, and EU eastern enlargement. Let us have a closer look at them.

The creation of the EU internal market is a particular challenge for Germany, because it removes Germany's artificial advantage, by accident of geography and population, of having a larger domestic market than the other countries. In the old Europe, which still had many trade barriers, the small countries were disadvantaged because of the limitations of their markets. Only the bigger countries, Germany in particular, were able to maintain large-scale industrial production networks and thereby maintain a higher level of productivity. German industry, from electronics to automobiles, profited from this effect, and it may be considered one of the essential reasons for Germany's superior productivity. The creation of the European internal market and the abolition of all tariff barriers in the early 1990s put an end to this. Now even a firm in Luxembourg has free access to the same 450 million European consumers as one in Germany. Obviously, the common market helps the small countries to overcome their size disadvantages.

Think of Nokia, which in 1990 was a small Finnish television manufacturer on the brink of bankruptcy. In 2000 it enjoyed the highest stock-market capitalization of all European companies. Without Finland's EU accession in 1995, Nokia could never have become the market leader of the European mobile phone industry, because it could never have matched the home bias of Siemens, its German competitor. Under the old system Nokia's engineers would have had to sell their patents to Siemens in order to enter the German market. The mobile phones might then have been slightly bigger, but Siemens would probably have been number 1 in Europe. In fact, however, Siemens gave up its mobile phone production in 2005.

Similarly, without the EU internal market, Ireland could not have become Europe's center of software production, and Portugal or Greece could not have become preferred locations for the large-scale production of electrical household appliances. The small EU countries are the big winners of EU integration; they are the tigers of Europe, as reflected by their marvelous growth performance. (See figure 1.5.)

German business representatives were way off the mark in predicting this result. They had always argued that a larger European internal market would result in German firms increasing their market shares. What the representatives overlooked, however, was that with the creation of the EU internal market Germany lost its comparative agglomeration advantages. Suddenly, much smaller countries also became attractive locations for large-scale production.

The EU also overlooked this effect, at least in its official research documents preparing the political moves toward the internal market. The famous Cecchini Report, for example, was right in predicting large gains from specialization for Europe as a whole due to the exploitation of economies of scale.[28] However, except for a short remark in its summary, it was surprisingly silent about the obvious implication that the small European countries would gain much more from this effect than the big ones.

To be sure, these considerations do not imply that Germany is losing from market integration in absolute terms. That would be a too hasty a conclusion, as will be explained in more detail in the next section. However, it does mean that the smaller countries now have relatively more advantages. There is nothing wrong with this. The idea of a united Europe rests in part on doing away with internal borders which have long encumbered the continent's economic development. Nevertheless it is important to realize that the creation of the internal market is one of the explanations for why Germany, like Italy, has been growing at a slower pace than the other European countries in the period 1995–2005.

The second uniquely German challenge is the advent of the euro. It has made the competitive environment for German jobs more difficult because the euro leveled the playing field in the capital market and deprived Germany of the advantage of comparatively low interest rates. As figure 2.3 shows, the euro has resulted in a dramatic convergence of bond rates in Europe. In 1995, the bond rates of many European countries were still four to five percentage points above German rates, and as no exchange-rate realignments had taken place in the meantime, these were real, not just nominal differences. At the time, exchange-rate uncertainty demanded that borrowers in these countries pay a high risk premium to international investors as compensation for possible devaluation losses. German firms, in contrast, under the protection of the deutschmark, enjoyed the great advantage of receiving financing terms other countries could only dream of. The solidity of its financial system was one of the reasons for Germany's prosperity. Only Dutch and Austrian firms shared this advantage, because their currencies were always firmly tied to the deutschmark, which effectively functioned as Europe's anchor currency and became the basis for the euro.

The mere announcement of the euro and the concrete preparations since 1995 for its introduction changed all that. Bond interest rates have

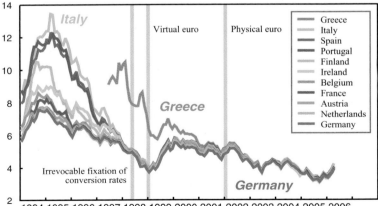

Figure 2.3
European 10-year bond-rate convergence caused by euro (percent per annum.) Sources: national central banks.

converged very rapidly, and all of these are now close to or already at the German level. Differences of 20 to 30 basis points (a basis point is a hundredth of a percentage point) are hardly worth mentioning and are too small to be seen in figure 2.3. Even Greece, which introduced the euro relatively late, has been able to benefit considerably from the convergence of interest rates.

Although interest rate convergence does not actually hurt German firms directly as interest rates are now low, for cyclical reasons, it helps the firms in other countries, robbing German business of the important competitive advantage it had previously enjoyed under the protection of the deutschmark. In the medium term, when the European economy recovers, bond rates may be higher than those to which Germany is historically accustomed. This could be the case because the other European countries, freed from their risk premia, may increase their demand for capital, pushing up interest rates and rerouting even more capital than is the case today to those countries—capital that would have otherwise been invested in Germany.[29]

Before its introduction, speculation abounded regarding the euro's economic impact on Europe. The advantages cited ranged from greater price transparency to saved exchange costs in international trade. By far the most important effect, however, has been interest-rate convergence and the creation of a uniform European capital market.

Today, the Southern European countries have markets for long-term fixed-interest rate loans that were historically rare in these regions but common in Germany. The loans, which permit firms to undertake long-term investments and to create high-quality jobs and individual households to improve living conditions, have been exported with the euro to Spain, to mention only one example. While Spain registered double-digit growth rates in credit volume, Germany suffered from a credit crunch, because its banks lost a substantial fraction of their equity capital and were forced to reduce their outstanding loans so as to avoid being downgraded by international rating agencies. In recent years, German banks have had to cope with the worst profit crisis of the postwar period, and not all of them have survived. The biggest victim was HVB, Germany's second-largest bank, which was sold to Italian Unicredit because it would have been unable to survive on its own. Even those German banks that overcame the crisis look enviously at the returns on equity earned by their competitors in the formerly high-interest countries.

Despite (or perhaps even because) of Germany's problems, the euro will likely have beneficial effects for Europe as a whole. The common capital market ensures that the capital collected by German banks from German savers can freely flow to the most remote corners of the euro zone and help finance investments that were unprofitable at the previous high interest rates. As these projects will typically yield a higher return on capital than the projects not financed in Germany, the reallocation of savings capital away from Germany is probably boosting European GDP.

The countries previously subject to high interest rates undoubtedly benefit from the reallocation, but what this means for German welfare is not clear. On the one hand German savers may earn higher interest income from lending their funds abroad. On the other, as less capital is invested in Germany, German workers will lose, either through wage cuts or through increasing unemployment. The net effect on German welfare will be positive, if the German labor market is sufficiently flexible. If not, more problematic outcomes are also possible.[30]

The third challenge for Germany is EU eastern enlargement. It is true that this affects all West European countries, not only Germany. However, due to its larger geographical and cultural proximity, Germany is more exposed to its effects than most other EU countries, Finland and Austria being obvious exceptions. The eastern EU countries offer excellent investment opportunities for German firms as well as new markets for their products. However, they certainly intensify the low-wage competition German workers are facing in this historical episode. German and Polish workers are now direct competitors for direct investment, and all too often the German workers lose out due to much higher wages and a less flexible labor market.

The recent decision of Sweden's Electrolux to terminate production at its Nuremberg AEG plant, which it had acquired only in 2004, and to move it entirely to Poland demonstrates the nature of the problem. AEG (Allgemeine Elektrizitäts-Gesellschaft), founded in 1899, was once one of Germany's proud producers of electrical equipment—the "German General Electric." In 1970 it employed about 180,000 people. The company had increasing difficulties to cope with international competition from low-wage manufacturers. Its decline took many years. One by one, its plants were closed or sold to competitors. The Swedish decision to relocate the last 1,700 jobs to Poland was only the final step in the sequence of events.

The Eastern European countries that joined the EU on May 1, 2004 (the Czech Republic, Estonia, Hungary, Latvia, Lithuania, Poland, Slovakia, Slovenia[31]) clearly are among the winners of European integration. At present, hourly wage costs in Eastern European EU accession countries are one-eighth of the West German level. The low wages attract capital, jobs are created, growth surges and wages rise in line with productivity. An economic miracle like that experienced by Germany in the postwar period is not a distant promise; it is already underway.

The downside is the restrained investment in Germany. (See figure 1.1.) In past years, many companies hesitated to invest in Germany because they were ready to expand their plants in Eastern Europe in anticipation of the next European boom. Today, they can produce beyond German borders without political constraints and with full legal security, and they are able to export their products to the old EU countries at minimal transport costs and without any tariff barriers.

With EU eastern enlargement, competition for location has assumed quite a different dimension from the 1970s and the 1980s, when German industry primarily had to fend off Asia's low-wage competitors. Asian competitors focus on low-weight high-value goods for which the costs of being shipped halfway around the world are minimal. Eastern European competitors extend the range of products to everything transportable, as the transport routes, especially to Germany, are extraordinarily short. Whereas in the past competition was concentrated on electronics, in the future building materials, perishable produce, primary products, raw materials, and many other goods will be subject to low-wage competition.

Furthermore, when Eastern European countries adopt the euro they will enjoy the additional benefit of low interest rates and will be able to attract a large part of European savings for their own purposes. Their workers will become even more aggressive competitors to German workers and, to a more limited extent, those in other West European countries.

If Germany continues to block the necessary adjustments to its wage rates, it will strengthen the overspecialization effects discussed above that manifest themselves in the pathological export boom and the bazaar effect, and will continue to jeopardize the textbook-type gains from trade that a flexible economy could generate from Eastern European enlargement.

The International Division of Labor: How to Profit from Globalization

If Germany is to prosper, it must find ways to harness the powers of globalization and continuing European integration by becoming more flexible internally. Trying to stop the forces of globalization and European integration is counterproductive and destined for failure, if only for political reasons. The wheel of history cannot be turned back. Blocking the effects of these changes would also be wrong because doing so overlooks the huge positive chances that the opening of markets offers to all countries, including Germany.

The creation of larger European and global markets by eliminating tariff and exchange-rate barriers is a source of increasing welfare because it makes possible gains from trade and specialization for all countries concerned. Countries have different strengths. Some are rich in capital, others in people; still others have good agricultural land and natural resources or a particularly well trained labor force. These differences result in very different relative goods prices as long as borders are closed. The different relative prices are the very basis of advantages of specialization and gains from trade that may be expected from an opening of the borders.

Many Germans tend to belittle gains from trade and do not place these advantages on the same level as the direct fruits of industrious human labor. Unlike the British, the German intellectual elite has a deep-rooted aversion against market processes and often faces difficulties understanding why the mere exchange of commodities could possibly be productive. The British still have a fresh memory of the gains from trade that made their Empire so rich, given that it basically ended only recently, with World War II. The memory that the Germany have of their "Hanseatic League," which for 500 years was Northern Europe's most important trading network, waned instead, being overshadowed by anti-free-market ideas ranging from Marxism to Fascism.

But the Hanseatic League, at least, should be able to convince the skeptics. The Hansa, which was chaired by the mayor of German Lübeck, included about 200 cities stretching from Russian Novograd, Estonian Reval (now Tallin), and Gothlandic Visby in the east to Norwegian Bergen and Flemish Brugge in the west. By abolishing customs and offering mutual protection, the Hanseatic cities were able to generate enormous wealth and prosperity which the tourist can still recognize today by looking at the imposing edifices remaining from that period. The Hanseatic League lasted for about 500 years, from around 1150 to 1650, eventually losing its importance when trade links to the Americas created even more wealth in Great Britain, Portugal, Spain, and the Netherlands.

No doubt there are welfare gains to be had from trade. Competition among merchants and the reactions of the producers who supply the goods to the merchants provide the chance for suppliers, be they individuals, firms, or entire countries, to concentrate on the production of those goods for which they have comparatively favorable conditions and may even realize economies of scale. The advantages accrue generally to all economies participating in trading in the sense that the average standard of living rises.

Today, the developing countries are among the particular winners of globalization and the elimination of tariff barriers. With globalization, the people of China, India, and many other Asian countries are experiencing a rapid improvement of their living standards. It is true that this improvement initially applies only to certain parts of these countries and certain segments of the population and will only gradually spread to the rest, thus increasing domestic inequality in the medium term. However, globalization makes a substantial contribution to overcoming the division of the world into rich and poor. In 1985, 14 percent of the world's people lived in the rich OECD countries and 86 percent lived in poor countries. With India, China, the East Asian Tigers, and the OECD countries, the proportion of people who live in countries that have escaped or are just about to escape the poverty trap now amounts to 55 percent. Of course, this does not in itself mean that every person in these countries participates equally in this progress. Increased inequality typically goes hand in hand with economic development, at least initially. Nevertheless, the proportion of humankind whose real income is below a standardized one dollar per day fell from 44 percent to 13 percent between 1980 and 2000.[32]

To some extent similar advantages are already visible in the still backward countries of Europe that have benefited from EU integration. Ireland's dramatic development was already mentioned in chapter 1. But in Spain, Portugal, Greece, and elsewhere, countries benefited not only from transfers from the EU but also from the free-trade benefits of membership.

Germany, too, has benefited much from globalization. Without world trade it would never have tasted economic success. During the second German empire, under the reigns of Wilhelm I (1871–1888) and Wilhelm II (1888–1918), German products were conquering international markets, making it possible, with the sales revenue, to buy those goods from the rest of the world that could not be produced in Germany at all or only at great expense. And without trade, Germany would not have recovered from World War II. The Wirtschaftswunder (Germany's postwar economic miracle) largely reflects the gains from trade that it was able to enjoy. The fact that Germany has had obvious difficulties in further increasing its gains from trade since the collapse of the Iron Curtain, does not imply that the country no longer reaps gains from trade. In fact, these gains are the basis of the high German standard of living that continue through this day.

In order for Germany to benefit from the new global economy, it is no longer possible to imagine a retreat into a closed economy. Germans do not want to use all the automobiles, all the refrigerators, or all the machine tools that they produce themselves, because they already have plenty of them. Instead they want to sell them in order to be able to import citrus fruits from Israel, petroleum from Saudi Arabia, natural gas from Russia, mobile phones from Finland, video recorders from Taiwan, and tourism services from all over the world.

The strong growth of the capital stock in the industrializing economies will make it possible for Germany to exploit the knowledge advantages it has in the area of capital goods, because it will produce a substantial fraction of machinery and industrial plants that represent this capital stock. It will take some time until the installed machines are able to themselves produce machines—that is, until the developing countries have built up an efficient machine-tool industry that can crowd out Germany's.

Germany can also turn the evolution toward a bazaar economy into a positive development, as indicated above. It can gradually become pivotal in trade between Western and Eastern Europe: a place where the intermediate products from low-wage countries are assembled into final products and tailor made for customers. This geographic location as a crossroads can become an advantage if the pace of Germany's manufacturing employment decline due to outsourcing and offshoring can be slowed and if more jobs are created in operating the trading post and in other services than are lost in direct manufacturing. There is great potential in the market for business services that has already grown by leaps and bounds in recent years. Many Eastern and Southeastern Europeans speak German, and many Germans are well versed in Slavic languages thanks to their communist past. These are natural advantages which need to be better exploited.

If Germany reacts wisely, it can still increase its gains from globalization even today, by specializing in the supply of those goods and services in which it has comparative advantages and is already well positioned. There will always be such products, as it is not possible for a well-functioning, flexible market economy to lose its competitiveness completely, and be unable to excel on any dimension. Even the most productive countries in the world import goods—goods exported by economically weaker countries.

The prerequisite for a successful reaction to globalization is that the market economy be allowed to work, and that means, in particular, that all prices and wages must react flexibly such that demand and supply achieve balance in all markets, most importantly the labor market. Only economies that restrict their markets and impose artificial constraints on prices and wages will lose their competitiveness and aggravate unemployment.

The adjustment processes demanded by globalization cannot be foreseen in all its minute detail. Only a completely liberal approach, leaving the reaction to free competition, can realize the potential gains from trade. As Friedrich von Hayek, the Austrian Nobel laureate in economics, once said, competition is a "discovery procedure" for finding out the capabilities and comparative advantage of each member of the social division of labor.[33] Germany would do well to understand this, and put this advice into practice.

Excessive Labor Costs

Herein lies the heart the problem. There are still powerful forces in Germany that distrust market processes. These special interests continue to oppose the forces of competition with a further expansion of the welfare state, an extension of co-determination (of employee participation in determining company policies) and the union's protectionist call. Many politicians and union bosses are trying to resist the market by pushing through higher wages or preventing structural change through the maintenance of subsidies and dismissal protection. They want to defeat the market instead of using it to achieve the goals of the welfare state. This is the reason for the much lamented high unemployment rate and is the underlying cause of the Germanys' economic crisis.

Of course, the problem is by no means trivial, as it concerns the income, the standard of living and the very existence of those affected. To specialize and to exploit gains from trade will entail the decline of some industries and the emergence of others. This causes frictions and burdens for those affected. To be sure, the losses are normally more than offset by the gains, and in the long run more groups are winners than is the case in the short run. Yet there are always losers who will be hard hit.

Think of the farmers who have been the losers to structural change since the 1800s because they could not keep up with the rising wages of the industrial workers. Many livelihoods were destroyed in this way, and competition left relatively few individual family farms in business. Around 1870, half of the German labor force was employed in agriculture; today this proportion is just 2.5 percent.[34] The shrinking agricultural sector had serious personal consequences for farmers, but the children and grandchildren of these farmers belong to the winners of the rapid economic globalization during the nineteenth century.[35] If no farmers had been made redundant and if the children of farmers had remained farmers, Germany's income today would resemble that of a developing country.

Other industries and occupations have experienced similar fates. The German textile industry or precision engineering, for which Germany used to be so famous, gave in to the pressures of globalization in the 1960s without inflicting any major damage on the German economy as a whole. Other industries took their place, often producing totally novel products.

However, the losers of the present globalization process include not only individual industries but also certain groups of workers. This makes globalization an issue of special social relevance. Unskilled workers are at the top of this list since it is they who, via goods trade and the competition for mobile capital, both indirectly and directly compete with the workers of the newly

industrializing countries of Asia, Southern Europe and Eastern Europe. Globalization puts pressure on their wages, because their productivity derives
primarily from the capital invested in the machines they operate. Capital,
however, moves wherever it finds the most favorable conditions. Highly
skilled labor is less affected, as skill itself represents a form of capital: human
capital accumulated through education and special training. In the end,
however, even specialized workers and other high-skill occupations are not
completely immune to the consequences of globalization.[36]

This is the fundamental problem of globalization for industrialized countries, which many critics of globalization fail to understand. In principle, globalization generates gains from trade for all countries. The average standard of
living rises everywhere. However, within the countries there are always losers.
The gains from trade come only in the sense that the winners gain more than
the losers lose, not in the sense that there are only winners. The reason for this
fundamental problem is that the market forces that generate gains from trade
are the same as those that bring about "factor-price equalization" (or, better,
factor-price convergence), in particular a reduction of wage differentials across
borders which obviously harms workers in the high-wage countries. If high-
wage countries try to counter the downward pressure on wages by holding
on to old wage patterns and wage agreements, increased unemployment is
inevitable, and there are no gains from trade. Firms go bankrupt without new
ones being established, and excessive amounts of capital either move to other
countries or are destroyed. This, in a nutshell, is the present German problem.
Here is the major cause of the weak investment activity and the trend, unin-
terrupted for 35 years, of higher and higher unemployment and lower growth
rates.

Politicians are not willing to admit this truth to their voters when they advo-
cate the integration of more and more economically backward countries into
the European Union. Thus, when they get up on their soapboxes, they tend to
convey the impression that by integrating substantial parts of Eastern Europe,
the old EU has managed to realize gains from trade and at the same time to
maintain wage increases among workers of the old EU. Any other claim is not
considered politically viable in Berlin or in Brussels. But from an economic
point of view, such a claim is basically equivalent to squaring the circle. All
reasonable economics models deem it impossible to generate gains from trade
by both expanding the union and maintaining the wages in Western Europe.
The hard laws of economics do not always match their wishful thinking. Gains
from specialization entail factor-price convergence, and if factor-price convergence is prevented, there are also no gains to be had from specialization.
You cannot have all of the benefits and none of the hassle.

If wages are defended against the forces of factor-price equalization, firms react by relocating production to other countries, as described above, and capital owners invest their funds in the international financial markets instead of in local entrepreneurial activities. The manufacturing industry undertakes excessive rationalization measures that lead to layoffs, and too few new firms are founded. And, as also explained, there are overly strong horizontal and vertical specialization effects whose devastating effects on employment are covered by a pathological export boom.

Moreover, when wages are rigid, the prices of goods supplied by other economic sectors that are more oriented to the domestic market do not fall, thereby preventing demand and employment from increasing there to compensate for the sectors shrinking due to international low-wage competition. Examples include the construction industry and much of the service sector. Lower prices in these sectors would lead consumers to turn away from manufactured goods and to spend their holidays at home rather than in low-wage countries.

Although the defense of old wage patterns can for a time help those people who, legally protected against dismissal, are keeping their jobs despite the structural changes, this is not sustainable over the long run. Over time, fewer and fewer young people succeed in finding jobs, and finally national income (i.e., the pie available for distribution to the entire population) shrinks. Unemployment means not only that those affected are no longer earning an income. It also means that total value added falls and that the incomes of those firms who could have collaborated with the unemployed fall as well. The entire society's economic activity drops, and in the end everybody loses, including those who are currently sitting pretty in their high-wage unionized jobs. In the long term there is no way to negotiate for high wages against the forces of globalization that foster lower wage rates.

This does not mean that nobody tries to overcome the laws of economics. The unions do not seem to be impressed at all by the problems of the German economy. Each year they demand higher wages that hurt existing firms and in many cases prevent the establishment of new ones. The consequences of this policy, which has been followed for many years, can be seen in figure 2.4. It shows, in an international comparison, the development of hourly West German manufacturing wage costs over the years 1970–2004.

With the exception of Denmark, Germany's industry has the highest labor costs in the world. But Denmark surpassed Germany only recently. West Germany had the highest labor cost per hour since the early 1980s (when it overtook Sweden) until 2001. In the past, when Germany enjoyed special advantages from particularly low interest rates under the deutschmark and

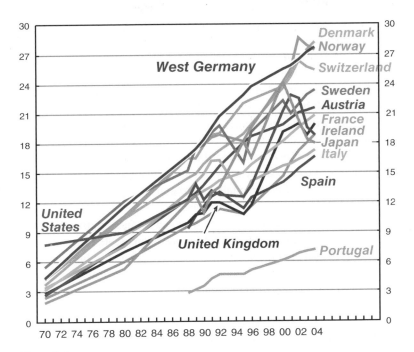

Figure 2.4
Hourly wage costs of manufacturing workers, male and female (euros per hour worked). Source:
Institut der deutschen Wirtschaft Köln.

from its relatively large domestic market, these higher costs were to some
extent affordable. This happy situation now is history.

Today, Germany suffers from labor costs that are much higher than in almost
all other OECD countries. Even Sweden, which was always considered a high-
wage country, now has wage costs which are only four-fifths that of Germany,
thanks to the market reforms of the 1980s and the depreciation of the krona
after the currency crisis of 1992–93. Scania, the Swedish producer of buses,
has hourly wage costs of 21 euros. MAN, its Munich competitor, must pay 28
euros per hour. It is hard for MAN to offset this difference by an increase in
productivity.

Needless to say, things have to change in Germany. The best a capital-rich
country such as Germany can do in the present situation is let market forces
freely determine wages and salaries. In that case, wages will no longer rise as
fast as Germans have come to expect, and in some cases they will even fall,
but unemployment will be avoided and Germany will benefit from the general
gains from trade that derive from globalization. As will be explained in the

next two chapters, a substantial reorganization of Germany's labor market and social system is necessary to achieve such an outcome.

To be sure, if wage flexibility is introduced, wages for unskilled work will in many cases be lower than is found acceptable from a social point of view. In that case the welfare state must step in by subsidizing the low-income earners. This topic will be discussed in detail in chapter 4, where a new system of social assistance will be presented. As will be argued, despite the necessary wage reductions, in many cases income losses may be prevented by wage subsidies. Of course, wage subsidies cannot be financed out of taxes that raise costs elsewhere or drive capital out of the country even faster. These changes can only be financed by fundamentally restructuring the existing welfare system.

An important question is how large the necessary wage adjustments will have to be. Germany's existing agglomeration advantages, its efficient legal system and its good physical infrastructure imply a sufficiently high productivity to prevent the wages for unskilled labor from falling near the level of Eastern European or of developing countries in the foreseeable future. Germany's unskilled do not have to choose between unemployment and Indian wage rates. Those who argue this thumb their nose at reality and make fools of themselves in the process. However, some wage reduction will be necessary.

According to research by the Ifo Institute, Germany's current rate of unemployment could have been largely avoided had wages of skilled workers stayed 10–15 percent below today's level and that of unskilled workers about one-third below current levels.[37] But these numbers refer to the past. Whether such wage cuts would be sufficient to return to full employment in the future is an open question, as the forces of international low-wage competition are likely to become even stronger. After all, China and India are only in the early stages of their participation in the international markets, and both countries have huge industrial reserve armies, to use a Marxist term.

Why Unit Labor Costs Are Irrelevant

Some will argue against the claim that Germany has a wage-cost problem by pointing out that wage costs per unit of output rather than wage costs per hour are the relevant metric—that is, that hourly wages must be divided by labor productivity in order to get a correct picture of competitiveness. If a comparison were made on the basis of unit labor costs, Germany would lie only a little above other countries. Productivity, these proponents say, is much higher in Germany than elsewhere, which justifies higher hourly wages without jeopardizing the competitiveness of German jobs. At first glance this argument may seem plausible, but it overlooks the problem of unemployment that is caused by wage increases and the increase in productivity induced thereby. The problem becomes especially evident when firms have to shut down because of wage increases. When wages rise, less productive firms experience difficulties and may have to declare bankruptcy. The employees are laid off and the number of wage and salary earners shrinks. Only the most productive firms survive. The economy's average measured productivity rises because the less productive firms together with their employees disappear from the statistics. In itself this reduces the unit labor cost, but it does not imply that there is no wage problem.

To understand why this is the case, imagine two types of firms in the same industry, robust firms and shaky firms. The shaky firms are close to bankruptcy and are just barely surviving at the existing wage level. The robust firms have no problem with the wage rate and make high profits. If collective bargaining now raises the general wage level marginally, the shaky firms go bankrupt, while the robust firms remain in the market. Measured productivity surges because only the robust firms are covered by the statistics now, but the output of the economy declines as some people have stopped working. Measured average unit labor costs, the ratio of the wage rate to average measured productivity, decline as the surge in measured productivity exceeds the small rise in wage rates. By focusing on wages per unit of output one may conclude that workers' competitiveness has risen. In truth, however, it has fallen as evidenced by rising unemployment and declining output. This example once again shows that the unemployment rate alone permits a true assessment of a country's labor competitiveness.

A similar pattern presents itself when wage agreements induce firms to implement more capital-intensive processes and lay off workers. Wage induced rationalization measures, which result in a reduction of the workforce or a shortening of working time, generate firm-level productivity gains that only seemingly provide a scope for income distribution because they are not matched by economy-wide productivity gains.

A look at history may be useful in this context. In the past 200 years, an increase in the ratio of capital to labor was the common indicator of technological change. Through saving, the capital stock could be augmented much faster than the labor force was able to grow. That is why repeated wage increases had to induce firms to use the available savings for capital deepening rather than capital widening, saving labor in this way. (Capital deepening means that firms invest more capital per workplace to increase labor productivity, and capital widening means that they create more jobs by investing more capital, given the labor productivity.) These wage increases were generated by the market itself as firms competed for scarce labor. Today many employees sit in front of computers or operate complicated control equipment, using their brains instead of brawn to do their jobs. That is a good thing and is the way in which an economy must develop.

It is not good, however, when interference in wage determination by unions or the welfare state generates a higher capital intensity in production than can be sustained by the available labor force, for this creates unemployment, and slows down output growth. Unfortunately, this situation describes the German problem. Since 1970, Germany has had much too much firm-level productivity growth and much too little economy-level productivity growth because overall wages have risen too fast. What was a rational reaction to wage increases from a firm's point of view, turned out to have problematic macro-economic consequences. The unions always raised wages to such an extent that unemployment was exacerbated. More and more firms were driven into bankruptcy, and the capital-labor ratio in production was magnified by reducing the labor input. An ever-bigger part of potential labor time remained unused, as reflected in both a reduction of time worked per employee and increased unemployment. Measured labor productivity increased beyond the level explained by technological progress and additional investment, and unions used this increase in the next wage negotiations to demand yet higher wages. This induced still more individual firm bankruptcies and still more rationalization measures. And thus, a vicious cycle of more wage increases, more redundancies, more measured productivity gains and new wage increases was set off.

All of this shows that the problem of competitiveness cannot be analyzed by looking at firm-level unit wage costs. A correct assessment of overall productivity should take the zero productivity of the time spent in unemployment and enforced leisure into account. A better measure of productivity is value added divided by potential working time, including the time during which the unemployed could work, if they had a job, and including the hours lost by the shortening of the working week. Only with this productivity measure can the issue of high unit labor costs be properly examined.

A look at developments in West Germany (including West Berlin) in the period 1982–2002 shows the scale of the problem. In this period nominal wage income per hour worked rose on average by 3.7 percent per year, and labor productivity, measured by gross domestic product per employee hour, rose by 2.0 percent per year. Consequently, according to usual calculations, nominal unit wage costs rose by 1.7 percent per year. However, if gross domestic product is related to potential employee hours by including the unemployed and fixing the working time per employee at the 1982 level, the aggregate productivity gain adjusted for layoffs is only 1.1 percent per year. About 0.9 percentage point of annual productivity growth is due to artificial gains caused by the wage-induced layoffs themselves and the parallel cut in working weeks by means of which the unions have tried to distribute the loss in labor time among a large number of employees. Correspondingly, the annual increase in unit labor costs was 2.6 percent instead of 1.7 percent, the number commonly cited. West Germany would need a 19 percent reduction of wage costs per hour just to offset the calculation error in wage agreements accumulated over the 20-year period considered.[38]

Worker layoffs and reductions in work time have obviously contributed substantially to the increase in firm-level productivity and to the reduction of measured unit labor costs. The measurement mistake has fed the illusion of gains which could potentially be redistributed, but in reality the declining growth observed proves that in hindsight there was much less to go around.

Better or Cheaper?

It must be admitted, of course, that productivity increases and unit labor cost reductions made possible by technological progress rather than layoffs would indeed be a useful contribution to solving Germany's unemployment problem. Whether a worker is competitive depends on how expensive and how good he or she is. Thus German workers have to become cheaper or better. Because becoming cheaper is uncomfortable, politicians tend to argue that wage cuts can be avoided with an innovation offensive. Technological progress, which will again justify the high wage level, is to magically materialize in order to enable German workers to compete with their low-wage counterparts in foreign lands.

If only it were that simple. The Chinese, the Indians, the Poles, the Slovaks, and the Czechs are no fools. They too are innovative and are jostling with industrialized countries to move to the top of the technology ladder.

Unquestionably, research at universities and in firms must be further promoted in order for Germany to defend its position in the world with new products and production processes. Some German states, especially Bavaria and Baden-Württemberg, show how this can be done. Their innovation policies have succeeded in producing many of Germany's silent stars, the unknown SMEs that are market leaders in their niches. Yet this region-by-region policy will no longer suffice to address the issues of globalization. Competitive pressures have become much too strong. The German model states, too, have a hard time preventing the loss of manufacturing jobs in times of globalization.

The problem is that innovative knowledge is easily transferable. You cannot glue it to the place where it was created. There is nothing to prevent German companies, which have a knowledge lead over their competitors, to utilize this advantage in their plants established in low-wage countries. International wage competition is difficult to circumvent by innovation offensives, for knowledge cannot be locked up.

To strengthen the competitiveness of German workers, the workers themselves must improve. Knowledge accumulated abstractly in company products and processes will not be of much use to them. Only embodied knowledge, stored in one's mind, makes one attractive to employers and justifies a high wage. In principle, therefore, only a broad-based education offensive can stave off wage declines.

It will take a long time, however, until the fruits of such efforts can be reaped. Even if the German school system were to be overhauled, even if everything were done to improve preschool education, it would take decades before a noticeably better-educated stock of people is available on the market. Nobody can wait that long. To be sure, to some extent it would also be possible to re-educate the existing workforce. By continuing their education and being willing to start an entirely new occupation, they must help themselves as well as they can given their age. But the extensive retraining programs financed by the German government thus far have shown only meager results. Those who lack the flexibility and willingness to learn must become cheaper by accepting lower wages. There is no other alternative.

Why a Currency Appreciation Is Not the Same as a Wage Increase

Another argument against the view that Germany needs lower wages points to exchange-rate adjustments. It is sometimes argued that the negative effect of wage increases on employment cannot be very large because it is similar to the effect of an appreciation of the country's currency, and the economy usually takes this in stride. The argument is that since the economy shows considerable robustness to appreciations, one should not worry too much about negative consequences of high wages.

This argument is not convincing either. First, appreciations are not really harmless with respect to employment. Take the example of Japan which, after the appreciation of the yen in the second half of the 1980s, slid into a long depression, and only recently experienced a recovery, after a simultaneous yen and dollar depreciation against the euro and other currencies. Finland and Sweden gained considerable wage-cost advantages through their depreciations of 1992–93, from which they still benefit. Second, labor-cost and exchange-rate effects are not identical. To be sure, wage-cost differences between countries at current exchange rates are decisive for location decisions. Whether German workers are expensive because labor unions agreed upon high euro wages, or because the euro is expensive relative to Asian or Eastern European countries may seem unimportant at first glance. Yet the parallels between wage effects and exchange-rate effects are limited.

Exchange rates are much more unstable than wages. Entrepreneurs can expect a faster correction of an excessive exchange rate than of excessive wage rates, making the incentive to relocate production considerably smaller. If they wait a bit, the exchange rate will normalize again. In contrast, waiting for wage rates to normalize can take a very long time.

Furthermore, exchange-rate changes affect decisions on the capital-labor ratio in production only indirectly. Whether a production worker is to be replaced by a domestically produced industrial robot depends on the cost of a worker relative to the costs of the robot, and this relationship is not altered directly by exchange-rate adjustments. If the wage rate rises, some additional workers are replaced by robots. However, if the currency appreciates, the relative price of robots and workers is not directly affected. Appreciation influences the cost relationship only indirectly by reducing the price of foreign robots and reducing the demand for domestic robots, which eventually also lowers their prices, inducing the replacement.

Above all, except for negligible migration effects, the exchange rate does not affect the domestic wage distribution. It is in the nature of an economy based on the specialized division of labor that individuals receive income because they are able to find someone else who buys their services. To secure employment for all people requires a certain natural wage dispersion that is determined in competitive labor markets. Thus, a taxi driver's wage relative to the wage of an industry worker must not exceed a certain level if the industrial worker is to decide to take a taxi. If certain kinds of work are artificially made more expensive relative to other kinds of work, unemployment results, and obviously this cause of unemployment is independent of the level of the exchange rate. As will be discussed in chapter 4, a good part of German unemployment may indeed be traced to an artificial compression of the wage scale, caused by institutional conditions.

Does Germany Need Higher Wages to Boost Aggregate Demand?

There is a very popular Keynesian counterargument to the view that Germany suffers from a wage-cost problem. It is made by some left-leaning economists[39] and is vigorously endorsed by the unions and parts of the German media, which all too often have a strong ideological orientation.

The argument, which was briefly touched upon above in the context of the export puzzle, is that wages are not too high, but too low, resulting in insufficient aggregate demand. Higher wages, so the argument goes, increase households' purchasing power. This translates into higher demand for consumer goods which enhances company sales. This, in turn, leads to increased employment which further boosts the demand for consumer goods. A multiplier effect would spread to all economic sectors. This argument is wrong for at least four reasons.

First, it is not obvious that wage increases stimulate aggregate demand, because overall demand consists of consumption and investment demand. It is true that higher wages will boost the demand for consumer goods should the employment level remain constant, but the demand for capital goods will fall. Purchases of capital goods revive the economy in much the same manner as the purchase of consumer goods. GDP can be used by eating it up or by piling it up. As a growing economy needs a permanently growing pile of capital goods to increase its capacity, this source of demand is as important as consumption demand. Wage increases reduce the profits that firms expect to earn on their investments, and thus push many technologically feasible projects below the profitability threshold. This implies that purchases of capital goods decline and that the capital goods industry earns less revenue and employs fewer people. Unfortunately, this effect is particularly important insofar as the business cycle results largely from fluctuations in investment demand, which is much more volatile than consumer demand. The risk of reducing investment demand by increasing wages could weigh more heavily than the hope to stimulate individual consumer demand.

Second, it is not clear whether labor income and hence consumption will rise at all, because employment will fall rather than stay constant if wages rise. If the percentage of jobs destroyed by the wage increase is larger than the percentage of the wage increase itself, aggregate wage income declines and so does consumer demand.

Third, demand is not restricted to domestically produced goods. High wages make many domestic labor services and goods with a high labor content more expensive and induce consumers to buy abroad instead. Tourism is a good example. Despite all their economic problems, Germany has continued to spend more money on international tourism in recent years than any other nation.[40] Thus, even if a wage increase would stimulate aggregate demand, it could reduce the demand for domestic goods.

Fourth, aggregate-demand problems and business-cycle problems are short-term and cannot, in principle, be used to assess a country's long-term problems. As figure 1.2 showed, the unemployment numbers have not fallen by much more than half a million since 1970, even during economic recoveries. Under present conditions, this would represent an unemployment decline 15 percent at best. In contrast, about 85 percent of unemployment is due not to cyclical causes but to structural ones, and this unemployment cannot be eliminated by demand stimulating measures even under the most favorable conditions. Even if the German economic stagnation of 2001–2004 had been followed by a super boom with full capacity utilization induced by an increase in aggregate demand, Germany would still have 3.5–4 million unemployed.

The difference between cyclical and structural problems, often not seen by laymen, is essential for understanding economic relationships. Regarding the business cycle, one looks at the capacity utilization of the production potential that is determined by the demand facing firms. With respect to structural problems, one deals with the potential itself. It is determined by, among other things, the economy's capital stock accumulated by past investment in buildings, plant, and equipment. Germany's capital stock has grown too slowly in recent years, and (as was discussed above) its labor intensity has been too low. A demand push can cause higher output and employment only up to the point where existing capacity is fully utilized. Additional output and employment effects can be realized only by capacity expanding investment. Whether such investment is made in Germany depends less on German demand than on the German business environment, and here wages play the key role as cost factors. German demand can just as easily be met from a plant located in the Czech Republic (which is now a member of the EU).

No, it is not more aggregate demand or more purchasing power that Germany needs. Germany needs lower labor costs so it can direct the existing demand toward its labor.

What Can Be Learned from the Americans and the Dutch about Labor Costs?

The decisive strategic variable for restoring Germany's international competitiveness is, above all, labor costs. To raise this issue is disquieting and threatening because labor costs deal with one's livelihood. Sometimes truths are uncomfortable, but the sooner Germans internalize them the closer they will get to solving their problems.

What is often overlooked is that, aside from local taxes, wages are a country's only important location-bound costs. It is true that at the firm level the costs of intermediate products are often more important than wages. But the costs of intermediate products are themselves mostly derived from domestic wage costs; where not, the intermediate products are imported and thus equally expensive for all locations. A similar remark applies to capital costs. As these have converged since the introduction of the euro, they are irrelevant for location decisions. As far as costs are concerned, only wage costs and local taxes determine a country's attractiveness as a business location.

The importance of wage rates in determining a nation's employment situation is exemplified by a comparison of the United States, the Netherlands, and Germany over the period 1982–2004 (figure 2.5). In the reference year 1982, the Dutch government implemented the so-called Wassenaar Agreement between the employers' associations and the unions, initiating a policy of long-term wage moderation. In the left-hand diagram, wage costs of manufacturing workers in the three countries are presented for lack of aggregate comparative data. In the right-hand diagram, the evolution of the total number

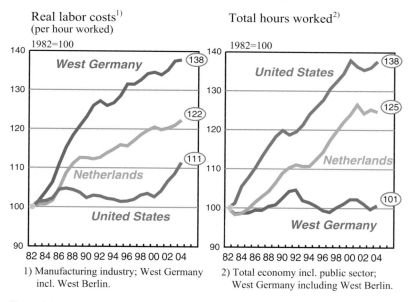

1) Manufacturing industry; West Germany incl. West Berlin.

2) Total economy incl. public sector; West Germany including West Berlin.

Figure 2.5
Wages and employment. Sources: Institut der Deutschen Wirtschaft, Köln (labor costs); OECD, Economic Outlook (employment in United States and Netherlands), Employment Outlook (average annual working hours per employee in United States and Netherlands); Statistisches Bundesamt, Wiesbaden (West German employment 1982–1991); Arbeitskreis Volkswirtschaftliche Gesamtrechnungen der Länder, Stuttgart (West German employment 1992–2004); *IAB Handbuch Arbeitsmarkt, Analysen, Daten, Fakten* (Campus Verlag, 2005) (average annual working hours per employee in West Germany 1982–1991); Ifo Institute calculations.

of man-hours worked (i.e. the total employment volume) is plotted. The curves represent indices,[41] showing the cumulative percentage growth of the various variables over time.

During the period 1982–2004, the wages of Dutch manufacturing workers rose by 22 percent in real terms; those of West German manufacturing workers rose by 38 percent. In the United States, the wages of manufacturing workers increased by only 11 percent, and most of this rise was driven by a steep increase in recent years. During the period 1982–2002, American wages, adjusted for inflation, rose by only 6.6 percent.

The change in the number of man-hours worked, shown in the right-hand part of figure 2.5, ran exactly counter to the wage development. Whereas the United States experienced an increase of 38 percent and the Netherlands an increase of 25 percent, Germany recorded a numerical increase of only 1 percent—less than the statistical margin of error in national accounting.

Unions argue that German labor costs have risen so much primarily because the federal government has raised social security contributions, which are part of labor costs. To be sure, social security contributions have risen a bit faster than gross wages. But gross wages (in terms of so-called direct earnings) rose by 36 percent—only 1.4 percentage points less than wage costs in the period 1982–2004. The rise in gross wages itself is completely out of keeping with international standards. The unions, not the state, are responsible for this development.

All three countries had to absorb a substantial amount of immigration during the period under consideration. Net immigration in the United States amounted to 9 percent of the 1982 population (20 million people). In the Netherlands it was 5 percent (704,000), and in West Germany it was 9 percent (5.3 million).[42] The percentage increase of the number of man-hours worked in the Netherlands and in the United States was obviously sufficient both to provide jobs for the immigrants and to reduce overall unemployment. In Germany, however, more immigration resulted in higher unemployment because German business was not willing to create more than a handful of new jobs in the face of surging wages. In the United States, the unemployment rate fell from 9.7 percent in 1982 to 5.5 percent in 2004, and in the Netherlands it declined from 8.1 percent to 4.6 percent, but in West Germany it rose from 6.7 percent to 8.5 percent.[43]

Sometimes it is argued that the Dutch employment successes are due to an increase in part-time jobs, and therefore Germany should try to solve its unemployment problem by a better distribution of work. This argument is wrong, as figure 2.5 shows that in the Netherlands the total number of man-hours worked rose by 25 percent and not just the total number of jobs. Because of the increase in part-time jobs, the latter increased even faster. The Dutch success is due not to a better distribution of existing jobs, but to an increase in the total number of full-time-equivalent jobs.

The inverse relationship between the level of wages and the employment rate shown in figure 2.5 is no accident. It is just the law of demand, one of the fundamental laws of the market economy. The lower the price of a commodity or a service, the greater the demand for it. In the case of the labor market, the law has been confirmed by a large number of econometric analyses of many countries and over many periods. A rough rule of thumb says that wage restraint of 1 percent relative to another country implies 1 percent more employment in the long term.[44]

It must be emphasized that these are long-term relationships. Measures that boost the economy temporarily are not meant here. As was mentioned above, about 85 percent of Germany's unemployment is structural; only about 15 percent has cyclical causes. Regarding long-term employment effects, it does not matter at all whether wage negotiations exceed or fall short of the usual target, defined by productivity growth plus the rate of inflation, by one percentage point within 3 or 4 years. Such small changes are irrelevant. If, however, the target is exceeded by nearly one percentage point each year for more than 20 years, there is the kind of problem one can see in figure 2.5. The longer the time span over which the problem has developed, the more difficult it is to resolve it through wage restraint.

In order to eliminate the cost disadvantage relative to the Netherlands that has accumulated since 1982, Germany's labor costs would have to be cut by 11 percent. Assuming that future Dutch wages rise in line with labor productivity, that would require Germany to keep wage increases one percentage point below productivity growth each year for about 11 years.

An alternative and complement to wage restraint would be a reduction of non-wage costs. Employer social security contributions amounted to 21 percent of gross wages and salaries in 2004, corresponding to 17.3 percent of wage costs excluding value-added tax but including these contributions. Of the 17.3 percent, pension insurance accounts for 8.1 percentage points, health insurance for 5.9 percentage points, unemployment insurance for 2.7, and nursing insurance for 0.7. Thus, the elimination of employer contributions to pensions and unemployment insurance would nearly suffice to bring about the required 11 percent reduction in labor costs. The revenue loss could be offset by a corresponding reduction in benefits with simultaneous partial privatization of the respective social security system or by the assumption of the employer contributions by the employees.

These options are well beyond anything that could find majority support in Germany today. However, in view of the new worldwide competitive conditions that came with the emerging Asian countries and the fall of the Iron Curtain, there is no way around finding some way of cutting wage costs. Only wage restraint and modesty in wage negotiations, which would at least result in a slowdown of the rise of real hourly wages, would make it possible to slow down the relocation of plants and the flight of capital out of Germany, which costs Germany so many jobs. Only restraint will give Germany a future.

3 Trade-Union Capitalism

Unions Then and Now

Unions bear direct responsibility for the misguided German wage policy since the 1970s. In bitter collective bargaining, they have successfully fought for the wage increases that have caused Germany so much trouble by undermining the competitiveness of its workforce. In order to understand Germany's problems, it is worth looking at the historical origins of the country's union movement.

This examination will also help explicate the economic problems of Europe as a whole, because the European welfare state is modeled on the German example. The cornerstone of the European model is social democracy, the idea of generating a more equitable distribution of income than that the one that results from the unfettered market outcome. Like socialism, social democracy is a German invention. Social democracy was a more reasonable and moderate means to accommodate workers' discontent with early capitalism than was the radical socialism of Karl Marx. Social democracy helped reconcile workers' desire for a better place in society with the economic gains reaped from the market system, avoiding the risk of revolution as happened in Russia.

There are two important players in the social-democratic system. One is the government, which engages in income redistribution. The other is the trade-union movement, which organizes groups of workers in order to bargain for better wages than they as individuals would have been able to obtain. While the rights enjoyed by European unions differ somewhat from country to country, these generally go well beyond those legal rights provided in the Anglo-Saxon countries, including the United States. In Germany, these rights are so extensive that to describe the system as trade-union capitalism is no exaggeration.

The origin of social democracy and union movements can be traced back to Ferdinand Lassalle, Wilhelm Liebknecht, and August Bebel, who organized German workers in the second half of the nineteenth century to empower them to partake in the benefits of industrial society.[1] Although the industrial revolution had unleashed gigantic productive forces to which even Karl Marx paid tribute, workers did not share in the fruits of their labors for a long time. Through much of the nineteenth century, industrial workers were the deprived proletariat, yet to find their place in society, both politically and economically.

The workers' economic problems and, in fact, the industrial revolution as a whole, largely resulted from the process of liberating the peasants that had peaked with the abolition of peonage in Austria in 1781 and in Prussia in 1807–1810.[2] The liberation of the peasants was the consequence, on the one hand, of growing population pressures since the demographic transition that began in the middle of the eighteenth century. On the other hand, this liberation itself stimulated population growth, as the newly liberated peasants now had the right to marry and start a family in their own right.[3] Population growth combined with the reduced fiduciary duties of the laird led to the further impoverishment of the rural residents. Germany found itself in a new era of widespread pauperism. People fled to the cities and became part of the growing industrial proletariat, about whom Marx and other social reformers of the time were so preoccupied.

Despite rapid industrialization, it was not possible to absorb the growing supply of labor in the cities. Therefore wage rates stagnated, remaining near subsistence level for a long time. Indeed, from the 1820s to the 1850s wage rates actually fell in real terms.[4] Workers' wages were decoupled from economic growth for decades—a pattern that threatens to reappear today in the context of globalization and international low-wage competition. Unemployment and mass poverty characterized this phase of economic development. As capital had become scarce and labor abundant, the owners of capital were the big winners in this historical development phase, and laborers were the losers.[5]

However, high returns to capital made possible its rapid accumulation, and so economic growth was extremely high. Germany was the second economy in which the industrial revolution took place. Germany became a serious competitor of British industry, and between the 1870s and 1914 it became Europe's most powerful economy. Germany's per capita income moved closer to that of Britain and reached 80 percent of Britain's at the onset of World War I.[6]

Per capita incomes are not wages, though. As long as there still was the "industrial reserve army" of unemployed peasants, to use a Marxian term, wages remained decoupled from the economy's performance. It was not until 1870 that the average wage rate regained its 1820 level. In a sense, the stagnation of wages for German workers had lasted half a century.

This was the climate in which the socialist movement flourished. Wages still were low, but due to their increased scarcity workers attained a more powerful position in the market, making it easier for them to successfully negotiate wage increases. To be sure, Bismarck had been able to weaken the workers' movement with his anti-socialist laws, and carried out his welfare reforms in order to take the wind out of the sails of the working class protesters. In a great 1881 speech before the Reichstag, Germany's upper house of parliament, Bismarck announced his extensive and later much emulated social reforms, ideas which before had been propagated by the "socialists of the chair" (Kathedersozialisten[7]). Bismarck emphasized that these social reforms were the "corollary" of the anti-socialist laws, with which he wanted to prevent the creation of socialistic parties and labor unions.[8] But the pressure of the workers' movement gradually became so strong that the anti-socialist laws could not be extended, and in 1890 they expired.

The workers' movement took off, and in 1890, with the founding of the Generalkommission der Gewerkschaften Deutschlands (General Commission of German Labor Unions), the union movement gained its first central organization. Workers' societies, the Sozialdemokratische Arbeiterpartei (Social Democratic Workers Party), and labor unions gradually embraced increasing segments of the working class. The pressure of the German masses was channeled into a legally sanctioned outlet, and a proletarian revolution, as later took place in Russia, was averted.

Over time, workers' organizations succeeded in pushing through considerable wage increases that greatly improved living standards. Although the wage increases had, to a large extent, been induced by the market forces, the putative bargaining successes further strengthened the labor movement.

Today, unionism is protected by the German constitution and union influence extends into the furthest reaches of economic, political, and social activity. Of the parliamentary members belonging to the Social Democratic Party coalition, 59 percent are union members.[9] Even the Christian Democrats, the right-of-center party, have a left-leaning faction, which has traditionally courted unions and which competes with the Social Democrats in extending the welfare state. Virtually each law passed by the Bundestag (the lower house of parliament) has to be approved by the unions. For parties in the ruling coalition, if not for other parties, wielding political power has entailed bedding down with the unions.

Because of co-determination, a form of giving workers a say in management decisions that is unique to Germany, unions also play an integral role in how German businesses are run. All corporations with 2,000 or more employees have to provide their workers with nearly half of the votes on the supervisory board, and smaller corporations with a staff of at least 500 have to provide them one-third of the seats. Unions typically have the right to fill a sizeable portion of these seats. All major policy decisions made by big German companies have to be coordinated with the unions, and all too often the unions use their power on the supervisory boards to significantly affect strategic business decisions—particularly when the shareholder's representative on the supervisory board are not agreed on any given course of action, as is often the case. Thus, unions have a unique historical legacy in Germany, and act to distort the labor market and business decisions to a degree almost unheard of in other Western countries.

While union power still is substantial in Germany, as it is in other European countries, the historical legitimization of unions is eroding, and union membership is shrinking. Since 1970, the German economy has been subject to rather different forces than those that in the nineteenth century gave birth to the Social Democratic Party and the union movement. Capital accumulation has slowed down considerably, while unemployment has been rising along a linear trend. (See figure 1.2.) A growing industrial reserve army is again waiting in vain to be let into the factory gates. Although labor scarcity has declined as a result of globalization, German unions have nevertheless continued their policy of wage increases and have pushed for the extension of the welfare state by exerting political pressure. A movement which historically enabled market development by permitting workers to share in the gains from the market economy is today grinding that same economy to a halt. Germany has developed its trade-union capitalism to the limits of what a market economy can tolerate. Only in East Germany unions have not been able to establish a similarly powerful position in the labor market after the obvious policy mistakes they made shortly after reunification. This will be discussed at length in chapter 5.

Throwing Mocha in the Ocean

As was shown in chapters 1 and 2, the wage policy for which unions have largely been responsible has overstretched the German economy. The unions' wage demands in previous decades have been so excessive that German workers are losing their competitiveness in comparison to the low-wage competition of the formerly communist countries, India, and some of the Asian

Tigers. Germany's unemployment rate has just kept growing along with its wage rates.

Why do the unions fail to realize the damage they are causing by their policy of high wages? Why are they so obstinate? Imagine the following scene. The chairman of the German Trade Union Federation publicly announces that he wants to end its high-wage policy and repeat the success of the Wassenaar agreement of 1982 (i.e., that he wants to get the economy going by restraining wages—see chapter 2), pointing to the new competitive situation in which Germany finds itself as a result of globalization. He declares that workers will agree to wage increases that would remain one percentage point below productivity growth for eleven years to offset the cost disadvantage built up since the Wassenaar agreement relative to the Netherlands. He says that he wants to signal to business that it pays again to invest in Germany and to create jobs there. Why is this scenario so unrealistic? Are union leaders stupid? They are not. They have no illusion about what they are doing to the country's economic welfare even if they cannot publicly admit it. But unions are what economists call cartels, interest groups that promote their own interests, and as such they condone the widespread unemployment their policies are causing. Germany's high unemployment rate proves the success of this policy. It shows that wages are above the market-clearing level.

In principle, a cartel is an association of the suppliers of a good with the aim of achieving a higher price than would prevail under competitive conditions and the free play of demand and supply. To understand a cartel's distorting effects, one must first understand how market competition works.

When there is competition in a market, a certain price defines the point at which demand and supply are equal. In this respect, the market for labor is not different from the market for apples. If the market price of apples is unregulated, the market finds a price at which buyers can buy as many apples as they wish and the growers can sell all the apples they produce. There is neither excess demand nor excess supply. As is well known, historical attempts to organize the labor market differently from other markets failed miserably in 1989, when the Iron Curtain fell and Communism collapsed. In reality, there is no viable alternative to an economic system in which human labor is exchanged according to the laws of the market.

In an unencumbered labor market with free wage competition, a wage rate would emerge at which demand would just equal supply. A lower wage rate would not persist, because the demand for labor would exceed the number of people willing to work. Firms would bid up the wage rate, meaning the price of labor. A wage higher than the competitive rate could also not persist, as it would cause an excess supply of labor (i.e., unemployment). Firms would offer only a few jobs, while many people would want to be hired. Those seeking a job would underbid each other, and the wage rate would fall. Firms would react by offering more jobs because with more employment they would be able to realize additional profits. Only the wage at which demand just equals supply can persist. In this situation, there can be low unemployment of only the frictional sort that results from the natural changes occurring in firms and peoples' individual circumstances.[10]

Israel provides a good example of what a labor market with flexible wages can accomplish. In the early 1990s, Russia permitted Jews to emigrate to Israel, which was then overwhelmed by Russian immigrants looking for work. Within just six years the Israeli labor force increased by one-third. Yet there was no increase in unemployment. Wages came under pressure, but practically all immigrants willing to work could be integrated into the workforce. At 8.8 percent, measured unemployment was even lower at the end of the 1990s than it had been at the beginning of that decade (when it amounted to 9.6 percent).[11] Another example of a flexible labor market is found in the United States. As figure 2.5 shows, this market was able to absorb the mass immigration of the past two decades without any additional unemployment. To the contrary, the high flexibility of the American labor market made a job miracle possible. From 1982 to 2004 the total number of man-hours worked rose by a stunning 38 percent.

All of this does not mean that market-determined wages are "fair." The market is efficient because it guarantees full employment, because it permits the best possible allocation of labor among industries and firms, and because, by wage differentiation, it signals to people in which occupations they may have the best chances. But the market is not equitable. It rewards scarcity, and scarcity has little to do with equity, no matter how you look at it. Those who received good chromosomes for high intelligence from their parents earn a higher wage than others. Those who trained for an occupation that many others also train for can expect a rather low wage, and those who are specialized in an area in which there are relatively few specialists have it made. Those with skills which are worth less now because of technological progress must accept a wage cut. All of this has little to do with equity or fairness.

That is why it is legitimate for society to correct the market outcome to a certain extent. But this is the responsibility of the government and not the unions. The welfare state can be given instruments that are compatible with the market, with which it can correct the income distribution between rich and poor. The fact that the German welfare state is overextended and partly uses the wrong instruments in no way contradicts this conclusion. In contrast, the unions' high-wage policy is a most unsuitable means to correct the inequities of income distribution. The wage rate is a price which has a central allocative function in the market economy. If one tries to change it artificially beyond its equilibrium level, one disturbs everything and inflicts a lot of damage.

The unions must understand this. As their precise intent is to push wages, in collective bargaining, above the market-determined equilibrium level, they cause the persistent excess supply of labor that is called unemployment. Unemployment is a necessary implication of a union policy that succeeds in bringing about a wage level higher than the one that the market itself would have established. Some groups succeed in getting a bigger piece of the pie, but they do so at the expense of making the pie smaller.

Unemployed workers in Germany would be willing to work for lower wages, but the union headquarters forbid such price competition by forcing all employees and firms to honor the industry-wide wage agreement they have negotiated. A cartel can function only if all members are effectively prevented from underbidding the cartel prices. That is why the unions insist that their wage agreements be honored at the level of the individual firm. That is how they create excessive unemployment in Germany.

One could raise the objection that the unions' cartel policy is limited insofar as the employers' associations are a heavy counterweight in the bargaining sessions. Both groups, it is said, would in their collective bargaining find the equilibrium that closely approaches the competitive market's equilibrium wage rate. But this objection fails to hold water, because the employers' associations are weak relative to the unions. The employers' associations cannot be interpreted as demand cartels (monopsonies) that assume the same position on the side of labor demand as the unions do on the suppliers' side.

A demand cartel sets a price ceiling that is below the competitive price. Because of the low price, the supply of goods is small, and each individual cartel member would like to buy more goods than it can. There is excess demand which cannot be satisfied. The individual demander would like to offer higher prices in order to get the goods, but is hindered by the cartel head-quarters in order not to spoil the price for the other members. If this demand scenario were translated to the German labor market, it would mean that there would be full employment, even an excess of job openings, and yet that the individual firms nevertheless would be prevented from hiring people away from other firms by offering higher wages. This is obviously not the situation in Germany today. There is no excess supply of jobs, no full employment, and above all the firms are free to hire away employees by making better job offers. To this extent, there are no indications of effective employer cartels. There is no doubt that the labor market is dominated by the wage-setting cartels of the unions.

The effects of the unions' wage-setting cartels are often felt further down the line. As wages are raised for all firms of an industry, all firms are forced to raise the price of their products. In effect, they end up acting like a supplier cartel that has agreed on prices, and passing on to consumers part of the disadvantage of the high-wage policy.

The cartel policy of the unions is extraordinarily inefficient and simply cannot be sustained in a country whose economy is gasping for breath. The victims of this policy include not only the firms (whose profits shrink) and the consumers (who must pay higher prices), but also, and particularly, the unemployed. They may not lose much income, because they receive social-replacement payments, but they forgo the chance to find fulfillment in work and be a respected member of society. Marx, Bebel, and Lassalle would pale if they saw how the unions' cartel policy is creating a new proletariat of people deprived of the hope of ever being integrated into the working society.

In order to avert the worst social consequences of their policies, the unions have always put their faith in the reduction of working hours. Given that lower employment is inevitable, it is better to have everyone work 10 percent less than to have 10 percent of the labor force not work at all, or so goes their thinking. There should be a fairer distribution of the continuously shrinking job pie, for which, of course, exogenous factors rather than their own policies are held responsible.

Indeed, the shortening of working hours in Germany has been substantial. In 1960 the average work week in industry was 45.7 hours. By 1980 it had declined to 41.8 hours, and by 2004 to 38 hours.[12] Even this is thought to be too much. A 35-hour work week is still the stated aim of the unions. Even in East Germany, where the overriding goal should be to achieve competitiveness, the metal workers' union tried to institute the 35-hour work week and called for strikes in 2003 to achieve this goal. In addition, more and more church holidays have been introduced.

In sum, this situation has resulted in putting Germany in the bottom range of the OECD ranking of working hours, as shown in figure 3.1. Only the Dutch and the Norwegians, who earn substantial incomes from the sale of gas, oil, and other raw materials and who often hold part-time jobs, work less on average. The French work as little as the Germans and indeed face very similar problems.

Fortunately, the countervailing forces of reason are also gaining ground in Germany. The East German metal workers' strike for shorter working hours failed, and the public mood seems to be turning. Longer working hours have been introduced in the Bavarian public service. The work week for new

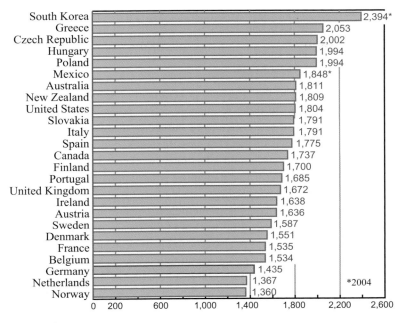

Figure 3.1
Average annual working hours per person in employment, 2005. Source: OECD Employment Outlook, 2006, p. 265.

employees below the age of 50 was increased there from 38.5 to 42 hours. Moreover, in many cases firm-specific agreements have been implemented throughout Germany without the unions' consent. Even the official negotiations of the private and public service sectors of the spring of 2006 resulted in an extension of working time.

The reduction of working hours that has characterized Germany in the past is sometimes interpreted as a social achievement. In truth it is—at least to the extent that it is due to union initiatives—primarily a means for hiding unemployment and for supporting the cartel price of labor. The shorter the working time, the higher the hourly wage. The extension of vacation time (in which Germany is already one of the world's leaders) and the prohibition of night work and of overtime are tools of the union cartel's high-wage policy. The wage increases and the quantitative reduction of working hours are two sides of the same coin, characteristic of one and the same policy.

It is no small irony that supporting artificially high prices was historically denounced by communists as a capitalist ruse. A popular ballad sung by the East German Ernst Busch contains these lyrics:

Go, go to Brazil
and throw the mocha into the ocean.
They are throwing the wheat into the fire,
they are throwing the coffee into the ocean;
when will the fat robbers be thrown in, too?

Here "the mocha" refers to the Brazilian government's "valorization" policy after the 1930 revolution. In order to support coffee prices, the government ordered 5.7 million tons of raw coffee to be burned or thrown into the ocean. "The wheat" is a reference to the U.S. government's policy of supporting agricultural prices. Today you could substitute "workers" for "mocha" and "wheat" in this song and get a fair picture of what unions in Germany and elsewhere are doing to keep wages high.

The unions' policy is fundamentally inefficient because it prevents useful economic activity. Artificially cutting working time means underutilizing not only the economy's labor force but also its capital stock, which has been built up in a cumbersome way by giving up consumption. Increasing the wage rate beyond its market-determined equilibrium level condemns millions of people to doing nothing productive. That is inefficient, as even a less productive person can be usefully integrated into the work process and make contributions to GDP. It is inhumane, too. Germany cannot afford to dispense with 5 million employable people for the sole purpose of letting the other 35 million earn slightly higher wages.

The reason Germany is no longer growing is that its labor market is captive to union power and thus no longer answers to the rules of demand and supply. An increase in employment is needed because that generates growth. The old formula that growth creates employment derives from the cyclical fluctuation of aggregate demand and capacity utilization and has never been true in the long term, which is influenced by deeper structural tendencies. The labor market gauges the health of an economy, and the economy is the basis of the entire polity. The cartel policy of the unions must be ended if the German economy is to flourish.

Industry-Wide Collective Bargaining as Cartel Agreements

Cartels in product markets, as Ernst Busch described in his ballad, were a serious problem for the market economy in earlier phases of capitalist development, but politics took care of this problem. Today antitrust laws prohibit such cartels in nearly all of the OECD countries. There is a broad consensus that a strong state is necessary to force firms to compete in product markets. Price fixing is generally prohibited, and effective merger control prevents the concentration of cartel-like market power. With its Federal Cartel Office and its Gesetz gegen Wettbewerbsbeschränkungen (Law against Restraint of Competition), Germany has effective instruments with which to foster competition in product markets. The economic conditions of the postwar period were largely designed by economics minister Ludwig Erhard, his permanent secretary Alfred Müller-Armack, and the advisory council to the federal ministry of economics, all of whom stood firmly in the tradition of so-called Ordo-Liberalism. An essential element of this economic tenet is a strong state that forces the firms to obey the rules of competition.

It is most surprising, therefore, that union cartels are permitted in Germany and are exempted from the Law against Restraint of Competition. From a legal point of view, unions are not even called cartels, although that is what they unambiguously are (at least, when viewed from an economist's perspective). In fact, the Betriebsverfassungsgesetz (Industrial Constitution Law) of 1972 and the Betriebsvertragsgesetz (Collective Agreements Law) of 1969 grant the unions extensive cartel rights that fundamentally contradict the rules of Ordo-Liberalism and thus harm Germany's economic basis. These laws establish a system of industry-wide collective wage agreements between the respective employers' organizations and unions that determine equal lower bounds on an industry's wages for each particular skill category that an individual company and their employees cannot undercut.[13] To be sure, sometimes the wage contracts allow for opening clauses that permit negotiations at the firm level; however, since the result of such negotiations is subject to the agreements of the collective partners, the opening clauses do not, in effect, imply more decentralization in wage bargaining.

One escape route that many firms (particular East German ones) have taken is to quit the employers' organizations. However, this step is difficult as the Collective Agreements Law (§ 3, Section 3) says that a collective agreement may not be terminated unilaterally. Firms often have to wait for many years until the respective Manteltarifvertrag (framework agreement) has expired.

The 1996 case of Viessmann, a producer of heating equipment, exemplifies the awkward construction of the German model of wage bargaining.[14] Viessmann intended to produce its new gas heater in the Czech Republic, where wages were much lower than in Germany. Offering to raise the weekly working time of all employees from 35 hours to 38 for three years, the employee council succeeded in having the new plant built in Germany instead, securing 60 new jobs. It even succeeded in negotiating the preclusion of all dismissals during this period. Nearly all employees (96.4 percent of the workforce) consented to this agreement and signed new work contracts. But even this marginal modification of the work contracts contradicted the industry-wide collective agreement. The union brought suit against the employee council, demanding the expulsion of its non-union members (who were in the majority). In addition, it brought suit against management, demanding the payment of a 250,000-euro fine. While the court dismissed both proposed actions, it essentially agreed with the union's stance. Although the changes of the contracts were legal for non-union members, they were illegal for union members. Moreover, the employee council was not empowered to negotiate with management about wages. The court refrained from removing the members of the employee council from office, as the union had demanded, only because it presumed an erroneous interpretation of the law.

But this story has a happy ending. Under pressure from a furious workforce, the union finally gave in to a settlement out of court, agreeing to a firm-level proposal of an unpaid extension of working time by 2 hours. The product line became a big success and instead of the planned 60 jobs, 600 new jobs were eventually created at the German location.

Other similar stories have not had happy endings. In 1999, the employees of Philipp Holzmann, a firm that used to be one of Germany's global players in the construction industry, tried to avert bankruptcy by offering to work for less pay but were not allowed to do so. Philipp Holzmann went bankrupt. Interestingly, not only the union but also the employers' association had opposed such a concession. The reason lies surely in the transference, described above, of the wage cartel to an implicit suppliers' cartel in the product market that would have been undermined by the wage concession. The firms competing with Philipp Holzmann, whose interests were represented in the employers' association and the labor union, were unwilling to agree to the wage concessions of the Philipp Holzmann workforce. They rather preferred that Philipp Holzmann went bankrupt, because they found that they could better service the market demand for construction work alone. This shows the serious nature of the market distortions that follow from the collective bargaining law in its present form. The events regarding Philipp Holzmann had little in common with the expected behavior of suppliers and demanders in a competitive labor market.

Viessmann and Philipp Holzmann are cautionary examples of a distorted legal environment whose origins are rooted in an era of class conflict and the exploitation of the working masses, but is no longer relevant to a country that because of laws and a welfare system favorable to workers and the unemployed, has nearly the highest labor costs of the world and suffers from mass unemployment. Industry-wide collective agreements are the instrument with which the unions implement their disastrous cartel policy. This instrument is badly outdated and in need of urgent reform.

More Autonomy for Individual Firms

Germany needs more competition in the labor market and, with rather mild reforms, this could be achieved by opening the agreements for firm-level and individual arrangements. This was proposed back in 1994 by the German Monopoly Commission, the legal arm of the Federal Cartel Office charged with safeguarding competition in Germany. The Commission demanded more flexibility and competition in collective bargaining, declared the fight against long-term unemployment of paramount communal interest, and questioned in their entirety the special labor-market rules that support the union wage cartel.[15]

An essential step would be having the collective agreements function as wage guidelines while permitting deviations on the firm level. Specifically, the bargaining parties could be forced by law to include an effective opening clause in each collective agreement that allows each firm to deviate from the collective agreement. Should circumstances warrant, the employee council and the management should be able to jointly change this agreement in either direction.[16]

There ought to be safeguards that a sufficiently large majority of the workforce approve the firm-level agreements. If an alternative agreement is reached with a two-thirds majority, it could be made binding for all members of the workforce including union members. The unions could only block such a firm-level agreement if they succeeded in convincing more than one-third of the employees. It would not suffice to just convince a handful of union members. If two-thirds of the workforce conclude that it is better to work longer hours for the same pay or to accept lower hourly wage rates in order to save the firm or to prevent relocation, then this decision must be accepted.

The necessary legal reforms can no longer wait because the number of company bankruptcies continues to be high. In 2002 and 2003, Germany experienced a serious banking crisis and a credit crunch unparalleled in the postwar period. Firm-level opening clauses that give workers threatened with unemployment the right to save their jobs by accepting lower wages or working longer hours without pay increases are urgently required to prevent similar crises in the future, and to provide for employment-promoting measures.

Working Longer

Agreeing on longer working hours without pay increases would indeed be a possibility to help solve Germany's labor cost problem. Reducing labor costs is painful if it implies cutting the paycheck. Working longer for the same monthly pay is comparatively harmless. This is a topic on which the Ifo Institute has started a public debate in Germany, and indeed over the last few years many wage negotiations have resulted in extensions of the work week without pay increases.[17]

The effects on employment of increasing the hours worked are similar to, but not identical to, those of reducing the monthly wage. The decisive advantage of working longer is the capacity effect that results in productivity gains. An increase in working hours not only increases the supply of labor, but also that of capital, as it permits a much better utilization of machinery and equipment. Except for cases where shift work already covers 24 hours a day, the hours for which the machine, the computer, or the office building is used increase in proportion to the human working time. It is as if God rewarded people with a free gift of capital for being more industrious. Capital that otherwise would have to be accumulated out of savings in a cumbersome process that takes many years is made available overnight.

Both factors of production, labor and capital, will become much more productive. More goods will be available in the markets. The transaction volume of the economy will rise, and so will national product and income.

Unions fear that there will be no positive employment effects. They argue that with longer working hours, any given volume of work could be done with fewer workers and that this policy will result in even lower employment. If this fear were justified then technological progress that increases the productivity of capital and labor should have had the same effect. The capitalist development of the past 200 years, which was characterized by powerful technological progress, would have resulted in continuously rising unemployment in the industrialized Western countries. Of course, this did not happen. Although there were recurring business-cycle fluctuations with rising unemployment resulting from coordination errors, and there were always countries like Germany, which had unemployment problems during long phases of history, there has been no systematic upward trend in unemployment due to technological progress. Unemployment in industrialized countries is no higher today than 100 years ago, even though technological progress has been immense. Technological progress has increased output and thereby enhanced people's standard of living; it has not resulted in a widespread destruction of jobs.

Consider what it would mean if the unions' argument were correct. One would have to immediately outlaw any research and development in Germany that result in productivity improvements, because, as the economic effects of research and development that enhance the productivity of capital and labor are essentially the same as those of longer working hours, increased unemployment would ensue. This is clearly absurd.

The great advantage of a lengthening of working time lies in the fact that, like technological progress, it directly triggers a growth surge in the economy without additional investment and without the firms having to redesign the production process. Such a growth surge would not occur after a direct reduction of labor costs.

A growth surge by itself does not generate an increase in employment, however. Employment growth may only be expected in a second phase, because an increase in weekly working hours in line with a higher utilization of capital results in an increase in the average and marginal productivity of workers. As workers generate more value added for their company without costing more, the profit maximizing firm has every incentive to hire more of them. More manufacturing firms will again decide to locate in Germany, and when they invest in Germany they again will build their plants in order to employ people rather than robots. In addition, household services will become cheaper, generating additional demand for such services, creating additional jobs.

Increasing working time will create more investment than cutting wages would. For one thing, the output of the capital-goods industry may rise even in the absence of its own additional investment because its working time and capacity utilization increases. In this manner, the buyers will immediately be able to get more capital goods to create new jobs in their factories. For another, the immediate expansion of capacity and output everywhere in the economy results in higher profits out of which such additional investment may more readily be financed. Viewed in this light, the increase in working hours is indeed the appropriate way to increase the competitiveness of German workers rapidly and to create additional jobs.

But why is the union's argument incorrect? Who will buy the additional goods produced by the additional labor supplied? Must it not be feared that the firm whose employees work longer hours will simply dismiss some of its workforce because it can now produce the same output with fewer people?

The answer is that working longer not only increases supply but also demand. The supply of goods and services entails demand for other goods and services, unless the revenues are hoarded as cash. Every firm that produces more at the same labor costs achieves higher value added and higher profits than before. The higher profits will be used to buy more consumer and investment goods, in turn benefiting other firms. Since all firms behave this way, sales of each individual firm rise. Indeed, the additional demand that can be financed out of the additional profits exactly equals the increase in the value of the final products due to longer working hours. Thus, there is as much additional purchasing power as there are additional goods and services produced by the economy as a result of longer working hours.

To be sure, there is a chicken-and-egg problem. The firms must first expect additional demand for their products before they increase output and sales, earn more and purchase more elsewhere. In the market economy there is, however, no linear chain of events from demand to production; rather, this type of economy is characterized by circular flows of effects and simultaneous microeconomic decision processes that are linked and synchronized by a complex system of prices. There is no need for an external demand surge to get the economy moving after working times have been lengthened and wage rigidities have been eased, because the necessary demand surge occurs simultaneously with the increase in working time.

If the individual firm gets more working time for the same wage—that is, experiences a reduction of hourly labor costs, it will produce more for this reason alone and will purchase more investment, consumption and intermediate products from other companies, validating the assumption that it will be able to sell the additional output. Since all firms will proceed in similar fashion, the demand for each individual firm's output rises even in the absence of price reductions. The economy moves rapidly to the higher level of output and income that corresponds to the longer working hours. This applies even if firms invest their additional profits in the financial markets rather than spending them. The additional investment in the financial markets means additional loans with which to finance the investment of other firms.

It is not even necessary for businesses to invest their profits domestically. If profits are invested abroad, and indeed if these constitute net capital exports, then an identical increase in export demand is induced by price cuts or by devaluation. No matter how one looks at it: the additional output of all firms combined generates additional aggregate demand of the very same volume, if money hoarding is neglected.

To be sure, the additional demand will be distributed differently than the additional output. To this extent there will be firms whose additional demand exceeds their additional output and others where the reverse holds true. Therefore the process will be accompanied by certain structural frictions, which will be overcome by changes in relative prices. Prices will rise where additional demand exceeds additional output and fall where additional demand falls short of additional output. In this way the additional demand is redistributed until its composition corresponds to the composition of the additional output.

Despite possible frictions, which occur until demand and supply are in equilibrium again, demand pessimism, derived from microeconomic analysis, is in no way justified if working time is increased on a broad basis and not only by one individual firm.

The real practical question is how much longer German working hours should be? If Dutch hourly wage costs are used as the benchmark, a 13 percent lengthening of working time would be necessary to cut hourly wages by 11 percent and close the gap between the German and Dutch wage growth since the Wassenaar agreement in 1982. To accomplish this, average annual working hours would have to rise by 182, from 1,435 to 1,617. Such an increase would correspond to an addition of 5 hours to the weekly working time of a person employed full-time, raising the number of hours from 38 to 43. Annual working time would then approximate that of Italy. There are worse things. As is well known, Italian working time is still compatible with *la dolce vita*.

Details aside, measures should be taken to extend working hours simultaneously in as many German firms as possible, preferably in all companies, for this increase would create the demand surge needed by each individual firm that would enable selling the increased output without a fall in prices. Only the state can guarantee the desirable synchronization of such measures. And it should do so aggressively.

Nobody knows, of course, whether the German economy will react in the same way Dutch economy did in the past. For one things, the world economy is much more global in 2006 than it was in the 1980s. Whether copying the Dutch example will suffice to actually increase employment against the negative trend of the past decades cannot be ensured in view of intensifying international competition. The Dutch, too, are feeling pinched, so much so that the bargaining parties agreed to another pay freeze in 2004 under pressure from the state.

Investment Wages

Another way of getting the wage costs down and making German workers competitive again is investment wages—that is, remunerating them partly with ownership shares instead of cash wages. Besides their wage income, employees could receive a share of capital income to protect them against wage losses resulting from international low-wage competition.[18] It was one of the greatest mistakes of German union movement that they missed the chance of entering large-scale investment wage programs in the 1960s or the early 1970s. At the time, there was an intense debate regarding whether

employees could become co-owners of their companies. The Christian
social philosopher Oswald von Nell-Breuning and the union leader (and, later,
Minister of Construction) Georg Leber supported the idea of investment
wages. Academics, too, argued in this direction. There was extensive scholarly debate on this issue initiated by one of the annual reports of the German
Council of Economic Experts and a voluminous study by Krelle, Schunck, and
Siebke.[19]

Unions also discussed investment wages intensively, but they decided in
favor of co-determination instead of workers' sharing in the ownership and
profits of a firm. The discussion about investment wages ended in 1976 when
the Mitbestimmungsgesetz (Co-determination Law) was enacted. Politically,
only one of the options was available to the unions.

As we know today, the choice of co-determination instead of investment
wages was a mistake. If 30 years ago the unions had encouraged workers to
save, and if they had bargained for attractive stock options and similar arrangements instead of higher wages, workers would have accumulated substantial
assets, the returns to capital would supplement their pensions nicely, and the
incentives of firms and workers would be better aligned. The workers would
not be the losers in a process characterized by a growing capital shortage and
increasing downward pressure on wages; instead they would share the gains
with the owners of capital, because they would also be capital owners. Today,
as the result of a decision against investment wages, a typical German worker
hardly owns any assets and must depend entirely on wages and salaries and
on pay-as-you-go pensions derived therefrom.

The union's decision in favor of co-determination instead of investment
wages has gained little besides plum posts for employee representatives. Co-
determination certainly has not resulted in higher wage incomes for workers.
Rather the opposite has happened, for the restrictions of co-determination on
the employers have contributed to the weakening of Germany as an investment location. Capital that would have been invested in Germany under more
liberal market conditions has gone elsewhere. With less capital, both labor
productivity and wages are lower.

Why the unions opted for co-determination is not known, but one can reasonably speculate that this option promised them more immediate access to
influential and well-paid positions than a policy of gradual asset accumulation
would have achieved. It has also been claimed that unions would have risked
losing their ideological base as their membership mutated into small capitalists, spelling the end of German trade-union capitalism.

It is likely that substantial income was forgone by refusing the equity participation option. From the end of 1965 to the end of 2005, the DAX, the

German equivalent of the Dow Jones, increased by 1,180 percent.[20] This corresponds to an average annual rate of return of 6.6 percent. Even a small wage concession invested in the stock market would have grown nicely.

It is not too late, however, to choose investment wages. There are still attractive investment opportunities for German companies either through domestic investment or via direct investment in foreign countries. That is why it would be opportune for the unions to bargain for participation plans in coming years in exchange for wage concessions.

Executed effectively, participation in a company could be used to facilitate the downward adjustment of wages necessitated by international low-wage competition. Company shares could be used to compensate the insiders (those who already have a job) for accepting a wage concession. The insiders could be satisfied, say over 5 years, with wage increases that are one percentage point lower than productivity growth (including the rate of inflation), and in exchange the companies could transfer to the employees some of their own shares whose value would equal the present value of the wage concessions. Investment wages would replace cash wages. If newly hired employees were not included in this deal but received only cash wages, the marginal cost of labor would decline, and the firms would be induced to invest and create new jobs in Germany. Everyone would be a winner.

The conversion of wage concessions into participation claims is initially only redistribution from one pocket to another: the old owners lose ownership shares but gain in terms of lower wages for those now employed. But because of the lower hourly wage costs for new employees, firms have an incentive to expand employment. New lines of business can be developed that generate more profit. The old and the new owners gain because they share equitably in these profits. In addition, newly hired employees benefit, because without the deal they might have remained unemployed.

In Germany, there are thousands of firms with partner participation models, including such well-known companies as BMW (automobiles and motorcycles), Otto (mail order), Bertelsmann (media), and TUI (travel). Many models have been designed and tested.[21] These range from direct stock purchases (common in large firms) to company loans and participation certificates (often used by small firms). Participation certificates are claims against the company that consist of a profit component and a guaranteed minimum rate of interest. All these models are suitable for deals that combine a compensated wage concession and a factual spread between the income of insiders, who have a job, and outsiders, who do not. This spread is the key to success because it allows implementing the wage reduction necessary for new hires without forcing the insiders to suffer losses.

The time when the proletariat was exploited by the capitalists is long past, and the age of cartelized unions exploiting firms in secret complicity with the welfare state also must end. Germany's old wage policy has come to face hard reality, and now the unions face the wrath of the populace. It is high time to consider modern wage models and to develop ideas for new ways of true firm-level partnerships with workers.

Less Dismissal Protection, More Job Security

Other rules and institutions of Germany's labor market are also badly in need of reform. The restriction on firms' ability to dismiss workers is a prominent example. Left to itself, a competitive labor market does not require special dismissal protection in order to provide job security. In such a market there is nearly full employment. Firms do not dismiss proven employees, and an individual who is dismissed for specific reasons usually finds another job quickly. In the United States, where the labor market is flexible, hardly anyone who is capable of working remains unemployed for long. It is true that jobs are often downsized and that people have to accept lower wages to find new employment, but they do find employment.

Statutory dismissal protection is closely linked to union wage policy. On the one hand, union members want protection against the unemployment that the high-wage policy causes. On the other hand, the unions can be more aggressive in wage demands when they know that their members are protected. The purchaser of labor is first obliged to buy, and then the price is agreed upon. It is clear that this will put the seller in a very comfortable position. It is others who suffer. The unemployed do not find a way back into the work force and young people who are looking for their first job face acute difficulties in finding one. The fathers and mothers who have become accustomed to secure jobs vote for high wage demands that prevent their children from entering the world of work.

Statutory dismissal protection, however, often fails to prevent the firing of employed workers, because the firms opt for a more extreme solution: closing down entire plants. The example of AEG moving to Poland was discussed in the previous chapter. In this type of situation even the best dismissal protection does not prevent unemployment. This statement should be qualified, insofar as firing people is extremely costly in Germany. Before people can be fired, "social plans" are negotiated between management and worker's council that specify the conditions of dismissal, and normally these agreements provide golden parachutes. The typical severance payments range from a year's salary to one and a half year's salary. Only in cases of bankruptcy is there no dismissal protection. Each year thousands of firms take leave of their union partners in this way.

Until 2003, statutory dismissal protection applied to all firms with more than five employees. This was relaxed somewhat in the context of Schröder's Agenda 2010. Since 2004, all firms with fewer than ten employees have been exempted from statutory dismissal protection. Dismissal protection gets stronger the longer someone has worked for a particular employer. Those who have been employed by a firm for 15 years or longer cannot, for all practical purposes, be fired. In this case, operating reasons no longer suffice for dismissing someone and personal reasons cannot, as a rule, be proven. In Germany, tenured positions are held not only by civil servants (who must sign a loyalty statement and are not allowed to strike) but by nearly all wage and salary earners who have worked for their companies at least 15 years.

To be sure, there are countries where the situation is worse than in Germany. In 2005 there was a revolt in France because the government wanted to introduce a two-year waiting period for young employees before dismissal protection started. The reform would have merely copied the existing German rules, but even so it went too far for French tastes. The protests by the unions and on the streets were so aggressive that Prime Minister Dominique de Villepin eventually had to withdraw this proposal. However, there are also much more liberal countries, among them Austria and Denmark, which in this regard do not differ much from the Anglo-Saxon countries. Both countries have had good experiences with their liberal approaches, as evidenced by their low unemployment rates and comparatively high growth rates The Danish labor-market system is often quoted as an example in the German debate. It entails much more than just liberal job-protection rules.

Denmark, otherwise a canonical welfare state, has long had liberal hiring and firing rules, much like the Anglo-Saxon system. During the 1990s, this system was complemented by a shortening of the duration of unemployment benefits combined with a more active labor-market policy requiring the unemployed to enroll in training or "workfare" programs to maintain eligibility for unemployment benefits. At the time of reform, many critics argued that the new Danish labor-market regime would result in unbearable hardship. In fact, however, the reforms contributed to a considerable decline in unemployment and hence de facto to an increase in job security. Unemployment, according to the OECD definition, fell from 9.6 percent in the initial reform year of 1993 to 5.5 percent in 2003. In Germany, unemployment rose from 7.5 percent to 8.9 percent over the same period. It is widely believed that the liberal firing rules in Denmark make Danish employers more inclined to add to their work force. Any employment may be ended as long as the bargained or legal period of notice is respected. Common periods of notice are 6 weeks for blue-collar workers (bargained) and 3 months for white-collar workers (statutory). Until recently, unemployment compensation in Germany was paid for a period of up to 32 months, and unemployment assistance, a generous second-tier unemployment benefit system, was granted indefinitely. In Denmark unemployment compensation is paid for a maximum of 48 months, but after a year of unemployment an unemployed person has to participate in time-consuming training or workfare schemes on a regular basis and is required to display considerable mobility across geographical areas or sectors of employment. Unemployment compensation averages 65 percent of the last net pay and is thus close to the German average of 63 percent. The Danish system is more generous only for low-income people. They receive, for 12 months, up to 90 percent of the last net pay.

Germany could follow Denmark's example and abolish its statutory dismissal protection for large and small firms alike. If employers and employees still want to have contracts with full job protection, they may sign them, but that requires no legal regulation. Those who want protection against dismissal will be able to get it from their employer in exchange for reduced pay. Everyone can decide individually whether he (or she) wants to have a safe job at lower pay or a less secure job at correspondingly higher pay. It is true that contracts without dismissal protection may become the order of the day if the choice is left to the parties involved. But so what? If a considerably higher level of employment with less job protection is what the market partners want, there is no need for countervailing government intervention. A work contract is distinct from a marriage contract, which has the character of mutual insurance and should therefore not be terminated at will. Employers and employees must at all times be satisfied with their working relationship, and if one party no longer is, it must be able to end it.

It is improper for the government to make itself an accomplice to the unions by providing dismissal protection. Doing away with statutory dismissal protection will no doubt incur the wrath of the unions. They will never agree to give up one of the most effective weapons for enforcing their high-wage policy. They will fight against it and send hundreds of thousands of workers into the streets. But it seems unlikely that the German labor market will prosper unless the unions are deprived of their weapon of dismissal protection. Without job protection, the unions would choose a more moderate wage policy and the firms would create more jobs. This would increase job security rather than weaken it. The success of the Anglo-Saxon countries and Denmark speaks for itself.

Doing away with dismissal protection would have two additional advantages.

First, the employed workers would be induced to work more, because each one would know that he had to earn his keep, and the working relationship would last only as long as the job is done well. If Germany's wages are too high relative to its productivity, then this is also one way to become more competitive relative to foreign workers and to secure jobs. The importance of improving work incentives is exemplified by comparing absences due to illness among Turkish employees of MAN (one of Europe's biggest truck producers) who work in MAN's Munich plant and those who work in MAN's Turkish plant. Whereas the absences in the Turkish plant are only 2 percent of the annual working time, it amounts to 8 percent for the Turks working in Munich. One weak explanation for this is that the bad German weather causes illness and depression among the Turkish workers. Another reason is German labor-market institutions. Germany's system of paid sick leave plus dismissal protection may have contributed to a much laxer work ethics of Turks working in Germany than of Turks working in Turkey.

Second, without statutory dismissal protection, firms would be more willing to hire people. Today, many entrepreneurs do not dare to hire additional people because they are afraid that they may never be able to get rid of them. Especially in uncertain times, when they are not sure where their next commission will come from, entrepreneurs are understandably reluctant to hire, knowing that this would entail a long-term commitment. Economic recovery would occur faster and be more robust, as many firms would start hiring earlier, which—via the increase in incomes—would start a multiplier effect.

Dismissal protection need not, and indeed should not, be abolished in one big reform, as it could lead to a wave of long-overdue firings, which might destabilize the economy. Such an important reform must be introduced cautiously. Thus, new employees whose contracts are signed after a certain date could be exempted from dismissal protection while existing tenure rights would remain untouched.

The current system of dismissal-protection exemption for small firms with fewer than 10 employees is also not particularly sensible, because it imposes a barrier to firm growth. Italy is a characteristic example. In 1970, Italy introduced dismissal protection for firms with fewer than 15 employees. As a consequence, many firms cut staff in order to avoid dismissal protection and others stopped growing in order to circumvent the law. This perverse result bolsters the case for abolishing dismissal protection among new employees in all firms.

Most civil servants should also be exempted from dismissal protection, as improved work incentives for them, too, would hardly be a mistake. Exceptions may be conceivable for those groups of people with security functions, those whose political independence must be guaranteed, or those who occupy central functions in the transport system, whose absence in the case of strikes would cause great damage.

In sum, abolishing dismissal protection only *appears* to disadvantage employees. In truth, it raises economic efficiency, encourages firms to hire additional workers and makes wage moderation possible, thus facilitating job creation. Abolition of dismissal protection for new employment contracts is part of a package of measures that would lead Germany back to full employment. Full employment is the best job protection one can get. Sometimes less is more.

The Welfare State as the Union's Secret Accomplice

Another way to make the labor market more flexible and initiate a policy of wage moderation is to curtail the numerous wage-replacement payments provided by the government, because such payments induce aggressive union wage policy. Wage-replacement payments include unemployment compensation and social assistance; even early-retirement benefits can be considered as wage-replacement benefits.

Until now, no matter how excessive the unions' wage demands and how much subsequent unemployment ensued, the welfare state took care of the collateral damage. This not only relieved the union bosses' conscience; it also reduced the population's resistance to increasing unemployment. Today Germany as a whole has more than 10 percent unemployment, and in some regions unemployment is as high as 30 percent. Without the welfare state's safety nets, there would be popular resistance to union policy, mass protests, and general upheaval. The welfare state has been the secret accomplice of the cartelized unions, and it shoulders much of the blame for Germany's labor-market misadventures.

But the welfare state is costing more and more money that must be raised from the working people. Non-wage labor costs have risen in recent years and have made hiring workers more expensive. Germany puts extremely high social security contributions and taxes on the value added of its employees, as will be shown in greater detail in chapter 6. This either leads to an additional increase in labor costs and a rise in unemployment or it results in the employees' direct income losses.

What is the explanation for the muddled policy arising from the concerted actions of German unions and the welfare state, which even harms the workers themselves? As has already been asked once in this chapter, are union leaders stupid? They are not. The explanation for the self-harming activities of unions, rather, is that individual unions that bargain with businesses have always been able to assume that the costs of the unemployment they triggered would be passed on to employees in other collective-bargaining regions and other industries. Whereas the advantages (higher wages) would accrue to their own members, the fiscal costs would be passed on to the mass of taxpayers who finance the welfare state. Of course, this also includes the union members, but it would affect primarily the members of other unions and other bargaining regions. Only a minute part of the increase in government charges caused by the union leader would be borne by his constituency. There is what economists call moral hazard in the behavior of unions: a certain degree of collective irrationality that results from the specific organization of the German bargaining process.[22]

Each individual union representative is, presumably, aware of these relationships when bargaining. But he or she will still not take a different course of action, for they cannot assume that their own restraint will be imitated by the other union leaders. Thus, all unions are involved in an excessive search for advantage that ends up harming everybody through the costs associated with an increasingly bloated welfare state.

Since the unions will not change their behavior, the government must change the rules of the game. The next chapter will discuss reforms to the German welfare system that entail a change in the conditions under which the welfare state provides its benefits. Although these reforms are motivated by the attempt to make individual workers accept lower wages, the reforms will also automatically weaken the incentives for an aggressive union policy.

Sweden's Ultimate Solution

If Germany's unions do not move and if German lawmakers do not limit their power, the only solution left is the Swedish one. In Sweden, the firms dissolved the employers' association SAF in 1983 in order to leave the unions without a bargaining partner in wage negotiations. This was a healthy shock for the unions that led to a sustained change in political conditions and resulted in a complete makeover of the entire wage determination system. Wage negotiations were shifted to roughly 50 different industry sectors, and the individual companies were given more autonomy with regard to wages. The industry results are not binding for firms; they serve only as guidelines for further wage negotiations at the firm level, where additions or deductions may be agreed.[23]

German employers could also dissolve their umbrella organizations. The wage agreements would continue to be valid, but no increases could be negotiated as there would be no negotiating partner. The unions would have to strike in order to force the firms to sign firm-level agreements, but it is doubtful that they would have the power to do this effectively. Firms cannot be blamed for pulling the emergency brake one day if the unions and the government remain entrenched in their positions.

The German government must act before such extreme measure are taken. It must reform the current set of protective labor laws and generous unemployment policies that act in concert to inhibit employment. In addition, it must limit its role as a competitor of private business in the labor market by reforming the incentive structure of the welfare state. This is the theme of the next chapter.

to the German ministers of labor, with the nagging question "Did they know what they were doing?"

4 Competing against the Welfare State

The Case for the Welfare State

Germans are proud to have one of the best-developed welfare states in the world. The welfare state stabilizes Germany's political and economic order. It compensates and appeases those who lose out to technological progress and to the expanding division of labor and world trade. It helps people with low productivity and prevents them from having to resort to fraud, theft, and other criminal acts. Above all, however, it insures the people against economic risks in a manner and to an extent that private insurance companies could not possibly provide, and thus benefits everyone.

As was discussed in chapter 3, a person's career does not only depend on his or her own achievements and own free will. Instead, a lot is determined by factors the individual has no control over. Whether one has a high income or a successful career depends largely on how hard one works. But it also has to do with whether one had good teachers in childhood, whether one is healthy, whether later in life one had the right contacts and opportunities at the right time, and even whether one has the "right" genes. These are not things most people have a lot of say in, and this means that, at least from an ex-ante perspective, there is a role for state-provided insurance protection via income redistribution. By taking from the rich and giving to the poor, people's career risks are reduced, and this insurance benefit is welcomed by most citizens. In Europe, the idea of solidarity is a popular way of expressing the principle of providing social insurance. The sense of solidarity with one's fellow man is part of the social contract that binds a nation together. Solidarity is only another name for insurance protection.

It is, therefore, only proper that the fathers of the German constitution set down the need for the welfare state. To the extent to which poverty cannot be considered the result of too little individual effort but of unknown influences beyond one's free will, state income redistribution from rich to poor may be interpreted as insurance protection. It is a useful economic service in the same sense as the protection granted by private insurance companies.

To some extent, the government is in an even better position to provide insurance than private insurance companies. Private insurance often simply comes too late in a person's life. Someone who wants to sign an insurance contract must already be an adult. But by the time one is an adult, life's dice have usually already been cast. By then the potential parties to an insurance contract have a pretty good idea about the insured's physical condition and intelligence. No private insurance can be designed against these two known differences, as the good risks who know that they are net payers would never play the game, and insurers would not be willing to accept the bad risks. People can only be privately insured ahead of time, before it is known who will one day be a net payer and who will be a net payee, but at that age they are too young to sign insurance contracts, and no Western legal system allows parents to sign the insurance contract for them. Only the government is in a legal position to effectively carry out a truly comprehensive insurance function.

Yet, just as there can be too little state insurance, resulting in an inadequate social safety net, there can be an over-provision of insurance protection, resulting in what economists call moral hazard. While insurance can exert beneficial effects on private behavior by enhancing productive risk taking, it definitely causes disincentives and distortions in the sense that individual initiatives to limit the insured risks are dwarfed by other considerations that can actually increase the risk. Examples are a company that reduces expenditures on night watchmen and sprinkler systems when it has fire insurance, the reduced incentive to look for inexpensive repair shops when covered by auto insurance, or excessive demand for health-care services or expensive medication when there is health insurance. As will be explained later in this section, Germany today suffers from a moral-hazard problem with respect to unemployment benefits and wage supplements.[1]

If the moral-hazard effects are strong, private companies cannot profitably offer insurance, Most risks people face in the course of their lives are not insurable because moral hazard would make insurance too expensive. The problem of state insurance is that all too often people are forced to participate even though moral hazard results in utility losses from an ex-ante perspective. But it is better to endure this abuse of the system than not to have one at all.

To be sure, government-provided insurance in the sense of income redistribution is also subject to some control to the extent that the political parties that make these policies must stand for election. But this democratic check is quite different from the market discipline imposed on insurance companies. Controlling government by way of votes is not only undertaken ex-ante, but also ex-post—that is, after citizens know whether they are net payers or net recipients of state benefits. To push the analogy, it would be as if the clients of a private insurer could decide the extent of their insurance after knowing whether or not they have suffered damages. This would be like having a major auto accident and then taking out coverage to pay for the damage. The majority decision after the fact is partly responsible for a state insurance system in which the number of net beneficiaries is continuously increasing relative to the number of net payers, and the basic idea of insurance—that many people help the few unlucky ones—is gradually being perverted to an unhealthy degree that poses grave problems for the country's overall economy.

Moral hazard in the welfare state was no problem for Germany until well into the 1970s. One reason was that the welfare state was still relatively small, and then, too, the behavioral change caused by the welfare state spread only gradually through the imitation of lifestyles that rely on government support. Since the late 1970s, the welfare state has become so large and has changed economic behavior so extensively that moral hazard can no longer be ignored. About 41 percent of German voters receive their income primarily from the state, and this share will rise in future years because of the increase in the number of retirees.

The problematic behavioral changes caused by the welfare state itself include increasing reluctance to invest one's time and money in education, to change one's occupation, to move if better jobs are available elsewhere, to secure one's consumption in old age by raising children, and, above all, to accept low-paying jobs instead of working in the underground economy or not at all. All these disincentives are characteristic of well-known deficiencies in Germany's society and economy, and they are caused, or at least exacerbated, by the country's too-generous welfare state. The last disincentive noted above is probably the most important at present, because, besides the wage policy of the unions, it is the main reason for rising unemployment in Germany since the 1970s. The remainder of this chapter addresses this topic in detail.

Wage-Replacement Income as Job Killer

It is not fair to attribute the population's reluctance to take up low-paying jobs to laziness, because nobody likes to be unemployed. As a general rule, the unemployed regard their predicament as a misfortune from which they want to escape as fast as possible. Voluntary unemployment is not an issue in Germany. The main problem is not a lack of job candidates; it is a lack of jobs.

However, the truth is a bit more subtle than it appears at first glance, because the lack of jobs is due not to some secret mechanism of the market economy, but primarily to the high wage demands or "reservation wages" generated by the welfare state itself. As a rule, an unemployed person starts by looking for a job that pays as much as the job he or she held previously. If the individual cannot find such a job, he wants to earn at least as much as the replacement income received from the state. Although this concern is legitimate and understandable, it is the core of the problem. There is no lack of jobs in Germany. There is just a lack of *well-paying* jobs which can compete with the wage-replacement income offered by the state. In the minds and at the desks of German employers there are plenty of jobs, but most of the jobs are not productive enough to allow the employer to match the reservation wages—that is, to pay as much as the welfare state does. The higher the social replacement incomes are, the lower the number of jobs that employers can profitably provide.

The reason why the welfare state generates high reservation wages is due to the circumstances under which assistance may be granted. Essentially, state funds flow only if the recipient is not working and therefore making no contribution to solving the problem. If the recipient works and earns some income, state assistance is withdrawn nearly to the extent of the income earned. The state does not primarily assist those who have suffered misfortunes and whose productivity is so low that they cannot earn a socially acceptable income by working, as any reasonable reading of the term "insurance" suggests. Rather, it assists those who do not work. It pays a replacement wage because it interprets poverty as being caused by the loss of a job rather than by low productivity. It is an open question as to whether the state acts this way because politicians consider unemployment a random, insurable event, or because it is simply acting as the accomplice of the union cartels, compensating for the collateral damage of their high-wage policy, as described in the previous chapter. In any case, next to the unions' cartel policy, wage replacement is the main reason for Germany's high rate of unemployment. It is responsible for the high reservation wages, which the market has been unable to match. This situation is a perversion of the welfare system as originally intended by the fathers of the German constitution. In the 1960s, providing for some unemployed and disabled people at the margins of a well-functioning economy was no problem for the German economy. But paying for a huge constituency that has been growing along a linear trend (see chapter 1) has created an unsustainable strain on the German economy. This trend, which began in 1970, cannot continue for another 35 years.

Wage-replacement incomes include, in the narrow sense, unemployment compensation and social assistance. In the wider sense it also includes pensions, especially those that are paid for early retirement. The state grants these kinds of assistance only if—and to the extent that—no labor income is earned. If labor income is earned, most of the assistance is cut. For each extra euro earned by working, the assistance is cut nearly by nearly a euro. It is as if the person's income were taxed at a marginal rate approximating 100 percent. This certainly acts to kill individual incentive and initiative, as the rules of the game are so skewed.

The wage-replacement incomes offered by the state create unemployment because they operate as wage floors. For one thing, hardly any eligible person will be willing to work in the private sector at a net wage that is not substantially higher than the wage-replacement income provided for doing nothing. For another, most employers are unwilling to hire someone who costs more than the value he or she adds, since to do so would entail making a loss. Therefore, there are no jobs for those people whose value added is either below or not far enough above the wage-replacement income for which they are eligible.

The German welfare state is thus caught on the horns of a dilemma. In its attempt to insure against unemployment, it ends up perpetuating and even causing it. The welfare state causes unemployment when an individual's wage replacement is too high or his productivity is too low. Perhaps the continuing growth of wage-replacement benefits in recent years could have been compatible with lower unemployment if the world around Germany had not changed, if there had been no globalization, no internal EU market, no interest-rate convergence among the eurozone countries, and no fall of the Iron Curtain. In view of the revolutionary changes that took place around Germany, the wage-replacement benefits granted by the German welfare state must be considered the major reason why wages cannot react flexibly to the changing events and why mass unemployment has come about.

By paying wage-replacement incomes, the welfare state has become a competitor of private business in labor markets. The welfare state is a powerful economic sector that pays well for doing nothing and, in the process, puts upward pressure on private-sector wages. Between the state's high-wage competition in labor markets and the international low-wage competition in product markets, German jobs are increasingly being squeezed out.

To make matters worse, private business is forced to pay a portion of its competitor's "wage bill" in the form of high taxes and social security contributions, which further compromise the competitiveness of German workers. Chapter 6 will discuss this in detail. Note, however, that even if this burden did not exist and somebody else footed the welfare state's bill, the welfare state would still cause unemployment, at least in the low-skill sector, because of the wage competition resulting from the payment of wage-replacement incomes.

In light of these considerations, the design of German unemployment compensation must be scrutinized before Germany's economic situation can be fully understood.

Until 2004, there was a two-tier system of unemployment compensation. First-tier unemployment compensation was paid for a period of up to 32 months, depending on age and work history, if contributions to unemployment insurance had been made for at least a year. Depending on whether or not the unemployed person had at least one child, he or she received 67 percent or 60 percent, respectively, of previous net earnings. After first-tier unemployment compensation had run out, second-tier unemployment compensation, called "unemployment assistance," took over. This provided 57 percent or 53 percent, respectively, of net earnings until retirement age. With its unlimited duration, unemployment assistance was a uniquely German institution, met with incredulity in the rest of the world. Both systems created reservation wages that were higher for an increasing number of individuals than the wages compatible with paid employment.

This situation has changed since Chancellor Gerhard Schröder introduced his Agenda 2010, also known as "Hartz reforms" after a commission chaired by Peter Hartz in 2002.[2] Schröder introduced the Gesetz zu Reformen am Arbeitsmarket (Law for Reforming the Labor Market), which shortened the period for which first-tier unemployment compensation may be received from 32 months to 12 months across the board. And with the fourth Law for Modern Services in the Labor Market ("Hartz IV") Schröder abolished unemployment assistance, forcing people to content themselves with the less generous Sozialhilfe (social assistance), a basic welfare payment available to everyone, regardless of the employment history. The two laws became effective in 2006 and 2005, respectively. Although both were justified by a need to tighten the government's purse strings, the true economic justification was to reduce the reservation wages of the unemployed. This reduction can be expected to result in lower actual wages and hence in the creation of new jobs, a mechanism that has never been openly mentioned by the German government. According to model-based calculations by the Ifo Institute, replacing unemployment assistance with ordinary social assistance in the low-wage sector would result in a 4 percent wage reduction relative to the current trend and about 260,000 additional jobs. At the time of this writing, it is too early to say whether these pre-dictions will hold true.

The abolition of generous unemployment assistance was courageous, as about a million West Germans and about a million East Germans were affected.[3] Understandably, there was enormous public opposition. For many months, "Monday demonstrations," which once toppled the Berlin Wall, were resumed in the East. Though Schröder did not give in, increasing opposition within his own party, the SPD, ultimately cost him his job. In 2004, he lost the chairmanship of his party and then, in early elections of his own choosing in the hope of finding more public support, he ended up losing the chancel-lorship to the CDU's Angela Merkel. Since 2005, Germany has been governed by a coalition of the Christian Democrats (CDU/CSU) and the Social Democrats (SPD).

Schröder's reforms were signals that Germany might be preparing for a turnaround. However, they were not a real breakthrough. Social assistance, the most important wage-replacement benefit in terms of its consequences, was left basically untouched. Renamed "Unemployment Compensation II," it was designed for those considered capable of working, and it is now a bit more generous than before, but apart from that it remained what it always had been: a wage-replacement system that provides funds only if, and to the extent that, people abstain from working.

The Accordion Effect; Low-Skilled Workers Are Priced Out of the Market

The redesign of Germany's welfare state will require rethinking social assis-tance, the new "Unemployment Compensation II." In contrast to Unemploy-ment Compensation I, this form of assistance is not tied to the wage previously earned and thus not to individual productivity. Every needy person is eligible, for it does not matter why one is poor, just that one is poor. Social assistance represents a fixed floor to the wage structure that cannot react to the level of wages but nonetheless forms the basis of the entire wage scale. Even though Germany has no formal minimum wage, its de facto minimum wage is derived from the replacement wage provided by social assistance. There is arguably no other component of the German welfare system that bears greater responsibil-ity for mass unemployment than social assistance. Low-skilled workers are the most affected, for the wage rate at which they could be profitably employed is often below the wage level established by social assistance. The lower a person's skill, the higher is the probability that he or she will be unemployed.

The effect of social assistance is much bigger than that suggested by the number of recipients of this type of unemployment benefit. In April 2006, this number totaled 5.202 million, not counting the additional 67,000 recipients of social assistance above the age of 14 who are not considered capable of working.[4] A large part of unemployment among those people who receive Unemployment Compensation I or are unemployed without declaring that they are looking for a job may also be traced to social assistance, because higher minimum wage demands imply higher wages even for the skilled, as certain differences in the skill differentiated wages must be maintained.

To explain the effect, consider for a moment a hypothetical market economy without a government, where wages are determined by supply and demand. In this economy, there would be very wide wage dispersion across skill levels, and the lowest wages would possibly be too low to provide for subsistence. However, there would hardly be any unemployment, except for the frictional kind.

Suppose now that a government were to step in and provide social assistance in order to ensure minimum subsistence-level incomes. The entire wage distribution would then be shifted upward and compressed from below like an accordion hanging in the left hand and pushed in by the right. The lowest wage has to be somewhat above social assistance in order to compensate for the work effort and a possible loss of black-market income, and the other wages will also increase due to a chain of adjustment effects. The second-lowest wage in the next skill category has to remain above the lowest wage, the third-lowest above the second-lowest, and so on, where the steps between the categories are necessary to provide incentives to qualify for better jobs and to work carefully and responsibly in them. The higher the social assistance, the more each wage will have to edge up above its market-clearing level, causing unemployment in all skill categories.

The wage increases will not be uniform, however, as the wage-adjustment effect will be weaker the further a wage is above the social assistance level. The wage increase of the unskilled worker will imply a wage increase for the supervisor and to some extent also of the supervisor's boss. The salary of the engineer, however, is too far above social assistance to be significantly affected. Thus, the paradox is that unemployment rate will be the higher the lower the wage rate. The accordion effect, which illustrates how jobs get pushed out of the economy because of this replacement wage policy, describes this situation.

Non-union and union wages alike are affected by the accordion effect, but let us look at union wages as they are better documented. In 2006, as this book is being written, the lowest collectively agreed wage in West Germany is about 8.70 euros per hour. This is what is earned, for example, by a janitor or by a worker in the clothing industry. At an average of 155 working hours per month, this corresponds to a gross monthly income of 1,350 euros. A single person with this gross income has take-home pay, after the deduction of taxes and social security contributions, of 968 euros. If he does not work, he is eligible for social assistance (Unemployment Benefit II), including a housing allowance, amounting to 673 euros. Thus, if he works, his disposable income is only 295 euros higher than if he doesn't work. At 155 hours, this corresponds to an effective hourly wage rate of just 1.90 euros. The disincentive to work is clear.

Things are similar for a married couple with two children. If the father works for the lowest union wage of 8.70 euros per hour, he must only pay the employee contribution to social security, but no taxes, and the state grants supplemental social assistance, including a housing allowance and child allowances, of 825 euros. In total, the family receives a net income of 1,886 euros to cover its cost of living. If neither the father nor anyone else in the family works, the family receives social assistance, including a housing allowance, amounting to 1,591 euros. This implies that the father again adds just 1.90 euro to the family net income for every hour worked. It should come as no surprise that this is simply not enough of an incentive for a large portion of the currently unemployed.

The minimum union wage of 8.70 euros is already so unattractive relative to social assistance that it is accepted primarily by those who are not eligible for social assistance or other wage-replacement incomes. This group comprises high school students, college students, married persons whose spouses work, and retirees. The unemployed, registered in the statistics of the Federal Labor Office, typically belong to a category of people who have higher wage demands because of the replacement incomes they receive.

The additional 1.90 euro per hour worked is so little that wage reductions below 8.70 euros are unthinkable for normal unskilled workers. The difference between the lowest collectively agreed wage and the rate of social assistance is negligible. The hourly wage cost (including employer contributions to social security and value-added tax) that corresponds to a gross hourly wage of 8.70 euros amounts to 12.20 euros. Skilled workers, who are unable to produce a value added of at least 12.20 euros, cannot, therefore, find acceptable jobs if they are eligible for social assistance.

The job-destroying effect of social assistance was not a topic of concern in 1970. Germany had hardly any unemployment, and social assistance was so far below the prevailing market wage rates that it was not a binding constraint on the wage distribution. Up to that point in time, the economy had been growing with wages that still were quite low by international standards. Social assistance was only a measure to fight poverty on the fringes of a well-functioning labor market, and, since recipients were socially stigmatized, social assistance was not considered a serious income alternative. Moreover, social assistance was much further below average wage incomes than today. Conditions have changed, however. German wages approached and then exceeded the levels of other Western countries, receiving state aid lost its social stigma, and social assistance has come close to the net incomes of ordinary lower-class workers. Average spending on social assistance per capita, including allowances for heating, and rent as well as benefits for children—in other words, everything that may be counted as current support to the cost of living—quadrupled from 1970 to 2000 in nominal terms. During the same period, the monthly net income of an average employee only tripled.[5]

The relatively brisk increase in the level of social assistance is directly associated with a hike in the number of recipients of social assistance in the former West Germany. This number increased from 528,000 at the end of 1970 to 2.2 million at the end of 2000. The percentage of foreign recipients increased even more. From the time of the first statistical survey at the end of 1980 until the end of 2000 it increased from 9 percent to 25 percent of the foreigners residing in Germany—in absolute numbers, from 81,000 to 567,000.[6] In 20 years, the number of foreign recipients of social assistance had increased by a factor of 7.

Since the abolition of the second-tier unemployment system, the number of recipients of social assistance (including Sozialhilfe and Arbeitslosengeld II) has grown out of bounds. The May 2006 estimate for East and West Germany together gives a total number of 7.3 million persons receiving this type of state aid.[7]

Even more important than these numbers was the indirect effect of the change in the level of social assistance on the wage level of the unskilled and the compression of the wage distribution—that is, the accordion effect. The accordion effect also results from the unions' policy of bargaining for lump-sum payments for those earning the lowest wages, in addition to the general percentage wage increase. Presumably the increase in social assistance has itself given rise to this policy, regardless of the fact that the unions contributed to the change in social assistance rates by way of political influence.

The German Council of Economic Experts has documented the compression of the wage scale for some bargaining regions and industries.[8] Thus, in a bargaining region of the West German metal and electrical machinery industry, wages in the lowest wage bracket (group 1) rose by 455 percent from 1970 to 1999, whereas wages in the highest wage bracket (group 8) rose by only 365 percent. And whereas in 1970 the wages of group 1 amounted to 75 percent of the wages of group 6, by 1999 the percentage had risen to 87. In the chemical industry, which has traditionally had very high wages, significantly above the level of social assistance even in the low-wage segment, the wage scale evolved more uniformly. The percentage wage increases were the same in each wage group. However, in the chemical industry, there had also been the same one-off payments with a lower percentage effect on the high wages than on the low wages. A substantial compression of the union wage scale was experienced by the insurance industry, the third industry looked at by the Council. There the wages in group 1 rose by 87 percent between 1980 and 1999, whereas the wages in group 8 rose only by 53 percent.

While Germany's social assistance policy in and of itself has tended to push the internal wage scale up, the forces of globalization have simultaneously tried to pull it down. International low-wage competition in commodity trade, low-wage competition for capital flows, and poverty-induced migration have all contributed to a gradual process of international factor-price convergence that has put downward pressure on the wages for unskilled labor in the Western world. The United Kingdom and the United States, which are characterized by flexible wages, have reacted by widening their wage scale and thus have succeeded in avoiding high unemployment. Germany, however, has resisted international downward wage pressure, accepting additional unemployment instead. The differences in the development of the wage distribution are shown in figure 4.1, which plots the ratios of the ninth to the first decile of the wage distributions for the United States, the United Kingdom, and Germany.

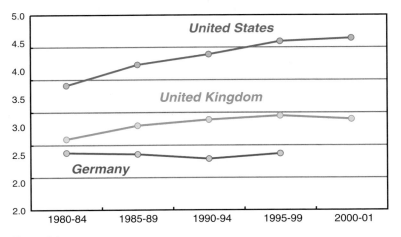

Figure 4.1
Earnings dispersion (9:1 decile ratio for gross earnings of full-time employees) in United States, United Kingdom, and Germany, 1980–2001. Source: OECD Employment Outlook, 2004, table 3.2, p. 141.

Obviously, the two Anglo-Saxon countries not only have higher wage disper-
sions than Germany, but also ones that increase over time. In contrast, the
German distribution has remained surprisingly unchanged, with wage inequality actually shrinking slightly from the early 1980s to the early 1990s.[9]

The implications for Germany's increasing unemployment rate are straightforward. Figure 1.2 showed that West German unemployment had risen cycli-
cally along a linear trend, from about 150,000 unemployed in 1970 to 3.43
million in 2005. As figure 4.2 shows, this trend can predominantly be attributed to the increasing unemployment of low-skilled workers. While the unemployment rate among people with a university degree increased by a factor of
2.1 in 30 years and by a factor of 2.7 for those who had formal occupational
training, it increased by a factor of 3.6 for the low-skilled, reaching a rate of
about 22 percent in 2005. This pattern follows the accordion theory's predic-
tion, explained above, that unemployment is inversely related to wage and skill
levels. The lower the skill category, the larger the wage distortions relative to
the respective market-clearing levels and the higher the rate of unemployment.
The wages of the low-skilled are greatly constrained by social replacement
incomes, and the wages of those with intermediate skills are indirectly affected
by subsequent adjustments, but the wages of the highly skilled are affected
but little.

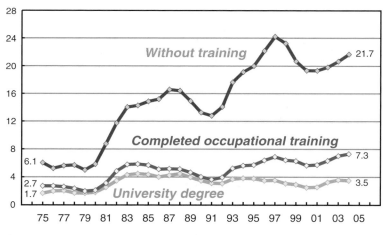

Figure 4.2
Qualification-specific unemployment rates (percent) for West Germany, including West Berlin:
unemployed persons as percent of civilian labor force (excluding trainees) with same qualification, men and women. "Completed occupational training" includes within-firm training, occupational school, special, master's, and technical training. Sources: Institut für Arbeitsmarkt- und
Berufsforschung der Bundesagentur für Arbeit (IAB-Werkstattbericht 4, April 23, 2002, p. 27;
IAB-Kurzbericht 9, June 13, 2005).

This shows that despite good intentions, social welfare policies may be counterproductive if these ignore the laws of economics. The attempt to secure a decent standard of living for the unskilled by way of social replacement incomes has driven too many of them into unemployment by perverting incentives to work. The continuation of these policies has introduced a serious structural problem into the German economy that must be addressed.

The German Disease: Why Germans Really Are Running Out of Work

A popular German sentiment suggests that growing unemployment among the unskilled is caused in a quasi-mechanical way by labor-saving technological progress and the forces of globalization. If there is no longer enough work for Germans, it is claimed, then this simply cannot be helped. This development must be accepted, and the welfare state must be used to make the consequences bearable for its victims. But this idea is wrong. Whatever the developments in international competition, technological progress, and the skill distribution of the workforce, there is a market wage structure securing full employment even of the unskilled. When wages change, firms change their production processes, technological progress adjusts accordingly, the prices of labor-intensive local services change, and the demands for the various skill categories of the labor market change.

Employment relationships are not rigid and God-given; rather, they react in large measure to the structure of wages and prices. Wages and prices help to organize the production process and the division of labor. They determine employment relationships and are, in turn, determined by them. In a free-market system, if demand and supply in the markets do not coincide, the wage-and-price structure will change, and with it the real economy, until the market equilibrium is restored in the sense that on all markets demand equals supply. A market economy that is left to itself will be able, with the help of wage and price signals, to fully utilize the employment potential in all segments of the labor market and to maximize economic welfare.

If, in contrast, intervention by the unions or the wage-replacement benefits of the welfare state disrupt the market mechanism by forcing an artificial wage structure on the economy, unemployment will result, especially in those segments that unions and politicians want to favor.

If there were any truth to the thesis of the quasi-mechanical increase of unemployment due to globalization and technological progress, then all countries that are involved in international trade and have access to the knowledge of this world would be similarly affected by unemployment among the unskilled. After all, technological progress is not unique to Germany. Clearly, this is not the case. In no other country has unemployment among unskilled workers reached the levels now experienced in Germany. Unemployment among this skill group is at the heart of the German disease.

As figure 4.3 shows, Germany is an outlier with regard to skill-specific unemployment. Here the definition of skill levels is slightly different from that in figure 4.2, for reasons of international comparability. In 2003, at an unemployment rate of 18 percent for persons with less than higher secondary education (that is, without a high school diploma or completed vocational schooling), Germany was at the top of the countries compared, whereas its unemployment rates for persons with higher secondary education were only marginally higher than those of other countries. Unemployment rates for university graduates hardly differed at all. Apparently, individual countries have reacted quite differently to globalization and low-wage competition. German unskilled workers, in particular, have become the victims of an ill-designed welfare policy that made them unable to react to international low-wage competition.

That German unemployment is primarily a problem of the unskilled is also illustrated by examining the composition of the unemployed workers. The

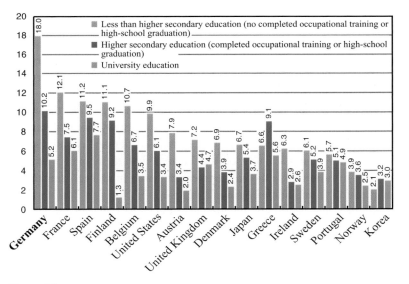

Figure 4.3
International comparison of qualification-specific unemployment rates (percent) for 25–64-year-olds, 2003 (no data for Italy and Netherlands). Source: OECD, Education at a Glance. 2005, p. 113f., table A8.4a.

percentage of Germans without occupational training among the unemployed is 34, but the percentage of Germans without occupational training in the total number of gainfully employed is only 13.[10] If unemployment were independent of occupational training, only 13 percent of the unemployed should be without completed occupational training. But the group of unskilled people include more than merely those without occupational training. Most of the recipients of social assistance may also be included in the group of unskilled workers because their occupational skills eroded during the long period of unemployment. East Germany is particularly affected by this phenomenon. It suffers from mass unemployment that, at a rate of about 20 percent in 2005, is about as high in percentage terms as unemployment among the unskilled in West Germany. And indeed the causes are also similar. To be sure, the formal qualifications of East Germans are high, and, unlike in the West, there are hardly any formally unskilled workers. The change in East Germany's economic system due to reunification, however, devalued many qualifications in the commercial area that had been acquired in Communist times. In addition, the businesses in Communist East Germany were largely obsolete and simply utilized pre-World War II technology. The true qualifications of many workers cannot, therefore, be equated with their formal qualifications. To make matters worse, many people have lost contact with the working world because of the already long duration of mass unemployment. Deficiencies in the infrastructure and geographical disadvantages are additional productivity reducing factors. Because of the low productivity of East German employees, the equalization of East and West German wages created similar problems in East Germany as wage compression has created among the unskilled in West Germany.

The alarming upward trend in unemployment in West Germany since 1970 and its further acceleration due to German reunification, as shown in figure 1.2, can be traced largely to Germany's attempt to equalize the distribution of income by directly and indirectly affecting the structure of wages, in particular by its wage-replacement policy. Moreover, most of the hidden unemployment can probably also be explained in this way. In chapter 1, the overall number of open and hidden unemployment was given as 6.7 million, or 16.1 percent. It can only be reiterated that the country cannot in any way afford the doubling of these numbers in another 35 years that must be feared if it sticks to its social model. The German social model has come to its historical end, and the welfare state must be refitted for the twenty-first century's globalized economy.

Assertion and Reality: Inequality in the Labor Market

The German welfare policy of providing more than proportionate wage increases for unskilled workers is driven by good intentions, but it overlooks the law of supply and demand in the labor market. Just as a good harvest lowers the price of apples so that all apples can be sold, so the wage rate for workers with a given skill set must be the lower the more of them there are in order to avert unemployment. It is worth repeating that the law of supply and demand has no inherent moral dimension. It is simply a description of how the market economy works, one that has to be accepted if this type of economy is desired.

The policy of wage compression across all skill levels, which has been pursued by the unions with the support of welfare policy since the 1970s, would be no problem for the labor market if Germany were a country with a homogeneous and well-trained labor force and if the share of the unskilled were declining. If, for example, the number of unskilled workers had become scarce because education policy had succeeded in raising the skill levels, especially among children of the poorer strata, then the remaining unskilled could have enjoyed faster wage increases. There is no evidence of this, however.[11]

On the contrary, the net immigration of about 3.2 million wage and salary earners in the period 1970–2004 has, in all likelihood, made unskilled workers more abundant.[12] As a general rule, the immigrants had completed no occupational training, which puts them formally in the class of the unskilled. In fact, most of them were not qualified for the German labor market for the obvious reason that they did not speak German and were ignorant of German working rules.

Many Germans believe that they live in a country in which class differences play no role. They are proud of the educational system that, they believe, gives everyone a fair chance to succeed in the market economy and supersedes the conditions handed out at birth. The policy of reducing wage inequality fits comfortably in this framework. Unfortunately, these Germans are deluding themselves.

The results of the PISA study, as reported in chapter 1, paint a sobering picture in this respect. Relative to other OECD countries, Germany stands out not only for the mediocre average proficiency of its 15-year-olds in mathematics and writing skills, but especially for the extremely large dispersion in the proficiencies of the age group under consideration.[13] With respect to inequality in educational outcomes, Germany ranked among the worst of all OECD countries—even worse than the United States, which is often criticized by Germans for its unequal educational opportunities. In absolute terms, the upper quintile of the skill distribution was comparable to the upper quintiles of the better OECD countries, but in the lower quintile few countries did worse than Germany. According to the OECD, which commissioned the study, the reason is supposedly the inability of the German school system to cope with students from different social backgrounds, which especially disadvantages the children of immigrants. In particular, Germany has not succeeded in effectively integrating the many Turkish children into its school system. This criticism is legitimate. Germany's three-pronged school system was originally designed to serve the upper, middle, and lower classes. This system continues to channel students into main schools, middle schools, and "gymnasiums" (Germany's high schools for college-bound high achievers) at the age of 10, thereby preserving and even fostering class differences in education. The school system does provide an exceptionally good high school education, leading to the degree known as the Abitur, that approximates the first two years of an American college education, but this comes at the expense of depressing the average educational quality for 15-year-old students.[14] Moreover, Germany's limited preschool education facilities and its half-day schools, which send practically all children back to their families at lunchtime, further reduce the equalizing effect of public schooling.

Addressing both inequality and mediocrity in educational attainment will require overhauling the three-pronged school system. Germany needs efficient preschool education and must introduce full-day schooling. In fact, Germany needs an entirely new education policy. But even if all the necessary measures were taken now, the effects of such a policy would not be felt in the labor markets until 15–20 years down the road, and another decade or so would have to pass until a sizeable stock of a better-educated workforce became available on the labor market.

In the interim, the unions' leveling efforts and the high social replacement incomes are at odds with the market system. In a market economy where wages are commensurate to skill levels, if one ranks top in skill inequality one cannot simultaneously try to rank top in wage equality. The policy of wage compression is bound to fail as it excludes more and more people from working life, thus compromising the social philosophy it purports to support.

The Slippery Slope

The absurdity of the German welfare system is primarily responsible for the leveling of wages. This fact may be better understood with the help of figure 4.4, which is based on calculations by the Ifo Institute. This figure presents

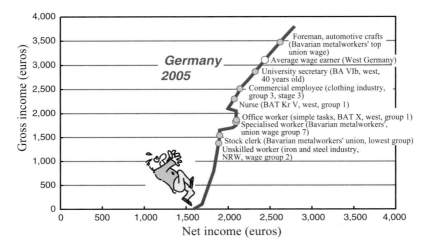

Figure 4.4
"The north face of the Eiger": the disastrous effects of the wage-replacement system. Labor income per month, Unemployment Compensation II, child allowance, child bonus; wage taxes; employee's contribution to social security system; family with two children.

the relationship between the monthly gross income and net income of a family of four for alternative effort levels resulting from the system of social transfers, taxes, and social security contributions, based on the legal rules applying after the Hartz reforms of 2005.[15] Despite some minor tax changes and adjustments in the social assistance level (Unemployment Benefit II), these rules are not fundamentally different from those of past decades. The vertical axis shows the gross wage and the horizontal axis the corresponding net wage (which takes account of personal income taxes, employee social security contributions, social assistance, housing allowances, child allowances, and a 400-euro tax exemption). If no member of the family works, net income amounts to 1,591 euros ($1,979) per month, not counting free health insurance, free accumulation of pension claims, and various in-kind benefits that are available on demand (refrigerator, washing machine, TV set, etc.). If someone works for a very low income of up to 100 euros per month, there are no deductions, and net income rises by the same amount. However, income earned beyond this is penalized by a withdrawal of transfer income and, above 400 euros per month, by imposing social security contributions adding to a marginal effective burden of 80 percent in the gross income range from 100 to 800 euros per month. Beyond 800 euros per month, the effective marginal burden of taxes, social security contributions and transfer withdrawals is 90 percent up to 1,500 euros (1,200 euros if there are no children). Thereafter, the marginal effective tax burden is 100 percent until the transfers have been fully withdrawn.[16]

The high withdrawal rates imply high wage demands, which in turn prevent job creation. Suppose that a low-skilled worker values his own time at 5 euros ($6.22) per hour. In the monthly income range from 100 to 800 euros, this person will have to demand a gross wage of 25 euros ($31.70), for 80 percent of this wage is taken away by the government. As no one is likely to be willing to pay him such a wage, he will remain unemployed. The situation at incomes above 800 euros per month is even worse; here the demanded wage for an additional hour of work will have to be 50 euros ($62.22) if a net income of 5 euros per hour is to result.

In many cases, the transfer withdrawal represents an insurmountable obstacle. It is like trying to climb the north face of the Eiger, a particularly dangerous Alpine route. Most people are not stupid enough to do it, and many who do end up falling to their death.

The trickiest part of the climb is when the family reaches a gross income of 1,700 euros per month. There, they find themselves at a particularly precarious ledge. If, at this point they work and earn a little more, their net income suddenly surges due to a special child benefit provided in this income range. But if they work too hard and increase their gross income beyond 2,100 euros per month, their net income falls. At this stage a number of complicated details regarding transfers change and among other things, the extra child benefit is withdrawn. It is only the strongest and the bravest (or the stupidest) who attempt to scale the overhang and climb on. Those who will never make it up the cliff include minimum union wage earners of 8.70 euros ($10.82) per hour. At 155 hours worked per month, they earn about 1,350 euros. That's simply too little to begin the climb, especially if they are married and have children.

Because of the unattractiveness of labor income in comparison to social assistance, this lowest wage group is virtually non-existent in the employment data. Figure 4.4 also shows examples of other wage classes. Thus, a stock clerk of the lowest metal worker wage group in the South German state of Bavaria (1,542 euros per month) will not make the climb. Even a highly skilled Bavarian metal worker of wage class 7 (1,862 euros per month, or 12.28 euros per hour) or an office worker (1,822.80 euros per month, or 10.93 euros per hour) would hardly be in a position to make the climb.

In order to just traverse the Eiger's midpoint ledge, one must earn a monthly wage of at least 2,100 euros—that is, about 13.50 euros per hour before taxes. But even then, one's net income is only 409 euros higher than it would be without working at all, corresponding to an effective net wage of 2.64 euros per hour in a full-time job. Why would anyone ever work at the lower wage rates? Anyone who would do so must be a student, a retiree, a second earner, or a new immigrant, all of whom are ineligible for social assistance. Or else he or she must be unmarried or must have no more than one child, because for this group the Eiger's north face ends at a lower gross income and starts further to the left in the diagram.[17] For a single person, for example, the Eiger's north face ends at a gross income of about 1,320 euros, corresponding to 8.50 euros per hour (before taxes) in a full-time job. A certain, if small, net income may therefore be realized by a stock clerk, an office worker, or a skilled worker whose monthly gross income is in the neighborhood of 1,500 euros or more (see figure 4.4) and who is unmarried and childless. That is not much of a consolation, as it means that people in these groups must choose between work and family. It just about pays to work if one is not married. But once someone has started a family and has children, working becomes unattractive: As far as net income for a family is concerned, it makes hardly any difference whether one works or not.

The only married people who can conquer the north face of the Eiger are those who are sufficiently productive to earn more than 13.50 euros per hour before taxes. Those who do not belong to this group of people are not permitted to move ahead. They are caught in the poverty trap and must spend their time working in the underground economy, watching television, drinking beer, playing neo-Nazi, or watching belly dancing. Working at a regular job is not a rationale choice under the welfare state's current rules of the game.

Mini-Jobs with Mini-Impact: The Crowding-Out Effect

The unbearable conditions in the low-wage sector are widely known in Germany. Policy makers are therefore trying to come up with low-wage models that supposedly improve work incentives. In April 2003, new measures for part-time employment (jobs paying up to 400 euros per month) and low-wage jobs (up to 800 euros per month) were introduced in order to get the low-wage sector moving.[18] Up to an income of 400 euros, workers in these new so-called mini-jobs need not pay taxes and social security contributions, and employers pay only a fixed charge of 25 percent of gross earnings, covering all tax and social security obligations (12 percent for housework and similar services). In the monthly income range from 400 to 800 euros, the employer pays the normal employer contribution to social security (21 percent of gross income), while employee contributions rise gradually from 4.5 percent of gross income to the full rate of 21 percent. Taxes, if any, are negligible in this income range.

At first glance this all looks very reasonable, and it seems plausible that hundreds of thousands of additional jobs could be created. At a closer look, however, it becomes apparent that, because of a lack of coordination with the social assistance system, no notable effect can be achieved. The rate of transfer withdrawal swallows most positive work incentives and makes state support of mini-jobs ineffective for recipients of social assistance and other transfer benefits (e.g., Unemployment Benefit I). For recipients of social assistance, the additional support of mini-jobs is offset by a reduction of social assistance by almost the same amount, and this largely eliminates the incentive to accept work at lower wages. The Eiger's north face does include the full mini-job support, and remains an insurmountable barrier for those whose wages are low despite the mini-job support.

The only people who effectively benefit from the support are those who are not eligible for social assistance or other transfer incomes, for they can keep what they earn. These are the students, second earners, retirees, and new immigrants mentioned earlier, who are ineligible for social assistance, as well as already employed persons who take a second job. Since most of these people do not count as unemployed, however, mini-jobs will not make a dent in measured unemployment. In fact, unemployment may even get worse. Because they are willing to work at somewhat lower wages, the overwhelming majority of mini-job beneficiaries may be expected to take the place of regular employees and to crowd these regular employees into unemployment which is cushioned by welfare benefits.

This crowding-out would not occur if those who are currently employed had flexible wages. In this case, there would be no replacement of regularly employed persons by students and others. Instead, more jobs would be created at lower wages and the mini-jobs would be added to existing jobs. The wage demands of those already employed are fixed, however, because for them social assistance is a feasible income alternative. Thus, the crowding-out effect is inevitable. The mini-job beneficiaries replace workers who before were regularly employed.

This mechanism follows from the so-called marginality principle, one of the iron laws of economics. Suppose there are two types of suppliers in a normal market for goods. Each has limited capacity and is characterized by either low or high unit costs. The suppliers facing the higher cost are the marginal suppliers; their cost determines the market price and thus also the trading volume. Assume now that new suppliers of the low-cost type enter the market. This will not affect the market price and the transactions volume as long as at least some of the high-cost suppliers stay in the market; the high-cost suppliers are always the marginal suppliers. The market price cannot decline, because even a slight price reduction would wipe out all high-cost suppliers and create an unsustainable excess demand in the market. Thus, the low-cost suppliers crowd out the high-cost suppliers one by one, given the aggregate transactions volume. Only if the low-cost suppliers are so numerous that they crowd out all high-cost suppliers can the market price fall and the transactions volume rise.

Things are very similar in the labor market. Here the high-cost suppliers are normal employees who would be eligible for wage-replacement benefits such as unemployment compensation and social assistance if they lost their jobs or while they are searching for jobs. The wage-replacement benefits create reservation wages that have a similar role as production costs in ordinary markets, because these costs also create reservation prices. The low-cost suppliers are the groups mentioned above who are not eligible for social transfers (students, second earners, new immigrants) or do not lose them when they work (pensioners). If more of these people enter, because the government subsidizes them and reduces their reservation wages, they will crowd out the normal employees, because neither the wage level nor the employment level will change.

Job-tenure rules complicate this picture somewhat, because they seem to protect normal employees from the crowding-out effect. However, the large annual turnover on the order of about 7 million employees that characterizes the German labor market should not be overlooked. People change jobs for natural reasons, and if they do, they are replaced by mini-jobbers. As the number of subsidized mini-jobbers is just several hundred thousand, there are always enough vacant regular jobs they can fill before new jobs are created.

Only wage decreases in the low-wage job sector can trigger a permanent net increase in the number of jobs available. But in the current system such wage decreases would only be possible if the marginal groups activated by the mini-job support were so numerous that they needed additional jobs even after they had crowded out all the regular low-wage recipients, which clearly is not the case. As popular as they are, mini-jobs cannot expand employment as long as regularly employed people are eligible for social replacement incomes.

The failure of mini-jobs to solve the unemployment problem is reflected in the numbers. The three years from April 2003, when the new mini-job law was enacted, to March 2006, witnessed the creation of 790,000 mini jobs, but there was a concomitant decline in social security contributions-paying employment by 1.08 million.[19]

These implications are similar to the crowding out of domestic wage and salary earners into state-supported unemployment by immigrants during the past 35 years. Regarding its economic effects, immigration is comparable to the activation of students, retirees, collaborating spouses, and moonlighters by way of mini-job support. In both cases, the additional workers push the regular employees into the lap of the welfare state because this lap prevents wages from falling and there can be no new jobs without a reduction of wages. Chapter 8 will deal in detail with the immigration question.[20]

Preparing the Welfare State for Globalization

Mini-jobs and Schröder's Hartz reforms cannot be the last word in terms of a permanent solution to Germany's job crisis. In an international comparison, Germany suffers from mass unemployment of the unskilled. This is the true German disease. In order to integrate the unskilled into the workforce, the welfare state must be redesigned in a fundamental way. Those who, despite great effort, do not succeed in earning an adequate income deserve assistance. But people must be helped to help themselves. As quid pro quo, even less productive members of society may be asked to work 8 hours a day just like everybody else, provided they can do so. Only the truly incapacitated must be allowed to receive assistance without offering something to society in return.

The solidarity principle requires that help continue to be granted to those on the losing end. The community of the insured into which one is born should not be questioned. Most Germans, including those better placed, want to keep the welfare state if only to protect their children and grandchildren against life's trials and tribulations. They want a system in which their own children give to the state if they are fortunate, and take from the state if they are unfortunate. Illness, accident, genetic weakness, bad influences in school and society, and plain bad luck can make life difficult and reduce one's productivity. This requires protection by the welfare state, even if the reduction of work incentives it calls forth very much limits the range of insurable risks. As described above, private insurance companies arrive too late in one's life to be able to cover these types of risks.

Most people would consider it perverse, however, that individual eligibility for state protection is conditional on making no effort to overcoming poverty—that recipients relax and do nothing, or hide in the underground economy. But this is precisely how the German system functions. Full assistance is provided only if one does not do anything. Indeed, doing something is penalized: in many income ranges state aid is cut nearly one-to-one for the amount earned. And at the Eiger's overhang (above the ledge; see figure 4.4), state aid is cut by much more than the additional income resulting from extra effort.

True, a recipient of social assistance is obliged to work if he or she finds a job. In theory, social assistance is cut if someone rejects a suitable job offered to him. But in practice it is very difficult to prove that a suitable job was available, since those who formally express their intention to accept a posted job without really being interested will easily succeed in convincing their potential employer that they are not suited. If a social assistance recipient rejects a suitable job, social assistance is cut with a low probability. If he accepts it, social assistance is cut with certainty.

Such a system is incompatible with the forces of globalization and international low-wage competition as it cements wages above the market-clearing level, preventing the international convergence of factor prices and causing mass unemployment instead. Firms try to avoid paying high wages by replacing people with robots, by moving from the labor-intensive to the capital-intensive sectors of the economy, and by not investing the funds supplied by domestic savers. Excessive increases in measured labor productivity, excessive structural change with too much value added in exports, and too strong a bazaar effect, as well as excessive capital exports as reflected by a growing current-account surplus, are the unavoidable consequences. The sick economy fools the ignorant public with superficial signals of success, while its health deteriorates further, as reflected by increasing unemployment.

An increase in unemployment is dangerous for any society. The less competitive are excluded from working life and labeled as belonging to the social underclass. They are publicly stigmatized and ostracized for not having a job. Only black-market work is a possibility to increase their incomes, as is conceded with a wink. The German welfare state provides weaker citizens with money and goods, but forbids them, under penalty of withdrawing the transfer incomes, to help themselves. The welfare state based on replacement income violates the already disadvantaged and their children (who see their parents' visits to the welfare office as income generating normalcy). It creates a new proletariat that can only seemingly avail itself of protection from a solidarity community, but is in truth excluded from it.

All of this can easily be avoided by an appropriate redesign of the welfare state. Instead of paying less productive people wage-replacement benefits, they could be granted wage-supplement benefits.[21] Supplementary payments that add to wages earned could replace the benefits that are paid in lieu of wages. The motto could be that anybody who can work shall work according to their individual ability, and that the state pays additional social assistance to those who nevertheless do not earn enough. The supplemental benefits would guarantee that the sum of social assistance and earned wages meets the social standards of society.

The big advantage of such a system would be that competition between private business and the welfare state in the labor market is ended. With regard to social assistance and work, there is no longer an "either/or." Since one is eligible for state aid if one works and is ineligible if one does not work, one is willing to offer one's labor at a very low wage. The floor of the present wage scale, currently determined by social assistance (Unemployment Benefit II), disappears. At lower wages it pays for firms or private households to create jobs. Plans for potential jobs become reality. Anybody looking for a job will get work and pay, and unemployment among the unskilled will disappear.

At the same time, competition between employers demanding labor would prevent the market-clearing wage from falling too low. If it falls to the point at which unfilled job openings are the norm, employers will outbid each other, raising their wage offers in their efforts to get the labor desired. According to calculations of the Ifo Institute, the wages for the unskilled would have to be lowered by about one-third to balance the labor market, and this would imply about 3.2 million additional jobs for the low skilled, not counting the additional jobs being created via a chain of wage-adjustment effects in other segments of the qualification scale.[22]

As less productive people would now be included in the labor force, there would be less measured productivity growth. As labor-intensive sectors would have higher survival chances despite international low-wage competition, less capital, fewer talents, and less unskilled labor would be operating in the capital-intensive export sectors, such that value added in exports would be lower again. As firms would have fewer incentives to curtail the labor-intensive upstream parts of their production chains, export quantities may even shrink in relation to value added in exports. And as investors would be willing to absorb a larger fraction of domestic savings, the current-account surplus would shrink. All of these developments would no doubt worry the general public and irk some Keynesians. However, it would be a mistake to interpret these as signs of failure. GDP would grow. There would be more jobs and an increased general prosperity of an economy that is better integrated in world markets, capturing further gains from the division of labor. This should ultimately convince the skeptics.

Activating Social Assistance: An Effective Weapon against Unemployment

How can the idea of switching from a wage-replacement policy to a wage-supplement policy be enacted in practice? Under the name of "Activating Social Assistance," the Ifo Institute has presented a proposal for the redesign of the German tax-transfer system that comes close to the idea, taking political feasibility constraints into account.[23] This proposal combines all support measures (including social assistance, housing allowances, and child allowances) as well as all public charges including social security contributions and taxes in an overall concept. Separate mini-job measures would no longer be needed. The Activating Social Assistance program would eliminate the competition between private business and the welfare state, the welfare state would achieve more of its objectives, and the burden on the public budgets would decline. The present welfare system is so inefficient with respect to the very objectives of the welfare state that the Ifo proposal would make it possible to achieve several objectives at the same time.

The basic idea of the Activating Social Assistance program is similar to the Earned Income Tax Credit of the United States, which has successfully reduced unemployment of the unskilled and has contributed to stunning economic growth there.[24] The proposal is adjusted to European social aspirations, however. It would provide higher income for the unskilled than in the United States, as the welfare-state precept of the German constitution must be respected.

At the heart of the proposal are three reform steps that concern only employable recipients of social assistance:

(1) Unlike today, social assistance will not be phased out beyond a monthly income level of 100 euros, but only beyond one of 500 euros. Up to a monthly earned income bracket of 500 euros, the transfer withdrawal rate is zero. For incomes above 500 euros, social assistance is phased out at a constant rate and merged with the tax and contribution system in such a way that the effective marginal tax burden of all components taken together is 70 percent instead of today's rates of 80–100 percent.

(2) In order to balance the government budget, transfers to employable people who are not working will be cut by about one-third.

(3) Those who do not find a job despite the new incentive structure can receive an income equal to today's level of social assistance from their local community, provided that they are working 8 hours a day in exchange. The local community may lease the work to private business by using private loan employment agencies. The fee charged to private customers is freely determined by supply and demand and will likely be way below social assistance. The local community may terminate the work contract at any time if the agreed work is not delivered.

Further details of the proposal include a 20 percent tax credit for the first 200 euros earned that is not subject to transfer withdrawal up to an earned income of 500 euros, as well as the normal employee social insurance contribution of about 20 percent for incomes beyond 200 euros per month.

Figure 4.5 shows the effects of the reform on the family of four considered earlier. Figuratively, the upper end of the Eiger's north face is broken off, and the rubble is used to build up a soft incline at the beginning of the slope. Now the person concerned will easily be able to leave the valley and to continue climbing the income mountain with some reasonable effort. Vertical parts of the climb, and even caves with dangerous overhangs, are avoided.

The Ifo proposal is designed in such a way that it becomes especially attractive to attempt first steps back to work instead of remaining idle. That is the reason for the tax credit that is available up to a monthly income of 500 euros. The idea is not to set the point at which the state offers most money at an effort of zero. Some effort must be shown in order to receive a maximum of public support.

It must be emphasized once again that the model's success would depend on the workers' accepting lower wage rates and on the employers' creating additional jobs at these lower wage rates. As explained before, someone who wants to earn a net income of 5 euros per hour, for example, today needs a gross wage of 25 euros per hour in the income range above 100 euros which no one would be willing to pay. With the Activating Social Assistance program, this person would need a gross wage of just 4.17 euros in the income

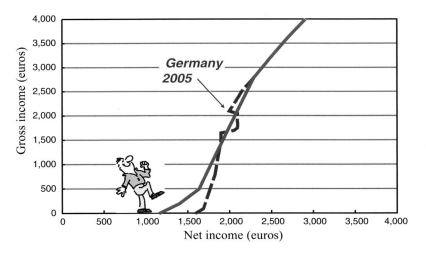

Figure 4.5
Activating Social Assistance: labor income per month, Unemployment Compensation II, child allowance, child bonus; wage taxes; employee's contribution to social security system; wage tax credit; family with two children.

range between 100 and 200 euros, and one of 6.36 euros in the income range between 200 and 500 euros. There would certainly be potential employers at such a low wage. Firms would no longer try to escape to robots, to capital-intensive sectors, or to other countries, and private households would provide jobs, too, because a lot of work can be done in the home at such low wages. These are only examples, however, to demonstrate the effects of the Activating Social Assistance model. According to detailed calculations of the Ifo Institute, the wages of the unskilled can be expected to fall by one-third. This would generate about 3.2 million additional jobs for the unskilled in the long term.[25]

Insofar as wages are co-determined by unions, the unions must cooperate to achieve this result. If they want to provide their members access to the attractive possibility of additional earnings, they will do so. In fact, practically all union bargaining models predict that the lower the reservation wages of the employed, the lower the negotiated wage. As the Activating Social Assistance program reduces reservation wages, union wages can be expected to fall. Should unions refuse to react, the low-wage sector ought to be taken out of collective bargaining for the benefit of society at large.

Nevertheless, it should not be overlooked that not all German employees are covered by union wages. As was mentioned above and as will be further explained in chapter 5, large portions of East German business are free of any union influence. Moreover, wage bargaining typically does not apply to house-hold services, where most of the new jobs are likely to be created. As social assistance is the binding constraint on wages in these two crucial areas of the German economy, the Activating Social Assistance program would definitely be able to mobilize the labor market even if unions failed to comply.

What about the living standard of the poor? Would the poor not be hurt by such a neo-liberal proposal? After all, the lowest wages would fall and other wages would also be affected negatively due to a wage adjustment chain extending well into the range of mid-level wages (accordion effect). More-over, the basic level of social aid would be cut by about one-third across dif-ferent family types in order to avoid any additional fiscal burden on the state.[26] In the case of a family with two children, as shown in figure 4.5, assistance without work would decline from the current 1,591 euros to 1,161.

The answer is that the poor would not be hurt, but would benefit instead, as they will easily be able to overcompensate these losses by working. If a person chose a part-time job with about 75 hours per month at the reduced wage of 5.90 euros, he or she would earn a net income of about 430 euros (including the tax credit) and would again arrive at the current 1,591 euros that are available without work. If, on the other hand, he or she decided to work more than 75 hours per month, the family would be even better off. Someone working 160 hours a month at a gross wage of 5.90 euros would receive a net income of 1,764 euros for his family. The Activating Social Assistance program would increase the living standard of the poor substantially beyond the level of the social assistance (Unemployment Benefit II) available today.

The well-being of the poor will even increase by more than these numbers suggest, because no account has been taken so far of the fact that, as a result of the reduction in labor costs in the low-wage segment, there will be a reduction in prices of goods and services purchased by low earners. The unskilled do not just sell their labor and buy manufactured goods whose prices are determined in the world markets, they also buy local goods and services whose prices fall in line with the wage reduction of the unskilled; and they will buy even more of those in the future as prices fall. These include things as varied as restaurant meals, cleaning services, and locally grown produce. True, some of those who take jobs may be unhappy because their leisure time shrinks. In fact, however, the overwhelming number of people, who now find a job in the private economy, will be glad to participate in regular working life, to be considered a valuable member of society, and to rescue their children from the fate of growing up with parents living on welfare.

Figure 4.5 refers to an unskilled worker with a family of four. The Ifo proposal shows similar positive effects on other types of families. It is always true that an employee would earn as much at a part-time job as he receives from social assistance today and that he would do substantially better if he took a full-time job.

What if the unskilled worker cannot find a job despite the reduction in wage rates? This possibility cannot, of course, be precluded in all cases, and it may be particularly relevant during a transition phase, before work habits have reacted to the new incentives and before the new jobs have been created. The answer is provided by the third design element listed above. If necessary, everyone could go to his local community and receive the same amount of total transfers as today—that is, the 1,591 euros instead of only 1,161 euros in the case of a family of four. But he would have to work 8 hours a day to get it. While this is an aspect that he may not like, it is a sure way to secure his income. Everybody who needs the money can rely on the social security net—a necessary feature of any politically feasible reform in Germany.

To ensure incentive compatibility, it is essential for the local communities to demand full-time communal work, at say 160 hours a month, in exchange for the full assistance payment, for otherwise it might not be sufficiently attractive to work in the private economy. As explained, in the private economy the same total income would be achieved with a part-time job of only 75 hours a month. If the corresponding work is not done, social assistance must be cut.

The requirement to do public work in exchange for receiving the full assistance is a self-selection device. Those who accept neither private nor public jobs simply cannot be needy. They must have hidden income from black-market activities or undeclared wealth on which they can draw. Their receiving a lower official income is not a social problem.

As has been mentioned, theoretically, social assistance can already be cut today if someone rejects a suitable job. In practice, however, there have been complicated questions of proof regarding the suitability of a job offered. In the system of Activating Social Assistance the question of suitability would be moot, as all communal jobs are suitable by definition. The local community simply defines and offers a job to anyone who wants one, and if it is not accepted only the curtailed level of social assistance is paid.

What kind of work should people allocated to local communities do? Should they clean the park for the umpteenth time, or should they carry out useful work that could also be done by local craftsmen? The answer is simple: People will do useful work, and local craftsmen will be happy about it. First, local craftsmen will have more customers. The customers of the former black-market suppliers will come to the craftsmen because their former suppliers no longer have the time for their old activities, since they are required to work 8 hours a day for the local community. Second, the craftsmen can hire the previous black-market suppliers from the local communities to work for them servicing the customers. It is essential that the community lend the working time of the welfare recipients allocated to them, via private loan employment agencies, to the highest-bidding private firms. And the private firms will, rationally, demand this time, because the fee to be paid for the labor services will be determined by supply and demand. There will be a non-negative fee, well below social assistance, at which the required private demand for this type of labor will be created. The proposal is a program for turning underground work and leisure time into legal employment with local craftsmen and other employers.

How is it that the government finds jobs in the private sector for people who fail to find these jobs themselves? If private jobs are lacking, how can the government create them? The answer to these questions is that the government has a lower reservation wage than individuals. Whereas individuals will not be willing to work for arbitrarily low wages in the private economy despite the abolishment of transfer withdrawals, simply because they demand compensation for the black market income they could earn elsewhere, the government can, in principle, lease loan labor for a fee way below this reservation wage. Any fee above zero would be better than the current situation where the government gets nothing in exchange for the social assistance it provides, and would therefore be acceptable.

The model of Activating Social Assistance anticipates a large number of people who will need a wage supplement permanently because their market income is too low in terms of the social standards of the German society. Many of the unskilled who are employed today will suffer a wage reduction, because otherwise the employer will exchange them for cheaper new employees. That is the so-called bandwagon effect. The Ifo model projects a total of 6.6 million people for whom a substantial bandwagon effect is to be expected. This band-wagon effect must be included in the plans. At a given location and for a given type of work there is only one level of labor costs at which full employment exists. Thus the number of jobs for the unskilled cannot be increased without a general wage decline for all unskilled, including those who are currently employed. One of the advantages of the Activating Social Assistance program is that it automatically takes care of these people by compensating for part of the income loss. The Activating Social Assistance program is granted broadly and permanently to the working poor.

No doubt the bandwagon effect will cost the state a lot of money. However, the present system of unemployment compensation and social assistance is also very expensive. The state must decide whether it wants to completely finance millions of people who are not working or to pay millions of people an earned income subsidy. Even though the number of people who permanently will have to be subsidized in the second case may be larger, the overall cost of the program could be lower. This is an empirical matter.

The Ifo Institute has done some detailed calculations. Together with additional revenues from taxes, social security contributions and loan employment earnings, and not counting any effects on early retirement, the state comes out a winner under the program. The budget surplus generated by the new system relative to the old one amounts to about 8 billion euros per year in the medium term and 21 billion euros in the long term.[27]

The Activating Social Assistance program shows the way to a more rational welfare state, one that pays the needy for participating in the workforce rather than staying at bay altogether. It will be the crucial reform to overcome the German disease: the excessively large rate of unemployment among the low-skilled. It will do wonders for the labor market. The market will recover in the entire low-wage segment and, because of the reversal of the accordion effect, the implications will reach far beyond the segment of social assistance recipients and into the normal job segment.[28] As more people work, GDP will rise, and Germany can return to a higher-growth path. Perhaps even more important, although the state will save money, the poorest members of society will be better off than today. With the combined total of earned income and the state supplement, they will have more money in their pockets than if they only received social assistance at today's level. In addition, they will be accepted by society as equals, will go about their daily work and will be able to face their children with dignity. Their children will then become used to the normalcy of regular gainful work.

Early Retirement: A Vicious Circle

Next to social assistance, early-retirement models are the second big obstacle in the German labor market. Although these models are not formally classifiable as wage-replacement systems, that is what they are. As they offer money for not working, they also make the government a competitor of private firms in the labor market, thus increasing wage demands and destroying jobs.

Germany's early-retirement models were created by Norbert Blüm, Helmut Kohl's minister of labor. Blüm belonged to the left wing of the Christian Democrats, Germany's conservative party, which governed the country for decades. He was in charge of German social policy from 1982 to 1998. As his policies were as social democratic as the policies of the Social Democratic Party itself, he was largely responsible for Kohl's winning four consecutive terms as chancellor. It is true that Blüm must be credited for introducing a number of measures necessary to keep the cost of Germany's defined-benefit pension system under control. In 1992 he carried out a major pension reform that indexed pensions to net rather than gross incomes of the current working generation, and later he prepared a further reform adjusting pensions for the foreseeable increase in the number of elderly relative to the size of the working population. He deserves less applause, however, for the various early-retirement models that he introduced, as these have had devastating negative effects.

Blüm's thesis was that the job pie was shrinking. Since he believed that technological progress would necessarily destroy more and more jobs, he wanted the remaining jobs to be distributed more equally. In his eyes, early retirement was an elegant way to make some existing jobs available to young entrants into the labor market.

Blüm's view was short-sighted, and his program turned out to be one of the biggest mistakes in postwar policy in Germany. In a well-functioning market economy, there is no such thing as a job pie whose pieces can be arbitrarily distributed. With flexible wages, it would not have been necessary to get rid of the older workers in order to employ younger ones. A well-functioning market economy has work for everyone if wages are determined by supply and demand.

Blüm's idea of a fixed job pie is approximately true only in a second-best sense, if unions or wage-replacement benefits prevent wages from reacting flexibly to the disequilibria of the market. Given this inflexibility, the possibility of retiring early at only minor benefit reductions induced millions of older people to quit, and presumably a substantial fraction of their jobs indeed became available for young entrants into the labor market.

However, the size of the job pie was not determined by exogenous forces, as Blüm believed, but was endogenously determined by his own retirement model. For one thing, the improvement of the options given to older employees increased the reservation wages, pushing actual wages up and hence destroying jobs. For another, the enormous public costs of the program had to be financed with additional social security contributions that increased the wage cost of ordinary workers. Both effects reduced the number of jobs that firms could profitably provide and exacerbated the problem that Blüm had wanted to solve.

Negative effects on the number of jobs can be avoided in early-retirement programs only with actuarially fair pension cuts. However, in the German system the actual pension cuts are much smaller than that. The present monthly benefit reduction amounts to 3.6 percent for every year a person retires before the age of 65. A benefit reduction of about 8 percent would instead be correct. Only that reduction would guarantee that, until the time of his death, the retiree would not receive more from the state than if he or she had retired at the regular age of 65.

An employee with the average income of the statutorily insured who, according to 2004 law, retires early at the age of 60 and thus reduces his years of pension contributions from 45 to 40, receives a gift from the state of about 46,000 euros, expressed in present value.

As the gift was provided under the condition of not working, it increased the wage demands of older employees. And as it had to be financed by active employees and employers in the form of higher social security contributions, it increased the wage cost. For both reasons, unemployment rose, and soon there were demands for more early-retirement schemes in order to provide more vacated jobs. This raised reservation wages and labor costs still more, and after a round of adjustments it resulted in even more unemployment. It is always the same game: Since unemployment is cushioned by expensive wage-replacement benefits, more jobs are lost, and more wage-replacement benefits are required. That is the inherent logic of the vicious circle in which the German economy and the German welfare state have been caught since Blüm's reforms.

Blüm initiated the vicious circle in 1984 by introducing early retirement at age 58 and in 1987 by increasing the duration of unemployment compensation for older workers to 32 months. In 1996 Blüm gave the early-retirement idea a further spin by introducing a system of part-time retirement (Altersteilzeit). Under this system older employees (at the earliest at age 55) are paid 83 percent of their previous wage if they agree to work only half time, which means a 66 percent increase in the wage per hour. Those who adopt the block model of part-time retirement (working full time for half the period and not at all for the other half) can, in some cases, stop working at the age of 57.

Blüm's successor, Walter Riester, a Social Democrat serving in the government of Gerhard Schröder, added to this with marginal reforms that facilitated the access to invalidity pensions for the unemployed. In this respect, his role was as dastardly as that of his predecessor, although, as will be explained in chapter 7, he must be lauded for adding a funded pillar to the German pension system.

When Norbert Blüm assumed the position of minister of labor in 1982, the average retirement age was 56 years if invalidity pensions are included. When Walter Riester left the office in 2002, the corresponding age had declined to 51.5 years.[29] The addition to the number of retirees due to unemployment or part-time retirement was especially dramatic. From 1982 to 2002 the number rose from about 40,000 a year to about 170,000 a year on average, peaking in 1995 at 300,000.[30] No fewer than 389,000 people took advantage of early retirement at the end of 2003, and 75,000 availed themselves of the part-time-retirement scheme.[31]

Hopes that the jobs so vacated would subsequently be available to young employees have been dashed because firms took advantage of the early-retirement schemes to reduce their workforces. Often jobs were eliminated rather than reallocated. In economic terms, the problem with this approach was the loss of wage flexibility resulting from the generous wage-replacement benefits offered for early retirement from a job. The uncompensated reduction of jobs was accelerated and the creation of new jobs was prevented. During the terms of Blüm and Riester, from 1982 to 2000, West German unemployment rose by 700,000, from 1.8 million to 2.5 million, East German unemployment added another 1.6 million.

Especially in view of the demographic problems that will be discussed in detail in chapter 7, the reward of early retirement was the opposite of what would have been economically desirable. If there are fewer and fewer children to support them in their old age, people should retire later, not earlier. Instead of reducing the retirement age, increasing it is the correct recipe against Germany's aging and pension problems. It is absurd for a country that must shoulder immense reunification costs to prevent willing and able people from working. This follows from common sense; it also follows from economic analysis. It raises the question of whether these two labor ministers knew what they were doing. It is possible that they did. There exist perfectly rational motives for their actions. One has to do with elections. Retirees do not count as unemployed if they do not work; young people do. It must, therefore, have been tempting to hide part of the unemployment in retirement. That the total number of jobs would shrink in the medium term because of high wage demands and high financing burdens was a problem that could be postponed. In the short run, it was more important to get the topic of unemployment out of the media and to win the next election. Or it may have been the close ties to the unions that induced the labor ministers to facilitate an excessively high wage by ensuring that the unemployment generated by this policy be withdrawn from the market in a socially agreeable way. Or perhaps it was the desire to generate higher wages by increasing the scarcity of labor and to help the unions in this way. All of this is just speculation. Only Blüm and Riester know answer.

Early Retirement with Unlimited Additional Earnings: The Better Way

Germany needs a new welfare state that is based on different principles than those underlying the ideology of wage replacement. Hiding unemployment, being secret accomplices of the unions, paying for not working, the welfare state competing with the private sector—all of this must end if the German economy is to stand a fighting chance. Older workers, whom Blüm and Riester wanted to take out of the work process, should work to the extent possible in order to take care of society and themselves. They should not be enticed by artificial incentives into becoming a burden on young workers.

All extant retirement schemes should be abolished, and only a radically changed scheme should remain. Those who want to retire early may do so; however, for each year between the early retirement and the official retirement age they must accept an actuarially correct benefit reduction of about 8 percent per year. A prerequisite for the new type of early retirement would, however, be that the pension remain at or above the rate of social assistance. Employees for whom this would not be the case should not be eligible for early retirement.

In order to augment the lower early-retirement income that the new model would yield, any additional earnings from a regular job should be allowed without a pension withdrawal. This is currently true for people who retire at 65, but not for people who retire earlier.[32] In order to prevent any abuse of this rule relative to the past employer, the old employment contract including potential tenure rights must be terminated before early retirement begins. It is then up to the parties concerned to sign a new contract if they so wish.

The possibility of unlimited additional earnings will have the effect of lowering the reservation wages of older workers. This will enlarge the job pie, and the additional employment of the older people will not be at the expense of the younger generation.

Most of those who retire early will seek a less burdensome, if lower-paying, job. Many will prefer part-time employment, either with the old employer or with a new one. A secondary labor market will develop in which one may work after one's regular career is over, similar to what is done in Italy, Japan, or the United States. Working in this secondary labor market would contribute to economic growth and to the general welfare of the country while reducing the burden on the welfare state.

to a West German bankruptcy lawyer who recently moved to the East, where
business is booming

5   The Withering East

The German Mezzogiorno

One year after reunification, Chancellor Helmut Kohl promised blooming
meadows in "three, four, five years." Desperate for East German votes in the
1991 federal election, Kohl promised East Germans everything under the sun.
And, in order not to irritate his West German voters, he led them to believe
that no taxes would be raised to finance reunification. With the wave of a magic
wand, a self-sustained upswing was to create a booming industrial economy
patterned after that in the West.

As we all know, this is not what happened. West Germany's economic
system, with all its collective bargaining and welfare rules that already presented a heavy burden on its own productivity, was imposed in its entirety on
the emaciated economy of the German Democratic Republic (GDR). This
obliterated any chances for a self-sustained upswing from the very onset.
Economists had warned against this course of action early on, but politicians
and the media turned a deaf ear.[1] To this day, Germans wait for the East
German miracle to come to pass.

In Italy, the region from Naples to Sicily, called the Mezzogiorno, perenni-
ally lags behind the dynamic economy of Northern Italy and shows no signs
of catching up. Today East Germany is Germany's Mezzogiorno.

At first, some really did think it possible that the East could have a successful start into the market economy. All the money that the federal government made available to East Germany, as well as the El Dorado politics of the
Treuhandanstalt, East Germany's privatization agency, which gave the capital
stock of the communist state away in exchange for pocket money, attracted
large numbers of adventurers from the West and created a euphoric mood.

After the initial breakdown of the East German economy that followed the end of communism, many expected an economic miracle. And indeed, in the early 1990s East Germany's standard of living began to rise rapidly, its roads and rails were modernized at an astonishing speed, and urban renewal transformed its cities.

The Regional Development Law (Fördergebietsgesetz), the Bundestag's generous subsidy program, played a special role in supporting East Germany's economic renaissance. Real investment was so heavily subsidized that the return on investment became a secondary consideration. Whereas typical industrial plants in the West had to generate at least 3.1 percent real return (before taxes and net of a risk premium) in order to yield the same net rate of return as a financial investment in the world capital market, in the East a real before-tax rate of return of *minus* 5.1 percent sufficed.[2] In other words, even if the invested capital generated an annual 5 percent gross loss of the invested capital, the investor could be happy, because the subsidies compensated for the loss and even provided an adequate net return. Needless to say, a lot of money was foolishly wasted under these permissive conditions.

The excitement was short lived. In 1996, when the privatization agency ended its giveaways and the Regional Development Law expired, the construction cranes were disassembled and economic growth slowed. Since then the East German economy has not been able to stand on its own feet.

Figure 5.1 shows the subsequent developments with a comparison of aggregate productivity in East Germany relative to West Germany. Here East Germany is defined as the former GDR (i.e., excluding West Berlin) in order to restrict the comparison to the formerly communist areas. The diagram shows aggregate productivity in terms of gross domestic product per person of working age. As the benchmark, West Germany is set equal to 100. East German productivity was close to one-third that of West Germany in the first year after reunification. East German productivity then rose rapidly, reaching 62.8 percent of the West in 1996. After 1996, however, relative productivity declined again, falling to 60 percent in 2001. Then it grew a little, and in 2005 it reached a value of 62.5 percent, about the same level as 1996. Ten years later (and 15 years after the collapse of communism) there still has been no further convergence to West Germany's overall productivity level.

And yet, for two reasons the comparative numbers still convey too optimistic a picture of the convergence process. First, national accounting systems measure the value added produced in the public sector by the wages of the public servants. Based on the 14.7 percent of gainfully employed East Germans working in the public sector, the policy of wage convergence, which was pushed with particular vigor in East Germany's public sector, created an

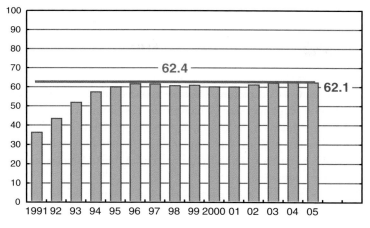

Figure 5.1
Aggregate productivity in East Germany (including East Berlin): GDP per person of working age (percent), with 100 representing West Germany (including West Berlin). Sources: Statistisches Bundesamt; Ifo Institute calculations. Regional differentiation of Berlin: Ifo Institute estimates.

ostensible economic convergence that lacks any economic significance.[3] In 2001, gross income of East German public-sector employees already amounted to 93.3 percent of the gross income of their West German colleagues.[4] If the public-sector employees are deducted from the East and West German numbers, then relative East German productivity is about three percentage points lower than that shown in figure 5.1.

The second reason for the lack of convergence is emigration. In the period under consideration (1995–2005), a good half-million more East Germans migrated to West Germany than West Germans to East Germany (including non-working people). These people increased the denominator of the productivity ratio in the West and decreased it in the East, which in itself implied an automatic increase in relative East German productivity of 2.5 percentage points.[5]

It is true that firm-level productivity data show a much more favorable picture of the convergence process than figure 5.1. For example, in 2002, firm-level productivity of the East German private sector amounted to 69 percent of the Western level.[6] However, firm-level productivities differ to the extent that wage rates differ, because those firms established after reunification could adjust to the wage level with the latest technological know-how, and all the old firms that could not afford East Germany's current high wages were obliterated. In a market economy, the development of firm-level productivity is always quite closely linked with the growth of wages because less productive firms and production processes that cannot afford the wages, must leave the market. Thus, firm-level productivity comparisons are not very revealing as a gauge for overall economic performance. For reasons that were discussed in chapter 2, unemployed wage and salary earners must always be included in the numerator of the productivity ratio for an aggregate economic comparison in order to get an undistorted picture. Otherwise one could create any productivity growth with wage increases which drive less productive firms that cannot meet the wage increases into bankruptcy. The problem may be neglected in a comparison of regions with similar rates of unemployment, but in a comparison of West and East Germany it is essential for understanding the actual macroeconomic situation.

East Germany's 60 percent relative productivity in recent years is approximately equal to that of the Italian Mezzogiorno. There, aggregate productivity in terms of gross domestic product per person of working age also is close to 60 percent of the Central and Northern Italian level, without showing any tendency toward improvement.[7] In this respect the Italian conditions have not changed over long periods of time. Even in 1936, the South-North ratio of aggregate Italian productivity amounted to 60 percent.[8]

During that same period, the area that is today called East Germany was in quite a different position.[9] Thuringia, Saxony, and Saxony-Anhalt, located in the middle of what then was Germany, were home to the most productive and innovative companies in all of Germany, if not all of Europe. From the airplane industry with Junkers in Dessau to the motorcycle and automobile industry with DKW/Auto-Union (Audi) in Zschopau and BMW in Eisenach, to the optical industry with Zeiss in Jena, the crème de la crème of German business was located in the eastern part of the country. The southern part of Mitteldeutschland, which is now East Germany, was the high-tech center of the world, the only present-day analogue being California's Silicon Valley. The chemical industry, with Buna in Schkopau, BRABAG in Schwarzheide, and IG Farben in Bitterfeld and Leuna, was world renowned. Correspondingly, Mitteldeutschland's aggregate productivity was 27 percent higher than West Germany's.[10] This makes it all the more remarkable that the economic performance of East Germany and that of West Germany are not converging. Figure 5.1 showed that relative productivity has stalled at around 60 percent. Not only is there no immediate sign of convergence; in an important sense, the two parts of the country have been diverging even more. While the economy of West Germany, including West Berlin, grew by 14.6 percent in the period 1995–2005, the East German economy (including East Berlin) grew by only 13.7 percent in real terms. And if West Berlin is treated as a part of

East Germany, as is done in the official statistics, the difference is even bigger. A 10-year growth rate of 15.5 percent in West Germany now compares with one of only 9.2 percent in East Germany. In only three of the ten years considered did the East grow faster than the West. In seven of the ten years it lagged behind. The reason for the bigger divergence in the growth rates with this second partitioning is that Berlin experienced a population drop of 7.7 percent between 1995 and 2005. When the western part of the city is added, the calculated growth rate is even more depressed.[11]

In Eastern Germany there is no trace of the "self-sustaining growth" or of the "blooming meadows" that Helmut Kohl had predicted within "three, four, five years." Neither are we seeing any "growing together of what belongs together," as Willy Brandt, Kohl's predecessor, had argued. To the contrary, the gap between East and West Germany is getting wider every year. The economic reality of the German reunification process is far removed from what responsible politicians had promised the people. In economic terms, reunification on the whole has been a failure.

It is true that behind the disappointing numbers are structural developments that cast a somewhat more favorable light on the progress of East Germany. While much of the relative decline can be attributed to a rapidly shrinking construction industry, manufacturing output has done very well in East Germany. It grew by a remarkable 86 percent in real terms from 1995 to 2005, whereas West German manufacturing output (including West Berlin) increased by only 17 percent.[12]

The manufacturing sector, however, is only a very small part of the East German economy. The Treuhand (East Germany's privatization agency) destroyed three-fourths of all manufacturing jobs, and what remains of this sector is so small that it cannot contribute much to aggregate growth, even though the percentage rate of growth of this sector is high. Whereas in West Germany 31 percent of all private-sector employees were working in the manufacturing industry in 2002, the corresponding share in East Germany was only 18–20 percent—about the same as in the Italian Mezzogiorno, where it amounted to 19 percent.[13] Moreover, the substantial growth in manufacturing output did not have any effect on the labor market. East German manufacturing employment actually declined by 7.2 percent from 1995 to 2005. It is small comfort that the decline in West Germany manufacturing employment was 11.6 percent in the same period.[14]

Especially disappointing is the low level of investment in East Germany. In order to achieve self-sustaining growth and convergence with West Germany, East Germany needs much higher per capita investment than the

West. Given otherwise similar circumstances, output can only catch up if the capital stock is increased to a level similar to that of the West. Unfortunately, the results of "Investor Accounting," which is regularly provided to the Federal Statistics Office by the Ifo Institute, were disappointing in this respect. Whereas in 1995 total private investment per employable person in East Germany amounted to 145 percent of the West German level, by 2005 it had shrunk to 86 percent, and investment in machinery and equipment, which is so important for industrial growth, had declined to 81 percent in 2005, down from 102 percent in 1995. All of this signals economic divergence rather than convergence.

It is no comfort that these numbers are a bit better than the corresponding ones in the Italian Mezzogiorno. In 1970, per capita investment in machinery and equipment there had amounted to about 80 percent of the level of Northern and Central Italy. It had declined thereafter and was only 40 percent around 2000. It is to be hoped that East Germany will not follow the example of the Italian Mezzogiorno in the years to come.

The East German labor market is also unpromising. Whereas employment in the old GDR amounted to 9.7 million people, in 2005 this number had declined to 6.1 million. Since the collapse of the Berlin Wall, about 360,000 East German employees have emigrated to West Germany (in net terms), and 640,000 have been commuting to the West, versus 180,000 West German employees commuting to the East. A million East Germans have left the labor market due to early retirement or other labor-market measures.[15] In 2004, 1.4 million people (18 percent of the labor force) were counted as unemployed— even more than the 15 percent registered in the Italian Mezzogiorno. The remainder of the 3.6 million people who disappeared from the employment statistics since the collapse of GDR are no longer working for a variety of other reasons.[16]

The number of employees subject to social insurance contributions is declining annually. Figure 5.2 shows the development in terms of an index based on January 1994—that is, after the initial dismissals by the privatization agency. Whereas regular employment has declined by only 5 percent in West Germany, it has declined by 24 percent in East Germany (about 2.2 percent per year) without any slowdown in sight.

Urban unemployment among young people, in particular, has reached frightening dimensions. In the city of Stralsund, 22 percent of the people under the age of 25 had neither a job nor a job training position in 2005. The situation was hardly better in Chemnitz (formerly Karl-Marx-Stadt), where 18 percent of the young people were jobless, and in Cottbus, where the percent-

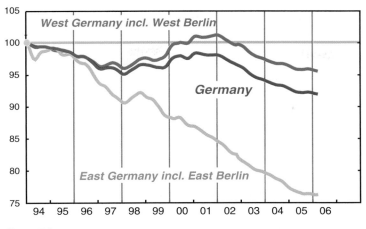

Figure 5.2
Percentage of employees subject to social insurance, seasonally adjusted, in West and East Germany, with 100 representing January 1994. Sources: Bundesagentur für Arbeit, from November 2002 regional differentiation of Berlin: Ifo Institute estimates; Ifo Institute calculations.

age was 20. The "champions" in this statistic were Döbeln (26.8 percent), Brandenburg an der Havel (26.2 percent), Stendal (25.3 percent), and Bernburg (25.2 percent).[17] One of the uglier consequences of this has been the rising popularity of neo-Nazism among young people.

Regional development in East Germany has been uneven at best. Some areas in Thuringia, including Sonnenberg and Jena, are doing relatively well, with overall unemployment rates of "only" 13 percent; however, Uecker-Randow's unemployment rate was 28 percent, and Demmin's was 26 percent. It is not surprising that at the margins of society there are increasing signs of decline, including drug abuse, vandalism, and other criminal activities.

Money, Money, Money

It is surprising that the political environment in Eastern Germany is still rather calm, that violent demonstrations have not occurred, and that there have not been any open revolts. With stoic composure, Germany's newer citizens have endured the mass unemployment that capitalism has bequeathed them. True, the new Monday demonstrations against Schröder's Hartz IV reforms in the autumn of 2004 showed that politicians were skating on thin ice. It is noteworthy, however, that the demonstrations quickly lost force as the agitators lacked an audience. Germany has witnessed no parallel to France's 2005 riots, in which fire was set to thousands of cars and hundreds of public buildings, factories and stores in a protest against economic reforms. The new citizens of the Federal Republic are not revolting openly despite all their economic problems.

This composure may be due to the relatively high income that East Germans are receiving despite mass unemployment. According to calculations of the Ifo Institute, 13 years after reunification average disposable East German income per capita was 81 percent of the corresponding West German level, implying a convergence of up to 88 percent in real terms, taking account of the fact that prices and rents in the West were about 8.5 percent higher.[18] Figure 5.3 gives an overview of the comparison of various income measures and productivity with West Germany.

East-West income convergence is likely to exceed that which has been achieved among West German regions. Although income *received* in West German government districts cannot be ascertained, income *generated* there, in the sense of gross domestic product, is known. In the West German government district of Lüneburg, per capita income is only 66 percent of the West German average; in Münster, another such district, it is only 74 percent of the West German average.[19]

East German pensions are especially high. Pensions paid by the statutory pension insurance fund per recipient are 14 percent higher in nominal terms, and 24 percent higher in real terms, than in West Germany.[20] This is only partly

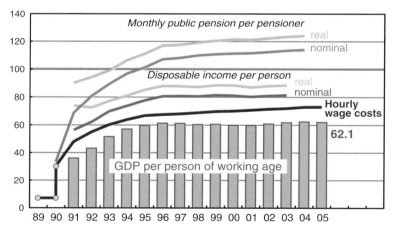

Figure 5.3
Productivity and income in East Germany, including East Berlin (percent, with 100 representing West Germany, including West Berlin). Sources: Statistisches Bundesamt; Arbeitskreis Volkswirtschaftliche Gesamtrechnungen der Länder, Länderergebnisse, Reihe 1, Tabelle 1.1 and Tabelle 13 (March 2006), Reihe 1, Band 5, Tabelle 5.2 and Tabelle 5.2 (2) (May 2006); purchasing power: Ifo Institute calculations. Regional differentiation of Berlin: Ifo Institute estimates.

due to the different employment histories of East German women whose labor force participation was much higher than that of West German women and who therefore had higher social security claims of their own. Even if only men are compared, pensions per social security recipient in East Germany are still 4 percent above the West German level in nominal terms.[21]

Tourist impressions also suggest that the quality of life in the cities of East Germany has substantially improved since reunification. The quality of the buildings and the state of renovation in some East German cities are admirable. Leipzig can boast of beautiful natural stone sidewalks and carefully restored façades of its magnificent late-nineteenth-century houses. Instead of the cheap dollar-store atmosphere around West Germany's Ulm cathedral, in Bautzen, the East German town on the Polish border, one enjoys the charm of a tasteful mall with high-quality retail stores. Of course, the picture is mixed. The walk from the train station in East Germany's Halle toward the city center is reminiscent of parts of the third world, at least until you reach the famous art nouveau quarter. But then again, the same is true of the area around Bielefeld's train station or Giessen's pedestrian mile. Casual differences of appearance within West and East Germany are now more pronounced than stark differences between the two parts of the country. In any case, one can no longer say that the cities of East Germany as a whole need to catch up with those of West Germany.

Yet some catching up may still be needed in the area of public infrastructure—that is, roads, railways, and train stations, wastewater disposal, sewage plants, and the like.[22] With Solidarity Pact II, an aid package worth 206 billion euros was passed in 2001 to meet this need over the next few years.

The emphasis on the recreational infrastructure in East German communities is particularly striking. Many swimming pools, tennis halls, golf courses, and "event parks" have been built, and the towns' public parks are well-maintained. While this is certainly nice, it costs a lot of money that may have been better invested in productive infrastructure that creates more attractive locations for business firms and increases the tax base. Many local communities have meanwhile found themselves in serious financial difficulties because they are no longer able to bear the maintenance costs of earlier investments in recreational infrastructure.

As all credit lines have been utilized to the limit, bizarre financial arrangements are being made to inject new cash into the coffers of East German communities. Dresden sold its trams to American investors in 1997 and immediately leased them back, and Leipzig used a similar arrangement in 2003 with its water supply. The economic rationale behind this transaction was that the American investors were able to enjoy tax benefits from an accelerated

depreciation scheme for leased assets. The US Congress had originally introduced such a scheme to help Boeing overcome its financial difficulties, but as
the scheme was not limited to domestic assets clever investors even applied it
to foreign infrastructure that was bought and leased back to foreign authorities. In the German case, the tax advantage to the American investors was large
enough to induce them to provide German cities with a profit of between 4
percent and 8 percent on the value of the items leased. Small wonder that the
method quickly became popular throughout Germany. About 150 similar
examples throughout the country have been counted, and until 2004, when
Congress abolished the law, German cities had collected about a billion euros
(1.24 billion dollars at the 2004 exchange rate) at the expense of American
taxpayers.[23] Although this was a lot of money in absolute terms, the share taken
by the Eastern cities was little more than a drop in the bucket considering the
size of the financial difficulties of the new Länder.

Even if only the openly shown debt is considered, East German states and
local communities had piled up more debt per capita during the first eleven
years since reunification than the West German states had during the 55 years
since the founding of the Federal Republic of Germany. In 2005, the per
capita debt of the East German states (including Berlin) amounted to 8,739
euros, whereas it only came to 7,677 euros in the West German states. Differences among the East German states are substantial, however. Whereas
Saxony-Anhalt and Brandenburg had piled up per capita debt of 9,066 and
7,263 euros, respectively, the per capita debt of Saxony, whose finances were
controlled by the iron hand of Georg Milbradt, then its finance minister and
now its president, stood only at 4,079 euros and thus below the West German
average.[24]

All things considered, East Germany is living far beyond its means. Aggregate income has almost reached the West German level, but aggregate productivity lies in the neighborhood of 60 percent. The discrepancies were made
possible by a gigantic transfer of public funds. The social security funds, especially the pension insurance and unemployment insurance funds, redirect West
German contributions to East German households. The so-called Solidarity
Pact East, which later became part of the fiscal equalization system among the
federal states, as well as federal expenditures on public infrastructure and
direct support of public and private investment also account for significant
amounts of transfer payments. On the other side of the ledger are only small
tax and contribution revenues from the East German states. By 2005, the sum
of net transfers of public funds from West Germany to East Germany since
reunification amounted to a total estimated 1,135 billion euros (1,412 billion
dollars).[25]

Oskar Lafontaine, the interim party leader of the Social Democrats, who lost the chancellorship election in 1991, understated the facts at the time when he spoke of "amounts in the three-digit billions" (in DM) as the total cost of German reunification, and presumed that costs would amount to "at least 100 billion deutschmarks," or 50 billion euros (60 billion dollars).[26] The total costs have long reached the four digit billion deutschmark range and since 2004 even the four-digit-billion-euro range—that is, they exceeded a trillion euros. Lafontaine was almost stoned for his remarks, and his realistic assessment certainly helped the Social Democrats lose the 1991 elections. Germans did not want to hear the truth. Helmut Kohl, the incumbent, who claimed that the transfer costs of reunification could be paid out of petty cash, was a much greater success with the people.[27] Ten years later, Wolfgang Schäuble, minister of the interior under Kohl, admitted at a conference on the event of the tenth anniversary of German reunification that Lafontaine's warnings had been correct. By the way, in 2004, Lafontaine founded a new socialist party, The Left, which has gained particular support in East Germany. (See chapter 6.) When he promised them more money, the East Germans quickly forgot that before reunification Lafontaine—who hails from the Saarland, a region bordering France—had argued that French Lorraine was dearer to him than East Germany, and that the two parts of Germany should not be reunited too quickly.

The net flow of public funds to the East now amounts to about 97 billion euros (120 billion US dollars) per year. This amount corresponds to 4.9 percent of West German gross domestic product and more than one-third (37.2 percent) of the federal budget (although only some of the funds are contained in this budget). This subsidy represents a heavy burden on West German business and on West German employees.

Since West Germany levies a "solidarity surcharge" of 5.5 percent of the personal income tax liability, one would think that this surcharge would largely cover the costs of reunification. This is not the case, however. The solidarity surcharge only raises 10 billion euros per year and, compared to the 97 billion euros, is therefore only a small amount of money.[28] The solidarity surcharge basically serves to hide the true costs of reunification and to calm the West German conscience.

The funds needed for the West-to-East transfer have essentially been raised by incurring a rapidly growing government debt (see chapter 6, especially figure 6.2) and by budget cuts in the Western Länder and in local communities, crowding out necessary infrastructure investment. Germany's violation of the EU Growth and Stability Pact as well as the clearly visible neglect of the West German public infrastructure are among the results of the transfer policy.

Since reunification, East Germany's own output, as measured by gross domestic product, has been continuously below the region's total use, or "absorption," of goods and services by private households, private investors, and the state. A country's excess of total purchases of goods and services over domestic production equals this country's excess of imports over exports, which is called the trade deficit. When there is a trade deficit, the country can live beyond its means because it enjoys a net inflow of goods and services from the rest of the world. As figure 5.4 shows, the East German trade deficit was initially about 80 billion euros and reached a level of 126 billion euros (157 billion dollars) in 2005, which was 45 percent of East German GDP. While private households, investors, and the government in East Germany purchased goods and services in the amount of 406 billion euros (505 billion dollars), the East German economy only produced goods and services in the amount of 280 billion euros (348 billion dollars). The net transfer of goods and services to East Germany was thus 126 billion euros (157 billion dollars). This net transfer of goods and services had to be financed by funds that came either from financial investment flows or gifts from the rest of the world. Three-fourths of the net transfer, the aforementioned 97 billion euros, was indeed paid for out of the public budget. One-fourth, or 29 billion euros (36 billion dollars), was financed by private loans or direct investment, and even this amount was not entirely private, insofar as 4 billion euros (5 billion dollars) was accounted for by new debt incurred by the East German states.[29] Just about 25 billion euros (31 billion dollars), or only 20 percent of Germany's

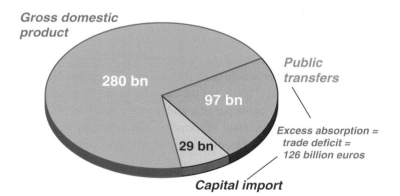

Figure 5.4
How absorption in East Germany (including East Berlin) was financed in 2005. Absorption is defined as the sum of private investment, public-sector spending on goods and services, and private consumption (national accounts). In 2005 it totaled 406 billion euros. Sources: Arbeitskreis Volkswirtschaftliche Gesamtrechnungen der Länder; Ifo Institute calculations. Regional differentiation of Berlin: Ifo Institute estimates.

total West-to-East net transfer of resources, was used to build up a productive private capital stock in the East. The lion's share of this transfer, 86 percent, went into public and private consumption.

In 2005, the net resource flow from West Germany to East Germany amounted to 45 percent of its total expenditures. Almost one in three euros that East Germans spent on final goods and services came from the West, primarily West Germany. About 75 cents of that euro came as gifts; about 25 cents were borrowed. In simple terms, this is East Germany's situation 15 years after reunification. It represents an utter failure to make progress toward becoming a self-sustained economy by any reasonable measure.

"Money for nothing," to quote Dire Straits, may well explain the East Germans' relative contentedness. At the same time, however, it also signals that this unbalanced situation is not sustainable. Instead of a stable market economy that can take its own place in the membership of industrial nations by relying on a productive citizenry, a mature legal system and an excellent infrastructure, a drip-fed transfer economy was created. If Germany is the sick man of Europe these days, part of the responsibility lies with the transfer economy sustaining East Germany.

Figure 5.5 shows the scale of the resource transfer to East Germany in comparison to other countries and regions. The Italian Mezzogiorno, Greece, Portugal, and Israel each receive a lot of money from Central and Northern Italy, the European Union, and the United States, respectively. However, at 5–14 percent of GDP, their transfer payments pale in comparison to the 45 percent East Germany receives from West Germany. There probably has never been a country or a similarly sized region of a country that has been so dependent on transfer payments as Eastern Germany has been since reunification.

The transfers, too, are proof of the dismal failure of Germany's economic reunification. Even the biggest pessimists envisioning what the situation would be like 15 years after the start of this process could not have imagined greater economic dependency upon West Germany by East Germany than is illustrated by the statistics cited in this chapter.

Why Currency Conversion Was Not to Blame

What is the reason for the failure of the economic reunification process? Many observers argue that the mistake was the internal German currency conversion with its one-to-one exchange rate. But as we will see, this argument is only true in a rather superficial sense. This section will explain why the actual reasons must lie elsewhere.

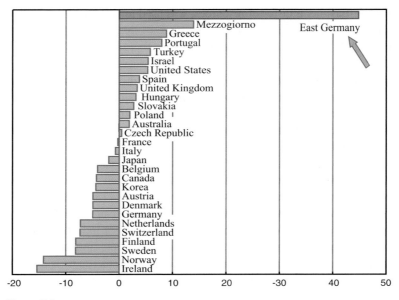

Figure 5.5
Excess absorption (trade deficit) as percentage of 2004 GDP. Sources: Eurostat; Israel, Korea: World Bank, World Development Indicators database; Mezzogiorno: SVIMEZ, Rapporto 2005, Sull'Economia del Mezzogiorno, table 1; East Germany (incl. East Berlin): Arbeitskreis Volkwirtschaftliche Gesamtrechnungen der Länder; Statistisches Bundesamt; Ifo Institute calculations.

Before the introduction of the euro in the period 1999–2002, Germany had an internal currency conversion. It took place in July 1990, three months before formal reunification, and it replaced the East German mark (sometimes called the ostmark) with the West German mark (sometimes called the deutschmark). Cash, life insurance claims, and wage contracts were converted into deutschmark cash or claims expressed in terms of deutschmarks. At the time, there was a major public controversy about the rate at which the conversion was going to take place, because there were two plausible exchange rates. There was, first, the average of the commodity-specific exchange rates, at which the communist GDR had been able to sell its exports to the world. It was 4.3 ostmarks for one deutschmark. Then, second, there was the internal purchasing-power parity between the two German currencies. This purchasing-power parity approximated one to one, as the communist East German government had made every attempt to assure its citizens that their currency was at least as valuable as the currency used by the capitalist enemy on West German soil. Thus, East German consumer good prices were much lower relative to export prices than they were in West Germany. Given that the relative prices differed, it was not possible to find a conversion rate for cash and wage contracts that would simultaneously preserve the competitiveness of the existing East German companies and maintain the living standard of the East German population.[30] One of these goals had to be sacrificed. Faced with an unsolvable dilemma, politicians decided in favor of the preservation of living standards and converted East German wages, life insurance claims, and most cash holdings one to one into deutschmarks. Choosing an exchange rate of 4.3 : 1 or even 2 : 1, as the (West German) Bundesbank had advocated, would have meant cutting the living standard of East German workers to one-fourth or one-half of what it was in the communist state. This simply was not a politically feasible option. Nevertheless, many economists and political observers maintained that the one-to-one currency conversion was the major economic mistake made in German reunification.

They were wrong. No doubt the economy of the former GDR, which had been in the lucky position of selling its goods to West German department stores and mail-order houses, suffered enormous difficulties as the one-to-one conversion of wage contracts effectively quadrupled their wage costs in terms of deutschmarks overnight. After the conversion, no company could continue to operate and sell its products to the West as they had done before the Berlin Wall had fallen. However, although a quadrupling of wage costs sounds excessive, the currency reunification raised East German wage costs to only 30 percent of the West German level. At this low wage cost, it would have been very possible to restructure the East German economy and to make it competitive again. Had this wage cost been maintained for a while, investors from all over the world would have queued up at the Treuhand to take over the old state-owned firms and make a go at them with new managements, new capital, new products, and new process technologies.

Just imagine the favorable conditions that would have existed. At only 30 percent of West Germany's wage rate, East Germany would have had the lowest wage costs in Western Europe (with the exception of Portugal and Greece), while a market of 380 million EU consumers could have been supplied free of tariff and language barriers. The breakdown of the communist countries' mutual market, the COMECON, which was often described as a big problem for East Germany, would have been more than offset by the new EU market, to which East Germany had access 15 years ahead of the other formerly communist countries. It was expected that East Germany's poor infrastructure would be modernized shortly with the help of West Germany. In contrast to other locations in Eastern Europe, the integration of East Germany into the Federal Republic gave investors a firm institutional and legal environment offering protection of capital investments as well as a solid base for long-term contracts. In addition, under the umbrella of the deutschmark, investors had access to an efficient capital market with low interest rates and to a pool of willing labor. There is no doubt whatsoever that East Germany would have enjoyed an economic miracle similar to that experienced by West Germany in the 1950s or Ireland in the 1990s had its wages remained in the neighborhood of 30 percent of the Western level for the foreseeable future.

But wages continued to rise. The truly problematic wage increases that deprived East Germany of its growth chances did not result from currency reunification, but occurred in later years. This is illustrated by figure 5.6, which compares the relative hourly wages in East Germany with wages in other countries. The level of hourly wages in West Germany is set equal to 100, and the wages of East Germany and other countries are expressed relative to that. Before reunification, and at the actual exchange rate between the ostmark and the deutschmark, wages in the GDR were 7 percent of West German wages. Intra-German trade took place at these relative costs, and the GDR's economy was competitive. By mid 1990, the one-to-one conversion of ostmarks into deutschmarks raised the wages by a factor of 4.3 to the above-mentioned

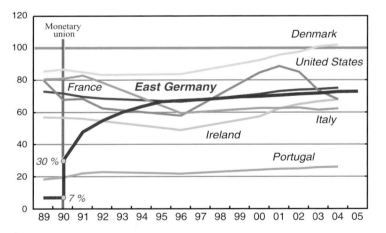

Figure 5.6
Hourly wage costs in the private sector relative to West Germany (percent, with 100 representing West Germany, including West Berlin). Here East Germany includes East Berlin. Sources: Denmark, France, Ireland, Italy, Portugal, United States, and West Germany: Institut der deutschen Wirtschaft Köln, hourly wage costs for industry workers. West and East Germany: Arbeitskreis Volkswirtschaftliche Gesamtrechnungen der Länder, April 2006, Reihe 1, Band 2, revision 2005, compensation of employees and number of employees in the whole economy; *IAB Handbuch Arbeitsmarkt, Analysen, Daten, Fakten* (Campus Verlag, 2005); Institut für Arbeitsmarkt- und Berufsforschung, Daten zur kurzfristigen Entwicklung von Wirtschaft und Arbeitsmarkt, May 2006, working time per employee in the whole economy; Ifo Institute calculations. Regional differentiation of Berlin: Ifo Institute estimates.

level of 30 percent. Thereafter, wages continued to increase at a fast pace. As early as 1992, East German wages were 50 percent of the West German level.

The German currency union raised wage costs only slightly above the Portuguese level, but with the ensuing increases, East German wages surpassed Ireland's in 1992, Italy's in 1995, and France's in 1996. Since then, wages in East Germany approximated those in France and exceeded those in Italy.

The dramatic increase of wage costs in the years after currency reunification is the main cause of East Germany's economic problems. It explains why international investors did not queue up in front of the Treuhand, and instead went elsewhere. Nobody wanted to take on French-level wage costs, higher than those in Ireland and Italy, as there were no other location advantages over these Western countries that would have justified these additional expenses. Investors are not charities; they want to make profits, and when they suspect that profits will soon be diverted into the pockets of the employees, they will stay away.

This does not mean that, after currency reunification, any wage increases would have been incompatible with a prosperous economic development. After all, a common labor market was established in Germany, and in such a market wage convergence would have been unavoidable. Firms that were attracted by the low wages that initially prevailed despite the one-to-one conversion would have bid up wages by competing for increasingly scarce labor. Wages would have risen as the result of investment and ensuing productivity growth. Moreover, some of the East German labor force would have moved west, depressing the wages there and raising them in the East as labor became increasingly scarce there. The wage increases would have also slowed down the capital inflows and labor outflows, but only to the extent to which the convergence of economic conditions to those of the West had already advanced. East German productivity and wages would have steadily converged on West German levels.

However, such a self-sustained process of growth and convergence clearly did not take place in East Germany. For one thing, the investment boom that could have triggered a demand-driven wage surge never took place. After the initial subsidies expired in 1996, investment declined rapidly, and although economic convergence would have required much higher investment than in the West, investment per capita fell even below the West German level after 2000. For another, figure 5.3 clearly revealed that the relative wage increase anticipated the relative productivity increase instead of following it, with no tendency to correct for the quadrupling of wages upon currency reunification. Thus, there must have been forces driving up wages other than those operating in a well-functioning market economy.

This is also suggested by comparing the speed of internal German convergence with the speed of convergence between other regions. Studies by Barro and Sala-i-Martin suggest that the gap in the economic performance of initially different regions usually closes at a rate of 2 percent per year, and in some cases convergence is even much slower.[31] The gaps between the countries of the European Union have closed on average by only 1.1 percent per year during the past 40 years.[32] Applied to the situation of East Germany, a 2 percent convergence rate implies that East German wages, which were about 30 percent of the West German level after reunification, should have only risen to 48 percent of the West German level by 2005. At the 1.1 percent European average, the corresponding relative wage level would have been 41 percent in 2005. Both numbers are far lower than the convergence to 73 percent that actually took place.

The overly rapid wage convergence is undoubtedly the true reason for the problems of East Germany. As was explained in chapter 2, among all the costs of a firm, in addition to local taxes it is only wages that are bound to the location and are decisive in a firm's location choice. If wages rise more slowly than productivity, investors are attracted because higher profits may be expected. If they rise faster, investors stay away because they foresee making losses. The sequence of first realizing productivity gains and then achieving wage growth cannot be reversed. Capital investment must come first and raise productivity, then wages can rise in response to this improvement. If one tries to reverse the steps, the capital investment stays away and one gets the disaster that is now bemoaned in East Germany.

Ireland is a good example for an economy that got the sequencing right. As was shown in figure 1.5, Ireland has surpassed West Germany in terms of aggregate productivity, but its hourly wage costs are still one-fourth below the West German average, and as figure 5.6 reveals, they are even below the East German level. Small wonder that the country continues to grow much faster than the two parts of Germany are doing. East Germany has tried to reverse the Irish sequencing strategy, violating the iron laws of economics. This is why it failed.

The question remains, however, as to how wages could rise so fast under the post-reunification market conditions. Why would the market generate wage increases that it cannot handle? Well, of course, it was not the market that brought about the wage increases. What it was will be explored in the next two sections.

Same Wages for the Same Work Only in the Same Location

From the beginning, East German wage rates were effectively removed from the impact of market forces. Although politicians pretended that they wanted to introduce the market economy to East Germany, they actually treated market principles with contempt by failing to establish competitive labor markets in the East and turning the wage into a political issue. The wage is the most important price in the market economy, however, as it, like no other price, determines the nation's competitiveness and hence its growth path. Making it subject to political influence is a recipe for disaster.

The new German citizens in the former GDR were not in a position to know that politics should have stayed out of this, as they had grown up in a system in which wages had no allocative function and were indeed determined by politics. The big West German parties that pushed for rapid wage convergence should have known better. The fact that even the conservative and market-liberal Christian Democrats (CDU) campaigned in East Germany under the slogan "equal wages for equal work" reveals both an intense sense of justice and enormous economic naiveté.

No question: To demand equal wages for equal work is a dictate of equity. But it cannot be repeated often enough that the market's function is not to achieve equity but simply allocative efficiency, and that it punishes all attempts to make market prices achieve equity goals. Responsibility for equity lies in the tax and transfer system.

The competitive mechanism of the market economy guarantees that in the long run the same wage is paid for the same kind of work in the same location, but it does not guarantee that the same wage is paid for the same kind of work in different locations. An apple in the South German city of Munich is a different good than an apple in Hamburg, located in Northern Germany; the price for a bottle of Bordeaux in the South of France is different from a bottle of Bordeaux sold in Dresden. These distinctions are reflected in geographically differentiated prices. And wages are no exception. To the extent that there are transportation and mobility costs for goods, capital, labor, and knowledge, wages will differ among regions, at least during a long phase of convergence that may take decades.

To this day, the differences in the location qualities between West and East Germany remain large. It is true that the East German population has better qualifications in a formal sense. If there was one achievement of the communist government, it was its success at reducing the number of unskilled people way below international levels. However, many skills needed in a market economy were nevertheless missing. There was, in particular, a serious lack of commercial and legal capabilities that for obvious reasons could not be acquired in the communist system. In addition, the GDR economy was backward and in part used pre-World War II production processes. It cannot be presumed that someone whose company was taken over by a government-run privatization agency in the early 1990s and was then sent into long-term unemployment really has the qualifications required by a twenty-first-century economy.

Other East German problems include the lack of business networks like those existing in the West, a deficient infrastructure, and (most notable) the lack of an entrepreneurial spirit. Entrepreneurial families with a high degree of inherited knowledge of markets and production processes and steeped in the tradition of risk-taking and responsibility represent the pillar on which the West Germany economy rests. Such entrepreneurial families were lacking in the East if only because—unlike in other formerly communist countries—most of them had moved to the West before the Berlin Wall was erected in 1961. Moreover, those people who had managed the communist economy and who might have been able to manage the transition from a communist to a market economy were systematically neutralized by West German politics. One of the mistakes of German reunification policy was that it had tried to build the new society on the poets and thinkers who formed the underground opposition in the East but lacked the practical skills needed in communist and market systems alike.

All these factors, the quantifiable hard ones and the more qualitative soft ones, combine to create very different labor productivities between East and West Germany despite free capital mobility. This was already alluded to in chapter 4. Government can surely try to help gradually even out the productivity differences, but to the extent that this fails, there cannot be any wage convergence without the productivity gains needed to justify these increases. To be sure, there are increasingly smaller location differences within Germany than between Germany and other countries. That is why relatively fast wage convergence could have been expected as the result of free-market forces. But "fast" could never have meant convergence in the "three, four, five years" that Kohl led the electorate to expect in 1991. To determine the pace of convergence between the two parts of the country should have been left to the market, not to elected politicians with their own agendas.

In the early 1990s, it was repeatedly argued that rapid wage convergence was necessary to prevent the East Germans from migrating west. This argument was not convincing, however. Even if there really had been large migration flows, if the market had been left alone, then convergence would have been accelerated, further obviating the need for political interference in wage determination.

Furthermore, the migration argument is weak because it implicitly assumes that it would have been possible to provide East Germany with attractive jobs in a very short period of time for which, at Western rates of productivity, Western wage rates could have been paid. But this unrealistic possibility did not exist. Even under optimistic conditions, practically all economic estimates of the ramifications of reunification assumed that the creation of a productive capital stock in East Germany, which would permit labor productivity similar to that in the West, would take two decades or so.

For the intervening period there were only two options. The first option consisted in letting a large part of the East German labor force wait idly for the buildup of a productive capital stock. The second option was to temporarily integrate those for whom there was no longer any gainful employment into the West German economy. If wages in the West had been reduced marginally, there would have been gainful employment possibilities for the number of people in question. At the same time, East Germans would have been given the opportunity to get acquainted with modern production methods and the rules of the market economy. Therefore, rational economic policy would have allowed migration instead of fearing the worst. The bulk of workers would not have migrated to the West, as most people would not have been willing to leave their homes even if they had been able to earn twice as much. But some would have moved and that would have been to everyone's advantage. In East German labor markets, labor would have become scarce early on, and because of the ensuing wage increases migration would have slowed on its own. The migrants would have been able to create income and assets for themselves in the West that were not available to them in the East.

Had this alternative scenario played out, Germany might not have had to bring in the 2.7 million foreigners who immigrated from non-EU countries between the beginning of 1990 and the end of 2004, most of whom settled in West Germany.[33] The simultaneous immobility of East Germans and immigration of foreigners is one of the perversities of German reunification. Of the 3.6 million people who lost their jobs in East Germany, about 2.2 million did not go to West Germany to find work. Instead they received their income from the welfare state in one form or another. At the same time, about 1.2 million immigrants from non-EU countries were legally hired by West German businesses, while presumably the same number found jobs in black markets (while German firms created 2.4 million jobs abroad).[34] In hindsight, it was not necessary for Munich restaurants to hire Poles, Czechs, and Hungarians instead of Brandenburgers and Saxons to meet their high demand for personnel, and even the 13,000 computer specialists who were brought into Germany from India and elsewhere by Schröder's "green card" scheme were not needed, insofar as there were nearly 13,000 unemployed computer specialists in East Germany.[35]

Temporary migration by part of a country's labor force to better-developed regions is a meaningful strategy for every nation in the catching-up process. Italy, Spain, and Greece have benefited from the immigration of guest workers. The money sent back to their home countries by guest workers increases income there, and most guest workers tend to return with their savings when economic conditions improve in the home countries. Many more people from East Germany could have taken advantage of this option if, instead of the high-wage policy, a more organic, market-based wage strategy had been chosen. Thus, the fear of migration was not a good argument for a politically enforced wage convergence.

Another argument for high wages, one especially popular with East German voters, was that high wages would "whip up" productivity and would encourage business to innovate most rapidly. Instead of copying the development strategy of West Germany and gradually moving toward a high standard of living via building up labor-intensive industries, they argued for leapfrogging over the West German level of technology. With its multitude of low-technology industries, the East was to jump directly into the information technology (IT) era. For this reason, politicians attempted to create new Silicon Valleys with the help of huge subsidies. Remarkable successes were indeed achieved in Dresden, in Sömmerda, and elsewhere. Yet the approach could not compensate for the larger mistakes made in wage policy.

In 2005, the East German IT industry employed just about 2 percent[36] of the total active labor force. What was created suffices to fill glossy brochures with pretty pictures and to impress state guests, but it has not really contributed to solving the unemployment problem.

High-technology industries are extremely capital intensive and create fewer jobs than other lower-tech industries. Having an excess of employable people in a country suffering from high unemployment is good if competent investors can be attracted, but does not constitute a development strategy. It also is necessary to encourage industries that lack the aura of the glittering cyber world. The economy must be humming across the board; the simple production processes and the modest activities that are relatively labor intensive and therefore create comparatively more jobs must also be represented. Shoe manufacturing, washing machine production, glass production, tin can making, and the food and machine-tool industries (to name only a few examples of traditional industries) must be represented, and a sizable fraction of the population must be employed in the sector of simple household and consumer services. It does not make sense to use high wages to whip up productivity by driving the less glamorous jobs out of the market. When such a strategy is chosen, firm-level productivity gains coincide with losses in aggregate economic productivity as part of the labor force is driven into unemployment and thus their labor productivity becomes zero.

Most of what politicians claimed at the time to be meaningful development plans were in fact naive dirigiste central-planning approaches that violated the rules of the market economy. Economic novices were at work, and with their fairy-tale view of the world they helped to steer many things into the wrong direction.

"No Japanese, Please": The Dubious Role of the West German Wage-Bargaining Parties

The influence of the political arguments notwithstanding, the true effects on the wage-determination process came about in quite different ways. Wages were driven by solid economic interests, not by mere political expediency.

The wage negotiations that determined the long-run development of East German wages occurred in early 1991, long before there were any East German entrepreneurs. Only the Treuhand could have negotiated on behalf of the employers (in order to protect the capital entrusted to it from being depreciated by excessive wage increases), but it stood aside. After the collapse of the Communist system, the Treuhand had become the owner of most East German companies. Birgit Breuel, head of the Treuhand, later admitted to having been told by the federal government not to participate in the bargaining sessions. In the absence of proper East German representation, West German employer associations, which had just set up offices in East Germany, negotiated on behalf of the East German firms, and the East German employees were represented by officials of the new East German labor unions founded by the West German unions. Important positions in these unions were held by West German union leaders, whose advice was fully relied upon in the process of wage bargaining. The West German employers and the West German employees bargaining to set East German wages reached an accord surprisingly quickly, agreeing on wage paths in the initial negotiations covering the electrical and metal industries that were to result in full wage convergence with the West (including all rules pertaining to work time) in just 5 years. Most of the other industries followed suit.

The miraculously harmonious wage bargaining has an obvious explanation: The decisions were not made by those whose interests were directly at stake. Rather, both employer and employee parties were represented by the West German competitors of the East German firms. The competitors pretended to strive for wage convergence for reasons of solidarity, but in truth they feared that East Germany would become as attractive a location as the politicians claimed and that hordes of investors from all over the world would come to usurp the German market. Understandably, the West German competitors were afraid that well-established and advanced foreign manufacturing firms (e.g., from Japan and the emerging Asian Tigers) that had followed Germany's development path would buy out the East German manufacturing firms. After all, East Germany had an oversized manufacturing sector with millions of skilled manufacturing workers, covering essentially the same branches of industry as West German industry did. The motto was: "Those who want to produce and supply in Germany unhampered by trade and language barriers must do so at the same wages as existing West German firms. Only fair competition is allowed!" East German cut-throat prices, at wage costs of one-third, were to be prevented by all means. While the politicians were trying to attract investors all over the world, the West German competitors' true motto in the bargaining poker was "Please, no Japanese in our back yard!"

Later, wages developed somewhat differently from what the initial bargaining parties had desired. The new entrepreneurs that came to the fore along with the increasing privatizations had no sympathy for the wage agreements reached by their West German counterparts, and in later negotiations they succeeded in stretching the period for wage convergence. Furthermore, many employers left the employer associations or, condoned by the East German unions, did not stick to the wage agreements. In 2001, 78 percent of the East German firms, employing 55 percent of the East German workforce, were no longer bound by bargaining agreements, because they had left the employer associations or were founded without ever belonging to them.[37] These late actions, however, were not able to offset the wage increases of the early years. The lead of wages over productivity could not be reversed, and the confidence of international investors was lost.

Except for Sony (which built a big corporate center in Berlin's Potsdamer Platz) and a few other foreign investors (including Vattenfall, the Swedish power producer, or Elf Aquitaine, the French petroleum company), all of which had been attracted by big government subsidies, few foreign firms came to the region. East Germany was not considered an attractive business location, because of its high wage costs and lack of other advantages. The

Treuhand statistics are revealing in this respect. In terms of jobs, 85 percent of the privatized East German companies were sold to West Germans, 6 percent to East Germans, and only 9 percent to foreigners.[38] Regrettably, there were a number of Treuhand sales to West German firms whose East German subsidiaries filed for bankruptcy shortly after being purchased. One cannot help thinking that, in view of the dearth of foreign buyers, the real point was to protect the home market against the entry of foreign competitors, rather than to produce at a new location.

The "proxy" wage negotiations by East Germany's competitors in the West were the major reason for the East German disaster. Autonomous wage bargaining by management and unions, anchored in the German constitution, could not have been legitimately interpreted as allowing contracts to be signed at the expense of third parties, as in fact happened. The federal government could have prevented the disaster by either asking the Treuhand to participate as the employer representative in the wage bargaining or, even better, by issuing a wage moratorium during the initial transition phase of the new market economy until the end of the privatization process in 1996. Private companies, which oppose the wage demands of unions in defense of their own profits, are a trivial prerequisite of any wage bargaining. It makes no sense to let arbitrary parties negotiate wages before such private companies have come into existence. The wage moratorium would have been a useful, if not necessary, means to get the East German economy going and to smooth the transition to a market economy. The moratorium would not have imposed legal problems, as all the German reunification treaties had constitutional status and had to be agreed upon by two-thirds of the Bundestag. It would not have been difficult to add an amendment to the treaty requiring a wage moratorium until the completion of the privatization process.

But politicians neither anticipated the problem nor wanted to prevent rapid wage convergence. For having refrained from taking steps against the abuse of autonomous wage bargaining, the German government bears the major responsibility for the failure of Germany's economic reunification.

The Dutch Disease

Disaster may have been averted if the new entrepreneurs hadn't had to compete with the German welfare state after they had begun to free themselves from the wage agreements signed by their competitors. The West German competitors could have been sent home and asked to mind their own business. The welfare state, in contrast, had been adopted from West Germany, and it became a serious competitor of private business in the labor market.

After economic and monetary union, which became effective in July 1990, the social union of October 1990 was the third pillar of German reunification. The West German welfare state, with all its provisions and nearly its level of benefits, was implemented in East Germany. The rationale for this was considered entirely self-evident. It seemed unimaginable that the German people, even only temporarily during a transition phase, could be exposed to different social standards in the East and in the West. Any politician who had dared to propose different standards would have been immediately attacked by his righteously indignant and politically opportunistic opponents.

There is little dispute that East German citizens deserved the full solidarity of their Western brothers and sisters, who had been lucky enough to find themselves on the right side of the Iron Curtain. East Germans had every right to demand the explicit social insurance protection enjoyed by their compatriots to the West. It was not necessary, however, to structure this solidarity in such a manner that new citizens themselves either did not or could not contribute to rebuilding their part of the country. Nearly half of the payments that flowed to East Germany were granted as social benefits, to a large extent conditional on the recipients' not working. According to an estimate by the Institute for Economic Research in Halle, purely social transfers amounted to about 45 percent of total transfers to East Germany in 2002.[39] Under today's conditions, this would be about 44 billion euros (55 billion dollars). A substantial fraction of these funds is thus paid to the East Germans each year on the condition that they do not participate in the economy. If this sounds perverse, it is because it *is* perverse.

The West German welfare system, with its wage-replacement benefits in the form of early retirement, unemployment compensation, and social assistance, was extended to East Germany. As a consequence, this policy had the same negative effects on the East German labor market that chapter 4 described for West Germany. Yet in East Germany, where productivity was lower, the welfare benefits had a catastrophic effect, pushing unemployment above 25 percent in some regions. The wage-replacement benefits, patterned largely after those in West Germany, set almost the same wage floors as in West Germany, but East German businesses were even less able to cope with these wage floors than their West German counterparts. Proxy wage bargaining had initially raised wages far above the level of productivity, and the wage-replacement income with which the welfare state competed with private business by defining high reservation wages now prevented wage rates from falling to a level compatible with full employment, even after firms had freed themselves of collective wage agreements. The social union and flawed collective bargaining for wage agreements combined to create and cement a labor-market situation that continues to block East Germany's economic recovery.

The situation in East Germany, created by the social union, is a reminder of the Dutch disease. In the 1950s, the Netherlands discovered large deposits of natural gas, which it began to exploit in the early 1960s.[40] The gas discoveries made the Dutch richer because the gas could be sold in world markets in exchange for goods that raised their standard of living. However, the rest of Dutch business suffered because the gas companies emptied the labor market and drove wages so high that the manufacturing sector's competitiveness declined. This situation was called "the Dutch disease."[41]

As a result of the social union, East German business suffered its version of the Dutch disease. Like the effect of the gas discoveries on Dutch business, the social union in East Germany contains powerful economic incentives that empty the labor market instead of encouraging employment. An important nuance is that, whereas people employed by the Dutch gas industry were paid for working industriously, East Germans are paid for not working. But from the viewpoint of the manufacturing industries in both countries, the problems are similar. The firms are faced with the difficult problem of satisfying the high wage demands that the competitive demand on people's time has created.

In addition to their job-destroying effects, wage-replacement benefits have hampered East-West migration. Because they made life without work in the East tolerable, they also kept many bound to the East who would otherwise have gone west to look for jobs there. Although this result is in line with the migration-deterrence ideology that politicians spread to defend rapid wage convergence, it has kept millions of employable individuals from taking up work either in the East or the West.

The major effect on labor markets has emanated from unemployment compensation and unemployment assistance. Unemployment assistance was Germany's second-tier unemployment compensation system, providing, after the period during which ordinary unemployment compensation was paid had ended, about 60 percent of the last earned net wage—if necessary, until the age of retirement.

Most of the unemployed East Germans put out of work by the transition process had initially been employed by firms taken over by the Treuhand. They had participated in the early wage increases negotiated by the proxy bargaining parties, but these increases never had a true economic underpinning and could only be paid with the help of huge subsidies to the Treuhand. When the Treuhand firms closed or dismissed their workers because their jobs turned out not to be competitive, the dismissed workers first received unemployment compensation and later unemployment assistance. With unemployment assistance as permanently provided secure income, many workers have been waiting in vain for firms that are able to pay even higher wage incomes. In May 2003, 960,000 East Germans were receiving unemployment assistance, which was almost as high as the 1.07 million West Germans on unemployment assistance. This near-equivalent number is despite the fact that West Germany's population is four times larger than East Germany's.[42] Unemployment compensation and unemployment assistance worked like a ratchet that blocked any downward adjustment of the wages that had resulted from the proxy negotiations of the initial reunification years and prevented the East German economy from gaining a foothold thereafter.

Recently, things have improved a bit. As was explained in chapter 4, Gerhard Schröder's government replaced unemployment assistance with social assistance (now called Unemployment Benefit II), which is a means-tested support system independent of previous earned wages and which is typically lower than unemployment assistance. Unemployment assistance had been a major income source in East Germany. When it declined, many of the affected one million East Germans decided to migrate. Since Schröder's reform, East German guest workers have been flooding the West German labor market and can even be found in the Austrian and Swiss tourist industries.

But from the very start, social assistance itself, which had been available to everyone as a basic wage-replacement income, provided such high reservation wages that East German business firms never had a chance to become competitive. In the meantime, the statutory social assistance to which East Germans are entitled has reached the West German level in nominal monetary terms, even though the cost of living is much lower in the East. Due to the lower prices and rents there, social assistance is about 10 percent higher than in the West in real terms.[43]

In order to induce someone take a job, he or she must at least earn a little more after taxes than the state pays for not working, to offset the loss of leisure. Table 5.1 presents the implied hourly minimum wage cost (including employer social security contributions) for the year 2000 under different assumed valuations of leisure and family status. Account is taken of the actual average hourly wage costs in West Germany of 27.18 euros as well as the specifics of East German subsidies and levies applicable to alternative types of family status and states of employment including: housing and child allowances, taxes and social security contributions, social assistance without work, the possibility of receiving supplementary social assistance while working and other elements of the German tax-transfer scheme.

The first row of the table refers to the case of full employment that generates exactly the same net income as is available without working through

Table 5.1
Minimum wage costs per hour in East Germany as a percentage of average West German wage costs implied by social assistance (2000). Figures in parentheses: social assistance East including rent allowance and child allowance. Working time East 1,700 hours per year. Working time West 1,645 hours per year. Average annual wage costs for wage and salary earners in manufacturing, commerce and banking: 44,706 Euro. Source: H.-W. Sinn and W. Ochel, "Social Union, Convergence and Migration," *Journal of Common Market Studies* 41, 2003: 869–896.

Value of leisure time (euros)	Single person (6,407)	Couple without children (10,447)	Couple with one child (13,571)	Couple with two children (16,579)	Couple with three children (19,457)
0	21%	34%	39%	43%	48%
2.50	39%	48%	54%	60%	66%
5.00	62%	67%	74%	80%	87%

unemployment assistance, and the rows below are calculated on the hypothesis that leisure is worth 2.50 euros ($2.31) or 5.00 euros ($4.62) per hour net, thereby representing the wage premium one must earn in order to prefer working to social assistance. The table presents the minimum East German wage cost as a percentage of the respective West German wage cost that ensures that the net income earned is enough to compensate for the loss of social assistance and leisure time.

The relevant numbers for minimum wage costs in the East relative to the West range from 21 percent to 87 percent, depending on the worker's family status and on the value this individual assigns to leisure time. The lowest number is derived for a single worker whose leisure time is worth zero, and the highest number is for a worker with a non-working spouse and three children who wants to earn an extra 5 euros per hour net in addition to the social assistance received for himself and his family. For a worker with a non-working spouse and two children, the absolute minimum relative hourly wage cost, at which he does not receive one cent more than if he does not work at all, amounts to 43 percent. If this worker values his leisure lost by working at 2.50 euros per hour, the relative minimum wage cost of regular employment amounts to 60 percent of the West German level. If he values his leisure at 5 euros per hour, which is a realistic assumption for someone who has access to the black market, minimum hourly wage cost amounts to 80 percent of the West German level. As has been mentioned, these data refer to the year 2000. Since this time, statutory social assistance has been fully equalized between East and West Germany, so the respective minimum wages are now even higher than those presented in the table.

As figure 5.6 shows, actual average hourly wage costs in East Germany were about 73 percent of the West German level in 2005. A comparison with table 5.1 makes clear that this number can hardly be lowered by market forces if East German firms are to successfully compete with the welfare state. For a married working person with one child who can work in the underground economy for at least 5 euros per hour, it is no longer attractive to work at the average East German wage, although this rate already implies wage costs of three-fourths of the average West German level and exceeds aggregate East German productivity which is just about 60 percent of the West German level. This applies even more to workers with more children, because the cut in the child allowance granted as part of social assistance works like an additional brake on taking a regular job. An East German worker with average skills and several children can benefit from regular work only if he values his leisure time at less than 2.50 euros per hour, which is not a realistic scenario.

The data shown in table 5.1 demonstrate in concrete terms what it means to East German business to have to compete with the welfare state's unemployment system. At home, the state harasses companies with high replacement wages, and abroad, competitors from China to Poland harass them with low-wage goods in international product markets. Thus, East German business is caught between a rock and a hard place.

An Attempt at Escape

Because of the proxy wage negotiations made by the West German competitors and the problematic decision in favor of a social union directly patterned on West Germany, the East German states never had a chance to become attractive locations for internationally mobile investment capital. Valuable years were irretrievably lost in the attempt to establish a flourishing self-sustaining economy. These were decisive years during which East Germany could have gained a solid lead over the other formerly communist countries, today also on the quest for the road to riches.

These other Central and Eastern European countries were initially fully occupied with climbing out of the rubble that communism had left behind, and did not have a better off brother to ask for help. With great effort, these countries had to establish a legal system appropriate to a market economy such as East Germany had received at the time of reunification. And above all, the Eastern European countries had to do without the immediate privilege of belonging to the European Union that overnight brought East Germany a stable market order and a huge market of hundreds of millions of consumers. This gain was more than an equivalent replacement for the shrinking markets in Eastern Europe, to which politicians had alluded so often to explain and excuse East Germany's economic problems.

In East Germany, the time after reunification in the early 1990s was simply wasted. People celebrated and cheered, renovated their homes and their inner cities, bought Japanese cars, Korean video recorders and trips to hitherto forbidden countries. They got used to the Western standard of living and to the continuous flow of money for a *dolce far niente* lifestyle, the sweet art of doing nothing, which fulfilled even demanding communist dreams and would have made the Italians envious. And while the East German soccer players failed to help Germany win the world soccer championship that the country hosted in 2006, well-funded East German tourists succeeded in making Germany the world's champion in international tourism. Unfortunately, however, East Germans were unable to create a new industrial base with successful companies that could have met the competitive challenge from the formerly communist countries. For this, they were simply too expensive. West Germany's postwar success, born of hardship and sacrifice, had created such a high level of aspiration among East Germans that they priced themselves out of the market.

After the EU accession of the Eastern European countries that court international investors with one-sixth of East German wages, a radical change of course is in order. Germany's new chancellor, Angela Merkel, comes from the East. She should know how urgent the necessary reforms are, but she should also know how difficult it will be to convince her fellow easterners.

The necessary reforms for East Germany are similar in principle to those that are required for Germany as a whole, but they are much more urgent. Most important are a change of the wage structure and a reduction of the reservation wages of those who still do not have jobs. These changes will require drastically reducing the wage-replacement benefits, with which the welfare state competes with private business, and supporting the living standards with wage subsidies instead. The required measures also include a new early-retirement scheme that makes fair deductions but permits unlimited additional earnings and in particular the introduction of the Activating Social Assistance program. To pay more assistance to those who work and less to those who are able to work but do not is the crucial element of a reformed welfare state that does not create a Dutch disease and is in partnership with private business instead of in competition with it. If all of Germany adopted the system of Activating Social Assistance developed in chapter 4, wages would become flexible and East Germany would automatically benefit much more than West Germany as a result of its more difficult competitive situation. Without these reforms, there will be no chance for the East Germany economy. With them there will be employment and prosperity. There is no denying that East Germany will be hard put to escape the double bind of the highly productive

West German economy and the low-wage areas in Poland, the Czech Republic, Slovakia, and elsewhere. It will be very difficult, but the escape must be attempted.

Simply pouring good money after bad cannot solve the problem and will only be harmful, for the reasons mentioned. There is only one option, and that is the market. The citizens of East Germany must meet the challenge of competition head-on, and that will require them to change their thinking and finally make peace with the idea of a truly liberal economic system, They must accept that the state does not owe them a living, and that a living can only be earned from one's fellow citizens who pay for the goods and services rendered to them. One has no God-given claim to an income without working for it. One is entitled only to the value placed on one's labor by someone who is willing to buy it. The citizens of East Germany must accept that people's incomes differ a lot and are regulated in part by a system of risk and reward. Entrepreneurs who choose self-employment, who try something new, who work day and night, and who take risks must be able to earn a lot of money if they are successful. The old socialistic envy must be relinquished for good!

There is no question of eliminating the entire system of state protection and leaving the East Germans alone and unprotected from competitive Eastern European countries. The transfers will have to continue flowing. Their big brother living in West Germany will not withdraw his support, as difficult as this may be in these challenging times.

But work can be demanded in exchange for welfare payments. Everyone who can work and gets benefits from the state must work. The argument of the supposedly lack of jobs is no longer appropriate. The Activating Social Assistance program is the way to create the needed jobs, even the socially desirable kind. With Activating Social Assistance and the ensuing reduction of firms' labor costs, the East German states can meet the Eastern European competition and create additional jobs. This region can become the center of trade and industrial production at the heart of Europe by utilizing their old contacts in the East and their firm integration in the Federal Republic of Germany, as well as drawing on their pre-World War II history as "the world's Silicon Valley." They will benefit from Germany's well-functioning legal system, from the commercial relationships with West German business, and from an excellent infrastructure relative to that in Eastern Europe. And by doing so, they will remind themselves of their pride and of old virtues that had made them into one of the most productive regions of the world before the war.

But they must be unshackled. It is not advisable to kept the East German Länder completely bound to the West German system of rules and regulations.

They must be free to go their own way—within limits—and to demonstrate
to the West what more liberal business laws can do. They should also be
allowed to introduce Activating Social Assistance by themselves should the
West not go along. Exempting Länder from constraining federal rules and
allowing them try economic experiments is the right way to proceed.

In the context of wage policy, special attention should be paid to ways of
letting employees participate in the capital and earnings of their firm, because,
despite their already considerable income, the East German households still
lack assets.

One of the disadvantages of the high-wage policy was the total devaluation
of the assets of Treuhand firms that were to be given in securitized form to
the population of the former GDR, according to the Reunification Treaty and
the Treaty on Economic and Monetary Union.[44] If a wage moratorium had
been agreed upon until the conclusion of the privatization activities because
there had been no true East German bargaining parties, and if conditions had
been created for competitive wage determination, then wages would have
remained at approximately one-third of the West German level in the initial
years and would have risen only slowly in the wake of productivity gains. The
Treuhand firms would have regained value because they would have offered
international investors the ideal basis for a successful new start with
new machinery, new products, and new markets. The task set down in the
Reunification Treaty, after all a task of constitutional rank, could have been
fulfilled. Investors would have fought for the Treuhand firms because they
would have seen their chances to supply the giant internal market of the European Union from a low-wage location that enjoyed the full legal protection of
the Federal Republic of Germany, was in direct proximity to the West German
industrial areas, and would soon have a very good infrastructure. The Irish and
Finnish successes could have been matched. Under these conditions, the
planned securitization would have made sense. The Treuhand would have been
able to find potent investors for jointly run firms that were, however, to be
controlled by investors, and instead of being paid in cash it could have
exchanged its old capital for a minority interest in the assets in order to distribute the latter to the population in a second step. Such a policy would
have been a healthier base for the start into the market economy, because the
lower wages would have created good investment conditions and because
the participation in the firms' assets would have been more than adequate
compensation for the wage restraint.[45]

Time cannot be turned back. However, it would be possible to partially
correct for earlier failings by letting employees participate in the equity of their
firms. The participation model described in chapter 3 should be introduced in

East Germany. If the firms were to "purchase" some wage reduction from individuals already on the payroll in exchange for shares or participation certificates, this could pave the way for hiring new employees at lower wages. There would be advantages for everyone. Those who already have jobs would be compensated for their wage concessions. Those who do not yet have a job would be more likely to be offered one, because their lower wages would make additional investment profitable. The firms and the co-owning workers would be able to increase their joint profits by expanding the business. With a little bit of imagination and courage, it should be possible to take this route.

In addition, to compensate for wage reduction, the real estate of the community housing associations and of other government agencies could be sold to the East Germans at low prices. Most of the housing built during the GDR era has been renovated and brought up to Western standards. Some of that housing has already been sold to West German and foreign investors and also to tenants, but hundreds of thousands of apartments should still be available.[46] By choosing sale prices that cover the cost of renovation but not the historical cost, the formerly publicly owned assets could be returned to the people. This program, originally proposed by an expert commission set up by the federal government, could be designed in such a way as to give everyone a fair chance to acquire property.[47] It could help facilitate a U-turn in wage policy.

The East German citizens entered the market economy destitute because politicians failed to change the national property of the Communist state into civil-law claims. By creating ownership in companies and housing afterwards, this failure may still be corrected in part. In exchange, it would be practicable to liberalize the labor market and move to an activating welfare state as the basic prerequisite for the creation of jobs. In the future, East German citizens would have secure wage incomes and another source of income in the form of capital income, be it as distributed profits, as interest, or as imputed rent on owner-occupied housing. And property ownership would help some people to dare taking the plunge into self-employment. They would be better prepared for the risks of globalization and eastern enlargement, with their foreseeable implications for the distribution of national income between profits and wages, than is the case today.

6   Taxes and Transfers: The Endless Loop

The State: Leviathan, or Gold Redistributor?

When the English philosopher Thomas Hobbes compared the sovereign authority of the absolutist state to Leviathan, a sea monster mentioned in the Old Testament,[1] he did not envision that this monster, with its voracious appetite, would become a description for the liberal political economists' assessment of the European welfare state. These economists view the European welfare state as a continuation of the feudal state that helps certain population groups to obtain sinecures based on ever-higher taxes and fiscal charges levied on others.[2] The firms that let themselves be subsidized by the state, the politicians who take advantage of the privileges provided by the state, and the "social mafia" that has been able to give its clients access to income earned by others are the examples on which these political scientists focus. This, however, is only one potential view of the state.

A starkly opposing view is held by left-wing theoreticians who consider the European welfare state a redistributor that provides all people with sufficient income. Everyone ought to contribute to the polity according to his or her ability, but those who cannot be asked to work or cannot find any work also should have enough income for an acceptable standard of living. Citizens are obliged to support one another as members of one big family. The old Marxist motto "from each according to his ability, to each according to his need" retains its popularity in Germany. Wealth, top executive salaries, and inheritances are considered unjust and can therefore be used for financing the welfare state. The gold mined by the rich is collected in the form of taxes and then distributed among the needy. Corresponding to this view, the regular delivery of the gold is considered a vested right of the needy, so any reduction in this delivery is viewed as unfair enrichment of those who mined the gold in the first place.

These two strictly opposing views are counterproductive for purposes of discussing the true form and mission of modern governments. The modern state is not a feudal state in sheep's clothing; it is a necessary consequence of the industrial revolution, of urbanization and of democracy. It provides transportation infrastructure in the form of road networks, canals, bridges, railroads, urban transport, and airports, the system that delivers fresh water and carries away waste water, the electrical grid, and the communications network. It operates schools and universities, and it provides an efficient legal and police system, without which a market economy could not function. In short, the public sector provides public goods that cannot be better supplied by the private sector, because these goods are used by everyone and are subject to economies of scale. The state also insures against the risks of life by its policy of income redistribution, a topic considered in chapter 4. All of this has little to do with the gluttonous sea monster that only takes and never gives back, and it is far removed from the Marxian ideology, according to which all incomes are redistributed in proportion to need. Neither the minimalist night-watchman state nor the exuberant communist state is appropriate as a model for modern societies.

Although there is clearly a role for a strong government in a market economy, its role cannot be merely to transport and redistribute arbitrary amounts of gold. There are limits to redistributing individually earned wealth that the government has to respect. For one thing, the government must ensure that the gold miners continue to do their job. If miners know that their riches are going to be handed over to someone else, they are not going to have much of an incentive to dig for gold in the first place. For another, it must keep the expectations of transfer recipients under control. If those receiving welfare payments know that they will get these funds only if they are considered needy, they are going to make sure that they preserve their need-based status, so all the gold may do in that case is replace what might, under a different set of incentives, be their own earned income from productive labor.

For Germany, the disincentives resulting from income redistribution are not simply a theoretical issue; they are the essential reasons for its internal difficulties. In chapter 4 we saw why the welfare state's wage-replacement benefits, which had been introduced to cushion the effects of unemployment, actually generate unemployment. These policies create entitlement wages that, in many cases, the market economy can no longer match. Through wage replacement, i.e. income paid for leaving the workplace and going to the welfare office, the state's generous policy functions as high-wage competition in the labor market that destroys jobs in the private economy.

But the public competitor differs fundamentally from private competitors, insofar as it finances itself by compulsory taxes and duties levied on its rivals rather than through the sale of goods and services in the marketplace. These compulsory taxes and duties add further distortions to the economic process by inducing changes in economic behavior among those who are taxed. In expectation of the gold collector, taxpayers increasingly do things just to evade the tax burden, compromising economic efficiency. Because of this, the economy underperforms, and the primary earned incomes are lower than these would have been in the absence of excessive government taxation.

There are plenty of examples of unreasonable economic escape behavior induced by Germany's high taxes. German firms relocate to low-tax countries like Ireland or Estonia despite their distance from most of the Central European markets. Instead of reinvesting their profits locally, company owners buy financial assets elsewhere in the world, where they can earn interest that German fiscal authorities cannot touch. By permitting generous depreciation allowances and loss-offset possibilities, the German state has opened a tax loophole, and as a result German investors have been co-financing a sizable fraction of the world's container vessels. In fact, Germany has by far the largest fleet of container ships. In terms of capacity, the German fleet is more than four times as large as the Japanese (which occupies second place), 11 times as large as the British, and 13 times as large as the American. Its world market share both in terms of ships and freight capacity is 34 percent.[3] Even the Hollywood movie industry has benefited from generous German depreciation models. The movies *Eight Millimeters* and *Crazy in Alabama* were nearly exclusively financed with German funds that have benefited from German tax credits.[4] Because of extremely generous accelerated depreciation rules and other investment stimuli, rings of empty office buildings were constructed around East German cities, which generate private profits even though the investment capital was obviously wasted. During retirement, money is burned instead of bequeathed, to prevent the state from benefiting as co-inheritor through the inheritance tax, which captures up to 50 percent of the bequest. Wives, who typically earn less than their husbands, refrain from taking jobs because the progressive tax structure works as a disincentive. Gifted pupils do not see why they should go to college, because the progressive income tax leaves them little net income from their extra efforts. Workers flee to the underground economy, although they cannot work as efficiently there as they could in a well-organized company, because their labor is not subject to taxation. Unemployed workers do not take jobs offered in another region, because the after-tax wage increase does not compensate for the subjective and objective costs of moving. Apart from taxes with an explicit steering function, such as the taxes on energy use and tobacco consumption, tax-induced changes in private behavior are almost always economically harmful, resulting in a smaller total income available for distribution to everyone than would have been the case without the tax,

Chapter 1 showed that, by international standards, Germany has fallen behind in recent years and is being passed in per capita income by one country after another. Apart from the union's monopoly power and the welfare state's wage-replacement policy, the high German tax burden, including social security contributions, also shares responsibility for this situation. The transfers and subsidies with which the welfare state provides its citizens imply high tax levies on productive economic activities.

Apologists would argue that certain efficiency losses must be tolerated if taxation is to provide for more equity and if the lot of the poor is to be improved. To a certain extent this argument is correct. One should not overlook, however, that excessive taxation can create a downward economic spiral that drags everyone along with it, including the poor who receive the welfare state's benefits. If even those who are supposed to benefit from redistribution are losing out, then the extent of reasonable income redistribution has arguably been exceeded. Germany may already be in this situation, for although its needy citizens enjoy relatively large benefits, the nation's meager growth trend seems to imply that a more parsimonious welfare systems, like that of Ireland or Britain, may be in order. By providing greater incentives for self-reliance, Germany should eventually be able to provide a higher living standard to those at the bottom end of the income distribution scale, even though this may initially create losers among them.

The GDR's communist system is an extreme example of how even the poorest citizens can lose from a redistribution policy enacted in their favor. In theory, the "proletariat" were on the winning side of communist redistribution policy, but in fact even they were substantially worse off in the GDR's system than in the capitalist system of the FRG. Before unification, the economy was in such a desperate shape that East German workers earned in real terms only one-third of the take-home pay of West German workers.

In view of these considerations, designing tax policy is a delicate matter. A judgment based on theoretical considerations must be carefully qualified with inter-regional and inter-temporal comparisons. As we will see, the picture has many subtle and interesting nuances.

Among the Sinners

Only after the Schröder government was re-elected in the autumn of 2002 was it acknowledged that Germany would have to go deeper into debt than was permitted by the European Stability and Growth Pact. As was explained in chapter 1, the country breached that pact in four consecutive years and had enormous difficulty straightening out its public finances. While the government even lowered personal and corporate income taxes, serious cutbacks in social spending had to be contemplated to keep the federal budget under control. After decades of expanding the welfare state and increasing its budget, Schröder's welfare reforms, as insufficient as they were, were a courageous step in the right direction.

The unions roared with indignation and demanded tax increases instead, arguing that, at only 23 percent of GDP, Germany had an extremely low tax burden by international standards. A prominent union leader claimed that, since Germany was charging its citizens relatively low taxes, these should be raised for the wealthy as well as for civil servants. The argument was short lived, however. It soon became obvious that this union leader had ignored employers' and employees' social security contributions, more commonly known in other countries as social security taxes. Only because social security contributions were not included in the tax comparison could he temporarily give the impression that Germany was a low-tax country.

In order to avoid any semantic errors in understanding how much the state interferes in the German economy and absorbs the citizens' incomes for its own purposes, it is instructive to look at the government share of GDP—that is, the ratio of the state's expenditures to the value of all final goods and services produced in the country during a given period. Instead of looking at expenditures, one may also wish to look at revenues, but it boils down to the same thing, as in the long run government expenditures must always be balanced by revenues; as in the United States and most other countries, the government is not permitted to finance public expenditures by printing money. It is true that current revenues may include borrowed funds. However, debt becomes a charge in the future when, including interest and compound interest, it must be serviced by taxes. The present value of these additional taxes is exactly equal to the debt.[5] Thus, the government share of GDP reflects both the public expenditure share and the citizens' actual overall tax burden.

Figure 6.1 shows an OECD comparison of government share of GDP of the major EU countries, Japan, and the United States. The years 2000 and 2005 reveal a somewhat surprising result: by European standards, Germany is indeed not a high-tax country. Germany occupies a middle position and has

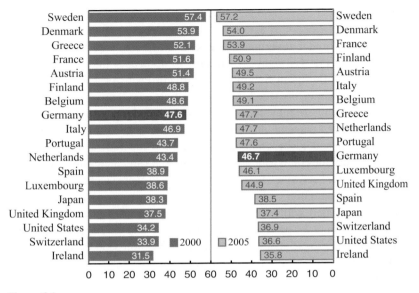

Figure 6.1
Government share of GDP (percent) in 2000 and 2005. For Germany, the 2000 number is adjusted for the 50.81 billion euros in revenue from selling mobile-phone frequencies (UMTS) that the official statistic counts as a negative expenditure. Sources: OECD, Economic Outlook 78, p. 187, table 25, December 2005; Germany: Statistisches Bundesamt: Fachserie 18, Reihe 1.4, p. 39, table 2.1.10.

actually reduced its share after 2000. It now ranks below the median of the distribution and is located surprisingly near the United Kingdom, which has jumped from 37.5 percent to 44.9 percent in only 5 years. Apparently, there is a historical tendency to move in cycles. Germany, much maligned, has been improving, while Britain has been slipping.

Germany has been improving because of the income tax reforms that Gerhard Schröder introduced in 2000, which were phased in gradually through 2005. These tax reforms, which will be described in more detail below, induced revenue losses for the government to the order of 2.5 percent of GDP. Even though some of the tax cuts were compensated for by additional borrowing, these did force spending discipline upon the state, explaining the slight drop of the government share of GDP, by 0.9 percentage points, between 2000 and 2005.

Unfortunately, the lower government share is likely to be reversed soon. Schröder's comparatively liberal reforms lost the backing of his own party, and he was not re-elected. Under new leadership, the Social Democrats returned to more traditional left-wing values. Even the Christian Democrats, with whom they have formed a coalition government under Angela Merkel, have been leaning toward the left.

In recent years, the political actions of the Social Democrats, moving forward and backwards abruptly to reflect changing moods and majorities within the party, have been confusing, and so have German politics in general. Before Schröder, the party did whatever it could to help expand the welfare state. Schröder introduced a cautious turnaround, and now his successors again lean more toward the left, while Kurt Beck, the new party leader who took office in April 2006, seems to be cautiously pushing again for a continuation of Schröder's course of reforms. The turmoil, in which the Social Democratic Party has found itself in recent years, stems from desperately trying to find a solution to the dilemma between its values that require an expansion of the welfare state and the forces of globalization that seem to imply its necessary shrinkage. It is telling that in the period 1996–2006 the Social Democrats had five party leaders, including ultra-left-wing Oskar Lafontaine, pulling the party in opposite directions.

Whatever the future course of the Social Democrats may be, and however responsibilities have been shared in the coalition government, the new government has carried out a major program of tax and expenditure increases— the largest program of tax increases in German history. In 2007, Merkel's government will increase the value-added tax by 3 percentage points, increase the insurance tax, reduce the commuting costs deductible, and introduce a "rich people's tax" that imposes an extra 3 percentage point tax on taxable income above 500,000 euros (622,000 dollars) for married couples. Together, these tax increases will generate extra revenues of about 25 billion euros (31 billion dollars), or 1.1 percent of GDP. While some of the money will be used to slightly reduce contributions to unemployment insurance and to depress the deficit share in GDP below the Stability and Growth Pact's limit of 3 percent, it will also make it possible to reflate the government budget. In all likelihood, Germany's government share of GDP will increase again in the years to come.

Even today, by international standards Germany is not a low-tax country. The United States, Japan, and Ireland still have government shares that are about 10 percentage points lower than Germany's. Germany is on the low side in comparison to other Western European countries, but certainly not in comparison to other global heavyweights. It is a mild sinner, but it is a sinner all the same. The real sinners hold the three top positions in figure 6.1. At 57.2 percent, 54.0 percent, and 53.9 percent, Sweden, Denmark, and France are true outliers.

In interpreting the government share, account must be taken of the fact that it relates public spending to gross domestic product, and not to net domestic product (the sum of all incomes generated by domestic and foreign residents in a country's territory). GDP equals the value of all newly produced final goods and services including capital goods. A substantial fraction of these capital goods, however, replace depreciated capital and are therefore not part of the net production or income originating in the economy. Although net domestic product is cited less frequently, theoretically it is the correct value to which the government budget should be compared. Relative to NDP, all public expenditure shares are higher than shown in figure 6.1. According to the Federal Statistics Office, Germany's NDP is only about 85 percent of its GDP. This means that in 2005 the actual government share of the sum of all incomes generated in Germany was not 46.7 percent but 54.7 percent (46.69/0.8542 = 54.66).[6] For Sweden, where NDP is about 12 percent lower than GDP, the corresponding calculation leads to a government share of 65.3 percent, and even Switzerland, which no longer is the free-market country its reputation would lead one to believe, has a share of 44.9 percent.[7]

All economic systems in advanced countries are mixed systems, lying between pure communism and a pure market economy. No modern Western country has ever had a pure market economy with a government share of GNP of 0 percent, and no country of the former Soviet Bloc was ever fully communist with a share of 100 percent. With a government share of aggregate income of 54.7 percent, Germany obviously belongs to those countries that are closer to Communism than to the market economy, if judged by the degree the federal government is involved with the macro economy. In this sense, the sociologist Arnulf Baring was right in calling the economic system of the Federal Republic "GDR light."[8] However, to be fair, one must admit that this is not a description that distances Germany from the other Western European countries. For example, in 2005 the old EU countries on average had a government share of NDP of 53.9 percent, which also was above the 50 percent limit. This once again stresses the point, made at various places in this book, that Germany's problems to a large extent are not idiosyncratic, but are just an extreme example of the problems with which most Western European countries have to struggle. In other parts of the world, the welfare state is less developed than in Europe. On average, the government share of the net domestic product of the OECD countries was 47.6 percent in 2004, while in the United States it stood only at 41.3 percent.[9]

Of course, many will shake their heads when confronted with such a characterization of the Western European welfare state, because it does not fit the European self-image that no longer wants to have anything to do with communism. In theory, a commitment to the market economy lies at the foundation of today's continent. But facts are facts and not ideologies or visions, and these facts speak clearly. If the government share of aggregate income does not fit the founding principles of the state, then either one should be honest about the violation of these principles and revise them accordingly, or one should reform the state in order to realign reality with principle. And the latter is without doubt the more attractive route.

The Road to Debt Is Paved with Good Intentions

Although Germany's government share of GDP seems moderate if compared with other European nations, there were periods when it was much lower than it is today. Figure 6.2 shows how this share changed from 1950 to the present. Until about 1955 the government share stood at about 31 percent. Then, during the administrations of Chancellors Adenauer (1949–1963) and Erhard (1963–1966) to the start of the big coalition under Chancellor Kiesinger (1966–1969), it rose to 39 percent, remaining constant until the first year of the social-liberal coalition under Chancellor Brandt (1969–1974), but exploding thereafter. Under Brandt and Helmut Schmidt, his successor in the same coalition

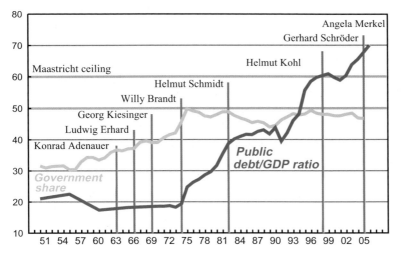

Figure 6.2
Government share of GDP (percent) and ratio of public debt to GDP in Germany. 1995 government share excludes transfers of assets in connection with assumption of debt of Treuhand privatization agency and housing authority of former GDR (122.46 billion euros). 2000 government share is adjusted for 50.81 billion euros in UMTS revenue that official statistic counts as negative expenditure. Sources: Public sector share: Statistisches Bundesamt; Ifo Institute calculations. Public debt/GDP ratio: 1950–1970 old Federal Republic, until 1959 excluding Saarland and Berlin; 1950–1970 only in five-year intervals, Council of Economic Experts; 1991–2006: Ministry of Finance monthly report, April 2006.

(1974–1982), the share increased to almost 50 percent, where it has remained under Chancellors Kohl (1982–1998), Schröder (1998–2005), and Merkel (since 2005), albeit with a recently declining tendency that is probably temporary.

During the second half of Willy Brandt's term in office, the rise in government spending was especially extreme. Against the bitter opposition of Karl Schiller, the economics minister who then stepped down in protest of this profligate spending, but with the overwhelming support of the electorate, in 1972 the Brandt administration decided to start down the road to a welfare state patterned on Sweden. Old-age insurance was opened to new groups of participants who could join on very favorable terms; pensions were raised for low-income people; German universities were converted from elite schools to mass institutions; university tuition fees were abolished; students were given generous public stipends to cover their living costs; social assistance was extended to people who formerly had to be supported by relatives; public health and accident insurance coverage were extended; child support was increased; and, last but not least, local communities received matching grants covering 90 percent of infrastructure investment, which made public swimming pools and other facilities of consumptive infrastructure pop up like mushrooms in Germany. The expansion of the welfare state was in the spirit of the time. In the aftermath of the European student revolts of 1968, the mindset of the German population tended toward efforts to establish socialist systems with more equality and more democracy in the state and in the economy. Only a few far-sighted people, including economics minister Karl Schiller (a professor of economics at the University of Hamburg), warned of economic overstretch.

The world's first oil crisis, which began in 1973, reduced growth and contributed to the rise in the government share, making it possible to sell the increase in public spending as a Keynesian policy measure to boost the economy. No one seemed to care that the increase in government spending was not an appropriate means to fight the supply-side crisis that beset Germany at the time, and that public spending was not reduced after the crisis was overcome. Up to this day, the government share of the German economy has not declined from the peak it reached under Willy Brandt.

When Helmut Schmidt, Brandt's Minister of Finance, became chancellor in 1974, he was initially successful in preventing a further rise of the share. Yet Schmidt failed to achieve a sustained effect, because he balked at rescinding the benefit laws introduced by his predecessor. With special labor subsidies that remained ineffectual, and with an expansion of public jobs, he even contributed to the expansion of the welfare state. In the early 1980s, a second oil crisis aggravated the situation by reducing growth again, thus raising the government share further.

The Kohl administration, which came to power in 1982, had good intentions, but as a result of unforeseen events it was not much more successful than its predecessor. Although it did lower the government share by a few percentage points during its early years in office, German unification in 1990 thwarted its plans.[10] The government share nearly hit the 50 percent mark, because it was not possible to shoulder the enormous costs of unification by rapidly cutting expenditures in the Western part of the country.

The ratio of public debt to GDP rose slowly at first but then accelerated considerably. This ratio, called the "debt ratio" for short, is also depicted in figure 6.2. In the 1950s it stood slightly above 20 percent. In the 1960s it was a bit below 20 percent without a rising trend. Konrad Adenauer, Ludwig Erhard, Georg Kiesinger, and (in a sense) even Willy Brandt restrained government borrowing.

But then came the Schmidt administration. Although it kept the public spending ratio under control, the debt ratio doubled within 8 years. Helmut Schmidt was confronted by his predecessor's social benefit laws, which he could not rescind, and he had no chance of getting his political coalition partner, the Free Democrats, to agree to tax increases. The debt-financed expansion of the welfare state was the easy solution. Even though Schmidt himself tended to be reactive rather than proactive, the social-liberal coalition is responsible for one of the biggest economic mistakes of the postwar period. The debt-financed welfare benefits that were introduced by his government are being repaid with compound interest by the present generation.

Although Helmut Kohl pursued a policy of moderation of public expenditures for 8 years, he did not succeed in keeping the debt ratio under control. The ratio increased, exceeding the 60 percent limit of the Maastricht Treaty in 1996 after the Treuhand debt had been transferred to the federal government.

The rise of German public debt under Helmut Kohl can largely be traced to German unification. Sixteen million East Germans had to be fed despite the collapse of their economy, and the ramshackle infrastructure left by the communist state had to be repaired and modernized. At the same time, the political aim was to raise the new citizens' standard of living to the West German level as fast as possible. All of this cost money, and the most expedient solution was for the Kohl administration to burden future generations, not the current electorate. Incurring more public debt was again the comfortable way to muddle through, at least for a while. Like Schmidt, Kohl did not dare present the bill for the gifts being handed out to his voting contemporaries.

The size of the gifts to the former GDR was enormous. As was noted in the preceding chapter, the net transfers that found their way to East Germany via the public budget amounted to about 1,135 billion euros (1,412 billion dollars at the 2005 exchange rate) between 1990 to 2005. During almost the same period (from the end of 1989 to the end of 2005) Germany's public debt rose by an estimated 985 billion euros (1,225 billion dollars). German unification was primarily financed by debt. This was the major reason why Germany violated the fiscal conditions for entering the eurozone and has been unable to stick to the Maastricht Treaty's debt criteria, as was explained in chapter 1.

Since then, the politicians have failed to get the debt ratio below the European Union's 60 percent limit. Democracies are often subject to the morbid addiction of distributing government benefits immediately and shifting the costs of these benefits to future generations that do not yet have a say in these decisions. German democracy, too, has succumbed to this addiction twice in the postwar period: first in the expansion of the welfare state in the 1970s, then with unification. As figure 6.2 shows, the debt ratio has again risen steeply in recent years, reaching a value of 67.7 percent in 2005. It is little wonder that Germany has consistently violated the 3 percent deficit ceiling of the EU Stability and Growth Pact.

Even if the 3 percent deficit ceiling were obeyed, Germany would not return to the 60 percent debt ratio at its current growth rate. As the real trend growth rate is just about 1.1 percent and the trend inflation rate is about 1.3 percent, the nominal growth rate can be taken to be 2.4 percent. By the mechanics of debt dynamics, the deficit to GDP ratio must not exceed 60 percent of this number (i.e., 1.4 percent) over the business cycle if the ratio of debt to GDP is to converge toward 60 percent. And in order for the debt ratio not to climb above 70 percent, the deficit ratio must be below 1.7 percent. As the deficit tends to hover by about +1 percent and −1 percent over bad and good times, this means that in the economic boom that Germany experienced in 2005 and 2006 the deficit should have been below 0.4 percent or 0.7 percent, respectively. As Germany was unable to meet this condition, a further increase in the debt ratio is in store.

Again, it could be pointed out that a number of countries, among them Belgium, Greece, Italy, and Japan, have debt ratios well above 100 percent. However, apart from the fact that the Maastricht Treaty has set a binding debt ceiling of 60 percent, the situation in these countries cannot be a yardstick for a rapidly aging society like Germany's. At the end of 2005, the German debt ratio ranked in the upper third of the EU countries, ahead of France, the Netherlands, or Sweden (whose debt ratios range from 50 to 67 percent), not to mention Great Britain or Ireland (whose debt ratios are less than 43 percent).[11] But stopping this development requires major rethinking of current government policies. Only when voters realize what legacy they are leaving to their children may the politicians then have the motivation and public support to end the permanent accumulation of debt that will be increasingly difficult to repay given future demographics.

Today's taxpaying adults are paying for the sins of their parents. They are bearing the cost of debt-financed welfare benefits enacted in the 1970s by the governments of Brandt and Schmidt, and they are financing German unification. Already today, the government proceeds from borrowing within the limits of the Stability and Growth Pact (3 percent of GDP) only just cover the interest on the debt accumulated in the past, and very soon these proceeds will fall short of the interest payments. The times for deficit financing of welfare gifts like those distributed in the course of German unification are gone for good. In 2005, the government's interest burden amounted to 63.4 billion euros (78.9 billion dollars), and the actual borrowing requirement came to 74.5 billion euros (92.7 billion dollars), while the maximum net borrowing permitted by the 3 percent rule was 67.42 billion euros (83.88 billion dollars). The interest burden is below the permitted deficit by only 4 billion euros (5 billion dollars). The situation will worsen when the eurozone's interest rates rise from their present exceptionally low levels. From now on, the bill must be paid when the meal is eaten. Buying on credit is no longer possible.

Where Is All the Money Going?

The treasury secretary who must administer the legacy of his predecessors is not in an enviable position. The debt cannot be increased and, as a result of the economic disaster in East Germany, the unification burden will not lessen. There just is not enough money, so the belt must be tightened. The only question is where to make the cuts.

This question has no objective answer. How it will be answered depends on citizens' voting preferences and on policy decisions made by the winning coalitions. A starting point, however, is to examine how public spending in Germany deviates from public spending in comparable countries.

A commonly voiced opinion in public discussions is that German civil servants are gobbling up too much money. According to this thesis, public expenditures could be cut substantially if the number of civil servants were reduced. This sounds plausible but misses the point, as Germany does not have many government employees. There are two kinds of government employees in Germany. "Beamte" (civil servants in the narrower sense) are privileged employees with super job security, who have no right to strike, and who have their own special pension system. Ordinary government employees serve under conditions similar to those of their counterparts in the private economy. The former category accounts for only 6.1 percent of total German dependent employment,[12] and according to the Statistisches Bundesamt the two categories together account for only 14 percent of total dependent employment. This number includes the employees in all layers of government, from local communities to the federal level. The wage costs of these employees absorb about 7.5 percent of gross domestic product, and their pensions amount to just 1.6 percent of gross domestic product.[13] Even if all Germany's public employees were dismissed immediately and the benefits of past employees as well as those of their widows and orphans were withdrawn, the government share of GDP would still be as high as it was before its explosive increase at the time of the social-liberal coalition in the 1970s. (See figure 6.2.)

Relative to other countries, the number of government employees in Germany is rather small. Figure 6.3 shows the total share of public employees in various countries, according to the OECD. The OECD measuring system is not fully comparable to the German system because it is based on a different treatment of quasi-governmental organizations (parafisci) and the like. Yet it allows an unbiased comparison across countries. At the 12 percent

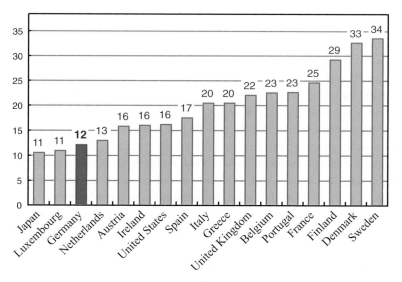

Figure 6.3
Government share (percent) in total dependent employment, 2005. Source: OECD data base, Economic Outlook 78, December 2005: Government employment, dependent employment.

the OECD statistics show,[14] Germany is extremely parsimonious with respect to its number of public employees.[15] At 34 percent and 33 percent, Sweden and Denmark have nearly three times the ratio of government employees of Germany, and even France, at 25 percent, has twice as many. Obviously, the reason for the large government shares in GDP of these countries, reported in figure 5.1, lies in this difference.

Government policies of absorbing a good part of the excess labor force has enhanced the employment statistics in the Scandinavian countries and in France. For one thing, these policies keep unemployment figures relatively low, and for another, GDP is inflated by the salaries paid to the large number of government employees. When Germany pays replacement incomes, the statistics treats the recipients as unemployed workers and the money they receive as redistribution with an existing GDP. When the Swedes give the same people a labor contract and a desk at which they can sit during the day in exchange for the public money, they are counted as employed, and the money they receive is counted as value added that augments Sweden's GDP. That way, any country can increase its measured GDP per capita to artificial heights by simply increasing its taxes and its share of government employees. On closer scrutiny, not all that glitters is gold.

With regard to public employment, Germany really is a thrifty state. Its government share of dependent employment is even lower than that of the United States, where public employment accounts for 16 percent of the total number of employees. The United States is a much larger country and is not known for excessive state influence. Contrary to popular opinion, a large number of state employees does not explain Germany's larger government share of GDP.

Neither are the salaries of German public employees exceptionally high relative to those in private business. With some exceptions in East Germany and in its structurally weak regions, salaries are generally lower than they are in the private sector. The times when state employees and civil servants enjoyed especially high salaries and true privileges are long past.

If it does not spend on its employees, does the German state expend large resources on education? The answer is No. German schools and universities do not belong to the state's high-cost expenditure categories either. The share of gross domestic product spent by Germany on public education is only 4.3 percent. Among the OECD countries, Germany holds a position below the average of 4.6 percent.[16] Thus, education does not help explain the high government share of GDP.

One reason for the German state's low education expenditures may be found in the small number of school-age children (see chapter 7). A land without

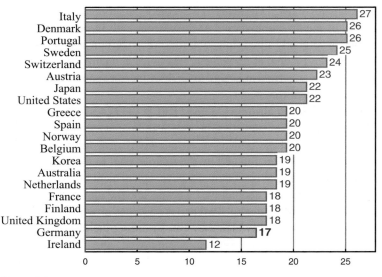

Figure 6.4
Educational expenditure per student in primary, special, and non-special primary schools in percent of per capita GDP, 2002. Source: OECD, Education at a Glance, 2005, p. 173, table B1.2.

children does not need schools. Even correcting for this fact, Germany still spends very little on schooling, at least at the compulsory primary school level. If primary school spending per pupil is taken as a percentage of gross domestic product per capita, Germany ranks second to last of 20 highly developed OECD countries. (See figure 6.4.) The United Kingdom is as tight fisted as Germany, and only Ireland spends relatively less per child.

The one category of public spending in which Germany is far from stingy is social protection, including pensions, unemployment benefits, and social assistance. In other spending categories, Germany is near or below average. With regard to social expenditure Germany has very deep pockets. As figure 6.5 shows, Germany hardly differs from the Scandinavian countries or France in this respect, but it ranks markedly higher than the Anglo-Saxon countries and most other continental European countries.

Figure 6.5 presents American and European expenditures on social protection as a share of GDP (for short, the social-expenditure share). The data from the European Statistical Office (Eurostat) underestimate Germany's true social-expenditure share because these figures exclude the employee savings premium or the owner-occupied housing allowance that are treated as tax benefits rather than government expenditures. Germany's Federal Statistical Office corrects for this error in its publications.[17] According to the definition

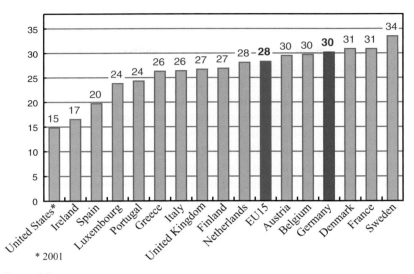

Figure 6.5
Social expenditure share of GDP (percent), 2003. Source: European Commission, Eurostat: European Social Statistics, Social Protection, Expenditure and Receipts, 1995–2003, 2006, p. 14, table B1.1; United States: OECD Factbook, 2006.

of the Welfare Report of the Federal Government, the German social-expenditure share is even higher than shown in figure 6.5, namely 32 percent. This makes it the second highest among all surveyed countries after Sweden, and Germany's government share of GDP, as shown in figure 6.1, would rise by three positions in the ranking, to just after Belgium.

One-third of Germany's gross domestic product or 697 billion euros (788 billion dollars) was absorbed for welfare purposes in 2003.[18] Of this, marriage and family benefits accounted for about 15 percent, health benefits for 34 percent, unemployment 10 percent, and old-age and surviving dependents for 38 percent or 268 billion euros (303 billion dollars).[19] The lion's share of expenditures arose in areas that will become even more important in the future as a result of population demographics, i.e. old-age pensions and disability pensions, health insurance and nursing insurance. If unemployment insurance, social assistance, housing allowances, unemployment compensation, social housing and other items are added, the costs are immense. In 2003 the German welfare budget per person employed amounted to approximately 18,000 euros (20,350 dollars).

Welfare expenditures are not only funded by employer and employee contributions to the pension, health, nursing, and unemployment insurance funds, but also by general tax revenues that help finance these expenditures. One quarter of the pension insurance, which is primarily funded by contributions, is financed by taxes, not least by the "ecology tax" on fossil-fuel consumption that in recent years has paid for part of the increase in the public support of pension insurance. In 2005, ecology tax revenues to the tune of 16.4 billion euros (20.4 billion dollars) flowed into pension insurance. Today, part of the pensions of parents and grandparents is paid at the gas station.

Germany's total welfare budget is more than 50 percent bigger than the volume of current social security contributions. The above mentioned 697 billion euros (32 percent of GDP) of 2003 welfare expenditures were only matched by social security contributions worth 447 billion euros (506 billion dollars, 20 percent of GDP), the rest being financed by general taxes.

In past decades, a growing part of the welfare state's costs were hidden in the general budget and were charged also to taxpayers who have almost no chance of ever enjoying the same benefits. But the shell game is becoming more and more difficult, and the sources from which the necessary funds can be extracted without great protests are drying up.

Voting for Transfers

The needs of the welfare state, which have increased as a result of demographic pressures, are magnified by the democratic process. The recipients of benefits have a vested interest in maintaining or even expanding their benefits despite scarce overall resources. And as the group of benefit recipients has grown, so has its political clout. The fact that the government share of GDP has risen so much over the past decades may also be traced to the increasing number of voters who live on government transfers. In drawing up its election platform, no political party, popular or not, can disregard the fact that growing parts of the electorate receive considerable welfare incomes from the state and that the group of those who would rather extend the state is gaining in political power.

In 2001, Germany had a population of about 82 million people, 61 million of which were at least 18 years old and thus had the right to vote.[20] At the same time, Germany had about 2.2 million recipients of unemployment compensation, 2 million recipients of unemployment assistance, 2.7 million recipients of social assistance, 0.7 million students receiving state support in the form of subsistence incomes, 19 million retirees (with 23.7 million cases of pension payments), 1.3 million public pensioners, 2.8 million recipients of housing allowances, 1.8 million recipients of benefits of statutory accident insurance, and 1.8 million residents of nursing homes. This total is about 35 million people out of the 61 million Germans eligible to vote. If double counting, non-voting foreigners, and minors are deducted, a rough estimate yields about 25 million people who receive their incomes primarily as social transfers from the state,[21] or 41 percent of those eligible to vote, and this percentage does not include government employees. The recipients of publicly provided social benefits constitute such large numbers that it would be suicidal for any political party's policy platform to disregard their interests. Cutting back welfare benefits is therefore a most difficult and politically dangerous matter.

This is especially true for politicians wishing to represent East Germans. Whereas about 38 percent of the 47 million West German voters receive their income primarily from the state, the corresponding share of the 14 million East German voters is about 47 percent. If all affected voting family members were included, the share of East German voters enjoying publicly provided social benefits would be considerably above 50 percent.

The unification has fundamentally changed the spectrum of political powers in Germany, and part of the country's inability to react to the forces of globalization has to do with this realignment. Germany's ultra-left-wing party, the PDS, which succeeded the ex-communist SED that ruled the GDR until 1989, was extremely powerful in East Germany, and in local elections often collected more votes than either the SPD or the CDU. In 2005 the PDS expanded to the West and merged with another left-wing party (WASG). Under the new Linkspartei and its charismatic leader, Oskar Lafontaine—the same politician who once had warned about the social costs of German unification—Germany has been at risk of becoming a different republic, one for which a market-liberal approach is more alien than ever. By explicitly targeting the huge number of recipients of social benefits in East and West Germany, the party may succeed in giving the country a new direction in the years to come, even if it is not able to directly participate in the federal government.

It is arguable that rumors about plans to found the new party were the main reason why Gerhard Schröder called for early elections in 2005, one year before the date originally scheduled. Afraid that a new party on the left would steal many votes from him and hoping that the summer break would make it impossible for his opponents to join forces, he scheduled the federal elections for September, only 4 months after first announcing he would bring forward the voting date. However, he underestimated the will and determination of his opponents. They nevertheless managed to found the party in time, participated in the elections and went on to win 8.7 percent of the popular vote, better than the 5 percent that is a requirement for entering parliament. Although there was hardly any time for an election campaign, Oskar Lafontaine and ex-communist East German leader Gregor Gysi, who had chaired the East

German PDS, triumphed, and Schröder lost his chancellorship to his opponent Angela Merkel, who became head of a coalition government of Social and Christian Democrats.

Since the Linkspartei is likely to win even more votes in the future, the chances for fundamental reforms that will permit the free working of market forces are small. In view of how the CDU/CSU had tried to overtake the SPD on the left on various accounts and how it currently bows to the post-Schröder SPD, which is itself paralyzed by the public support for the Linkspartei, the country will have a hard time ever managing a turnaround. Yet despite its considerable economic problems, Germany still can be saved. The necessary and sufficient policy moves, summarized in chapter 9, emerge directly from the analysis of this book. The real question is whether the Germans will consent to being saved.

This unwillingness to undertake the necessary and sometimes painful reforms may be even more pronounced, as the inevitable aging of the population will rapidly increase the number of transfer recipients in the future, a topic that will be discussed in chapter 7.

The only hope is that people will realize that this is a dead-end road and that everyone will be hurt in the long run. Only if those seemingly favored by the state's redistribution policy vote for a reduction of the benefits received because they realize that otherwise the economy is bound to decline, will the turnaround in Germany succeed despite the large number of voters already dependent on the welfare state. For this to happen, the country needs a knowledgeable and courageous politician who is able to convince the people and willing to incur the risk of not being reelected. Margaret Thatcher once said that she would not have been able to carry out her policies had she aimed to maximize public support. In fact, it was the Falklands war rather than agreement with her economic policies that brought her reelection and gave her the chance to turn Britain around by overcoming its economic stagnation. Luck, dedication and benevolence rather than tactical calculus are the attributes of the politician that Germany needs to master its future. With Bismarck, Adenauer, and Brandt it has had such politicians. But Germany is still wondering whether Angela Merkel will turn out to be a distinguished successor who is able to confront its current challenges.

Wasted Energy: Taxpayers versus Beneficiaries

Many Germans believe that the concern about expanding the welfare state is exaggerated. They view the redistribution exercise as being analogous to the state taking the money from one pocket and transferring it to the other. As long as the taxes paid and the benefits received are equal, on aggregate, they assume that the balance will amount to zero. What one group loses is equal to what the other gains.

Unfortunately, this conclusion is erroneous. Although the money flows balance, the private economy is distorted because the citizenry's economic incentive structure is altered. The taxpayers as well as the welfare recipients change their economic behavior and this hurts the economy at large. Those who pay act in such a manner as to minimize their taxes, and the recipients change their behavior so as to increase the benefits they get. Economic efficiency is compromised in the process, resulting in a smaller national product than would have resulted in the absence of redistribution. The pie gets smaller as one tries to distribute it more equitably.

Taxes *and* social expenditures paralyze the German economy, and these paralyzing forces add up instead of netting out. Think of the labor market. While the taxes on labor push people out of work, the spending on social replacement payments pulls them away. Employment shrinks, and economic growth diminishes. Direct increases in labor costs and indirect ones attributable to the welfare state's acting as a competitor in the labor market were discussed in chapters 4 and 5.

Sacrificing productive activity in the market economy is bad in and of itself. It is still worse if people channel their energy and effort in unproductive activities. Economists speak of rent seeking here, meaning the costly search for state sinecures or costly defensive activities against income seizure by the tax state.[22] Potential value added that would contribute to making the pie bigger is not created.

A market economy functions because people earn their own income by selling a valuable service to someone else. This is a difficult business, as the buyer decides whether the service is worth its price. But this is exactly why only useful economic activities are selected that benefit the buyers enough to compensate the sellers for their costs. This is the mechanism by which the market economy generates the true the welfare of a nation, as Adam Smith details in *The Wealth of Nations* (1776).

Instead, if people no longer have to make the effort of selling their own services to other people, but have the chance of either taking income away from others via the welfare state or trying to avoid being included in the group from which income is taken away, then more and more effort will be directed at doing well in the redistribution game.

Thus taxpayers try to keep their burden as low as possible by staying away from taxable activities and by expending a lot of time, money and effort on their tax returns and the legal design of their income situation. They consult books, attend courses, study laws and ordinances, collect receipts, keep records of their expenditures and buy professional advice. In Germany, armies of lawyers and tax accountants are busy with helping their clients avoid taxes and leading them to the edge of legality in these avoidance schemes. This evasive action keeps some of the country's best minds from productive activities. Instead they are only trying to do win the redistribution game between taxpayers and benefit recipients. No true economic value is generated. On the contrary, economic value is being destroyed by wasting valuable time that could have been used for productive activities or for leisure.

It is similar for benefit recipients. They get used to going to some office in order to queue up for their welfare benefits, to fill in forms, and to beg from civil servants. With their acquaintances they exchange the latest information on which benefits they may be entitled to, and how they have to present their cases in order to get access to the subsidies. Some take courses to learn about their rights or they get advice from specialists in social law. This knowledge translates into a behavioral pattern in dealing with the rules of the welfare state that is passed from one generation to the next.

In the past, there was shame associated with going to the welfare office, and many did not go although they were needy and entitled to these benefits. Today, going to the welfare office has become daily routine for many Germans. A good part of one's energy is spent on identifying and exploiting the various support measures.

The benefit recipients expend energy to pull money out of the taxpayers' pockets, and the taxpayers expend energy to prevent that from occurring. Both fight with each other in the legal jungle, in front of government offices and in the lobbies of parliament. In so doing, they use up energy that they could have used for productive activities. It would be wrong to call this criminal activity, because people are just reacting with legal means to economic incentives, but it surely is wasteful, harmful energy.

Chasing Subsidies

It is not just recipients of welfare benefits who are scrambling for various sources of support. Private firms are also seeking rents, to use Gordon Tullock's term.[23] Whenever the state puts money on the table, it redirects people from the private market to public entities, and in many cases it causes them to make economically damaging decisions in their efforts to get some of the public funds. Precious labor time is wasted on filling in forms, on writing voluminous reports, on applications for public subsidies, and on walking the floors of local offices. In East German companies, in particular, the subsidy departments are often bigger than then the accounting departments because there is hardly a major investment that is not financed out of public money.

According to the Subsidy Report of the Federal Government, subsidies in terms of financial support and tax privileges amounting to nearly 60 billion euros (66.4 billion dollars) are granted in Germany every year.[24] If a broader definition of subsidies is chosen, the government pays out more than 150 billion euros in subsidies per year, more than 7 percent of GDP.[25] Subsidies do not only include useful support measures benefiting non-profit public activities and emerging technologies promising considerable knowledge transfer, but also absurd payments to increasingly obsolete or declining industries like coal mining that have counterproductive effects on the overall economy.

"Save the coal!" was the slogan with which massive subsidies were demanded in the 1960s in order to save miners' jobs. Today none of those miners are still working. Instead, their grandchildren and newly hired Turkish guest workers are working in the mines. If no coal mining subsidies had been paid in the 1960s, these new workers would have gone to other, competitive sectors or they would not have emigrated to Germany at all. The social problem that is supposed to be solved with coal subsidies today would no longer exist.

As the extraction of German coal costs four times the price of imported coal, the country harms itself by using its own resources. Today, each employee in the coal industry accounts for 56,000 euros in subsidies per year. For that money, he could be sent on a year's holiday to Mallorca. Coal subsidies have slowed down the necessary structural change in the Ruhr region, Germany's industrial heartland, in the middle of West Germany between Cologne and Hannover, and contribute to the region's remaining structural problems.

The coal policy cannot even be justified on the grounds of guaranteeing a long-term domestic energy supply, as the subsidies lead to a particularly fast exploitation of the existing coal reserves and contribute to exacerbating the CO_2 problem. Some day, when energy reserves become so scarce that difficulties arise in supplying energy to German industry, people may wish to fall back on the Ruhr region's coal reserves. But because of today's subsidies of premature extraction, no coal will be left in the ground. The slogan should be "Save the coal, don't mine it!"

Agriculture is another big recipient of subsidies. Until EU enlargement recently forced through a change of policy, these subsidies created awkward economic incentives. By offering guaranteed prices, in a figurative sense the EU created mountains of butter and milk-filled lakes that were only reduced when, in 2005, price guarantees were partially replaced by direct income supports that are independent of output. The direct and indirect subsidies that EU farmers enjoyed by way of receiving government funds and being able to charge above world-market prices accounted for one-third of their income.[26] Clever Dutch entrepreneurs bought agricultural land in East Germany only to let it lie fallow and cash in on EU acreage reduction premia. Pigs were carted all over Europe from their birthplaces to the slaughterhouses simply because the EU subsidized the transportation cost.

Policies like import tariffs and quotas long protected European farmers from foreign competition, drove up prices above the world market level, induced farmers to expand production and forced public storage agencies to spend tax revenues buying up the surpluses only to then destroy them.

The list of state-produced nonsense in agriculture was long. All of it served to support the incomes of the farmers and to safeguard the wealth of agricultural land owners. This was not only hugely expensive and a burden on the taxpayer; what was even worse was that intensive agriculture destroyed the natural environment and tariff barriers closed off the markets to products from developing countries.

In 2002 and 2003, the prices of sugar, veal, and beef in the EU were about three times the prices on world markets. Pork cost 31 percent more and poultry 56 percent more. Milk was 85 percent more expensive.[27] The incomes of the poorer population groups were supported with tax money and, through a complicated web of taxes and agricultural subsidies, much of this additional income was funneled into the pockets of the farmers and land owners.

Fortunately, EU eastern enlargement has put a stop to some of this nonsense insofar as it enforced the abolishment of the system of price controls and induced the EU Commission to replace output related payments with lump sum payments supporting agriculture as such. The old system of price supports would have become prohibitively expensive if all Eastern European farmers and agricultural cooperatives were included in this program. Poland's accession alone doubled the number of EU agricultural workers, and the Polish agricultural sector would have been likely to grow further with EU support. However, while the new system will have the effect of lowering prices, it will not change the fact that much too great a part of the East European labor force will remain in agriculture as public funds do continue to flow to agriculture.

Germany Wins the World Cup for Marginal Tax Burden

The German government will not be able to afford these kinds of subsidies in the future. It will neither be able to fulfill the wishes of the subsidy recipients nor will it be able to meet the demands of an increasing number of welfare recipients. The tax screw cannot be tightened further, and the public debt is already above the limit set by the Maastricht Treaty.

A comparison of marginal tax rates on the value added produced by average workers of various countries shows that additional tax increases in Germany are hardly possible. On the contrary, a dramatic tax reduction is necessary to get the fiscal drag of the tax system under control. The marginal tax burden is the percentage of the value added resulting from an additional unit of labor input of a worker that must be paid to the state in the form of taxes and contributions. It is this marginal tax burden that causes the fiscal drag rather than the average burden that represents the percentage of the worker's total value added that must be paid to the state. A progressive tax system always has a marginal tax burden that is higher than the average tax burden.

In order to clarify what is meant here, let us suppose that a customer asks a painter to paper and paint a room. The painter's employee, who already has enough to do, accepts the job on the condition that he is paid for the additional hours of work. After the work is done, the bill is presented to the customer. Besides the paint, the wallpaper, the brushes, the transport costs, and a contribution margin for other materials used, the bill amounts to 1,000 euros (including the value-added tax) for labor. These 1,000 euros are the value added by the additional labor for painting and papering the room. The question is how much of the additional value added can be paid to the employee after taxes and contributions and how much goes to the state. The latter, in percentage terms, is the marginal tax burden on the worker's value added.

Figure 6.6 shows the calculations for various countries. The columns present the marginal tax burden, and the sections show how the marginal tax burden is composed of the personal income tax, the employee (EE) social security contributions, the employer (ER) social security contributions, and the value-added tax or related taxes on the sales of the painter's firm. The calculations refer to a standardized employee as defined by the OECD for its purposes. The employee receives the average wage income of a typical manufacturing worker in each country, has two children and is married to a spouse who earns an additional one-third.

At a marginal tax burden of 65.2 percent, Germany is at the top, followed by Sweden, at a marginal tax burden of 59.1 percent. There is probably no other country where the marginal tax burden imposed on the average employee is as high as in Germany.[28] While the complicated calculations have been done only for a limited number of countries, these include the usual suspects, the Scandinavian countries in particular. But even Sweden and Denmark do not reach the German level. At the low end are the United States and the

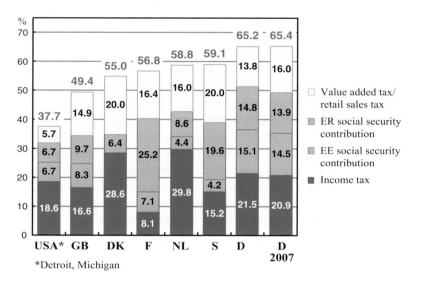

Figure 6.6
Marginal tax burden of labor, 2005, in percent of value added, for family with one full-time earner, one earning 33% of average earnings, and two children. Sources: OECD, Taxing Wages, 2004–2005; Ifo Institute calculations; Germany 2007: Ifo forecast.

United Kingdom, with marginal rates of below 40 percent and 50 percent, respectively.

Of the 1,000 euros of value added (i.e., of the labor costs paid by the customer), 652 euros went to the German state in 2005, given the assumed constellation of family status and income. Only 348 euros were pocketed by the employee. This is a rather small amount for which it hardly pays to work, and the 1,000 euros to be paid by the customer are an exorbitantly high amount for which it hardly pays to have a room renovated.

It is clear, then, that the next room will be painted in the evenings and during the weekends. It is little wonder that the amount of moonlighting has increased during the past few decades, leveling off slightly only recently.[29] Value added produced in the German underground economy is estimated at 15 percent of the officially measured GDP. At this level, Germany occupies a middle position in Europe, but it is no longer the shining example that it used to be in this respect.

And if the employee is unwilling to work in the underground economy for fear of incurring the wrath of his customer, the customer may go to a hardware megastore, buy paint and brushes, and do the job himself. It may take three times as long for him to do the job as it would take a professional, but the saving may still be substantial. This is not to criticize hardware megastores. However, much of their success stems from the overdrawn tax system that undermines the division of labor and distorts economic activities.

As has been mentioned, Germany passed another tax reform in early 2006. Effective January 1, 2007, the value-added tax will be increased by 3 percentage points, and both employers' and employees' contributions to unemployment insurance will be cut by one percentage point. Merkel's government sold this increase to the public as a measure to mobilize the labor market by reducing non-wage labor costs. The last column in figure 6.6 shows how this will affect the calculations. The marginal tax rate will not be reduced. Instead of 65.2 percent, it will now be 65.4 percent. Because the customer will hardly care about the labels the government attaches to the various levies contained in the painter's bill, the labor-market mobilization that is the ostensible reason for this increase is hard to imagine. Because the value-added tax (levied according to the "destination principle") does not apply to exports, there will only be a positive effect on companies that sell their products internationally. For these firms, however, labor costs per hour, which were 27.60 euros for a manufacturing worker in 2004 (see chapter 2), will decline to 27.35 euros. This does not sound like the radical reform that will get the German labor market going either.

It must be emphasized again that the calculations presented in figure 6.6 refer not to the average tax burden on the workers' value added but to the marginal tax burden that alone is responsible for the economic disincentives in the labor market. The high marginal tax burden does not necessarily imply a high average tax burden. Because of Germany's large tax brackets protecting low-income people, it does, however, signal a highly progressive income tax—that is, a sharp increase in the average tax burden as taxable income rises.[30]

The highly progressive nature of the German tax system is also revealed by the findings of a study conducted by the Cologne Institute for Business Research. According to this study, more than two-thirds of German income taxes are paid by only 20 percent of the taxpayers, whereas the lower half of the population pays just 8 percent of the tax and the lowest 40 percent pay nothing.[31]

Germans must decide which mix of economic liberalism and communism they want their tax system to reflect. The argument for a progressive tax system is based on improved insurance protection implicitly provided by the state with its system of taxes and contributions: The fortunate ones may not be able to climb very high, but at least the unfortunate do not fall too far down. On the other side of the coin are the deterioration of work incentives and the ensuing erosion of the formal labor market and the increase of unproductive energies spent on tax evasion. In view of the visible dominance of these problems, the judgment is clear that Germany has moved too far in the direction of excessive taxation and welfare spending.

Are Wealth Taxes Just?

The international comparison in particular suggests that the German tax system is too progressive. The marginal tax burden on labor income is much too high to be compatible with a functioning market economy. If an ordinary manufacturing worker bears a marginal tax burden of two-thirds, something must be wrong with the system.

But the welfare state does need the money. A knee-jerk reaction to the high tax rates on labor income is to shift the tax burden to capital income and wealth. Unions, in particular, argue for this, playing Robin Hood. As long as there are people who possess some wealth, they say, the society cannot have financing problems; it just has to take the money from those who have it. Frank Bsirske, the leader of Germany's biggest union, Verdi, does not even shy away from pillorying individual rich people by name, arguing that unions do not have to exercise wage restraint in order to save these citizens from paying higher taxes.[32] Though such arguments find much support among an envious German public, the unions are wrong in arguing for a wealth tax, both with respect to equity considerations and with respect to the true interests of labor.

With respect to equity, they are wrong because they overlook the fact that wealth is always accumulated by saving (i.e., non-consumption.) Savings derive from income that has already been taxed. Taxes on capital income and wealth violate the postulate of "horizontal equity." Two people receiving the same amount of labor income but having different consumption preferences ought to be taxed in such a way that the amount of their consumption shrinks by the same percentage regardless of what goods they want to consume. If someone consumes his income as apples, he should sacrifice the same percentage of apples as the pear eater has to sacrifice of pears, provided that both consumers have the same labor income to spend.

If interest income or wealth is taxed, this postulate of horizontal equity is violated, since those who save their net income will have to give up a higher percentage of their future consumption than those who consume right away. To see why this is the case, assume that the income tax is 50 percent and that the interest rate is 6 percent. Those who want to consume their income today must give up 50 percent of their consumption. Those who want to consume their income later must give up half of their savings but must also give up half of their interest income and half of the interest earned on reinvested interest income. Thus, the percentage of their consumption that the government forces them to sacrifice is higher the later they want to consume their initial labor income. Because of compound interest, the sacrifice is very large under realistic conditions. Suppose the individual wage earner is 30 years old and wants to save some of his income for retirement consumption at the age of 80. It can be shown that, in this case, the amount of consumption that the individual could have afforded absent the state shrinks by not just 50 percent (as it would with immediate consumption) but by 88 percent, which is a blunt violation of the principle of horizontal equity. Taking a higher percentage of the apple eater's consumption away than of a pear eater's, as apples are cheaper per pound than pears, would be the same thing.

Note that, in the example chosen, at an interest rate of 6 percent, a 3 percent wealth tax would be fully equivalent to an income tax of 50 percent on interest earned. Wealth taxes, too, are special taxes on those who prefer to consume later rather than sooner.

Of course, wealth does not always originate from labor income as was assumed in the example. One can gain wealth by striking unexpectedly good deals, by making monopoly profits, by enjoying windfall profits from urban zoning decisions, or by benefiting from a purely speculative rise in the value of stocks and other assets. It is possible to make an argument for a tax on such sources of wealth, provided the normal interest on one's invested capital is exempted. But this is not an argument in favor of the taxation of interest income or the general taxation of wealth. If the principle of horizontal equity is accepted, then those who own such sources of income should also be subjected to the same shrinkage of their consumption as wage earners regardless of the time of consumption, which precludes the taxation of interest earnings and wealth. Taxing the source of wealth is compatible with horizontal equity, but not the taxation of the wealth itself or of the normal interest earned on this wealth.

As an alternative to taxation of the sources of income, a consumption tax would also comply with the principle of horizontal equity. If the original income were tax exempt and the consumption tax were levied at the same rate in all time periods, the quantity of consumption would be reduced by the same percentage, regardless of when consumption took place. Such a consumption tax need not be invented; it already exists in the form of the value-added tax. The necessary tax reductions in Germany should therefore affect the value-added tax last, which of course does not imply that Germany should, as it has just done, increase this tax.

Why Capital Cannot Really Be Taxed

More important even than equity is the workers' own true self-interest. At first glance, it seems in the interest of employees that employers (capitalists) be fleeced. With the tax money received by the state, tasks could be financed that would otherwise have to be funded by social security contributions or other levies on employees, or the money could be directly handed over to the employees. But this would be naive, as it disregards the negative repercussions on workers of the evasive maneuvers of those taxed. The evasive reactions are by no means harmless. They touch upon the fundamental functions of the market economy. The unions are forgetting that the productivity gains that made past wage increases possible may be primarily traced to the growth of capital inputs extending labor's leverage factor and improving technology. Today's workers do not earn more than their fathers and grandfathers because they are more industrious. They earn more because they work with better and more expensive machinery, which has been financed by savings and wealth. If there are no savings, and if wealth is invested in other countries, there will be no more productivity gains to be had. Unions can try, but will fail, to extract from German business the wage increases to which they have become accustomed.

Indeed, there is a considerable risk that, with a high tax burden on wealth and investment income, the capital from which the workers derive their income will no longer be available. First, savings will fall; second, stocks of assets will be shifted abroad.

Germany's demographic pressures promise to place a large enough financial burden on wealth owners as it is. In this situation, the labor union's efforts to pillory the rich could have fatal effects. If people point their fingers and the wealthy live in fear of being stripped of their assets to finance future public deficits, who will make the effort of accumulating wealth on which to live in old age?

Potential capital flight is an even bigger problem. If the tax screws are tightened, more and more wealth owners will leave Germany, or at least send their capital abroad. Many countries accept tax fugitives with open arms. Switzerland has benefited from German tax policy for decades. Two-thirds of the assets invested by Germans abroad are held in Switzerland, and it is estimated that 85 percent of the earnings on these assets are no longer taxed in Germany. Switzerland even offers tax fugitives from Germany and elsewhere the opportunity to settle there with their assets and to pay a freely negotiated flat tax instead of the Swiss income tax (a flat tax that, in most cases, amounts to just one-tenth of what the Swiss themselves must pay).

Switzerland is not alone. Tax paradises, including the Cayman Islands, Guernsey, the Bahamas, and Liechtenstein, abound. Even EU member countries are playing the game. Ireland taxes business profits at a corporate tax rate of only 12.5 percent, and Lithuania, which joined the EU in May 2004, has announced that it wants to copy the Irish model. Estonia, now also a member of the EU, charges no corporate tax at all on retained earnings. The Netherlands and Belgium have special rules for financial institutions and are happy to tax only a minimal base rather than the true capital income these institutions earn in their countries. Even Denmark, Finland, Norway, and Sweden have introduced low taxes on capital income in order to attract financial assets from other countries or to prevent the emigration of their own capital. Austria is doing likewise and has become a popular destination for flight capital. All these countries have given up the principle of the so-called synthetic income tax, according to which all sources of income are combined and subjected to the same tax rate. Similar to Germany, they levy a progressive income tax on labor income, but they levy on interest income only a low flat tax, ranging from 25 percent (Austria) to 30 percent (Sweden).[33]

In view of these circumstances, it would be sheer folly for German workers to plead for extension of the policy of taxing the very wealthy. Workers would only hurt themselves by accelerating the flight of the very capital that makes their high productivity and their high wages possible. These are not theoretical considerations; this is the bitter truth in a country that has been suffering from stagnation, increasing unemployment, and huge capital exports. As was shown in chapter 1, Germany's current net capital export is about twice as large as domestic net investment—a huge deviation from normality.

When the state increases the taxes on capital, it initially reduces the net rate of return on capital and thereby causes capital flight. The result is that the capital remaining in the country becomes scarcer and therefore can earn an ever-higher gross rate of return at the expense of wages. Wage rates will come under pressure because there will be fewer firms demanding labor. If wages do not fall initially, because unions or the wage-replacement benefits of the welfare state prevent it, capital flight will continue unchecked. The result will be mass unemployment culminating in a collapse of the economy. If, however, wages decline, or grow more slowly, there will be less unemployment, because the remaining firms will choose more labor-intensive production processes and because fewer firms will leave the country. The firms' relocation will come to an early standstill because, from the point of view of the owners of capital, the lower wages offset the higher taxes at home. The gross rate of return earned by capital in the home country would then be sufficiently high, despite the taxes, so that the net rate of return can keep up with the rest of the world. But then a larger share of investment income will be earned abroad, beyond the reach of German tax authorities, and labor incomes are low.

The wealth owners are only burdened by the additional taxes on wealth and investment income during the transition to the new equilibrium. After wages have fallen, they no longer face any real disadvantages because they earn a net rate of return on all assets that is determined in world financial markets. The local taxes on wealth and investment income do not affect them, but they affect the workers of the country levying the taxes. The wealth owners pay the taxes, but they can shift all of the tax burden to the workers and other income recipients who cannot easily escape by leaving the country.

For an individual country, it does not make sense to levy taxes on investment income except for taxes that merely cover the cost of using the public infrastructure. From the perspective of national economic efficiency, it is always wise to keep capital in the country up to the point where the last available unit of it earns as much gross income net of infrastructure costs as this unit of capital could earn abroad after foreign taxes. This condition can only be met if capital is not asked to contribute to the financing of the state budget in excess of the infrastructure benefits it receives. The attempt to demand taxes over and above this drives out too much capital and leads to an equilibrium in which the gross rate of return on the remaining capital net of its infrastructure cost would exceed the rate of return, net of foreign taxes, which could be earned in world markets. Pulling some of the capital back home by lowering domestic taxes would, at home, generate more income earned by the state, workers, and domestic wealth owners combined than would be lost by domestic wealth owners abroad.[34]

But couldn't higher taxes on capital still be better for the workers themselves? After all, the government would have extra revenues that it could distribute to the general public. The slogan could be "It is better to get a large piece of a small pie than a small piece of a large pie!" But if the pie (i.e., the sum of all national incomes, including those that domestic wealth owners earn abroad) becomes smaller as a result of tax-induced capital flight, the very portion accruing to the workers will also become smaller. Why? Because the government budget must be balanced, and capital owners will again receive a fixed net rate of return on all of their capital, including that invested at home, determined by the international financial markets. Thus, logically, only labor can bear the burden of having a smaller pie. Even if the state were to distribute all of its tax receipts from charging capital more than the infrastructure cost to the workers, the money would not suffice to compensate them for the falling wage incomes. Workers would suffer net losses.

It must be reemphasized that this result does not mean that mobile capital cannot be taxed at all. Taxes as prices for the use of the infrastructure are both feasible and reasonable. Only taxes that contribute to the financing of the general government budget, as demanded by the unions, should not be levied. Labor would only hurt itself. This statement must be qualified. It refers only to the taxation of new capital, i.e., net investment and replacement investment. To the extent that income taxes are levied on the profits on previous investments, whose location is already determined and cannot be changed, things are different. Indeed, some of the wealth trapped in a country can be expropriated.[35] However, it would obviously be short-sighted to choose a tax system that eliminates new investment simply because it generates some revenue from taxing old investment. Switzerland, Austria, Ireland, Switzerland, and the Scandinavian countries have understood this well and have implemented it in their policies. They know that it is in the interest of labor to pamper the capitalists with low taxes on investment income instead of scaring them off. They are betting that the indirect gains via a revival of the entire economy will more than offset the revenue losses of the state, and evidence supports their assessment. Sometimes it seems that only Germans fail to understand this.

Tax Reform 2000: A Step in the Right Direction

One must give credit to the Schröder government for having stayed its course. With the 2000 tax reform, it took an important step in the right direction by cutting the corporate tax rate (the tax on retained earnings of corporate firms) from 40 percent to 25 percent. The total tax burden on retained earnings from the corporation tax, the solidarity surcharge, and the trade tax, which had been very high by international standards, was thereby reduced from 51.8 percent to 38.6 percent, assuming a typical municipal loading factor of 400 percent for the trade tax. In this respect, Germany now holds a middle position among the OECD countries. (The data are summarized in table 6.1.)

The tax relief on distributed corporate earnings is small, however, for distributed earnings will now not only be subject to the corporate tax and the trade tax, but also to half of the personal income tax of the shareholders. The latter is called the "half-earnings procedure." For a shareholder at the top of the income tax progression this means that the tax burden on distributed profits has declined from 61.5 percent to 52.2 percent after the last stage of the tax reform. The comparatively small relief on distributed profits is justified insofar as taxes on dividends do not discriminate against investment as long as debt or retained earnings are the marginal source of finance, and these sources indeed represent the lion's share of corporate financing.[36] However, dividend taxes discriminate against new share issues and thus against the foundation and expansion of new firms.

Taxes on labor income have also been reduced. The top rate on labor income of the wage tax and the solidarity surcharge was reduced from 55.9 percent to 44.3 percent in steps. Not counted here are the voluminous social security contributions that are not considered as taxes.

Unincorporated firms have also enjoyed tax cuts, but the tax level is still rather high. For the owner of such a firm, who has arrived in the upper range of progressive income taxation, the burden of income tax, solidarity surcharge, and trade tax has fallen from 54.5 percent (1998) to 45.7 percent. This is a high level by international standards. As owner-managed firms still dominate the German labor market, this is still a major concern.

No doubt, the Schröder government's 2000 tax reform has made some contribution to the restoration of Germany's tax competitiveness. However, despite this reform, the tax system is not yet in a satisfactory state. Neither a government share of net domestic income of nearly 55 percent, nor a profit tax of nearly 46 percent for most firms, nor the world championship in terms of a marginal tax rate of two-thirds of the value added of an average worker is compatible with a well-functioning market economy. Germany needs an even more courageous reform.

Any such reform would also have to simplify the tax system. The many special rules and exceptions that have been added to the system over time make it virtually impossible for a normal person to file his tax forms by himself. If he does so without consulting a tax advisor, he can be sure he is overpaying. That need not be. Other countries have simpler tax systems. In Canada, the local tax office tells you how much tax you must pay, and this is almost non-negotiable. Moreover, because only very few exemptions exist, filing a tax return is easy.

From an economic standpoint, only interest earnings should be given special treatment. From the point of view of equity and efficiency, it makes little sense to tax them exactly like original sources of income. Interest earnings can only be taxed to the extent that the tax covers the cost of the infrastructure used by capital. How might such a reform look?

A Dual Income Tax for Germany

The idea that Germany needs a new income tax to make the country more attractive for international investment is widely accepted, and thus the current

German government announced that it will carry out a major tax reform in 2008. Among the candidates for a reformed system of income taxation is the "dual income tax" of the Nordic type. Such a tax has been proposed by the German Council of Economic Advisors; a bit earlier, it was presented in the first edition of this book as the proposal of the Ifo Institute for Economic Research.[37]

The advantage of the dual income tax is that it simultaneously satisfies the requirements of horizontal equity, simplicity, and provision of better investment incentives. The basic idea is that interest earnings are not taxed like labor income but have a tax burden of only 20 percent. The tax on labor income and other source income is higher, following a step scale with different but fixed marginal tax rates (as in the United States).[38] The tax relief for interest income includes imputed interest on a company's equity capital, which is also taxed at the rate of 20 percent. Only earnings above this imputed interest income are taxed at a higher rate. Interest to be paid on company debt remains deductible.[39] This ensures financial neutrality for the firms.

There would be only four tax rates for source income: 0, 15 percent, 25 percent, and 35 percent. In figure 6.7 the tax scale is depicted in comparison to Germany's current tax system. The first bracket, in which no tax is levied, goes up to a basic exemption of 7,500 euros (9,330 dollars); the second bracket, with a marginal tax rate of 15 percent, goes up to an income of 17,500 euros (21,770 dollars); the third bracket, with a marginal tax rate of 25 percent, ends at an income of 35,000 euros (43,540 dollars); above this, the marginal tax rate is a uniform 35 percent. The solidarity surcharge may be deducted from the total tax due, similarly to the trade tax on business, and thus is already contained in the tax rate.

The proposed tax scale will substantially benefit employees and, in conjunction with Activating Social Assistance, will help reduce moonlighting. The average industrial worker, with two children and with a spouse who adds another third to family income, will now be subject to a marginal tax burden on his value added of 61.4 percent instead of the current 65.4 percent, which is close to the marginal tax rate in the Netherlands and Sweden.

One advantage of this proposal is the simplicity of the tax scale. Everyone can remember the margins and the tax brackets and can compute the taxes that must be paid. Exceptions are broadly abolished. Tax consultants would have to start worrying about their livelihoods.

The simplicity also extends to business taxation. A corporate tax of 25 percent and a trade tax of 10 percent would be levied on the retained earnings of corporations in excess of the normal return to equity, yielding a total tax burden of 35 percent. The profit in excess of the normal return to equity of

Marginal tax including wage tax and solidarity surcharge

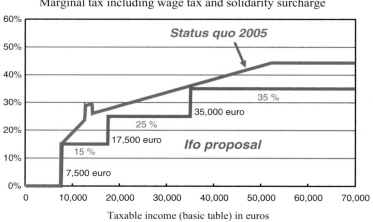

Taxable income (basic table) in euros

Burden of wage tax and solidarity surcharge

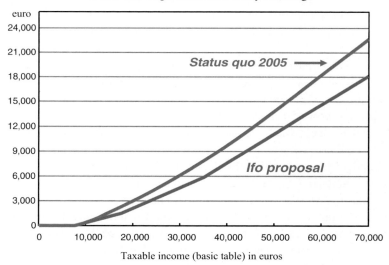

Taxable income (basic table) in euros

Figure 6.7
The Ifo Institute's proposal. Sources: Ministry of Finance; Ifo Institute calculations.

Table 6.1
The Ifo proposal compared with the status quo as of 2005. All tax rates include solidarity surcharge. Trade tax is based on a factor of 400 percent. Income tax is always for the top stage of the progression.

	Status quo	Ifo proposal
Corporations		
Retained earnings	39%	35%
Distributed earnings	52%	46%
Unincorporated businesses	46%	35%
Wage income	44%	35%
Actual and imputed interest on equity and debt capital	39–46%	20%

unincorporated firms would be subject to the personal income tax. Although they also pay a trade tax to the local communities, this tax is deductible from the income tax due and is therefore irrelevant for the taxpayer. If the owner of the firm earns more than 35,000 euros (43,540 dollars), his marginal income tax rate would also be 35 percent.

In this way, the differentiated treatment of retained earnings of unincorporated businesses and corporations would be eliminated. For corporations that presently pay 38.6 percent, the tax relief is somewhat more modest than for unincorporated firms which currently pay 45.7 percent. Table 6.1 compares the Ifo Institute's reform proposal with the tax rules that have applied since 2005.

The "half earnings procedure" is also retained in the Ifo proposal, albeit at lower rates. Accordingly, the marginal tax rate on distributed profits would amount to 46 percent or about 6 percentage points less than today. The corporate tax would account for 25 percentage points of this marginal tax burden, the trade tax for 10 percentage points, and the personal income tax for 11 percentage points.

Roughly speaking, the Ifo tax would reduce the state's revenues by about 32 billion euros (40 billion dollars) and could thus cut the government share of GDP from today's 46.7 percent to 45.3 percent. That percentage was last reached in Germany at the end of the 1980s. It would be low by European standards, though still high in comparison to the United States or Japan. Yet the tax reform could herald a new environment in Germany—an environment of less government, more private initiative, and more economic growth.

to Konrad Adenauer, Germany's first postwar chancellor, who believed that people would have children no matter what

7 The Birth Dearth

Why Is the German Population Aging So Dramatically?

Up to 2005, Federal Republic of Germany found itself in one of the biggest economic crises of its history, but even this crisis looks harmless relative to the creeping stagnation expected in the coming decades as a result of demographic problems. The share of old people in the population will increase sharply in the next 30 years, and the average age of Germans will rise substantially. The consequences of this population shift for Germany's innovativeness and vitality can be easily predicted. The country that made such momentous contributions, good and bad, to human development is now facing the ravages of old age, losing dynamism and vitality. A similar development is taking place in most advanced nations. Population aging is evident in all developed countries. Only the populations of developing and newly industrializing countries in Africa, Asia, and Latin America are staying young. But the problem of aging is affecting Germany more strongly than most other OECD countries. At 42.1 years, the median age in Germany (the age that separates the population into an older and a younger group of equal size) is already very high and higher than in France, at 39.3 years, or the United States, at 36.1 years.[1] And it will continue to rise in coming years.

Figure 7.1 looks ahead to what the future might hold for Germany, showing the results of the most recent projections of the UN Population Division for the year 2020. At 46.9 years, the German population is projected to have the third-highest median age in the world which means that there will be only two countries, Italy and Japan, where the division in the older half of the population begins at a higher age. On average, at that time the median age of the EU population will only be 44.7 years.[2] Remarkably low are the figures for the

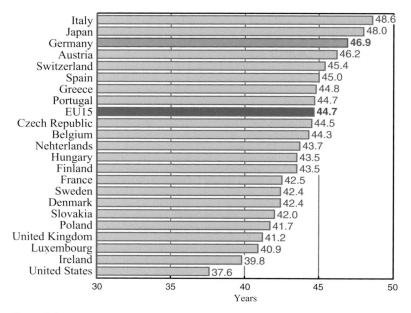

Figure 7.1
Median age in 2020. Source: UN, World Population Prospects, 2004 Revision, Highlights.

United States (37.6 years), Ireland (39.8 years), and the United Kingdom (41.2 years). The new EU countries in Eastern Europe also will have a markedly younger population than Germany.

Why will the Germans be so old? Do they live longer than others? Do they live healthier lives, have a more robust constitution or enjoy access to better physicians and hospitals? Such flattering suppositions are occasionally spread by politicians, but unfortunately these miss the point.

To be sure, German life expectancy keeps rising. Every six years it increases by a year. "Every six years the Germans become one year older," one could say, tongue in cheek. But that is not the reason for the fast rise in median age. Among all advanced nations, life expectancy is also rising, and whether it actually will rise faster in Germany is hard to predict. To be sure, at present German life expectancy is not higher, but lower than that of most comparable countries. As figure 7.2 shows, Germany ranks way below the average of the old EU countries, though significantly above the United States. Japan, Switzerland, Sweden, Spain, France, Italy, and many other countries have a higher life expectancy than Germany. The relatively large share of the foreign-born population that comes from countries with even lower life expectancies and the German diet, which is replete with good beer and rich sausages, rank

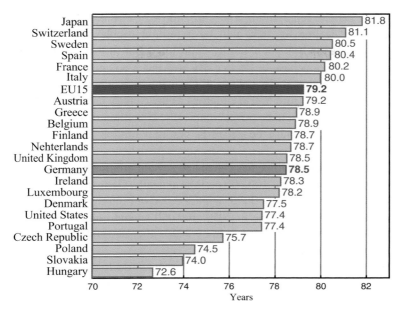

Figure 7.2
Life expectancy at birth in 2004. Source: World Bank, World Development Indicators database, May 2006.

high among the possible explanations. But neither suffices as the main reason for the high and rising median age of the German population? The truth is more fundamental.

A Country without Children

The real reason for the comparably high median age of Germans is not a high life expectancy but the small number of births. The lower the birth rates, the smaller is the share of young people in the population and, consequently, the higher is the median age. A rapidly growing population has many children and a low median age, whereas a shrinking population has few children and a high median age.

Germany belongs to the second category. Today, 82.5 million people live in Germany, including 15.3 million people with an immigrant background (immigrants and children of immigrants), 7.3 million of whom are foreigners.[3] The latest forecast of the Federal Statistical Office indicates that by 2050 the current population of 82.5 million people, including their children yet to be born, but excluding new immigrants and their potential children, will shrink

to 62 million people, representing a loss of almost 21 million.[4] The foreseeable population decline by 2050 will be 5 million people more than the
increase in population brought about by unification. But further immigration
will compensate for much of the decline. By how much no one knows, as this
will depend on the course set by politics. If Germany opens the gates, as many
people will come from Third World countries as the country decides to admit.
If the population decline is to be offset completely, 20 million new immigrants
including their children must be added to the 15.3 million that are in the
country already.

The Federal Statistical Office has calculated several arbitrarily chosen scenarios. If net immigration was 100,000 persons annually, Germany would have
about 68 million inhabitants in 2050; with 200,000 net immigrants per year,
it would have 75 million people in 2050. 100,000 annual immigrants translates into 6–7 million additional people by 2050, after accounting for births
and deaths within this group of immigrants.

The lack of children being born and the consequent decline of the present
resident population in Germany is a fact that must be considered, whatever
one's assessment of possible future immigration. Based on the circumstances
of 2004, 100 German women can be expected to bear only 137 children.[5]
Hence, the fertility rate in terms of average number of children per woman is
1.37.[6] This is very low. The fertility rate would have to be 2.08 to keep the
population constant. Two hundred children born per 100 women would suffice
if as many boys were born as girls and if the girls never died before having
children of their own. If account is taken of the natural mortality of girls until
they reach child-bearing age (about 1 percent) and the fact that 7 percent more
boys are born than girls, then it follows that 208 children per 100 women are
needed to maintain the population. This number guarantees that exactly 100
girls reach child-bearing age and that the population is maintained. Taking the
maintenance of the population as the point of reference for a natural number
of children, 71 children would have to be added to the 137 currently borne by
100 German women.

Although this phenomenon affects all developed countries, Germany is, in
a sense, more adversely affected than any other developed country in the
world. Figure 7.3 presents an international comparison of birth figures, using
two different fertility measures. One is the fertility rate as defined above, the
other the birth rate given in the number of children born per 1,000 inhabitants.
It can be readily seen that the two measures yield rather different results. In
terms of the fertility rate, depicted on the left-hand scale, with a value of 1.37
Germany ranks among the lower range of countries, but not at the bottom. The
fertility rates for Italy, Spain, and, in particular, the East European countries

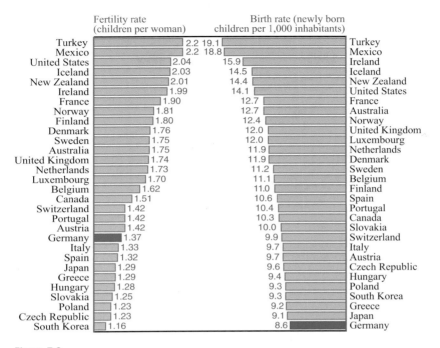

Figure 7.3
Fertility and birth rates in OECD countries in 2004. The fertility rate of a particular year is defined as the average number of births per woman, assuming age-specific fertility rates of this year stay unchanged throughout the life of a woman. The birth rate of a year is defined as the number of live births ocurring during this year per 1,000 inhabitants. Sources: World Bank Group, World Development Indicators database, 2006.

are lower, although the differences are tiny. Most countries with lower fertility rates than Germany's have birth rates in the neighborhood of 1.2 to 1.3, about 0.8 points behind the United States (which, with a value of 2.04, boasts just about enough births to preserve the size of its population). Only South Korea lags behind, with a value of just 1.16. Nine OECD countries have lower fertility rates than Germany. The surprising result is shown on the right-hand scale. In terms of births per thousand inhabitants, Germany, at 8.6, clearly ranks lowest among OECD countries. It even lies behind Spain, Italy, the Czech Republic, South Korea, and Japan, all of which have much lower figures than the United States, whose 14.1 birth rate reflects a stable population.

Why do both rankings differ so much from each other? The explanation lies in the timing of the decline in fertility rates. In Germany, this decline started much earlier than in other countries. As can be seen in figure 7.4, the

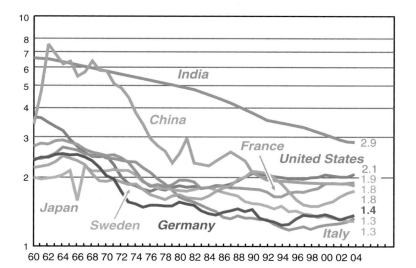

Figure 7.4
Number of children per woman. Source: World Bank, World Development Indicators database, May 2006.

Japanese or Italian fertility rates, for example, declined about 6–10 years later than the German ones. As a result, the generation of potential parents nowadays is smaller in Germany than elsewhere. There are about 40 percent fewer people in the age group around 30 than in the group around 40. (See figure 7.6.) Germany suffers from two simultaneous problems: it has a relatively low fertility rate, though not the lowest, and it has a very small number of people in their reproductive years. The two problems reinforce each other, putting the country at the bottom of the developed world in terms of births per thousand inhabitants.[7]

If death rates are subtracted from birth rates, the native population's own growth rate can be calculated. By this measure, which does not count immigrants, Germany is also at the bottom of the developed world. Germans are currently dwindling faster than any other people in the developed world.

Figure 7.4 shows that most countries have experienced a decline in fertility rates during the past few decades. The Chinese rates started to decline some 20 years later than the German ones, and even the Indian rates have been coming down. Some countries, however, notably the United States and France, have been able to check the downward trend. As will be discussed below, the French successes are largely due to an active population policy it has administered for more than a century.

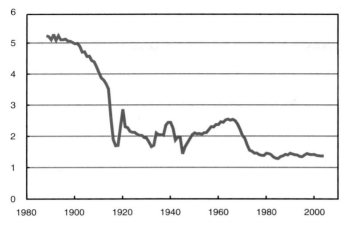

Figure 7.5
Number of children per woman in Germany since 1888. Sources: Institut Für Bevölkerung und Sozialpolitik (IBS), Bielefeld 2000; Statistisches Bundesamt, Fachserie 1, Reihe 1 1999, Fachserie 1, Reihe 1 2000–2003, 2004; press release, March 17, 2006.

Germany's current low birth rates are remarkable insofar as by the mid 1800s Germany had the third-highest birth rate among the world's leading economies.[8] The nineteenth century was a period in which the size of the German population virtually exploded. As was explained in chapter 3, one of the reasons was the liberation of the agricultural workers from peasant bondage and gaining the freedom to marry. The increase in the number of new families was followed by a corresponding rise in the fertility rate. German excess births induced mass emigration to the United States, making Americans of German descent, at one-seventh of the population, the largest population group there today, even ahead of those Americans claiming British ancestry.[9] Yet this robust population growth has been relegated to the past. In 150 years, Germany has moved from one extreme to the other in the international ranking of birth rates.

As figure 7.5 shows, in 1900 an average German woman still bore about five children, a rate that leads to more than a doubling of the population within one generation. Since some women had no children at that time, the number of children in some families had to be very high to reach this average. The grandparents or great grandparents of today's Germans often had ten siblings or more.

In the past, children were considered a sign of prosperity. Everyone strived to form a family, and those who had children, or more children, had to worry less about surviving during their old age in an era before the social safety net provided by the welfare state. Today, in contrast, children have become a nuisance in Germany. They cost money, limit consumption and downgrade lifestyles. Being single is becoming the normal state and loose partnerships a substitute for marriage. If a couple marries, starting a family is usually postponed. The first child tends to be born when the mother is about thirty, and often he or she remains an only child. The DINK (dual income, no kids) family is even more popular, and has become the slogan for an increasing number of young couples: with two incomes and no children life is better than with one income and three children.

How dramatic the changing German demographic trend has been is illustrated by comparing the age pyramid of 1875 with that of 2000, as depicted in figure 7.6. The age pyramid represents the number of people in various age groups, separated into men and women, for a given year. Natural mortality makes the number of people in an age group decline with rising age, such that the age pyramid narrows toward the top. Instead of a pyramid, however, mortality with replacement births generates a beehive shape. A pyramid shape such as that shown for Germany in 1875 results from population growth.[10] The higher the population growth, the larger is the fraction of young people in the population and the broader therefore the lower part of the pyramid.

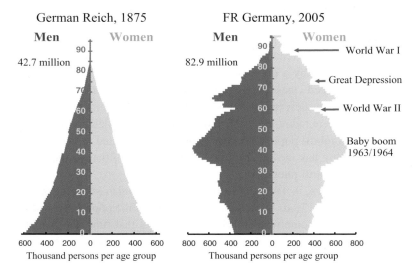

Figure 7.6
The German age pyramid at the time of Bismarck (1875) and today. Sources: Statistisches Bundesamt, 2006, Kaiserliches Statistisches Amt, Statistisches Jahrbuch für das Deutsche Reich, 1878.

Figure 7.6 shows that the 1875 pyramid has since morphed into an odd-shaped Christmas tree or a bush, whose thicker middle branches represent an age around 40. 1964 was the year Germany had the highest number of births in its history. The bad postwar times had been overcome and the pre-war cohorts, which had sprung from the Baby Boom of the 1930s, were now themselves having children. By 2004, those children were already 40 years old.

In the following years, from the middle of the 1960s to the middle of the 1970s, the birth rates declined dramatically as a result of the birth-control pill and the smaller number of potential parents due to the decline in births during World War II. As was mentioned above, the size of the population cohorts in the range of up to 30 years of age is about 40 percent lower than that of the Baby Boom cohorts.

Figure 7.6 clearly shows the consequences of the two world wars and the Great Depression on Germany's population growth. The dents around 88, 73, and 60 years of age are due to these events which resulted in declining births.

The area of the pyramid corresponds to the size of the population. Germany's present population is much larger than it was in 1875. Today Germany has a population of 82.5 million, whereas in 1875 it had only 43 million. Yet today the number of one-year-old babies is more than one-third lower than it was then even though one-third of these babies have immigrant parents, and the declining trend is continuing.[11] The 1875 pyramid is characterized by a growing, dynamic people that was moving to the top in economic terms. In contrast, the 2005 Christmas tree, with its bulbous middle, characterizes a saturated, listless society that is also falling behind in the global race for economic growth.

The Road to Gerontocracy

What will Germany be like when the German population is markedly older than it is now? The demand for cakes, decaffeinated coffee and wellness spas will boom, while the producers of baby food, diapers and baby carriages will be laying off workers. Sales of Benetton and McDonald's will shrink. Instead, specialty stores for orthopedic and medical products as well as health-food stores will gain in popularity. Meals on Wheels Inc. has already been admitted to the DAX 30 index, the German equivalent of S&P 500, closely followed by the Rhön Hospitals and the Methusalem fund for retirement-home shares. Playgrounds will give way to shuffleboard courts, and discos to dance halls for mature audiences. Cruises will boom whereas backpacking will be out. Television will no longer seek the young German singing star. VIVA and MTV will have either gone bankrupt or evolved into "golden oldies" platforms, while the German folk music will get record audience ratings. Many nursing jobs will not be filled in spite of green cards for Thai nurses, and the government will vote for turning two-thirds of all youth hostels into retirement homes. This is a caricature, but one that may well provide a rough picture of the demographic evolution of the German economy.

All of the above may not be a real problem, as tastes are known to differ. A true problem is, however, that technological progress may flag due to a lack of young innovative researchers. According to a 1967 study by Guilford on the average age of all disciplines, scientists reach their maximum productivity at age 35.[12] Today, the strongest age cohorts in Germany are already markedly older, in the range of about 39–45 years in 2006. These cohorts will bring dynamism to Germany for a few years yet, but after another two decades these people will be at an age at which one does not conduct research worthy of a Nobel prize but rather prepares for retirement.

This demographic evolution reinforces another trend that is already evident, brought about by Germany's poor school system. Germany has few young people from whom a certain degree of dynamism can be expected, and even those few, on average, are being trained poorly in terms of academic skills.

Some people presume that the age-related reduction in the labor force is advantageous to the job market, as it causes the unemployment rate to fall. This presumption is dubious, however; it springs from too simplistic a view of the economy, and it overlooks the fact that the aging process removes not only employees but also employers from the labor market. New companies that create additional jobs are founded by young people. The average age of company founders in Germany is 34 or 35 years, identical to the age of maximum scientific productivity.[13] Therefore, the continual aging of the German population will not result in a reduction of unemployment; on the contrary, it will result in an increase in the current scarcity of new firms that create new jobs. It is absurd to imagine that a country whose population consists primarily of older people will have lower unemployment than a country of young and dynamic people.

The aging of the population will further reduce Germany's innovative capacity, upon which its international competitiveness depends. In an international comparison, Germany still occupies quite a good position among the top patent-producing countries. Yet since the 1980s the number of patents issued to Germans has grown more slowly than the number issued to Americans. Whereas in 1980 Americans registered twice as many patents in their country as Germans did in theirs, today patent registrations by Americans are three times higher.[14]

Anticipating the demographic problems, investors are already cautious. If German markets shrink and social security taxes rise, profit opportunities from an investment in Germany do not seem promising. Germany's position as having one of the lowest net investment shares among OECD countries may be largely attributable to the awkward demographic situation. Some sectors will boom, however: Germany's future obviously will lie in retirement homes and resort facilities, the owners of which will undoubtedly prosper.

Aging will have sustained effects on the political decision-making process. The decisive variable in a forecast of political majorities is the median age of the voting population. In a democracy, no decision can be taken against the interests of the median-age voter, because it would not find a majority. The parties will therefore always try, regardless of their ideological leanings, to develop programs that come as close to the preferences of the median-age voter as is possible. Today the median age of German voters is 47, but in 20 years it will be 54. This will bring about a significant change in politics.

From the time path of the median age of the voting population one can calculate whether and how long strategic majorities will exist for certain redistribution measures between the generations. For a pension-reduction scheme that would cut both pension contributions and pension claims and thus would favor the young at the expense of retirees, 2015 will be the critical year.[15] Until then, majorities may still be found for such a reduction policy, but afterward it will be difficult, because the losers will account for more than 50 percent of the voters. Reforms of this type will hardly be possible. Germany's political system will mutate to a gerontocracy: the old will rule over the young.

The Collapse of Pension Insurance

The effects of the German population's rapid aging on the pension system are a major concern. Many people believe that their pensions are paid out of the contributions they made to the pension system during their active lives. Indeed, the German pension system, which is based on individual accounts, gives this impression. A person who has paid in 10 percent more than his neighbor during his working life will receive a 10 percent higher pension. According to the opinion of Germany's Supreme Court, such a person's claims are even protected by the constitution.[16]

In truth, the German pension insurance system lives from hand to mouth. Its capital stock guarantees only 6 days of payments. If no new contributions are made, no pensions can be paid out. German pension insurance is a pay-as-you-go system, as are nearly all pension insurance systems around the world. A pay-as-you-go system is like a chain letter, where it is hoped that more and more people participate. The more that do so, the higher is the payoff. By taking care of the generation of one's parents in their old age, one acquires a claim against the generation of one's children to be taken care of in one's own old age: thus, the higher the number of children born, the higher the expected pension relative to wage income. But there are fewer children today than there were in the past. That is why Germany has had to push through one pension reform after another since the early 1990s, cutting back the expected pension claims.

Because of the individual accounts in the German system, the size of a claim against the generation of one's children depends strongly on the amount of money with which one supported the generation of one's own parents. Other countries, especially the Anglo-Saxon ones, have systems in which the relationship between contribution and claim is much looser. Although the claim depends on the number of years of contributions, as in Germany, it does not depend on the amount contributed each year. The "contribution equivalency" of the pensions is a cornerstone of the German system, because it is considered just and efficient. However, nearly all systems, whether with or without contribution equivalency, are pay-as-you-go systems and are only able to pay pensions to the extent to which new contributors participate, whether as children or immigrants.

The pension problem may also be understood by comparing the German age pyramid with a "population-preserving pyramid"—a fictitious age pyramid of a population that remains constant over time, because its fertility rate is 2.08, and has the same number of people in the active age groups from 25 to below 65 years of age. This comparison, represented by the shaded area in figure 7.7,[17] shows that Germany not only lacks young people but also old people. In view of the "excessive" pension burden that the media often cite, this may be surprising, but it is a fact. For one thing, the deaths of many young men in World War II sharply reduced the number of older men; for another, and more importantly, today's old had relatively many children, which implies that there are few old people in comparison with a stationary population that has the same number of people of working age. In view of this, the complaints of the working generation about the high pension burden and the high non-wage costs do not ring true. It is the next generation that can complain, because it will have to support today's numerous 40-year-olds when they retire. In contrast, the present working population finds itself in the extremely comfortable situation of having to support neither the normal number of old people nor the

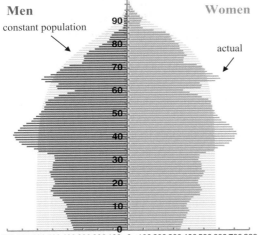

Figure 7.7
Actual and population-preserving age pyramids, 2005. Actual age pyramid on December 31, 2005; a population-preserving age pyramid assumes a population with a birthrate of 2.08 children per woman and whose age distribution is not affected by wars or fluctuating birth rates, but follows the actual pattern of age-specific death rates of the base year. The population preserving age pyramid is chosen in such a way that it includes the same number of people in the age group 25 to 64 years as the actual pyramid (45.6 million people). Sources: Statistisches Bundesamt, 10. koordinierte Bevölkerungsvorausschätzung, medium variant 5, and Sterbetafel 2002/2004; Ifo Institute calculations.

normal number of children. In other words, the life of the DINK family is very nice not only because it has two incomes and no children to raise, but also because it can share the support of its parents with many siblings.

It is only fair to admit, however, that this double benefit does not only accrue to today's working generation. The pensioners are also better off relative to the standard of living of the working population than any past generation of pensioners, and arguably any future one. In addition, the few children that Germans do have are growing up in historically extraordinary luxury. If one has one or two children, they can be granted a different standard of living than if one has five or ten.

The demographic situation will change fundamentally until the mid 2030s, for the present lack of old people will turn into a surplus. Today's strong working generation will then be in retirement, and the thick branches of the Christmas tree, which in 2004 reflected the number of 42-year-olds, will move to the 70-year-olds. At the same time, because fewer children will have been born, the thinner branches will move to the life range when one is typically in employment. It takes just one glance to see that this is bound to cause problems for the pension insurance system, as the unusually favorable constellation that still exists today will turn into an extremely unfavorable one. Judged by the number of dependents that have to be fed, the current German working generation is leading the life of Riley. Probably never in German history was there such a small number of old and young taken together that had to be fed by the members of the working generation, and there will hardly ever again be such a favorable combination.

In Germany the old-age dependency ratio (that is, the ratio of people 65 and older to those from 20 to 64) stood at 27.5 percent in 2001. This ratio will double by the mid 2030s, according to the most recent report of the Federal Statistical Office. This already assumes an immigration rate of 100,000 people per year. If immigration were to amount to 200,000 per year, this development would be postponed but not prevented. A doubling of the number of old people relative to young people is then expected by 2050.[18] Roughly speaking, today nearly four people of working age are supporting one pensioner, while in 30–50 years there will only be two bearing that burden. That is the problem.

You do not need a mathematical pension model to realize what this implies for the pay-as-you-go system. Either pension contributions will have to double relative to gross wages or pensions will have to be halved relative to gross wages. Policy makers may select any combination within this range, but they cannot correct the deficiency itself within the pay-as-you-go system. If Adenauer's pension formula of 1957, which tied the average pension to the average wage of the current working generation, were still valid, then the first variant would be relevant. An increase of the contribution rate from today's 20 percent to 40 percent would have to be expected. However, in 1992 Adenauer's pension formula was replaced by a new formula based on "net wage adjustment." From then on, pensions were only to grow in line with the increase in wages net of taxes and social security contributions. Net wages were expected to increase more slowly than gross wages, as the demographically induced increase in the contribution rate would increase the wedge between gross and net wages. A kind of automatic overrun break was built into the system that was to prevent too fast an increase in pensions. Of course, this effectively meant a pension cut relative to what Adenauer's formula had promised. Additional pension reductions were passed in 1999, in 2001, and in 2004, and these are unlikely to be the last ones.

How the shift in the age composition of the German population will affect the pension system, given today's legislation, was calculated by the Ifo Institute using the CESifo pension model.[19] The calculations are based on the ninth coordinated population projection of the Federal Statistical Office (variant 2) and assume uniformly a far-reaching reduction of unemployment as well as a further increase in women's labor market participation rate above the trend. Table 7.1 presents an updated variant of these calculations.[20]

The first line of table 7.1 shows the current circumstances. The pension insurance contribution rate amounts to 19.5 percent, and the level of gross pensions is 47.3 percent of gross wage income. The gross benchmark replacement rate is defined as a benchmark gross pension in percent of the average gross wage of contributors to the system. The benchmark pension is the pension received by someone who has paid into the system for 45 years and has always earned the average wage of all pension contributors. Unfortunately, the benchmark pension is only an artificial construct. It is not identical to the average pension received by someone who has contributed for fewer years. Because of the lower number of contribution years, the average pension is only about 70 percent of the benchmark pension. But in discussions of German pension insurance it has become the norm to work with the artificial figure of the benchmark pension. That is why the table refers to this construct.

In addition, table 7.1 shows the burdens created by the large tax subsidies given to the pension insurance system. At present about one-third of the expenditures of the statutory pension insurance system is not financed by contributions but by federal subsidies that are funded by general taxes. About 40 percent of these federal subsidies (i.e., about 15 percent of the retirement

Table 7.1
Pension levels and contribution rates. Source: Ifo Institute.

	Gross benchmark replacement rate	Formal contribution rate	Federal subsidy to normal pension[a]	Effective contribution rate[b]
At present 2035	47.3%	19.5%	2.6%	22.1%
Pension reform 2004	37.5%	24.1%	3.9%	28.0%
+ retirement age of 67 years	41.3%	22.6%	3.5%	26.1%
Old pension, frozen[c]	35.6% ⎫ 47.3%	19.5% ⎫ 21.9%	2.6%	22.1% ⎫ 25.6%
+ Child pension	11.7%[d] ⎭	2.4% ⎭	—	3.5% ⎭

a. Excess of federal subsidy over non-insurance benefits as percentage of gross wages.
b. Total burden as percentage of gross wages.
c. Including higher retirement age of 67.
d. At three children.

pension budget) covers non-insurance benefits. These include the pensions for ethnic Germans who immigrated from the Soviet Union and other immigrants who were included in the pension system after the fact. The remainder— almost 60 percent of the federal subsidies, or about 18 percent of the pension budget—is a gift from the taxpayers to the normal pensioners of the statutory pension insurance system. As passed by the "Red-Green" coalition government (1998–2005), this gift is funded primarily by increases in the "eco-tax" on fossil energy and in the value-added tax.[21]

The federal subsidy does not reduce the pension burden on the working population; the burden is merely being hidden, for the taxes needed to fund the subsidy are also a burden on the active population. Converted to the wage bill of the members of the statutory pension insurance system subject to contributions, the share of the federal subsidy in excess of the non-insurance benefits is now 2.6 percent. The effective contribution rate including this hidden tax burden is therefore 22.1 percent rather than 19.5 percent, the statutory contribution rate. This is the last number in the top row of the table. Pension calculations that fail to show the federal subsidy are based on false reasoning and thus are misleading.

The demographic problem will cause the contribution burden to rise sharply during coming decades, despite a reduction of the level of pensions needing funding. The second line in the table shows the values that are to be expected in 2035 if the 2004 pension law remains in effect.[22] Evidently, the formal contribution rate will rise to 24.1 percent despite the fact that the level of pensions will fall to 37.5 percent of gross wages. Adding the additional tax burden of 3.9 percent hidden in the federal subsidy results in an increase of the effective contribution rate to 28.0 percent.

The low pension level and the large effective contribution rate are an alarmingly unattractive mix. In 2005, the total burden of all social security contributions to be paid by the employer and the employee on the gross wage of a typical employee amounted to 41.4 percent, or 45.3 percent if the tax burden due to the federal subsidy to normal pensions is added. The first of these numbers is broken down into 19.5 percentage points for pension insurance (as shown in table 7.1), 13.7 percentage points for statutory health insurance, 6.5 percentage points for unemployment insurance, and 1.7 percentage point for long-term care insurance. According to a projection by the Ifo Institute, the effective total burden could increase from the current 45.3 percent to about 63 percent by 2035.[23]

On top of this, people will have to bear the normal personal income tax and the value-added tax. As was shown in chapter 6, the marginal tax burden on an average industry worker amounted to 65.2 percent of value added in 2005.

Even cautious calculations imply that this percentage will rise to about 77 percent by 2035 if the present pension and tax systems are retained. One will have to work 3 hours for the state for every hour worked for oneself. This is so greatly beyond anything compatible with healthy economic developments that something must be done now to reduce these burdens that threaten Germany's economic future.

Pseudo-Solutions

There are two general types of solutions to the pension problem: those that help strengthen the economic base for pension payments in later year and those that try to manage the impending deficit more efficiently by distributing the income between and within generations in a different way.

The second category includes an even more drastic increase of the federal subsidy to the pension insurance system than that already envisioned. It would amount to no more than a bigger cosmetic trick to reduce the calculated burden, and not to a real solution. Under the label "value-added charge," ways are being discussed to tap, besides wage income, capital income for financing the pensions. But such attempts will fail because international capital mobility prevents the effective taxation of capital in a country. (See chapter 6.) At best, a small shift of the burdens to other groups could be achieved via the value-added tax, which exempts value added contained in investment, but even this tax hits primarily private-sector workers.

At times, demands have been voiced to introduce "citizen insurance" for all groups of society. Citizen insurance would also include civil servants, the self-employed, and those whose incomes exceed today's maximum income subject to contributions, and it would provide everyone with the same pension, sacrificing the principle of contribution equivalence (also known as individual accounts). It is true that such a reform would alleviate the financing problem of the statutory pension system by extending the security tax base and depriving the well-to-do pensioners of some of their entitlements.[24] However, citizen insurance would only be another form of deficit management by redistribution within a generation. It would not be a means to really overcome the lacking resources thirty years from now, when the old age dependency ratio and hence the demographic crisis will be at its peak. Apart from that it would be strange to move from a system of individual accounts to one with flat benefits given that the much applauded Swedish pension reform of 1998 implied exactly the reverse move.

A more serious proposal concerns raising the retirement age, as suggested by many scholars and, most prominently, by German Labor Minister Franz

Müntefering (SPD). Each year by which an individual delays retirement beyond the standard retirement age offers double relief for the pension system. The person pays contributions for one more year and receives a pension for one less year. Of course raising the retirement age is equivalent to a pension reduction that only distributes the deficiency in a different way, but among all conceivable reduction measures it is likely to be the one that will meet with least resistance. Germans must work longer in order to compensate for the low supply of young people. It has always been that way in the history of the world. Those with no children to support them in old age had to continue working for as long as possible, and despite the collectivization of pension insurance this reality still holds.

To be sure, increasing the retirement age to 67 (perhaps by copying the American solution of gradually raising it to 67 for people born in 1938 or later) would be helpful. In Germany, at present, the legal retirement age is 65, but the average retirement age is 63.1 if disability pensions are ignored and 60.8 if these are included. By way of increasing the legal retirement age to 67, the average regular retirement age could be raised to 65 and the average overall retirement age to 63. Table 7.1 shows that, if this measure were introduced, a somewhat higher level of pensions, at 41.3 percent rather than 37.5 percent of gross wages, might be expected in 2035, while the effective contribution rate would decline from 28 percent to 26.1 percent.

However, the demographic problems are much too large for the increase in the retirement age to deliver more than a marginal alleviation of the pension problem. If the present level of pensions were to be retained until 2050 by only raising the retirement age, then, according to United Nations calculations, the legal retirement age in Germany would have to be raised to 77 instead of 67.[25] That is, as the UN emphasizes, too absurd to be seriously considered as an option for public policy. According to a forecast by the Federal Statistical Office, the remaining life expectancy of 60-year-old men will be 24 years in 2050.[26] Raising the retirement age to 77 would imply working all one's life to receive a pension for just 7 years. Only women, who on average will live for another 28 years from age 60, would enjoy their pension a bit longer.

The true solutions to Germany's demographic crisis are to be found not in ever new ideas on how to change the distribution of income within a pay-as-you-go system, but in measures that tackle the imminent scarcity of resources. A good policy must see to it that during the critical mid 2030s, when the number of pensioners will peak, there are either more savings or more people to finance the pensions. The key measures, therefore, are increased funding of pensions, more immigration, and improvement of the fertility rate. Which of these is the most promising is debatable. Immigration, in particular, is much less helpful than it seems at first glance, and as to the increase in the fertility rate, it may be too late to master the imminent crisis. However, in principle, all three measures can basically to be viewed as parts of a sensible package for a real solution to the emerging pension problem. The following sections will deal with these problems and will suggest solutions.

Human Capital or Real Capital, But No Free Lunch

One suggested reform of pension insurance that goes beyond management of the projected scarcity of resources is partial readjustment of the pension insurance system from a pay-as-you-go scheme to a funded system. Each generation ages, and it can get by in old age only if it has made its own provisions during its younger years. Either it must have borne and raised children or it must have saved in order to live by drawing down its savings. In the language of economists: To enjoy a pension in old age, one must have formed human capital or real capital or both. A generation which has done neither must go hungry in old age, because there is no such thing as a free lunch.

At present, for any number of reasons, Germans form much less human capital than their forebears. The relative loss of income which people sacrifice for their children is much lower than it used to be, for the very reason that they have fewer children. If they still do not want to lead a life of deprivation in old age, they only have the option of saving substantial parts of their present income so as to secure a pension via capital formation that the fewer future contributors cannot be asked to provide. Real capital must be formed to the extent that human capital is lacking. This is the central idea behind the 2000 pension reform, which is associated with the name of Walter Riester, Minister of Labor in the Schröder government, and which had been prepared by the Scientific Advisory Council at the Economics Ministry as well as the Center for Economic Studies (CES) in Munich.[27] According to the calculations made by CES for the Scientific Council and the Ministry, savings of 4 percent of income would suffice to form enough capital to fund one quarter of the pensions by the middle of the 2030s, when the demographic crisis will be at its worst. A substantial part of the reduction of the statutory pensions made unavoidable by the lack of children could be offset in this way and financed out of one's own savings. Partial funding, based on subsidized individual savings decisions, has meanwhile become law. It offers one way to reduce the problems of the German pension insurance system.

The decision in favor of partial funding was not uncontroversial. Many social policy makers felt that partial funding could not contribute to a solution of the pension crisis because its economic effects were not essentially different from those of the pay-as-you-go system. Their arguments stemmed from Gerhard Mackenroth, a German sociologist[28] who half a century ago argued that funded and pay-as-you-go systems were essentially identical, as all social spending can only come from the national income of the current period. Therefore it does not matter how old-age security is organized. Thus, replacing the lack of human capital by real capital cannot contribute to solving the German pension crisis. But as popular as this view is, it is nonsense.

The Mackenroth thesis is misleading and wrong. It is misleading because it suggests that future national income is independent of today's savings. In truth, however, national income rises if savings are higher. Savings invested abroad result in more interest income earned by domestic residents that is part of national income. Via faster real capital formation, savings invested at home furthermore result in higher capital income and higher wages that are also part of national income. In contrast to the suggestion of the Mackenroth thesis, one can therefore very well assume that additional savings will lead to higher future national income, out of which social spending will be easier to fund. The Mackenroth thesis is wrong because social spending cannot only be financed out of national income, but also out of consuming the saved-up capital stock itself. Savers cannot only consume their interest earnings in the future, but their assets as well. This aspect is not only true from a microeconomic but also from a macroeconomic point of view. A closed economy without foreign trade can finance social spending out of the existing capital stock by not replacing depreciated capital. An open economy with foreign trade can bring home the stock of capital built up abroad in the past by realizing a current-account deficit—that is, by importing more goods and services from abroad than it exports. All of this makes the financing of social spending possible without the use of current national income.

A similar response may be given to the related argument that the demographic crisis does not only present a problem for the pay-as-you-go system, but also impairs the way capital may be utilized, because capital will melt down if everyone wants to sell their assets. There is something to this argument. By way of example, if no other forms of savings existed besides real estate and no new houses could be built, the attempt to save more would only result in higher prices for these houses, while in old age, when pensioners want to draw down their savings, these prices would fall again. Funding would then indeed be affected by the demographic crisis in a similar way as the pay-as-you-go system.

The assumption that the formation of real capital is impossible is unrealistic, however. Via the banks, the savers can contribute to the credit financing of firms' real investment. In addition, even the purchase of existing real estate is accompanied by the formation of real capital, as the former owners will invest at least part of the proceeds in the financial markets and thus make more real investment possible. Although there are not more people to cooperate with the bigger stock of real capital, capital deepening will increase output. Future national income will increase during the years of the demographic crisis and there will also be a larger capital stock that can be consumed by not investing for the capital depreciation. Both constitute a solid base for a true improvement of the pension situation in old age.

The pension situation will even improve if the return on capital should fall due to additional capital formation. As long as the rate of return is bigger than zero, future national income will be higher than in the absence of capital formation, and even if the rate of return should fall to zero, more capital would be available in old age.

Apart from that, a decline of the return on capital need not be feared for the simple reason that the financial markets will see to it that additional savings flow abroad before the domestic return is pushed below the world level. Germany is part of the system of communicating tubes of the international capital market. Since there is no lack of people worldwide who can cooperate in a useful way with German savings, the international level of interest rates will not fall. Germany is much too small to exert any noticeable effect, and even the OECD countries together have only one-seventh of the world's population. Furthermore, it is worth remembering that the real world interest rate has remained remarkably stable, at about 4 percent, during the past 200 years, despite all the turmoil the world has seen. There is every reason to be optimistic for the next 200 years. The Marxian law of the falling rate of profit and similar theories that amount to a fall of the rate of return on capital have not proven true empirically. No, all these aspects do not refute the idea that savings are indeed a successful route to overcoming the pension crisis that Germany will face in the 2030s. The human capital gap has to be filled by real capital in order to solve the imminent pension crisis.

A False Argument in Favor of the Funded System

While the above argument only implies partial funding (i.e., funding to the extent that human capital is lacking), there is another argument in favor of the funded system that claims the general superiority of this system. If true, that argument would imply full funding.

The argument is that funded pensions are more efficient because they earn higher rates of return than pay-as-you-go systems. Countries should replace their pay-as-you-go systems by funded systems in order to realize these efficiency gains. Yes, there would be the difficulty of transition, because the claims built up by the old would have to be covered by taxes when the pay-as-you-go system is abolished. But this would only be a temporary problem. Having a higher rate of return forever weighs more strongly than any temporary transition problem.

As plausible as this argument sounds, it is false. While it is true that the market rate of interest exceeds the rate of return available to the pension system, it does not follow that the pay-as-you-go system is inefficient. The reason is that the pay-as-you-go system is an intergenerational redistribution device shifting resources from later generations to the introductory generation without altering the value of these resources in present-value terms.[29]

The rate of return disadvantage can be interpreted as an implicit tax charged to all future generations to service the implicit pension debt resulting from the gifts to the initial generation, the debt being rolled over from one generation to the next. The present value of this implicit tax is exactly equal to the initial gifts, and at each point in time the then-existing claims against the pension system are equal to the present value of the implicit taxes to be paid from there on to infinity. Thus, switching to a funded system without expropriating the old requires an explicit tax whose present value is exactly equal to the implicit tax in the pay-as-you-go system that is to be abolished. The transition would simply concentrate the tax burden on one generation, which is of dubious political and economic value.

It is true that this concentration can be avoided if the government borrows the funds needed to finance the pensions of the transition generation, as was proposed by the G. W. Bush administration for the United States. However, as the public debt would have to be serviced with future taxes, little is gained relative to the existing pay-as-you-go system. The present value of the explicit taxes needed to service the public debt equals the present value of the implicit taxes in an ongoing pay-as-you-go insurance system up to the very last cent, and with an appropriate borrowing strategy even the time path of the implicit tax could be mimicked exactly.

No, the rate-of-return argument in favor of the funded system leads nowhere. The truly effective arguments focus on the management of the imminent pension crisis and the substitution of human by real capital, as was explained above.

Voluntary, or Mandatory?

A much debated question in Germany is whether partial funding should be voluntary. This is the current German solution. The government recommends saving 3 percent of gross income (4 percent from 2008) and provides an incentive to do so by paying a premium on the account and possibly tax benefits. However, the success of this solution is not overly impressive. By the end of 2005 (5 years after the introduction of the scheme), only 16 percent of those eligible for government subsidies participated in the savings plans.

Why is this so? Are people stupid? No, they just react to other, more dominant economic incentives that follow from the construction of the social system. If low income earners save voluntarily, they will not gain much because they will reduce their claim to the base level of social assistance to which everyone is eligible in old age depending on the extent of their individual poverty. Each additional euro of private saving will drive social assistance down by one euro. Because of the demographic problem, it is not only today's low-income earners who are affected by this problem. If the contribution rate is fixed and the share of the federal subsidy in the total pension budget is kept constant then, according to table 7.1, the gross pension of the benchmark retiree with a complete work record will decline from the present 47.3 percent of the insured's average gross wage to 35.6 percent by 2035, which approaches the level of social assistance at today's standard (32 percent). This already assumes that the retirement age will be raised to 67 years and that some other favorable events will happen—in particular, a rise in women's rate of participation in the labor market and a decline in the unemployment rate. As the average pension is just 70 percent of the benchmark pension, it will be just about 25 percent of then-prevailing gross wages, way below the level of social assistance. Obviously, therefore, most people would not see one cent of their additional savings if social assistance remained at its current relative level. Thus, voluntary saving does not make any sense for an individual, as important as it may be from a macroeconomic point of view.

In addition, even the well-off retirees, who can expect their pensions to come in above the social assistance rate, must always fear that further reforms will deny them the pay-as-you-go pension in old age because they possess sufficient resources of their own. Social legislation already uses such arguments today, and society's backing of this policy will increase with rising old-age poverty.

That is why it is individually rational not to save and why saving must be made mandatory. State intervention in the form of granting social assistance to the elderly urgently demands another intervention in the form of mandatory insurance for the young. Whoever ruminates over the high value of the freedom to make his own personal savings decisions overlooks the hard facts of the German welfare system.

Many people consider the burden of additional saving unbearable and oppose its mandatory nature, as one may be forced to sell one's car or forgo a vacation trip. However, as the standard of living of today's working generation is much higher than that of all past generations. It would still be higher if this generation were to forgo the same share of its income for raising children as used to be the case in the past, be it in the form of expenditures on the children or in the form of income losses due to the time needed to raise children. No, such a point of view contradicts the empirical facts. The general prosperity and the lack of children make the funds available to finance the savings for pensions. That the funds may not be equally available to all members of society, as many do raise children, is another story. This all will have to be considered in the redesign of the pension system.

Why Immigration Really Won't Help Solve the Problem

In view of the burden of additional savings, it may be tempting to look instead at immigration as a solution. The idea is that if there is a lack of native-born German children who will some day become contributors, additional contributors may be invited from abroad.

Immigrants would indeed help to finance the pensions. Permanent immigration that leads to full citizenship, implying that the children and grandchildren of the immigrants will also remain in Germany, helps most. With such immigration one can presume that the entire gross contributions during the working life of an immigrant become net contributions to the fiscal system, because the pension claims of the immigrants will be financed by their own children. According to a rough calculation, at the end of the 1990s the pension insurance system would have received a discounted value of 175,000 euros from a 20-year-old immigrant earning an average income, and hence making average contributions to the pension insurance system.[30]

Of course, most often immigration is not permanent. Ten years after immigrating, more than half of the immigrants return home, and after 25 years this ratio climbs to 75 percent.[31] Such temporary immigration yields much smaller advantages to the pension insurance system, as the pension claims of the migrants remain intact after they return home and are not serviced by their own children, but by the whole of the German contributors. A person who immigrates at the age of 20, works until he is 65, and leaves no children behind to help fund the German pension system yields only 40 percent of the above amount (i.e., up to 70,000 euros)—and only if he earns an average income and pays average contributions, which is not usually the case.

One should also not overlook the fact that immigrants not only relieve the pension system but may become a burden on the welfare state elsewhere.[32] Immigrants benefit from the redistribution in favor of poorer population strata, provided by the entirety of state levies and expenditures, as the levies are positively and the benefits from the expenditures are, if anything, negatively related to income. As will be shown in more detail in chapter 8, the annual financial burden on the state of one immigrant who spends less than 10 years in the country amounted to around 2,400 euros in 1997. This already includes the discounted value of the advantages accruing to the pension insurance system from the employer and employee contributions. In this light, the picture changes substantially relative to considering pension insurance alone.

The inability to solve Germany's demographic problems by increased immigration becomes clearer when looking at the number of people who would have to immigrate in order to stabilize the pension system in such a way as to keep constant the age composition of the population (in the sense of the old age dependency ratio). For the sake of argument, assume the unrealistic proposition that all immigrants remain young and are permanent contributors to the pension system. The net immigration that then would be necessary by 2035 would amount to about 43 million people. Germany's total resident population would have to increase to about 100 million. Today, excluding the naturalized immigrants, 7.3 million foreigners reside in Germany. Thus, in 2035 half of the resident population would consist of foreigners, ignoring any additional naturalizations.

Of course, assuming that immigrants remain young is unrealistic. They are subject to the same demographic problems as Germans, as they too grow older and retire. If they have the same age composition as the existing population, nothing will be gained. Even an infinite number of immigrants would not help. Immigrants have to be younger than the average German in order to alleviate the problem. United Nation calculations of the required replacement migration to stabilize the pension system, which took account of the actual age distribution of immigrants, paints a much more pessimistic picture. According to these calculations, no fewer than 190 million immigrants would be needed by 2050, or 3.4 million immigrants per year, in order to stabilize Germany's old age dependency ratio at the 1995 level.[33] The immigrant population living in Germany would rise to about 300 million, 80 percent of whom would consist of the immigrants since 1995 and their descendants. These are astronomically high figures, which will never be realized and are not meant as a recommendation by the United Nations. But the size of these figures clearly shows how little immigration can be expected to help solve Germany's demographic problems. In public discussions this topic is completely overestimated, and it is misused to postpone the harder reform decisions.

The labor market may not need special measures to increase the immigration flows either, at least not from non-EU countries. For one thing, Germany now suffers from mass unemployment, i.e. a lack of jobs and not a lack of people. For another, the time has not yet come when the labor force starts to decline for demographic reasons.

Figure 7.8 presents projections of the German Institute for Labor Market Research in Nuremberg that illustrate the timing issue. It is evident that with a moderate immigration rate of 200,000 people per year, as is to be expected as a result of EU enlargement (see chapter 8), in 2017 the German labor force will be roughly the same as in 1995. And if immigration of 300,000 people per year is assumed, the break-even point will occur around 2022.

This does not imply that a program of increasing immigration to Germany could not contribute to solving the emerging demographic problems. It is evident, however, that the time has not yet come to look at additional immigration programs to solve these problems. In order to get a grip on the pension system and to stabilize the labor market, Germany does not need additional adults who work and pay contributions today, but it needs them 20 to 30 years from now, when today's 40-year-old Baby Boomers begin to retire. The demographic problems in Germany will not become virulent until 2020; they will culminate around 2035, and will very slowly abate thereafter.

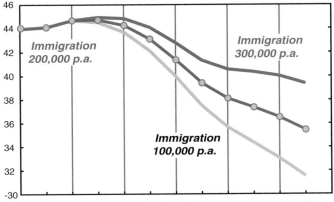

Figure 7.8
Germany's potential labor force (millions). Source: Institut für Arbeitsmarkt- und Berufsforschung. IAB-Kurzbericht 11, July 26, 2005.

Adenauer's Error, or Why Germany Needs an Active Population Policy

Given these various future scenarios, we now return to the present causes of the demographic problem in general and the pension problem in particular: Germany's bottom position among OECD countries in terms of the number of children being born. Instead of fighting the symptoms of the crisis or substituting real capital for the lacking human capital, Germans could also consider doing something against the causes by pursuing an active population policy with the aim of raising the fertility rate. If the birth rate could be raised to the level necessary for a stationary population, the population would gradually become younger again. The pension problem would be solved, the labor market would be stabilized, and the country would regain its dynamism in business and science, so say the optimists.

Here, too, illusions are out of place, for, although it is too early to liberalize immigration, it may already be too late to raise the birth rate with respect to the pension crisis expected to peak in 2035. German Baby Boomers born in the mid 1960s are nearly past their childbearing years. Furthermore, children born now will not start to enter the labor market until 20 years from now, shortly before the last Baby Boomers retire. (Germany's Baby Boom came much later than America's.) A large stock of additional labor will not have been built up by then. Even if the fertility rate were to rise at once to a normal value of 2.08, which characterizes a stationary population, the stock of employable people would only increase by 10 percent by 2035. Assuming that the number of working people rises by the same percentage, this would reduce the combined burden of the federal subsidy and the contribution rate by about three percentage points.[34] Larger effects require more time than this. Thus, without partial funding of the pension system, there is no true solution to overcoming the crisis of the pension system that will peak in 2035.

Still, 10 percent more employable people and three percentage points off the contribution rate may be better than nothing, and in any case the stock of additional employable people would grow rapidly in the ensuing years. As early as 2040, when the last Baby Boomers turn 80, the employable population would be 18 percent higher than at the old fertility rate. The combined contribution burden could then be about 4.5 percentage points lower. In 2050, the employable population would be 30 percent larger, and the contribution rate could be seven percentage points lower, or almost one fourth less, than without an increase in the fertility rate. In these years, the population structure would gradually normalize, and in the second half of the century Germany would have overcome its demographic crisis. So much for the mechanics of population growth, which at least follows clear rules and supplies rather certain forecasts over very long horizons.

The real question is political: Should a population policy that aims at changing the birth rate be pursued at all? This topic is fraught with taboos from misuse during the Nazi period, and politicians thus far have not dared to touch it. Yet there are facts that are of utmost importance to the future of the country and simply cannot be tabooed away any longer. The population trends presented above are so dismal that ideological circumspections are not helpful. If a nation's population shrinks faster than that of any other developed country in the world, that nation should be able to discuss the issue rationally.

But can it not be left up to each couple to decide how many children it wants to have? Is it the state's business? Should the government not keep out of the fertility decisions of its people and take the consequences as given, whatever they may be? "If the German people want to die out, then let them!" could be the position of more than just a liberal economist who respects "consumer sovereignty."

Indeed, the state must stay away from people's bedrooms. Family planning is none of its business in a legal system based on individual freedoms. But the state does intervene. For more than 100 years it has massively intervened in family planning, and that is the problem.

Of course, the state only intervenes indirectly, in a way that is hardly noticeable. People do not notice how their family planning has been influenced by political decisions. And they are not supposed to notice. But it happens because the state redirects the contributions that the working generation pays to their parents' generation, from their own parents to the parents of other contributors as well as to older people who are not parents at all. The state collects the contributions in one big pot and then redistributes them to the elderly generation, without taking account of whether those elderly have contributed to the potential payment of pension contributions by having raised children. Children are human capital. By way of a collective mandatory pay-as-you-go pension system, the state socializes the earnings of human capital.

This is not a fundamentally wrong approach. There are good reasons for organizing a pension system collectively on the basis of mandatory contributions. One reason, which played a special role for Bismarck, is safeguarding the parents' claim against children unwilling to pay. Another is the insurance against undesired childlessness caused by biological factors or by being unmarried.[35] Indeed, pension insurance via the pay-as-you-go system is, at its core, an insurance plan against childlessness and ensuing poverty in old age. Even if one cannot have children oneself, one need not live in want in old age, as one will be supported by other people's children.

Unfortunately, this insurance against childlessness eliminates some of the economic reasons for having children. Developing countries are not the only places where people have children in order to protect themselves against poverty in old age; the same motive prevailed in the past in Germany and in other Western countries. Before Bismarck introduced pension insurance, safeguarding consumption in old age was a dominant motive in Germany for getting married and having children. Those who had children were better off, and those who had none were usually poor. Today it is those with children who are relatively poor and the childless who belong to the richer population groups. The self-protection motive is no longer relevant in Germany, because having one's own children is no longer needed to safeguard one's consumption in old age. It suffices if other people have children who will foot the pension bills. One of the major economic motives for having children has disappeared under the protection of pension insurance because the fruits of human capital investment have been socialized by the pay-as-you-go system.

Today few young couples connect the desire to have children to the question of how to provide for their old age. There is no relationship in people's minds between wanting to have children and pension considerations. But this shows clearly the dramatic way in which the state pension system has influenced social norms. Before Bismarck, everyone had to have this economic relationship in mind when starting a family and some marriages would not have been entered into, if the destitute childless old people had not been a warning example for the young. After Bismarck, everything changed.

It is no coincidence that Germany, which was the first country to introduce comprehensive state pension insurance, has the lowest birth rate in the world today. Since the introduction of statutory pension insurance in 1889, generations of Germans have learned that one gets by all right in old age without children of one's own. Thus, by way of imitation, new life patterns spread from generation to generation that were adjusted to the new institutional conditions. One saw that one's childless uncle or aunt could live well in old age because they still received their pensions, and thus one learned that in planning one's life there were alternatives to the traditional nuclear family. Childlessness lost the social stigma of personal misfortune, and the number of people who decided in favor of a life without children became larger and larger from one generation to the next. Today, loose partnerships and one-person households have even become attractive life patterns, and children are considered dispensable. The number of young couples, who at least for the time being do not want to have children and do not plan to marry, has increased sharply since Bismarck, bringing down the fertility rate as shown in figure 7.5. The economic reactions to pension insurance emerged slowly, and in steps.

But today, more than a hundred years later, they can be seen clearly in the birth statistics and marriage registrations.

In the past, childlessness was a threat to one's own life that was to be avoided by all means. Today, childlessness leads to massive material advantages that more and more people aspire to attain. The new car and the exotic vacation can be financed by the money that was saved by not raising children or that the wife could earn because she decided to work instead of bearing children and staying home to raise them. Especially for the lower middle class of society, which used to have high birth rates, childlessness has become a way to facilitate material advancement.

The threat caused by childlessness still exists today, but it is no longer an individual threat: it has become a threat to society at large. Germany is aging, the country's dynamism is waning, the welfare state is in crisis, and yet the individual has little to gain from helping to prevent this development by deciding to have children or more children.

The relationship between childlessness and pension insurance has been discussed and documented at great length in the economic literature under the topic of "social insurance hypothesis." In studies covering 57 countries, Ehrlich, Chong, and Kim were able to prove a significant negative effect of the introduction and expansion of pay-as-you-go pension systems on family formation and the number of births in the period from 1960 to 1992.[36] Similar results were found by Cigno and Rosati,[37] and in a more recent study these authors present clear evidence, especially for Germany, in favor of this hypothesis.[38]

When Adenauer gave Bismarck's pay-as-you-go system the form it has today by introducing the "dynamic pension" (a system tying the average pension level to average wages), he probably was told of the risk of falling birth rates. Wilfrid Schreiber, Oswald von Nell-Breuning, and other advisors had recommended taking account of the individual number of children as an important part of an adult's pension formula, although it was not quite clear whether they focused on incentives or on fairness.[39] Adenauer, however, did not see the need to include children in the pension formula. People were having children anyway, he was said to have remarked. Today we know how wrong he was. Many pensioners will experience the consequences of this erroneous policy during the coming decades.

The fiscal effects on birth behavior are as large as the pensions and contributions themselves. These can be calculated by finding the present value of the fiscal advantages created by a newborn child, who during his lifetime has average earnings and has children of his own, for other members of the pension system. The child grows up, pays pension insurance contributions until reaching his own retirement age and then receives a pension, which is paid, of course, out of the contributions of his own progeny. In 1997, the present value of the contributions of a newborn child amounted to 90,000 euros, assuming that the contribution rate does not rise despite the demographic problem, but remains at 20 percent. In 2003 this corresponded to 100,000 euros (113.000 dollars).[40] Using a more realistic assumption about the likely increase in the contribution rate, a sum of 139.000 euros (157,000 dollars) was calculated in an extensive study by the Ifo Institute.[41]

Of course, one may hold the opinion that the state subsidies to child-raising, including free schooling, should be subtracted from this amount. But then one should also take into account that a child, when adult, will also contribute taxes and enjoy the public goods that the government provides for free. Trying to take account of the total fiscal cash flow a child and its own offspring generates for the state, the Ifo study found a net present value of 77,000 euros (87,000 dollars).[42] Thus, even in a broader perspective, there still is a substantial socialization of human capital in the system.

The pension contributions are a gift that parents who decide to have a child are giving to other groups of society. They are equivalent to a child tax, levied by the state on the parents at the time of the child's birth, but deferred at market rates of interest until the child has grown. If the state were to offset the effect of this tax by handing the parents a check for 139,000 euros, or at least one for 77,000 euros to compensate for the net overall fiscal effect, many more children would be born than is the case today.

This is the case for an active population policy that grants financial incentives for having children. It is not about letting the state intervene in family planning, but quite on the contrary, about getting it out of this planning. In Germany's liberal basic order, based on individual rights, the reference point for the assessment of a policy measure must never be the status quo in which the state already intervenes. Rather, the reference point must always be the situation without state intervention. Against the background of the German pension insurance system, a fiscal incentive for increasing birth rates is not a state intervention in private family planning, but the opposite: a reduction of state intervention! This must be advanced with determination, because there are many politicians who have become victims of their own superficial sound bytes in this respect.

The massive intervention in family planning undertaken by the state through pension insurance was certainly not done in order to reduce the number of children being born. It is a fact, however, that this intervention has had such an effect and has distorted the fertility decision. Therefore, politics can no longer avoid the question of how to reduce the undesired distortions.

The French Example

The French state has fewer ideological problems with an active population policy than the German state. Since the Prussian war was lost in 1870/71, and even more so since World War I, France has actively tried to raise the birth rate with policy measures. As figure 7.4 showed, it has been successful. Throughout the postwar period, the French birth rate has been consistently higher than the German one.

Above all, it is remarkable that in France the share of childless women is smaller than in Germany, and that those who have children decide to have three or more children more often than their German counterparts. Table 7.2 presents an instructive statistic regarding the number of children born to German and French women who themselves were born between 1945 and 1960 and who were between the ages of 43 and 58 in 2003. Two representative groups of 100 German and French women are compared. For example, in Germany 19 out of these 100 women had no children, whereas in France only 8 remained childless. A further example: 22 French women out of 100 had three children, compared to only 13 in Germany. Multiplying the number of children by the respective number of women yields the number of births, as shown in the second and fourth columns. The table shows that 100 German women bore a total of 162 children and the same number of French women a total of 210 children. The last column shows the cause of the lack of children in Germany relative to France. Obviously Germany has a dearth of families with several children. The larger share of French women with three children alone is responsible for France having 27 children more per 100 women than Germany.

In the meantime, the differences have grown further. The most recent comparable figures from 2001 show 135 children per 100 women born in Germany

Table 7.2
Births per 100 women born in the period 1945–1960 (average of years 1945, 1950, 1955, and 1960). Source: Eurostat, Population Statistics, 1960–1999, pp. 108–113.

Births per woman	Germany		France		German birth deficit
	Women	Children	Women	Children	
0	19	0	8	0	0
1	27	27	20	20	−7
2	34	68	40	80	12
3	13	39	22	66	27
4	7	28	11	44	16
	100	162	100	210	48

and 191 children per 100 women in France. The difference thus already amounts to 56 children. These numbers include the birth rates of the foreign women resident in the two countries. A hundred foreign women living in Germany still have 190 children. This partially offsets the fact that 100 German women have only 130 children.[43]

The high French birth rate will change the relative population sizes of France and Germany. In 2001, Germany, with 82.4 million inhabitants, Germany had 734,500 births. France, with 60.9 million inhabitants, had 804,100. Although the French population is smaller than the German one, clearly it already has more children. It is only a matter of time until France overtakes Germany and becomes the most populous country in Western and Central Europe.

This is the mirror image of a development that took place in the nineteenth century. Around 1820, the French population amounted to 31 million, whereas the German population was only 25 million. Just 90 years later, the relative sizes were reversed. In 1919, the French population totaled 40 million people, but the German population had grown to 65 million.[44] Whereas Germany's population pyramid really deserved this name (see figure 7.6), the French, with its large older cohorts, instead resembled an urn, not dissimilar to the projections of the Federal Statistical Office for Germany in 2050.

The shift in the relative population sizes of France and Germany led to frictions in the balance of power among the European countries, resulting in three wars and leaving the French with a long-lasting negative population shock that deeply imbedded itself in the consciousness of the political classes. Even today, the country looks with suspicion at its German neighbor and observes the development of its population and economy with a mixture of envy, admiration, and concern.

The experiences of the nineteenth century have caused France to pursue an active population policy in order to raise the birth rates again. As was mentioned, this policy was started back in the 1870s and was perfected from then on, and very successfully so. French children have received more financial and material support by the state than the children of other countries, Germany in particular.

How this support may affect fertility was shown by in a unique experiment in German history: the switch of the Saarland from French to German administration. After World War II, the Saarland was under French administration, subject to the same laws as France itself. After the Saarland was returned to Germany (as the result of a plebiscite held in 1956), all state rules and institutions, including the family support system, were replaced in one fell swoop with the corresponding German rules and institutions. The effect on the birth

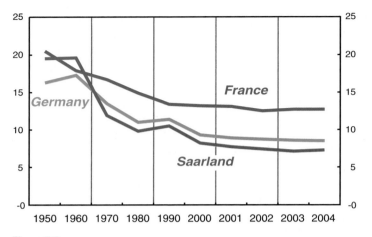

Figure 7.9
Live births per 1,000 inhabitants (Saarland: after accession to Federal Republic of Germany).
Sources: Statistisches Bundesamt, Statistisches Jahrbuch für die Bundesrepublik Deutschland and
Statistisches Jahrbuch für das Ausland: various years; Statistisches Landesamt Saarland,
Bevölkerungsbewegung 2004.

rate was not long in coming. In the 1950s and the 1960s the Saarland's birth
rate stood at the relatively high French level, but thereafter it declined
markedly, even slipping below the West German level, then converging gradually toward the German level.[45] Figure 7.9 illustrates this development.
Similar, by the way, was the reaction of birth rates in East Germany to the
change from the relatively high incentives for children in the GDR to the rather
meager incentives in West Germany.[46]

French population policy is not limited to financial incentives. In fact, one
of the most important aspects of this policy is the generous child care facilities, in particular the famous "école maternelle," a preschool where children
of ages 2–5 even learn to read and write. Figure 7.10 provides an international
comparison of kindergartens and similar preschool facilities. Because of its
école maternelle, France stands at the top of the league, whereas Germany is
positioned in mid-field, between Japan and Sweden. While 100 percent of the
French children aged 3–5 are placed in preschool facilities, in Germany the
figure is only 73 percent, and it is primarily nursery schools rather than
the true preschools patterned on France.

Preschool facilities and kindergartens are a topic that should be of special
interest to Germans, for kindergartens were developed and promoted by
Friedrich Fröbel, a German educator. Although the Prussian state initially prohibited them, kindergartens spread to the entire world. The road led to the
United States, where in the middle of the nineteenth century, Margarethe

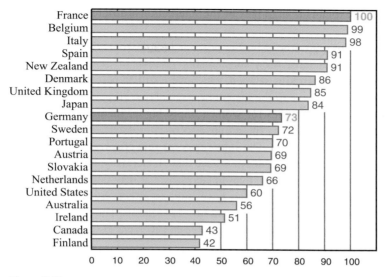

Figure 7.10
Attendance of kindergartens and pre-school institutions (percentage share of 3–5-year-old children in total age group, 2000). Source: OECD, Society at a Glance 2002; Social Indicators, table SS 15.1.

Schurz, the wife of Carl Schurz, a German revolutionary émigré who served as U.S. Secretary of the Interior, introduced the German kindergarten system.[47] Now, the country that invented kindergartens has fallen behind France and a number of other countries regarding early childhood education.

Even more pronounced are the differences in full-day schools. There are hardly any countries with half-day schools like those customary in Germany. In most OECD countries full-day schools are the rule. In Germany, half-day schools mean that women in most cases must decide either to pursue a career or to raise children, encountering a lifestyle that is not much different from "the three big Ks," the traditional stereotype of German women: Kinder, Küche, Kirche (children, kitchen, church). As the three big Ks have lost their attraction, very often today the decision goes initially against having children, postponing them until the woman has achieved a career and has secured her job, and as a rule this results in fewer births. In fact, while the age-specific relative birth frequencies of women above 30 in Germany have not changed in the last decades, the birth frequencies of women below 30 have collapsed. Women no longer have babies while in their twenties, and they do not make up for this in their thirties. The lack of preschool facilities and kindergartens implies a substantial income loss for women who decide in favor of children. Presumably this income loss represents the largest part of the costs of raising children and explains a large part of the international differences in fertility rates.

This is all the more true as in the postwar period women's incomes from wages and salaries have risen substantially relative to those of men. The salaries of full-time working women, which were still 55 percent of their male colleagues in 1960, have in the meantime risen above 70 percent.

Higher wages and salaries for women imply bigger income losses during child-raising, and that is why these may also be considered an explanation of falling birth rates over time. The importance of this effect may be doubted, however, as birth rates are higher in France than in Germany, although women earn more there relative to men than in Germany.[48] It may rather be presumed that the higher incomes of women have indirect effects by reinforcing the effect of lacking preschool facilities and full-day schools. The higher the wage income of women, the higher the incentive not to have children if no such facilities are available.

Besides preschool facilities and full-day schools, there are also big differences between France and Germany in the tax treatment of children. While in Germany a uniform deduction is granted for all children, the French state allows family splitting (quotient familial), which reduces the tax burden in a similar way as the splitting in Germany by the joint tax assessment of spouses who earn different incomes. Family splitting considers up to five children, with the first two children receiving half a weight, whereas the third, fourth, and fifth children receive each a full weight. Although the advantage of splitting is limited for a larger number of children and concerns only the income tax and not the social security contributions, it can be substantial for families with several children and higher incomes, because it considerably reduces the tax progression.

Especially for the middle income strata, these tax advantages are a big incentive to have children. Such a system contradicts the idea, prevalent in German politics, that the ability to pay taxes is independent of the number of children and it is therefore only fair for the state to support child-raising with fixed, equal-size amounts of money. In France, by contrast, the prevailing opinion is that children reduce a family's ability to pay taxes and this should therefore be taken account of by reducing the income tax progression by way of a joint assessment of all family members. Given the per capita income within a family, in Germany the average tax rate of this family increases sharply with the number of children which is a blunt violation of the principle of horizontal equity.[49]

Disregarding these legal considerations, in terms of incentives the French system is clearly better than the German one. Whereas in Germany the fiscal incentives to have several children focus on the poor and poorest families, in France they are also of importance to middle and higher income families. The French way sets down clear incentives for bearing and raising children also in socially intact families of the middle class. This results in a better education of the children, and at the time of inheritance it quasi-automatically (that is, without state intervention) results in a more equal distribution of wealth.

The French incentive system is not restricted to family splitting, however. It also comprises additional incentives, including a child allowance (which is progressively scaled according to the number of children) and a family premium for the needy with at least three children. The French incentive system does not offer very much support for the first child, but correspondingly more for the second and especially the third child, assuming that the decision for the third child is more sensitive to economic incentives than the decision to have children as such.[50]

Ifo Institute calculations that consider the entire fiscal incentive system, with all its complicated aspects, show that the French "policy of the third child" indeed has a financial basis. Whereas the first child is offered more support in Germany than in France, in France the second and third child receives more support than in Germany.[51] A French couple with three children and one earner, receiving the average wage of an industry worker had a net income higher by 9.1 percent in 2000 than a couple with two children and the same gross income. For Germany the corresponding increase of net income was only 6.5 percent. When the second spouse earned an income equal to one-third of the average, the increase of in net income due to the third child amounted to 7.5 percent in France and 5.9 percent in Germany. When the income of the second spouse was equal to two-thirds of the average, the net income increase due to the third child was 7.7 percent in France and only 4.8 percent in Germany. Especially if the wives work, the families receive much more support in France if they decide to have a third child than is the case in Germany.

Even larger are the differences in the incentives for middle-class families with above-average incomes. If the total family income amounts to three times the typical wage of an industry worker, which in Germany corresponded to 95,679 euros in 2000, net income rises by a mere 3.5 percent with the birth of the third child, whereas in France (at a corresponding income of 62,428 euros) it increases by 6.5 percent.

Of course, all of this implies revenue shortfalls and expenditure increases for the state. The budget burden is even greater. But Germany could consider reallocating its state's welfare expenditures. Perhaps the system of wage-replacement incomes, which has a very negative effect on the labor market, could be reduced, and perhaps pensioners should bear a greater burden in favor of better schools for their grandchildren. After all, a country does not only have a past; it also needs to have a future.

Child-Funded Pensions for Parents and Wealth-Funded Pensions for the Childless

Germany could learn from France, which in the nineteenth century was in a similar situation to Germany's today regarding its birth rate and which has achieved a significant change in trend with energetic policy measures. Copying the French incentive systems is one possible way. There are many arguments in favor of a joint assessment of children and adults in the tax system in order to take account of the reduced ability to pay taxes of families with children. Furthermore, the number of places in kindergartens relative to the number of preschool children could be raised sharply, at least to the customary international level, and all-day schools could be introduced on a large scale in order to increase the efficiency of the education system.

Less useful is additional financial support of families with children. Although such support can, in principle, strengthen the desire to have children and raise the number of births, it amounts to a double intervention by the state. By socializing the pension contributions in the statutory pension insurance, the desire to have children is reduced while it is rekindled by other, offsetting public expenditures that socialize the cost of raising children. Such a double intervention by the state does not make sense because both interventions cause behavioral distortions besides the change in fertility that do not offset but reinforce each other and lead to net disadvantages for the citizens. For example, pension insurance gives rise to artificial incentives to retire early, to give up working or to moonlight, and the family allowance may encourage the immigration of families with many children as well as increase wage demands that cause unemployment due to its construction as wage-replacement income. If a government intervention creates excessive disincentive effects in the economy, it is always better to scale down this intervention rather than to try to reestablish the proper incentives with further interventions.

In the case at hand, where the disincentive effect concerns child-raising, it is better to diminish the primary intervention in family planning, as embedded in the pension system, by reducing the extent of the fiscal redistribution from families with children to people without children.[52] A possible starting point for a reform is the subsidized funded pension introduced in the context of the 2000 pension reform. As has been explained, the correct consideration behind this reform is that Germans are forming less human capital today than in past generations and therefore must save more to accumulate real capital to fill the protection gap: as the "child-funded" pension weakens, a "wealth-funded" pension has to come in as a replacement. The wealth-funded pension has not been thought through completely, however. It cures the symptoms of the German disease, but not its causes. It does not diminish the disincentives for family planning. In particular, it results in unbearable burdens on those who are already making their full contribution to the financing of future pay-as-you-go pensions by having children and, in addition, are supporting today's pensioners with their contributions to pension insurance.

Instead of placing collective responsibility on an entire generation, the pension cuts that will become necessary after 2020 because of the demographic crisis that will peak around 2035, could be concentrated on the childless. Those who do not bear and raise children can be asked to accept somewhat bigger cuts in their pensions than parents who are not responsible for the demographic crisis. Of course, the pensions of the childless should not be reduced to zero, because this would negate their major economic function as insurance protection against the economic consequences of childlessness and would leave out of consideration that the childless provide, by way of the family allowance system, a certain, though small, contribution to the financing of children. A more than proportional cut in the pensions of the childless appears to be appropriate, however, to manage the crisis of the pay-as-you-go system.

Those affected by the pension cuts must be asked to accumulate enough savings to compensate for the lack of means in old age. But a savings rate of only 4 percent, as now envisaged for the childless, will not suffice to offset the loss of pay-as-you-go pensions. A rate of about 6 percent would be necessary according to calculations by the Ifo Institute. Such scaling of the pay-as-you-go pension and, inversely, the funded pension according to the number of children will help change family planning in the desired direction. And to reiterate the crucial point made above: this is not about involving the state in family planning, but quite the contrary, it is about partly extricating the state from it, because the degree of socialization of the fruits of human capital investment is reduced.

Regarding the cut of pensions for the childless, the claims and entitlements already built up at present must not be touched, however, because they are considered to be ownership rights protected by the German constitution. The reform, therefore, only concerns today's young people who are still in the process of accumulating pension claims by working and paying contributions. The reform does not take anything away that belongs to somebody. Today's young people have sufficient time to secure a comfortable pension by way of saving or raising children. The older a person is, the more claims he has built up in the old system, and the smaller the need for an offsetting funded pension. Therefore, older people will hardly be affected by these reforms, which is an important prerequisite for their political feasibility.

The introduction of a pension system that depends on the number of children would not only be able to reduce state intervention in family planning and let the natural motives for having children come to the fore again. It would also be fair, as it follows both the causality principle and the ability-to-pay principle.

Those who have no children, and therefore caused the pension crisis, have to bear the consequences in terms of pay-as-you-go pension cuts and by being forced to save. They also have the ability to save and pay for part of their own pensions because they have no child-raising costs. They are comparatively liquid and can invest those funds not spent on child-raising in the financial markets.

One may object to the proposal by noting that young, childless people are already making a provision for their own pension by paying the pension contribution, and it would therefore be unjust to force them to make a second provision by way of additional saving. This argument ignores, however, that in the generational relationship each generation has to bear a double burden: During one's working years one must support one's parents *and* one's children. The former burden is borne by parents and non-parents in the form of pension contributions that flow entirely to today's pensioners. The latter burden, however, is borne by parents alone. Forcing parents to save means imposing a third burden on them, which is one too many. Instead of asking parents to bear three burdens, it seems more equitable to ask non-parents to bear the second burden. Regardless of why they have no children, whether they decide not to have any or because they cannot have any, they do have the funds that other people need for child-raising, and they may well be asked to invest them in the capital market.[53]

Ready for the Future: The Three Pension Pillars

These basic ideas can easily be framed in a way that is legally and politically feasible in Germany (and, one hopes, in many other countries that are in a similar situation). There are three pillars to the new pension system.

The first pillar is the statutory pay-as-you-go pension in its present form. It continues to operate as before, but it does not receive more and more funds. It becomes a defined-contribution system: the contribution rate will be frozen at the present level of 19.5 percent, and federal subsidies in excess of non-insurance benefits will also be frozen in relative terms. The demographic crisis will then be reflected in a corresponding slowdown of pension increases, countered only by the rise in the retirement age to nominally 67 years. The special state pensions of Germany's super-tenured public employees (Beamte) will be indexed to the statutory pay-as-you-go pensions and thus follow the same reduced growth trend. According to calculations by the Ifo Institute, the benchmark pension will fall from the present 47.3 percent of the pensioner's average gross earnings to about 35.6 percent by 2035. The next-to-last row of table 7.1 shows this result.

The distribution rules within the old system will not be touched, and no one will lose in relative terms. The cuts result solely from the demographic effects, for which the generation of pension recipients itself is responsible. As the distribution structure within the existing statutory pension system is not changed, there can also be no reservations on constitutional grounds. The small number of children does, of course, have its financial implications.

The benchmark pension of about 36 percent of the gross wages of contributors will not by itself suffice to feed the retirees; it will just be in the neighborhood of social assistance, and many people will be receiving much less than this assistance. This necessitates two supplementary pension pillars.

One of these supplementary pillars is the "child pension," an additional pay-as-you-go pension especially for parents. For the benchmark parent pensioner, it will fill the gradually widening gap between today's relative level of pensions and the actual relative level of pensions resulting from the demographic crisis. The child pension claims may be accumulated, beginning at the time of the reform, by raising children. The maximum child pension will be reached by raising three children. Combined with the statutory old age pay-as-you-go pension, it provides the benchmark retiree with today's pension level of just over 47 percent in the crisis years around 2035.[54]

The child pension is financed by all wage and salary earners, including civil servants and the self-employed, for all of them have parents. It is a citizen's pension paid by the grown children to the generation of their parents, because the parents have cared for them. All parents are eligible, including civil servants, the self-employed, and inactive persons.

The contributions to the child pension creep in to the extent to which the replacement rate of the statutory pension system declines, for demographic reasons, below the present 47 percent, because it is this gap that the child pension will fill. A sizeable contribution burden to the child pension will arise only when the German Baby Boomers now about 42 years old begin to retire, from about 2020 on.

As the child pension is reserved for parents, people without children have to save instead to augment their basic pay-as-you-go pension from the statutory system. Savings are the third pillar of the new pension system. Savings are obligatory in order to preclude any speculation of being able to rely on social assistance in old age and therefore enjoying a good life today instead of providing for one's old age.

Young people who enter the labor force are obliged to start immediately with the required savings of 6 percent of their gross income. After the birth of their first child, the obligatory savings rate will be reduced by one-third, and one-third of the savings accumulated by then will be paid out. Similarly, the second and the third third of current savings and accumulated savings will be reduced or paid out, respectively, when the second and third children are born. This provision ensures that young families will be able to enjoy more liquidity at the very time when they need it.

The system presented here will safeguard the pensions at the present level for parents and non-parents alike despite the demographic crisis, without implying higher contribution burdens than the present system. In addition, it creates pension claims even for the non-working parent that are based on child-raising. The funded pension provides the childless with solid resources in their old age. In such a new system the pensions of parents and childless people will truly be guaranteed.

The exact financial implications of the new system have been calculated with the CESifo pension system and are shown in the lowest two rows of table 7.1. As was explained the present system will suffer from severe pension cuts. Even if the pension age is increased to 67, the relative pension level will fall from today's 47.3 percent of gross wages for the benchmark pensioner to 41.3 percent, while the effective contribution rate will rise from 22.1 percent to 26.1 percent. By contrast, the new system will preserve today's relative pension level without increasing the overall effective contribution rate beyond what the present system would imply. Actually, with 25.6 percent, the effective contribution rate will even be a bit lower than it otherwise would be.

The main advantage of the new system is that it no longer leaves young people in the dark about the economic basis of their pension. The microeconomic incentive structure matches the macroeconomic reality that pensions come either from children or savings—that is, from human or real capital. Everyone knows that they must invest in children and/or in the capital market if they want to make ends meet in old age, and no one can escape the burden this involves. The childless will still be partly financed by other people's children by way of the statutory old age pension system, but the degree of socializing the contributions of the children will not continue to rise as it would if the present system were continued. The new system rekindles, at least partially, the economic reasons for having children, which were driven out of people's minds by the system of Bismarck and Adenauer. Germany will become young again.

8   EU Enlargement, Migration, and the New EU Constitution

The Difference between European and German Unification

May 1, 2004, was the day on which the postwar division of Europe was finally overcome. Eight Eastern European countries joined the European Union, together with Malta and Cyprus. Bulgaria and Romania are waiting in line and will join in 2007. After half a century of communist dictatorship in Eastern Europe, the division of the continent has finally been overcome. With 457 million people, the new political union has a substantially bigger population than the United States of America (300 million).

And it is possible that Europe will be enlarged further. Turkey, with a rapidly growing population approaching 71 million, is waiting, as is Croatia (4 million). The Ukraine (47 million) has also expressed its interest in membership. Currently, Turkey is the most serious candidate. An Associate Member of the EU since 1963, it applied for full membership in 1987 and received formal candidacy status. The EU began negotiations in June 2006, but whether Turkey will in fact become a member is quite uncertain. Chancellor Angela Merkel of Germany and Minister of the Interior Nicolas Sarkozy of France have argued against Turkey's accession to the EU because they fear a mass influx of immigrants as well as economic and cultural frictions. On the other hand, the Turkish case has found strong support across the Atlantic. Turkey is "Europe's Mexico," but while the United States is building a fence at its Mexican border to stop immigration it is pushing hard for Turkey's EU membership for strategic reasons.

Cyprus's new EU membership has further complicated the decision about Turkey's entry. The failed referendum on the unification of the Turkish and Greek parts of the island and the fact that Turkey has not recognized Cyprus as an independent state have resulted in a difficult legal situation.

It is too early to tell how this will affect the likelihood of Turkey's EU membership.

As table 8.1 shows, the countries that became EU members in 2004 have a total population of 74 million. Including the additional 30 million in Bulgaria and Romania, the two countries that will join the EU in 2007, the EU is being enlarged by the same percentage (27 percent) as the Federal Republic of Germany was by reunification. In this light, EU eastern enlargement is the second major challenge facing Germany during the last two decades.

The challenges and the opportunities are enormous. The Eastern European countries will enter into close economic relationships with Western Europe. This will bring about gains from trade and a better division of labor for all parties. The capital-poor but worker-rich countries of Eastern Europe will be able to focus on labor-intensive production processes, while the West will be able to specialize in capital- and knowledge-intensive high technology. Thanks to their geographic and cultural proximity to the East, Austria and Germany in particular will profit if they respond suitably to the challenges. Germany will be able to buy inexpensive consumer goods from Eastern Europe in

Table 8.1
Additions to EU population by eastern enlargement, in millions, as of January 1, 2004. Source: Eurostat website, June 7, 2006.

2004 entrants	
Poland	38.2
Czech Republic	10.2
Hungary	10.1
Slovakia	5.4
Lithuania	3.4
Latvia	2.3
Slovenia	2.0
Estonia	1.4
Cyprus	0.7
Malta	0.4
Total	74.1
2007 entrants	
Bulgaria	7.8
Romania	21.7
Total	103.7
Candidates	
Croatia	4.4
Turkey	70.7

exchange for machinery and equipment in which it still holds the leading international position as an exporter. (See chapter 2.) Germany may also become the hub of East-West trade and see its bazaar economy prosper.

Eastern enlargement will bring peace and prosperity to Europe. Under the forces of the market economy, the former communist economic systems will grow rapidly and will experience a development similar to the German postwar economic miracle, the rise of Japan in the 1970s, and the subsequent boom in other East Asian and Southeast Asian countries. Integration into the European product, capital, and labor markets will help Eastern and Western Europe converge during the coming decades. The workers in Eastern Europe will especially benefit from this development. In coming years, Europe will grow rapidly and will gain in economic importance.

Some fear that European unification will face problems similar to those that arose during German unification. But the analogy with German unification is not well founded. The big difference between European and German unification is the fact that the EU, at least until now, has been only a loose confederation and has been unable to interfere with the internal policies of its Eastern European members as West Germany did with respect to East Germany. While the political weakness of the EU poses its own challenges, it protects the Eastern European countries against the kind of political distortions of the market mechanism that Germany encountered after its unification, as was described in chapter 5. For example:

• It will be impossible for the unions and employer associations of the old EU countries to negotiate an overly rapid wage increase in the East so as to protect their own industries.

• The old EU countries cannot prescribe Western standards for wage-replacement benefits that would also lead to excessive wages.

• The old EU countries are unwilling to make financial transfers to the Eastern countries similar to the internal German transfers after unification that would alleviate the consequences of mass unemployment.

• The old EU countries cannot use debt financing to shift the burden of these transfers to future generations.

As long as the political constraints that bar the old EU countries from repeating the misguided German policies remain in place, a repetition of the German debacle need not be feared.

Yet fear that eastern enlargement will be expensive for the West has been voiced repeatedly. If the eastern enlargement of Europe were to be as costly as the eastern enlargement of Germany, then the old EU countries would have to live with a transfer burden of 4–5 percent of gross national product for some time. That is not to be expected, however. In 2002, the entire budget of the EU amounted to only 1.1 percent of the EU's GDP, and in 2005, a year after eastern enlargement, the contributions of the old EU countries to the EU's budget had even decreased to 1.0 percent of their GDP.

Even Germany, the biggest net contributor to the EU's redistribution system, would not face an insurmountable burden. German gross payments into the EU's budget amounted to 18.9 billion euros—one-fifth of the EU's budget. Of this Germany received 11.5 billion euros back. Thus, net payments amounted to 7.4 billion euros or about one-third of one percent of GDP.[1] In 2005, Germany's net payments had risen to 9.8 billion euros (0.4 percent of Germany's GDP). Even though this financial burden is likely to grow via political processes, it is most unlikely that financial burdens similar to those of German unification will ever arise.

Thus, from an economic perspective, the challenges posed by European unification have little in common with the problems brought about by German unification. In principle, the conditions for prospective gains from trade, prosperity, and full employment in Eastern Europe are being met.

This does not mean that there are no challenges for Western Europe, Germany in particular. Migration into Western welfare systems and extreme low-wage competition in product and factor markets crowding out domestic jobs are the most important problems to be expected. Interestingly enough, they are similar to the potential problems at which German politicians had hinted at the time of German unification in order to make the case for a social union and rapid wage convergence. This chapter will deal with these new challenges and potential policy reactions.

The Problem of Extreme Low-Wage Competition

From a German point of view, the most urgent challenges of European enlargement concern the labor market and the potential relocation of German industry to Eastern Europe. The greater competition suffered by German workers since the mid 1990s stems in special measure from the integration of the East European economies that followed the fall of the Soviet Union.

For German workers, Eastern Europeans are particularly strong competitors for three reasons. First, they have a well-trained labor force. The communist countries' universities and training systems were competitive in technological areas, and the cultural background of Eastern Europe is comparable to that of Western Europe. Second, the accession countries are close to Western Europe. Short distances mean low transportation costs for people, capital, and goods, and therefore intensive competition. Third, wages in Eastern Europe are still very low.

Figure 8.1 compares the hourly wage costs of workers in Eastern Europe, Germany, and several other countries in 2004, converted at actual exchange rates.[2] One can see that West German labor costs are about 8 times higher than in Poland, 6 times higher than Hungary, and 19 times higher than Bulgaria. Even East Germany is in a different league. Its wages are 4–6 times higher than those in Poland and Hungary, and 14 times higher than those in Bulgaria.

These differences will narrow over time, but the adjustment process will take many years. During the period 1963–2000, "sigma convergence" in Western Europe amounted to 1.1 percent per year,[3] which means that, on average, the relative gap in European per capita incomes shrank at an annual rate of 1.1 percent. In other regions and other historical time periods, an even higher convergence rate of about 2 percent has been observed.[4] Assuming a high convergence rate of 2 percent a year, Polish hourly wages, which were 12 percent of the West German level in 2004, will still be only 22 percent of West German wages in 2010, 36 percent in 2020, and 48 percent in 2030. And if the internal German East-West wage convergence is also 2 percent per year, Polish wages will have reached 46 percent of the East German level by

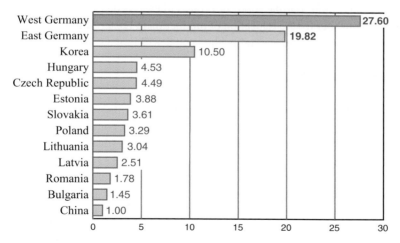

Figure 8.1
Average labor costs per hour in manufacturing industry, 2004, in euros. Sources: Institut der deutschen Wirtschaft Köln; East Germany: Ifo Institute estimate. For Bulgaria, Romania and the Baltic countries, the figures for 2000 were extrapolated on the basis of the Eurostat press release 35 of March 17, 2006 or the ILO database Laborsta, respectively. China and Korea: 2003 estimated from data of the ILO database Laborsta; Ifo Institute calculations.

2020 and 57 percent by 2030. Presumably, however, there will be a correction of the artificial wage convergence in East Germany in the early years of European unification, so that the gap between East Germany to Poland may close faster than these figures suggest.

Current wage differences are so extreme that one need not be an economist to recognize that the German labor market will be subject to enormous pressures. Financial capital that the banks collect from German savers will continue to be exported to the East to finance the many profitable investment projects there. German manufacturing firms will relocate more and more plants to Eastern Europe. In particular, the small and medium-size firms that can repeat on a smaller scale what the large firms have already done in Asia will be lured away from their expensive German locations. As was discussed in chapter 2, Germany's evolution in the direction of a more concentrated bazaar economy will continue, as it increasingly specializes in downstream activities ranging from design and assembly to marketing, leaving the labor-intensive upstream activities to the Eastern Europeans. Brand fraud, with Eastern European products that merely get labels slapped on them in Germany, will also continue. The developments described in chapter 2 will continue unabated.

At the same time, there will be substantial migratory pressure exerted by Eastern Europeans seeking their fortunes in the West. Politicians will try to prevent the migration, but the more rigorously they proceed the greater will be the forces pushing for the relocation of production to Eastern Europe. Either the people will move to the capital or the capital will move to the people.

How Many Will Be Coming?

It is not easy to predict how many Eastern Europeans might come to Germany, as it is impossible to gauge how quickly the political constraints will be removed. One can only estimate the potential migration—that is, how many would come if they could.

In 2006, about half of the old EU countries still restrict immigration using the option provided by the accession treaties. These are Austria, Belgium, France, Germany, Italy, Luxembourg, the Netherlands, and, to some extent, Denmark. While tourists, students, and self-employed persons from Eastern Europe may freely migrate across the former communist borders, the number of dependent employees who may do so is limited to well-defined exceptions. Germany is one of the EU countries that have used the option and decided to keep its gates closed for Eastern European immigrant workers for the time being. In all likelihood it will continue to do so as long as it will be permitted to do so—that is, until May 2011. After that date, no restrictions on labor migration will be permitted under EU law.

A starting point for forecasting the potential migration that is going to take place after liberalization is a look at Germany's present immigrant population. According to a new study of the German Statistical Office, about 15.3 million people with an "immigration background" lived in Germany in 2005, accounting for 18.5 percent of the population.[5] The figure includes the children of immigrants as well as ethnic German immigrants, who primarily came from the Soviet Union and from Transylvania (Siebenbürgen) in Romania.[6] Ignoring the children born in Germany (that is, counting only the foreign-born population), one gets 10.4 million, 12.6 percent of the currently resident German population. As figure 8.2 shows, this share exceeds that of other big countries (including the United States, where the respective percentage is 11.1). Only Canada and New Zealand—classical immigration countries—have a larger percentage of immigrants. Germany has already experienced huge immigration inflows.

Figure 8.3 sheds some light on the source countries of the immigrants. One can see that about 3 percent of the Turkish and Greek populations currently live in Germany, and 1 percent of the Portuguese and Italian population.

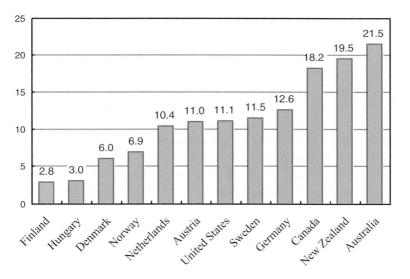

Figure 8.2
Foreign-born persons as percentage of population (most countries 2001, United States 2000, Germany 2005). Sources: OECD, 2004: Trends in international Migration: Sopemi 2003 edition; Statistisches Bundesamt, Wiesbaden, 2006: Leben in Deutschland—Ergebnisse des Mikrozensus 2005; Eurostat, Population and social conditions, Statistics in Focus 8/2006.

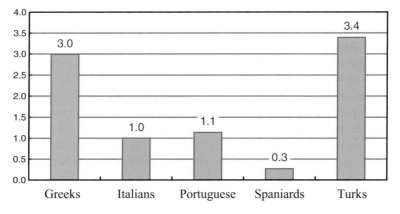

Figure 8.3
Immigrants living in Germany as percentage of population of the respective countries, 2004.
Sources: Eurostat, Population and social conditions database; Statistisches Bundesamt, Wiesbaden, website, April 6, 2006 (Ausländische Bevölkerung in Deutschland); on request: naturalizations; Ifo Institute calculations.

Spaniards, in contrast, were obviously not inclined to come to Germany. Immigration from Eastern Europe will be comparable to these numbers, perhaps with the exceptions of Spain and Portugal.

Many commentators downplay the potential role of immigration from Eastern Europe by pointing to the low flow of Spanish and Portuguese immigration after the accession of Spain and Portugal to the EU in 1986. The comparison is misleading, however. First, most European migration is to the neighboring EU countries. Just as the Spanish and Portuguese immigrants went primarily to France, most of the Poles, Czechs, Slovaks, and Hungarians who elect to leave their home countries will likely prefer to move to Germany, Austria, Finland, and other neighboring countries. Second, income differentials were much smaller in the case of southern enlargement. When Spain and Portugal joined the EU, their average wage income was nearly 50 percent of West German wage income.[7] In contrast, in 2003, a year before the accession, average annual wage income in the East European accession countries amounted only to 15 percent of West German wage income.[8] There are correspondingly higher economic incentives for Eastern Europeans to move to Germany. According to the 2 percent convergence rule mentioned above, it will not be until 2030 that Eastern European wages relative to West German wages arrive at the relative levels of Iberian wages at the time of Portugal's and Spain's entry into the EU, and if the convergence rate is only 1.1 percent (as it has been in Europe) the critical year will be 2051. A convergence rate of 2 percent corresponds to an initial growth rate of 11 percent, while a 1.1 percent annual convergence rate corresponds to an initial growth rate of 6 percent. The actual average growth rate of the eight Eastern European accession countries was 4.8 percent from 2003 to 2005. The reader may judge which of these scenarios is more likely to affect Germany. Third, in the period 1960–1975—that is, in the 15 years before the Franco and Salazar dictatorships ended and Spain and Portugal applied for EU membership—there had already been mass emigration from those countries. Although both Spain and Portugal had also been experiencing particularly high immigration from their former colonies at the time, 5.5 percent of the Iberian population emigrated during that period in net terms.[9] The potential exhaustion of the migration-prone part of the population should not be ignored when looking for parallels between the past and the situation created by Eastern Europe's accession.

Whereas the dictatorships on the Iberian Peninsula let their people emigrate, the Soviet Union sealed off its empire with an Iron Curtain that only very few surmounted, at the risk of life and limb. When the Iron Curtain came down in 1989, many Eastern Europeans did go west, especially to Germany, claiming asylum. In the period 1991–1995, gross immigration to Germany was 6.2 million, and net immigration was 2.6 million (about 520,000 per year). But then immigration slowed. In the period 2001–2004, average annual net immigration was only about 180,000, with a declining tendency.

One reason may have been that Western European nations had found ways to replace the barrier posed by the Iron Curtain by tightening their immigration and asylum laws. Even Germany, which in the past had Europe's most liberal asylum policies, anchored in its constitution, became more restrictive toward asylum seekers, moving toward the tighter constraints of the other European countries. Moreover, later, after EU eastern enlargement in 2004, the country postponed free labor migration to 2011, as was mentioned above. Since then "tourist migration" (into the black market) and migration of self-employed people, both of which are still possible, have increased considerably. There are no statistics on this available—for good reasons. Only personal observations and anecdotal evidence, such as the fact that the number of tilers in Munich increased from 119 in 2003 to 971 in 2005, hints at the magnitude of this type of migration.[10] In general, at the time of writing, there is still a huge pent-up migration pressure in Eastern Europe, particularly if Romania and Bulgaria, which are about to join the EU, are taken into account.

An econometric study by the Ifo Institute tried to forecast the potential official migration from Eastern Europe on the basis of experiences with earlier migration flows.[11] The study found that about 4–5 percent of the population of the accession countries joining in 2004 would immigrate into the old EU countries within the next 15 years if immigration were not restricted.

Until 1998 (unfortunately this is the most up-to-date information available at this time) nearly two-thirds of all Eastern European immigrants into the EU came to Germany. One-third went to the other 14 EU countries.[12] Assuming that this ratio will also hold in the future, then within 15 years after granting free movement in 2011, an additional 2.5 million people are expected to immigrate to Germany from the countries that acceded in 2004. This will correspond to an annual rate of about 200,000–250,000 in the initial years.

The numbers are correspondingly higher when immigration from Romania and Bulgaria is included. A rough guess, based on relative population sizes, is that another million immigrants may come to Germany. However, owing to the extreme poverty in these two countries, this number is probably at the lower end of reasonable estimates.

Why Migration Is Essentially Good

There are different opinions as to how to assess the expected migration flows, and one often finds a correlation between this assessment and the numbers quoted. Either one is in favor of free movement and hence presumes smaller figures to allay fears or one is against it and presumes large figures to fuel fears. The right-wing Austrian politician Jörg Haider keeps stoking the fear of immigration by forecasting mass immigration movements, whereas the EU tends to avoid discussing the potential problem by projecting negligible numbers.[13] This polarization leads nowhere and makes both sides lose credibility. What does economics have to say about the usefulness of migration?

In theory, assuming that labor markets are functioning and are free of distorting state interventions, the free movement of people can be expected to be advantageous for Europe and all countries involved. This statement is true independently of whether the volume of migration is small or large.

The potential wage bill of immigrants in Western Europe far exceeds the GDP lost in their home countries due to their emigration, and because of the marginality principle, what they earn in the West is normally less than what they contribute to Western GDP. The wage rate of all migrants is determined by what the last migrant contributes, but earlier migrants contribute more than later migrants, as the most productive jobs are filled first. Therefore, both sides stand to gain. This is still true if the subjective and objective costs of migration are taken into account, because these costs are calculated by the individual immigrant upon making his decision to migrate.

A migration equilibrium will be reached after the wage rates in the countries concerned have converged as a result of migration. In the country of origin these rise as labor becomes scarcer, and in Western Europe they fall as the supply of labor increases. The fall in wages in the West induces companies to provide the additional jobs needed by the immigrants, and the reduction in the wage gap between the East and the West makes immigration less attractive until it stops.

Many people believe that this migration equilibrium causes real income losses in the West, as it is accompanied by lower wages for Western workers. But this is not true. While those occupational groups that offer similar services on the labor market as the immigrants do suffer from the erosion of their wages, this erosion is merely a redistribution effect that implies gains elsewhere in the economy. Firms' profits increase as their wage costs fall, and the incomes earned by other factors of production, such as land and skilled labor, rise as the demand for these factors increases with immigration. Moreover, wage declines reduce the prices of labor-intensive products, raising the living standard of those who consume them. Although there are many losers and severe internal distribution problems, the marginality principle implies that, on average, Western Europeans stand to gain from immigration.

The migration equilibrium is reached at a point at which the international wage difference is equal to the last immigrant's personal cost of migration. This is also a situation where the stock of immigrants is efficient in the sense that the joint GDP net of migration costs is maximized. It is higher than it would be with any other international distribution of the available workforce. If migration were higher, the increase in the resulting joint GDP would fall short of the additional migration costs, and if migration were lower, there would be an unexploited scope for increases in the joint GDP.

The distribution of the working population between Germany and the migrants' Eastern European home countries will not remain constant over time, but is itself subject to change as the economies of these countries improve and the demand for labor rises. Over the course of time this will result in further wage convergence. This will reduce the stock of immigrants in the West, which implies that many of the foreigners who have come will and should decide to return to their home countries.

Such a two-way migration flow has indeed been observed in past migration processes. For instance, most of the Italians who immigrated to Germany in the 1960s have since returned to Italy, and the Greek immigrants, too, are gradually returning home as their native country's economy improves. Only the Turks seem to be prepared to stay longer, which may be due to the fact that the economic differences between Germany and Turkey are still very large.

The widespread distrust of free migration is thus misplaced from an economic viewpoint. Especially because of the large wage and productivity differences in an enlarged EU, mass migration of labor from the less developed to the more developed areas is part of a rational convergence and growth strategy for Europe. Just as the migration of guest workers from Italy that Germany absorbed without any problems in the 1960s brought advantages to both countries involved, so the migration of guest workers from Eastern to Western Europe is among the desirable aspects of the European convergence process.

However, all of this is true only in theory—that is, under the assumption of free markets and no distorting effects of the welfare state. In reality, immigration to Germany if not Western Europe during the past 35 years looked quite different from the optimistic picture painted above, and that is the topic of the next section.

Migration into Unemployment

Wage flexibility is the major prerequisite for the welfare-enhancing effects of migration, as an adjustable wage rate directs job creation and immigration in such a way that both are in equilibrium and at an optimal size. Employers will only want to create new jobs for the immigrants if there is a decline in the wages of those occupational groups which the immigrants join. Only in this case will there be additional output in the country of immigration, only in this case will it be possible for this additional output to more than offset the reduced output in the country of origin as well as the costs of migration, and only in this case will the flow of immigrants be stopped at the right point.

Israel and the United States, whose labor markets have been able to absorb large numbers of immigrants, are characterized by such wage flexibility. In Israel, the unemployment rate rose only from 9.6 percent to 10.3 percent between 1990 and 2002, although the population grew by 38 percent during this period. In the United States, population growth from immigration amounted to 8.6 percent (nearly 20 million) from 1980 to 2002. Yet the unemployment rate fell from 7.1 percent in 1980 to 5.8 percent in the low-growth year 2002.[14] Neither country experienced any particular problems of integration due to immigration, and both succeeded in translating immigration into a growth surge. If the labor market is left alone, immigration is an advantage to the economy.

Germany seemed to have had much greater difficulties with immigration, suffering mass unemployment at the time the migration took place. (See figure

1.2.) From 1970 to 2004 its overall population (including the East and the West) was augmented 5.7 percent by the immigration of 7.8 million people. During this same time, its rate of unemployment increased from 0.7 percent in the West and 0 in the East to 10.5 percent. As was explained in chapters 3 and 4, German institutional rules do not allow for the kind of wage flexibility that would allow the creation of a sufficient number of jobs for the immigrants. In particular, the wage-replacement benefits of the welfare state, such as unemployment compensation and social assistance (now Unemployment Benefit II), imply that unskilled domestic employees are unwilling to compete with the immigrants by offering their services at lower wages.

This reason does not play a similar role in Israel and the United States. In both countries wage-replacement benefits comparable to the level of German social assistance are unknown. In the United States, people even receive the Earned Income Tax Credit, a wage subsidy to the poor, which makes it attractive for people to accept low-paid jobs. Those who have nothing must work, and because this is the way it is, they do work. Those who have no job must look for one, and they usually find one if they offer their labor more cheaply than others. With competition, the wage rate falls until there is more work for everyone and unemployment disappears except for a small transitional remainder.

In Germany, the wage rate follows the politicians' idea of equity, as implemented by the welfare state's wage-replacement system, instead of the dictates of the free market. This is why no additional jobs are created for the immigrants and why there is also no self-limitation of migration. Instead there is mass immigration into unemployment.

Mass immigration into unemployment does not imply that the immigrants themselves are moving into unemployment, for the sole reason that immigrants are not eligible for wage-replacement benefits before they have worked or lived in the host country for a sufficient period of time. As will be explained in more detail, it is one of the basic design principles of the European Union that only "active immigrants" and their dependents have full social-inclusion rights. Pensioners, tourists, students, and other "inactive immigrants" are excluded from receiving social benefits. While this principle has recently been eroded by the new Directive on Free Movement for internal EU migration, it still applies to immigrants from non-EU countries. Germany does not differ much from the other EU countries in this regard. As a rule, active immigrants from EU and non-EU countries are fully included into the welfare system after a year, inactive immigrants from EU countries are included after 5 years, and inactive immigrants from non-EU countries are not included unless they are granted asylum.

Thus, the large majority of immigrants take regular jobs, and, because hardly any new jobs are created, German citizens become unemployed instead. The revolving door of the labor market spins quickly. Each year, about 7 million people lose their job in Germany, and nearly as many find another job again, without this having any effect on the average number of unemployed workers. The immigrants usually succeed in occupying many places in the revolving door that then become unavailable to the nationals. Unemployment among immigrants, as a rule, occurs only after the immigrants themselves have become eligible for wage-replacement benefits.

Again, a look at the relevant German statistics may be useful. Multiplying the above mentioned 7.8 million people who immigrated from 1970 to 2004 in net terms by the labor force participation rate of foreign residents in Germany (51 percent) yields a total increase of the German work force due to immigration of 4.0 million people. About 0.8 million of these (20.5 percent) were unemployed and 3.2 million were working. This is nearly identical to the 3.6 million unemployed nationals (4.4 million unemployed minus 0.8 million unemployed immigrants) that Germany had in 2004.[15]

While these numbers are telling, they do not constitute a causal relationship between immigration and unemployment. Rather, such a causal relationship follows from the logic of the economic marginality principle, already discussed in chapter 4 in the context of Germany's mini-job rules. To repeat, the marginality principle says that, in a market, the price and transactions volume are determined by the high-cost suppliers who just manage to survive, while the low-cost suppliers secure their sales by charging only marginally less than the high-cost suppliers and enjoy high profits. If more low-cost suppliers enter the market, their supply gradually crowds out the supply of the high-cost suppliers, while the market price and the transactions volume do not change as long as at least some of the high-cost suppliers remain in the market. In the labor market, the high-cost suppliers are the nationals who have high reservation wages because they lose their welfare benefits if they accept a job. The low- cost suppliers are the immigrants who are not entitled to replacement benefits but lose their low income abroad if they accept a job here. Being the low-cost suppliers, the immigrants can underbid the nationals by accepting slightly lower wages or by working slightly longer hours for the same amount of pay. They take the jobs, and the nationals accept being crowded out, moving to the easy chair offered by the welfare state. The total employment volume does not change as long as some nationals remain employed, which, given the quantities involved, is a condition that is normally satisfied.[16]

One might argue that firms could keep their domestic employees and, in addition, employ the immigrants at lower wages. However, replacing nationals by immigrants is the more profitable alternative from the point of view of competitive employers since additional jobs could only be created at declining returns. Thus, the immigrants are employed first, and the nationals become the marginal suppliers. As their reservation wage is constant, being determined by the given replacement income offered by the welfare state, it is not profitable for firms to increase overall employment. There is indeed perfect crowding out.

This scenario becomes even more problematic if account is taken of the fact that the artificial increase in domestic wages resulting from the wage-replacement system has destroyed a sizeable number of profitable jobs in the first place and is luring in more migrants than would have come at competitively determined wages. The German-type welfare state destroys jobs, induces excessive immigration, and makes the immigrants crowd out the nationals from the labor market. It is little wonder that Germany has had relatively more immigrants than even the United States and is OECD champion in terms of unemployment among unskilled workers. (See figures 8.2 and 4.3.)

Of course, in practice, some qualifications of this result are in order, as the immigrants do not only consist of people seeking jobs in the low-skilled segments of the labor market where the replacement incomes of the welfare state effectively constrain wage flexibility. There are quite a number of immigrants who, armed with above-average skills, have helped to get German firms going again and to increase the demand for less-skilled German employees. In addition, there are many entrepreneurs among the immigrants who start their own businesses and thereby create jobs, especially in the area of local services. Such positive employment-creating effects of immigration should not be ignored. Nevertheless, these are side effects. Massive crowding out, numbering in the millions, is the empirically dominant event.

The crowding-out effect can be experienced on a daily basis in Germany. What waiter, road worker, garbage collector, cleaning woman, harvest helper, unskilled construction worker, or assembly-line worker is still German? Yes, there still are some Germans who take these types of jobs, but their numbers are shrinking. A large and growing share of these occupational groups consists of immigrants. The Germans who used to do this kind of work are sitting at home today and collecting unemployment compensation, social assistance, or early-retirement benefits.

This shows how pointless immigration policy has been under Germany's institutional conditions. The Germans affected by unemployment accepted being crowded out of the labor market. They were not happy about not working, but neither were they condemned to hardship. They just accepted the wage-replacement income offered by the state and got used to it. Today people do not want to relinquish their social assistance or unemployment assistance in order to work as garbage collectors at only marginally higher earnings than they get in terms of welfare benefits. As long as the welfare office sends the money, people do not mind foreigners doing the work. But from an economic point of view one should mind, because someone has to generate the income redistributed by the welfare office. The foreign garbage collectors are bad for the German economy if their laid-off German colleagues stop working but get an income nonetheless.

Warnings against chiding foreigner immigrants are in order. It is entirely legitimate and understandable for someone to migrate to another country for economic reasons. Reproaching foreigners on moral grounds is therefore inappropriate. What is appropriate is a moral reproach directed at the politicians who, lacking any knowledge of economics, designed the German welfare system in such a way that it turned the labor market into a shambles. The mistake lies with the rules of the game, not with those people who play by these rules. One cannot bring millions of people into the country and fail to adjust the institutional framework so that it can cope with the influx. A policy of wage compression, an expansion of the welfare state by way of the wage-replacement system, and mass immigration are three things that simply do not fit together. Germany must change its institutional framework if it wants to handle immigration from the new EU countries and realize the basic welfare gains described in the previous section.

Under the current institutional framework, structural German unemployment is likely to grow as a consequence of EU eastern enlargement, as the difference between Eastern European wages and German wage-replacement income is much too large to allow a moderate adjustment process. Table 8.2 shows the actual differences between the net wage incomes in some of the Eastern European countries and West German social assistance in the case of long-term unemployment (not including a rich set of in-kind benefits). It can be readily seen that West German social assistance to a family of four (Unemployment Assistance II) is about 3.5 times the net wage earned by an employee with an average gross wage and two children in Poland, Hungary, and Slovakia, and about 2.5 times the net wage in the Czech Republic. In 2005 the corresponding values for East Germany were only slightly lower than those for West Germany, and since then they have come even closer to the West German level. (A full equalization of the basic social transfers with West German levels became effective in July 2006.) Under these conditions, a type of migration that encourages German nationals to hand their jobs to foreigners and retreat into the arms of the welfare state rather than make wage concessions is well nigh unavoidable.

Table 8.2
Social assistance in West Germany and wages in Eastern Europe, 2005, in euros. Sources: OECD, Taxing Wages 2004–2005, Paris 2006; Deutsche Bundesbank, Devisenkursstatistik, April 2006; Ifo Institute calculations.

	Monthly net wage of a single employee with average gross wage	Monthly net wage of a family of an employee with average gross wage (one earner two children)
Poland	422	433
Czech Republic	471	611
Slovakia	364	454
Hungary	401	487
West Germany	1,995	2,660
West German social assistance (Unemployment Benefit II)[a]	673	1,591

a. For a family of four, including child benefits and housing allowance, excluding free in-kind benefits and health insurance.

But it does not have to be this way. To prevent the crowding out of national workers after European enlargement from exacerbating Germany's problems, the labor market and the welfare system reforms described in chapters 3 and 4 should be implemented immediately. These changes include breaking up industry-wide collective bargaining agreements and switching from a welfare system based on wage-replacement benefits to one based on wage supplements. The Activating Social Assistance proposal made by Ifo, which has been accepted by both the German Council of Economic Experts and the Scientific Council at the Federal Ministry of Economics, shows how to eliminate the minimum wage constraint in the German social system without sacrificing the goals of the social-democratic state.

If the welfare state would no longer pay benefits on the condition of not working but instead would make working a prerequisite for receiving assistance, then the reservation wages and the actual wages at which the unskilled are willing to work would decline. This would make a decline of actual wages possible, which, in turn, would induce employers to create additional jobs. Immigration would no longer lead to crowding out of native German workers; it would lead to an increase in employment.

The Welfare State as a Magnet for Immigration

Even if the aforementioned measures were to be implemented, a second problem would stand in the way of optimal migration. That problem arises from state income redistribution as such. Since it is in the nature of the welfare state to take from the rich and give to the poor, even if immigration is distorted. Skilled immigrants who earn above-average labor income in Western Europe must pay a state entrance fee, whereas less-skilled immigrants who earn below-average income in the West receive a migration premium that increases the incentive to immigrate beyond what can be explained by wage and productivity differences. For these reasons, the welfare state works like a two-pole magnet for people who are willing to migrate. With one pole it pulls in welfare recipients; with the other it repels net payers whose contributions would alleviate the state budget.[17]

As was explained above, a magnet effect already occurs when the welfare state, while excluding the immigrants, offers its citizens wage replacement (that is, income on the condition of not working), which keeps wages artificially high, destroys jobs, and attracts immigrants, who crowd some native Germans out of the remaining jobs. This indirect magnet effect is reinforced by the redistribution activities of the welfare state that benefit immigrants directly. These include replacement benefits (for which immigrants become eligible after having worked in Germany for a while), social housing, and subsidized health insurance (to which they have immediate access). Even more important, they include so-called public goods—regular infrastructure costs in the state budget which in public discussions are not considered means of state redistribution. Think of the free availability of roads, bridges, parks, public offices, judges, policemen, schools, and universities. The state levies taxes that rise in line with income, but it makes these public goods quite uniformly available to everyone.

To date, immigrants to Germany have been predominantly unskilled workers, or at least people who could only earn a below-average income in Germany. To some extent this may simply be in the nature of things, as immigrants usually lack facility in the language of their new country. But it is also an endogenous implication of a selection process exerted by the redistributive state. Because of their low incomes, the unskilled immigrants receive, in addition to a wage matching their value added, a migration premium. Although they and their employers paid their taxes and social security contributions, they receive more in benefits from the state than they have paid for, and this effect is the stronger the lower the immigrants' skills, and thus the lower their wages.

To be sure, fiscal incentives may not have played a role for many people who decided to migrate. Those who had strong motives for migration accepted the gifts of the state but were not influenced by these in making their decision to migrate. But there were also people who were induced to migrate by the

state's redistribution policies, who would not have come without these policies and who, in fact, should have stayed home from an economic efficiency
perspective. This list includes people who have particularly low skills, a fact
that makes their redistribution gains especially large, people who by migrating create only a small net addition to the aggregate GEP of the participating
countries, and people whose subjective or objective migration costs are high.
The migration of these people would have been inefficient even if there had
never been the problem of migration into unemployment (discussed in the previous section). In fact, it can be shown that the arrival of the last immigrant,
who is nearly indifferent to having come or stayed home, involves a social
waste whose size is equal to the net fiscal benefit this immigrant receives from
the host country.[18] The state gift received by the last immigrant does not
increase his standard of living compared to having stayed home because it just
compensates for the disadvantage of migrating, but the taxpayer who foots the
bill incurs a sizeable loss. The migration equilibrium is utterly inefficient, with
too much migration taking place.

While this is a strong theoretical point, the question arises as to the actual
size of the gifts Germany offers to immigrants. In an extensive study based
on the German socio-economic panel, the Ifo Institute estimated the flows of
state benefits to the stock of immigrants in Germany in 1997. Account was
taken of taxes, social security contributions, pensions, welfare benefits (including the replacement incomes that were received after having worked), and benefits from the provision of public goods. However, the indirect fiscal costs of
immigration resulting from crowding out domestic residents into unemployment were not included.

As has been mentioned, public goods include roads, bridges, parks, schools,
environmental protection, courts, public administration, police, and fire departments. If the quality of these goods is not to deteriorate as they are used by
more people, the government has to provide more of them if immigration takes
place, and this provision is expensive. Thus, the average cost of providing
these goods was included in the calculation as a measure of the redistribution
gain from their free availability.[19]

The study's findings, presented in table 8.3, show that immigrants paid less
into health insurance than they received from the state, but that they made high
net payments into the pension insurance fund, because the discounted value
of their payments exceeded the pension claims established. Unemployment
insurance gained from those immigrants who had lived in Germany for less
than 25 years and lost from those immigrants who had been in Germany
longer. Because the latter were not very numerous, the unemployment insurance system gained on balance. But the immigrants paid less in taxes than they

Table 8.3
The financial effects of migration on the German state. Using the socio-economic panel (6,810 surveyed households in Germany), the stock of immigrants in West Germany was surveyed in 1997. These were persons of non-German citizenship who lived in West Germany, naturalized persons, and persons with mothers of non-German citizenship. Sources: H.-W. Sinn, G. Flaig, M. Werding, S. Munz, N. Düll, and H. Hofmann, *EU-Erweiterung und Arbeitskräftemigration: Wege zu einer schrittweisen Annäherung der Arbeitsmärkte.* ifo Beiträge zur Wirtschaftsforschung, No. 2, Munich 2001; Sozioökonomisches Panel (SOEP).

Balance of state revenues/expenditures (euros per immigrant per year)	Length of stay (years)		
	0–10	10–25	25+
Health insurance	−590	−43	49
Pension insurance[a]	1.376	1.606	2.148
Nursing insurance	95	117	176
Unemployment insurance	127	217	−519
Taxes and tax-financed benefits	−3.375	−3.227	−1.001
Total balance	−2.367	−1.330	853

a. Present value of payments made and received excluding any child effects.

received in tax-financed welfare benefits and public infrastructure services. In these areas, the net effect is that the state experienced a big deficit.

Immigrants who had been in Germany for less than 10 years could realize, on balance, a net gain from redistribution of nearly 2,400 euros per year per capita. This net gain can be interpreted as a migration premium. It is not small. A Turkish family with three children that came to Germany in 1997 and stayed for 10 years would have received a total of 118,000 euros as a migration premium, based on 1997 conditions. It is obvious that such a sum can influence the decision to migrate and distort it substantially.

If the immigrants stay longer, they succeed in integrating better into the German labor force. As their occupational knowledge and language proficiency improve, their productivity and wages rise. At higher wages, they have to pay higher taxes, and the redistribution gain becomes smaller. Migrants who were in Germany for at least 10 years but less than 25 years received, on balance, only 1,331 euros per year from the state, and migrants who had already been in Germany for longer than 25 years made net payments to the state of 853 euros per year.

Unfortunately, as a rule, the immigrants did not stay long enough in Germany to assume the status of a net payer. About half of the immigrants had returned home after 5 years, and after 25 years more than 80 percent had either died or returned to their home country.

Immigration into Germany is rather different from immigration into the United States. Immigrants move to the United States with a view to staying there for good. Immigrants into Germany usually come as guest workers with the idea of eventually returning to their home country. The data available on return migration leave no doubt that immigration represented a significant losing bargain to the state.

These calculations can be modified by taking into consideration the contributions made by the immigrants' own descendants. When the children of the immigrants grow up, they join the state's fiscal system as taxpayers and contributors. In this way these children contribute to financing the pensions of their parents. Similarly, the pensions of these children, when in pension age, will be paid for by the generation of grandparents, and so on.

The gross contributions of the immigrants to the pension funds would in this case be equal to the net gain for the state. The corresponding present-value calculations show that the annual state loss for the first 10 years after immigration by the parents would decrease from 2,367 euros to 1,241 euros with this modification, that in the following 15 years it would be practically zero, and that for immigrants who have been in the country for at least 25 years the balance would be clearly positive, at 2,610 euros. Yet given that most immigrants do not stay for 15 years or longer and no less than half of them return to their home countries within the first 10 years, taking their children with them, immigration remains a losing game for Germany from a fiscal perspective.[20]

In addition, it must be emphasized again, the costs of indirect migration into unemployment due to the crowding of nationals out of the labor market are not included in these calculations. Such indirect migration into unemployment has been the dominant aspect of the German immigration pattern over the last three decades at least. Though it is difficult to calculate the resulting fiscal costs, it is clear that the deficit indicated in table 8.3 would be much bigger if they were also taken into account. A substantial fraction of the annual cost of German unemployment, which in 2005 amounted to 104 billion euros or 4.6 percent of German GDP, would have to be included in the immigration budget for an overall assessment of the fiscal implications of immigration.[21]

In light of these problems, one may wonder about what political actions are required in Europe as it confronts eastern enlargement. How should the rules of the game be changed so as to avoid the distortions resulting from welfare migration, and just how will these policies be changed? These questions can only be discussed meaningfully before the background of Europe's new laws and directives, in particular the new constitution, or what was meant to become the new constitution before the French and Dutch electorates defeated this in mid 2005.

The New EU Constitution: The Road to a European Social Union

In 2003, when former French president Valéry Giscard d'Estaing presented the draft of the new EU constitution (which had been prepared under his guidance by a committee of representatives from all the EU countries) to the European heads of state, he was confident he had erected a new legal roof under which the continent's unification and its progress toward peace and economic prosperity could continue. But he was mistaken. Though Germany and 14 other EU countries had ratified the constitution by May 2006, it was the French and the Dutch who eventually rejected it in national referenda, putting a hold on subsequent ratifications planned in the other EU countries. Prime Minister Tony Blair must have felt great relief that he did not have to present the constitution to the British, who probably would also have rejected it.

However, this may not yet be the last word, because German Chancellor Angela Merkel, with backing from several the governments of several EU countries, has announced that she will revive the topic during her EU presidency in the first half of 2007. As Germany was able to ratify the constitution and, according to popular polls, a majority of the population seems to support it, Merkel feels obliged to act and make an attempt to set in motion a new discussion process that would ultimately rescue the constitution with minor amendments yet to be specified.[22]

Whether or not Merkel succeeds, popular opposition in some EU countries clearly shows the widespread discontent with the European unification process. Many people in the richer Western European nations feel overwhelmed by the speed of this process and are afraid that leveling the European playing field will reduce their living standards and jeopardize their entitlements, if not their jobs. While they may not have good economic or political theories on what they see happening in Europe, their fears are not unjustified, as the above discussion of direct and indirect immigration into the welfare state has shown. Welfare migration indeed waters down the domestic workers' entitlements to receive protection from a redistributive state, and it does create unemployment under the present social wage-replacement systems. These are undeniable facts despite all the politically correct sermons given in Brussels and elsewhere. How much the welfare states of Western Europe will be pressured by EU enlargement and other integration measures depends not least on the ease of immigration into the welfare state provided by the European legal system. Politicians deny that pressure exists or believe that it is an unimportant side effect of the constitution. They emphasize that the draft constitution defines the basic rights of the citizens of the EU, the decision-making bodies, the division of responsibilities among the European Union and the individual countries, and much more, which is all true and useful. However, the draft does have implications for the European welfare state system, by definition a hallmark of Western Europe. After achieving the economic and monetary union, the EU now tries to prepare the road to a European social union.

It is true that such a social union has already been realized in large measure by previous treaties, directives, and decisions of the European Court of Justice in recent years.[23] The constitution essentially only summarizes existing EU law. However, it grants constitutional status to certain rules, thus elevating these above simple directives. If the new constitution becomes law, it will be more difficult to change the direction of the social unification process, as the old directives and treaties will be carved in stone and the direction of future reforms will be predetermined.

The topic of social union should make Europeans sit up and take notice, as the German example has shown how difficult it is to handle a social union satisfactorily. (See chapter 5.) If the same things that happened in Germany after unification were to happen at the European level, there would be every reason to think twice about ratifying the constitution.

The constitution considers the basic elements of a European social union in many articles that deal with social coherence, the fight against poverty, solidarity and similar things. Of particular economic and political importance to Germany and many other Western European nations are the following statements:

Article I-4, Fundamental freedoms and non-discrimination

2. In the field of application of the Constitution, and without prejudice to any of its specific provisions, any discrimination on grounds of nationality shall be prohibited.

Article I-10, Citizenship of the Union

1. Every national of a Member State shall be a citizen of the Union. Citizenship of the Union shall be additional to national citizenship; it shall not replace it.

2. Citizens of the Union shall enjoy the rights and be subject to the duties provided for in the Constitution. They shall have . . . the right to move and reside freely within the territory of the Member States. . . .

Article II-94, Social security and social assistance

1. The Union recognises and respects the entitlement to social security benefits and social services providing protection in cases such as maternity, illness, industrial accidents, dependency or old age, and in the case of loss of employment, in accordance with the rules laid down by Union law and national laws and practices.

2. Everyone residing and moving legally within the European Union is entitled to social security benefits and social advantages in accordance with Union law and national laws and practices.

3. In order to combat social exclusion and poverty, the Union recognises and respects the right to social and housing assistance so as to ensure a decent existence for all those who lack sufficient resources, in accordance with the rules laid down by Union law and national laws and practices.

These articles do not sound implausible. Union citizenship and free choice of residency are essential steps for a united Europe, and what Europeans would want to discriminate against the citizens of other EU countries! The connection between the prohibition of discrimination according to article I-4 with the right to migration according to article I-10 and the social-inclusion rights according to article II-94, however, may have dire consequences. Taken together, on the face of it these articles imply that citizens of the EU may reside wherever they want, that they are entitled to the host country's full social security benefits and social assistance, and that they must not be treated differently from the country's own citizens, which are extensive rights indeed.

However, when interpreting the articles, the amendment "in accordance with the rules laid down by Union law and national laws and practices" should not be overlooked. This amendment basically leaves more things open than a straightforward interpretation of the constitution would suggest, because it refers to the treaties and directives on which the EU is currently built as well as to previous national practice. Taking all this into account, things would stay unchanged for the time being.

Currently, the right to free movement and the right to inclusion in the European welfare state fully apply to *active immigrants* and their dependents, with the exception of the above-mentioned transition period for East European employees, which ends in May 2011. Family members of active immigrants may follow freely and then enjoy the full protection of the welfare state. For active immigrants who are self-employed or who work for a foreign company offering services in Germany, there is not even a transition period if they come from Eastern European countries. A Polish worker will be able to freely immigrate to Germany only after May 2011, but even today a Polish citizen who opens a store in Germany or a Slovene who works permanently for his Slovene company in Germany faces no restrictions.[24]

Direct immigration into the German welfare state would therefore continue unchanged for active foreigners. Foreigners who work in Germany and pay their taxes and social security contributions have free access to all state benefits, just like all German citizens. But since the welfare state is an institution that redistributes income from top to bottom, and since most migrants have low productivity and earn a low income in the initial years, they tend to receive considerably more from the state than they contribute. The state's net redistribution gift of about 2,400 euros per person per year for the first 10 years of their stay in Germany continues to be at their disposal.

Indirect immigration into a welfare state, in the sense that immigrants displace domestic workers who are pushed into the easy chair provided by the welfare state, would also continue. As was shown in table 8.2, German social assistance to people able to work, which determines the wage floor for the German union wage scale, is higher than the Polish net wage by a factor ranging from 1.6 to 3.7, depending on family status. Even with very rapid wage convergence, artificial migration incentives for Eastern European immigrants will remain in place for a very long time.

In short: Once the EU constitution becomes effective, there is no hope for a change in European law to alleviate the huge mistakes regarding immigration into the welfare state described in the preceding sections. Indeed, conditions may even worsen.

How to Immigrate into the Welfare State without Having to Work

Although the inclusion rights for gainfully employed Europeans have been EU law for a long time, only recently have the inclusion rights of foreigners who do not immigrate for the explicit purpose of taking a job been extended. Until the 1990s, EU residents who were not in the labor force, such as pensioners, students, or tourists, were excluded from welfare benefits in countries other than their home country, except of course for emergency medical treatment. In addition, residency permits could be made contingent on sufficient financial resources to prevent the needy from becoming a direct burden on the host state. Recently, there have been dramatic changes to these laws.

The European Court of Justice has significantly expanded the inclusion rights of EU foreigners through various individual decisions. On September 20, 2001, a pioneering decision occurred in the case of a French citizen who had been studying in Belgium and had asked the Belgian government for social assistance because he had run out of money. Unlike Belgian citizens, who in the same circumstances would have been eligible for social assistance, the French student was denied these benefits. The Court, overturning precedent, decided in favor of the student, arguing that the Belgian policy violated the inclusion principle.[25] A host country is now obliged to provide social assistance if the immigrant's need was unforeseeable at the time of entry—provided, of course, that its own citizens receive state support under similar circumstances. This "equal protection" was required by "solidarity" among the citizens of different EU member states as postulated in the Maastricht Treaty of 1992. Even an unemployed EU citizen legally residing in another country may not be denied the protection of that country's welfare state. After the Court's decision in the case of the French student, it was no longer true that the citizen must hold a job or work as self-employed, as had been the case before the decision.

It is not necessary to speculate regarding the extent to which the case of the French student could be generalized. Since this decision a new Directive on the Freedom of Movement and Residence has very clearly defined what are the new rights for non-employed migrants among the EU member countries.[26] The directive was passed by the European Parliament on March 10, 2004, and had to be translated into national law by May 1, 2006, an obligation which was met in time by most EU countries and will most likely also be met soon by the remaining countries (Belgium, Italy, Luxembourg, and Finland). It was prepared simultaneously with the constitution and exudes the same spirit, showing what the articles cited above mean in practice. Basically, it allows free entry of non-employed EU citizens into any EU country with unlimited inclusion rights after a waiting period of 5 years.

The directive stipulates that an EU citizen may stay in another EU member state for more than 3 months if he has health insurance protection and has the means of subsistence for himself and any dependents, so they will not to have to require any of the host nation's welfare benefits during this stay. The individual would receive a permit granting a residency right for the desired length of stay, up to 5 years (article 11.1). The requirement of resources and health insurance protection applies during this stay.[27] After this period, the immigrant will automatically enjoy permanent residence status, even if by that time he no longer has any resources or health insurance (article 16.1). In contrast to previous law, he is fully eligible for social assistance and other welfare benefits in the host country, just like a national.

Germany, like the other EU countries that have implemented the directive, now does allow direct immigration into the welfare state for someone who will never work in the official labor market, subject only to the requirement that he finance himself for the first 5 years. After these 5 years, the immigrant will be automatically granted permanent resident status with full social rights even if his individual financial resources are exhausted and he cannot afford health insurance.

If the individual is able to work but cannot find a job, he or she is entitled to receive Unemployment Benefit II. This means, for example, that a family of four receives state support in the amount of about 1,600 euros (1,980 dollars) per month, including housing allowances. In addition, the immigrant and his dependents will receive free health insurance, and they will build up pension claims (if he is able to work) as well as old age nursing home insurance claims, even though no social security contributions are made. They will also enjoy various in-kind benefits, including the initial outfitting of an apartment (TV set, stove, fridge, cupboard, bed, etc.). If after 5 years of residence the immigrant is unable to work because he is sick or is 65 or older, he receives the ordinary social assistance that a German citizen would receive, which currently amounts to 673 euros (837 dollars) a month for a single person and 1,048 euros (1,304 dollars) for a married couple without children, including the housing allowance. Again, free health insurance and the above-mentioned in-kind benefits are also provided.

If, say, a Polish couple at the age of 60 feel that their savings will not last for the rest of their lives, they may come to Germany and use up these savings or work as self-employed until they are 65; they will then receive German social assistance for as long as they live. The Polish net wage income is currently about 422 euros at the going exchange rate and 806 euros if converted at Polish-German purchasing-power parity.[28] The Polish net pension level is about 52 percent of Polish average net earnings.[29] Thus, the couple could raise its living standard in retirement by 150 percent even if they had to give up their Polish pension.

The migration incentives would be even larger for people from Romania, Bulgaria, and Turkey, three big countries that are even poorer than Poland and whose accession to the EU has either been approved or is still being discussed. This may be one of the implicit explanations of the large political resistance in Germany to Turkey's accession to the EU.

Immigrants who after entering Germany work for at least a year are particularly protected by the new directive. They need never demonstrate sufficient resources. Any foreigner from an EU country, even one who does not intend to immigrate permanently, who works for at least a year and subsequently becomes involuntarily unemployed, enjoys the full rights of residence and the corresponding eligibility for support, just like a German citizen (article 7.3 b). In Germany, earnings-related Unemployment Insurance I benefits are granted for 6–18 months, and there are no time limits for means-tested social assistance (Unemployment Insurance II). As the right of residence is not restricted once the status of being gainfully employed is achieved, the funds provided by the state will always be available. Whoever enters as employed or self-employed shortly before the legal retirement age has the right to permanent residence and thus *is eligible* for social assistance (Sozialhilfe) when he or she reaches retirement age (article 17.1 a). The directive does not mention a minimum period required between entry and a claim for social assistance. Only if retirement is based on an early-retirement arrangement are 3 years of residence and at least a year of employment required. In Germany, there is no explicit restriction regarding a minimum employment period before an immigrant can claim social assistance with unlimited duration after he or she has reached the legal retirement age.

It will take a number of years before the empirical implications of the new directive become visible and lend themselves to econometric research. Undoubtedly, however, opening the doors of the European welfare states will have dramatic consequences for the way national governments operate. Heretofore, one was able to interpret the redistributing nation state as a homogeneous community that insured and helped those who had become needy through no fault of their own (as was discussed at the start of chapter 4). This interpretation will no longer apply in the future, for this community will admit so many poor risks from outside its country, who have never paid and will never pay their premiums, that the level of protection will necessarily decline.

The Erosion of the European Welfare State

Easier entry into the Western European welfare states will imply a gradual erosion of protection. For one thing, the available funds will have to be spread over more people, an effect that can be offset only to a limited extent by higher taxes and is already in full swing in Europe; for another, governments have an incentive to reduce the benefits granted in anticipation of budgetary problems: they fear the immigration of welfare recipients. Both effects will lead to a kind of deterrence competition, with governments undercutting each other's benefit levels.

Indeed, migration flows can be expected to react to different benefit levels. People willing to migrate from Eastern Europe and elsewhere will compare potential destinations and will go to the countries where they will be treated best. Although migration is a serious personal decision with many non-economic considerations that will not be changed by small economic advantages, once the decision to leave one's home country has been made, the choice about which country to emigrate to is determined largely by the economic conditions in the countries under consideration. Even small differences in welfare benefits can therefore bring about considerable migration effects.

In this situation, individual countries are well advised to think about the welfare benefits they want to offer. If they are too generous, they will attract free-riders and they can expect substantial expenditures. Each country will therefore tend to be stingier than its neighbors. If, however, all Western European countries try to be stingier than their neighbors, the European welfare state will gradually erode.[30] The European social model will be destroyed by deterrence competition.

This must be expected especially if migration is strengthened by network effects—that is, if the initial immigrants from a certain country are likely to be followed by more immigrants from that country. The fear of network effects forces the welfare states to be wary of giving benefits to migrants. Small gifts that can be financed may become financial burdens that can no longer be borne without a large cutback in general welfare.[31]

The combination of inclusion and migration rights that characterizes the new Europe implies that Europe will gradually move in the direction of the United States. The American welfare state is much less developed than the European one, offering significantly lower levels of protection. The reason is not necessarily that Americans would not want more social protection under different rules of the game; it may be, rather, that they have rules that prevent more protection. In the 1960s, under Mayor John Lindsay, New York City had tried to introduce more generous welfare rules along the European pattern, in order to get the poor off the streets. As a consequence, poor people from all over the United States soon came to New York City and drove it to near bankruptcy. Eventually, in 1975, the banks refused to extend any additional loans to the city. This forced the politicians to reverse direction and return to the harsh welfare rules that prevail in the entire country to this day. The city of Washington had similar experiences when it had to cut back its initially generous welfare programs because the cost increase caused by the inflow of poor people spiraled out of control.

To be sure, such processes develop slowly. The European countries' reactions may take many years. But they are subject to fairly powerful forces that will markedly change the European-style welfare state in the long term. Germany already finds itself in the throes of deterrence competition. Reactions like Agenda 2010 are a good example of what deterrence competition can bring forth. Some other countries have already reduced their benefits, and still others will follow. Slowly but surely the European welfare state will wither unless the rules of the competitive game among the European states are changed. Just as the welfare state was successively expanded in the past, it may shrink again in the coming decades. This result will certainly not have been desired by the politicians and lawyers who strengthened the inclusion rights of immigrants. But, as is often the case with well-meant protective laws, economic reality turns the desired effect into the opposite result. The economic reactions of the advantaged citizens and the burdened states provoked by free movement and inclusion will lead to the destruction of what the legal system wanted to protect.

In order to stop the erosion of the European welfare state, Europe should not follow the route proposed by the draft EU constitution, but should develop different rules of the game. In principle, there are only three ways to prevent the consequences described:

1. Free movement of EU citizens is prohibited.
2. The social-inclusion rights of immigrants are reduced.
3. Welfare systems are harmonized across Europe.

The first alternative would not be feasible, as it would violate the Treaty of Rome and would prevent the efficiency gains of migration. The second has been proposed by the author and the Scientific Advisory Council at the German Ministry of Finance. The third would, for obvious reasons, prevent erosion by competition.

It is highly likely that the EU will opt for the third alternative. Welfare migration can be expected to trigger ever louder calls for the harmonization of European welfare rules. Such calls can already be heard from social policy makers from all countries, demanding a social union for Europe in addition to the economic and monetary union. Such harmonization would be consistent with article I-15 (3) of the draft constitution, which explicitly provides for EU initiatives to coordinate the social policies of the member states. This would perfect the social union.

But a social union presupposes great similarity of economic conditions in Europe. If there are large differences in the economic strengths of different regions, a social union with harmonized standards cannot work. As was described in chapter 5, that is exactly what Germany experienced as a result of unification, and what the Italians have also learned from their Mezzogiorno, which has been stagnating for more than half a century. Neither country has found a way out of the permanent stagnation that a social union created in its weaker regions.

A European social union, at least one based on wage-replacement incomes, would imply uniform minimum wages in all countries. Welfare incomes that are acceptable in the richer nations would raise wages in the economically weaker countries above the level that is compatible with full employment. The resulting mass unemployment would have to be financed by the richer nations, making the substantial problems already affecting Germany and Italy a chronic, widespread European illness.

The quantitative significance of this problem is illustrated by figure 8.4, which compares the net wages of various countries and regions with the West German level of social assistance. Harmonization of social assistance on a

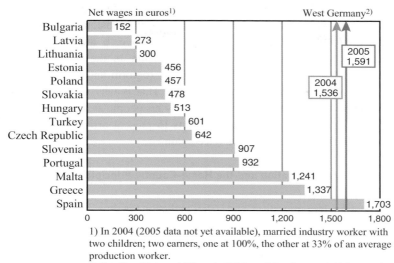

1) In 2004 (2005 data not yet available), married industry worker with two children; two earners, one at 100%, the other at 33% of an average production worker.
2) Family with two children, in 2004: social assistance 1,536 euros; in 2005: newly introduced Unemployment Benefit II 1,591 euros.

Figure 8.4
Monthly net wages in Europe compared to West German social assistance. Sources: Eurostat, Population and social conditions database; West Germany: Ifo Institute calculations.

level that Germany still considers appropriate would, via enforced wage increases, be tantamount to sounding the economic death knell for entire regions within the European countries as well as some entire countries. Not only would this affect the Eastern European countries, which would be sentenced to an East German type of stagnation; in addition, many regions in the old EU would be unable to pay wages in line with a harmonized social standard on the German level. Spain, Portugal, and Greece, in particular, would have to expect economic decline in large portions of their countries. There would be not two but twenty "Mezzogiorni" in Europe. Like Eastern Germany and Southern Italy, these twenty Mezzogiorni would have to be kept afloat by funds transferred from the economically functioning regions. The numbers mentioned above for the EU budget would no longer apply. These would be a multiple of what they are now, and the EU would begin to become financially problematic for the member states. As was shown in chapter 5, West Germany now transfers nearly 100 billion euros of public funds per year to East Germany. It would probably have to raise another 100 billion euros if a social union based on German standards were to come into being for the EU. Perhaps the politicians will recognize this potential trap and set the standards so low that even the weaker European countries can keep up. However, in that case welfare migration would undoubtedly lead to the erosion of the better-developed European welfare states, as described above. If the right to free movement is combined with the right of inclusion in the welfare state, Europe's only choice will be between many Mezzogiorni and the demise of the European welfare state as we now know it. That is why Giscard should see the rejection of the European constitution by his people as an opportunity. He could reconsider whether he really wants to present article II-94 in its present form to the European people once again.

Selectively Delayed Integration and the Home-Country Principle

Social protection, free migration, and social inclusion are three important goals of the European Union; however, these values are incompatible. If history proceeds along the paths that Europe's legal structure has defined, social protection will erode. If that result is to be prevented, either free migration or social inclusion will have to be sacrificed. Free migration, however, is undoubtedly the higher goal. It is a prerequisite of individual freedom and prosperity, and therefore it was rightfully proclaimed in the Treaty of Rome of 1957. Thus, the inclusion principle should be sacrificed, or at least inclusion rights should be much more limited than is stipulated in Europe's treaties and directives. Doing without the inclusion principle is the lesser evil.

The Scientific Advisory Council at the German Finance Ministry, and earlier the Ifo Institute, recommended a strategy of selectively delayed integration into Germany's welfare structure for gainfully employed immigrants.[32] During a transition phase after immigration, the tax-financed social benefits provided for the immigrants should be limited in such a way as to completely balance the fiscal accounts, and full integration should be possible only after this period. The dictum should be that every EU citizen who wants to come is welcome to do so, to work, and to earn a competitive income, but that he or she cannot expect to receive any gifts from the state.

With selectively delayed integration, the working immigrant is fully subject to paying taxes and making payroll contributions, and he receives all entitlements to contribution-financed benefits as is the case today, but tax-financed benefits would not be initially granted in full. Most state benefits, including free access to the public infrastructure and protection by the police and courts, cannot and should not be limited. But housing allowances, social assistance, allowances for children remaining abroad, and the opportunity to move into public housing (which at present is available to only one-fourth of the eligible German nationals) should be limited. The limitations should be fine-tuned in such a way that the fiscal account of the state is balanced. The deficit of nearly 2,400 euros for the annual net cost to the state during the initial 10 years (table 8.3) would be reduced to zero. If, despite working, a migrant needs additional support, he must claim it from his home country. Only after the transition phase would he be entitled to the full protection of the host country. The transition phase should be long enough for immigrants to be, as a rule, so well integrated that they earn the average income of the host country, and that they are no longer net recipients of state benefits.

It follows from the spirit of the above-mentioned proposal that the migratory constraints that currently exist in Europe should be lifted. For example, Germany should immediately waive the immigration restriction for Eastern European workers, which otherwise would be expected to last until May 2011. If, in addition, Germany were to introduce the system of Activating Social Assistance proposed in chapter 4, it would be able to fully capture the gains from free migration described at the beginning of this chapter. So much for the migration of working immigrants.

For inactive immigrants from other EU countries, the Ifo Institute has proposed the home-country principle. Pensioners, students, disabled persons, tourists, and others who would like to take up residence in another EU country should face no restrictions to doing so. However, they should not be able to direct financial claims against the host country. They may, of course, make free use of the public infrastructure and the legal system, just as citizens do. However, if foreign immigrants are or become needy, their claims would have to be directed to their home countries. Because the home countries are all EU members whose entry conditions included the meeting of European social standards, this solution should not be problematic. There is nothing to be said against a welfare recipient moving to another EU country while he or she continues to consume the benefits provided by the home country. However, there is much to be said against the automatic social inclusion that forces the host country to take over the social burden from the home country.

Selectively delayed integration for working immigrants, combined with the home country principle for inactive immigrants, would reduce the artificial migration incentives. It would take the pressure off the welfare states to curtail their welfare benefits, and it would limit the erosive forces of competition among the welfare states. Europe would not develop twenty Mezzogiorni, but would prosper in the existing economic variety. Driven by the natural economic processes described above, it would gradually converge. For this to happen, the Directive on Free Movement—and, accordingly, Article II-94 of the constitution—would have to be reformulated. Section 2 of that article could read as follows:

Everyone gainfully employed who resides legally in the European Union and legally changes his residence is entitled, after an appropriate period of time, to the full social security benefits and social advantages of his host country. During the transition period, tax-financed services may be limited. Inactive citizens may direct their claims at their home country, independently of their country of residence.

This would suffice, at least at the constitutional level, for establishing the principle of selectively delayed integration for active immigrants, and for establishing the home-country principle for inactive immigrants. The other articles cited above would not be inconsistent with this formulation, and would not have to be changed. However, the precept of non-discrimination according to article I-4 could no longer be interpreted in the sense of inclusion in the host country's welfare state.

Unquestionably, Europe will forgo many opportunities for its future if it fails to give itself a constitution. It is nearly inconceivable that such a confederation of states with a common currency and an already far-reaching transfer of legislative powers to the European level can be successful without a formal constitution. The rejection of the draft constitution presented to the people of Europe provides a chance for correcting mistakes made and for redirecting the economic and social development of Europe toward true social cohesion and economic prosperity.

to the children of Europe, who will inherit the liabilities of the welfare state unless today's adults take action now

9 Rethinking the Welfare State: A Reform Program

Options for Europe and Germany

Not only have Germany's attempts to achieve social objectives by going against the rules of the market economy failed; many other West European welfare states, too, have been bent on attempting this untenable feat and have bloodied their noses trying to achieve it. These countries are suffering from deep structural crises that result from their inability to cope with the forces of globalization—forces that are not compatible with the older rules that, in a less open world economy, helped foster the generous welfare states of old.

The German welfare state is at the center of attention here, because Germany is by far the biggest European economy and because many Western European countries have modeled their social systems on it. With a few exceptions (among them Ireland and Great Britain), all Western European nations have in one way or another been influenced by the social developments in Germany. Germany is the country where socialism was invented and where its milder form of social democracy originated. It is the country where politicians first tried to appease the masses by developing the social welfare state and where later the welfare state was pushed to its limits. It is little wonder that the problems of the aging welfare state are becoming visible in this country with particular force. Germany's current predicament is the tip of an iceberg with which the European ship could collide should it continue on its current course.

In the so-called Lisbon agenda of 2000, a program to foster growth in Europe by means of government intervention in the innovation process, the heads of state of the EU-15 countries had proclaimed that by 2010 Europe would "become the most dynamic and competitive knowledge-based economy in the world, capable of new economic growth with more and better jobs, and greater social cohesion."[1] At this writing, with the ten-year period more than half over, there is not the slightest glimpse of this predicted success. From 2000 to 2005, China grew by an annual 9.5 percent rate, the Middle East by 4.9 percent, Asia absent China and the Middle East by 2.7 percent, Africa by 4.7 percent, central and Eastern Europe by 4.3 percent, the United States by 2.4 percent, Latin America by 2.4 percent, and the old EU-15 only by 1.6 percent. Even the enlarged EU grew only by 1.7 percent, much less than any of the world's other big regions.[2] Instead of showing signs of becoming the world's most dynamic region, Europe has turned out to be its laggard.

The reason behind the embarrassing failure of European policy is that the politicians have focused on the wrong priorities (and in fact have done very little even to pursue the priorities on which they focused). Emphasizing the roles of research and innovation, they have ignored Europe's labor-market problems and its demographic problems, the two most important impediments to growth.

Innovations are necessary. However, they must be carried out by private business rather than by government, and the gains disperse quickly to the rest of the world. Although many innovations can be patented, no one can stop the owner of a patent from exploiting his knowledge in a low-wage country. The competitive pressure on European workers can hardly be mitigated by simply throwing EU money at the innovators. More important for an improvement in the competitiveness of the European population are government actions in the field of education. Indeed, the human capital stored in the minds of people enables them to sell their services at higher prices on the world labor market. Moreover, good education policy provides equal starting conditions and helps a country satisfy equity goals. Unfortunately, however, education policy will have its effects only in the long term. It takes a full generation until a sizeable impact on the labor market materializes. Thus, to solve Europe's imminent competitive problems, there is hardly an alternative to liberalization of the labor market coupled with reform of the social welfare system.

The strong winds of globalization have brought international low-wage competition from the formerly communist countries and India to Western Europe. This greater competition has effected more rapid structural adjustments than ever before in the peaceful eras of Europe. While European wage scales are pulled down by the forces of factor-price convergence threatening to produce more inequality than Europe's democratic systems are willing to tolerate, the countries of Western Europe are desperately searching for viable policy responses that maintain the living standard of their lower income strata and avoid social unrest.

Despite their similarities, the countries of the western hemisphere have sought different responses to the forces of international low-wage competition. Four different approaches can be defined, and the counties of Europe must make up their minds which one they want to pursue further:

1. the Franco-German way of permitting strong union power and paying voluminous wage-replacement incomes that keep wage scales compressed, crowding out jobs that would otherwise exist,

2. the Thatcherite-British way of full liberalization of the labor market with a fight against unions, a widening of wage distribution and a downscaling of the welfare state,

3. the Scandinavian way of social cooperation with the unions that results in keeping the demand for labor high by employing those who cannot earn enough in the market economy in the government sector,

or

4. the American way of supplementing a liberal labor market with the payment of wage subsidies.

The Franco-German way is an attempt to overcome the forces of factor-price convergence. Thus far, to be sure, it has been successful in terms of maintaining the incomes of the unskilled. However, it leads to more and more unemployment, which, apart from pushing an increasing part of the population to the offside und causing social unrest and violence, will not be financially feasible in the long run.

The Thatcherite way succeeded in achieving more employment and growth, but it failed to avoid the problem of poverty. Because it asks Europe to give up its social objectives, and because it jeopardizes the achievements of a century of social development, it does not find much support on the European continent . Britain itself has watered down Margaret Thatcher's model by implementing major corrections to satisfy social objectives. (See chapter 6.)

The Scandinavian way keeps the wage distribution scale compressed, avoids the problem of social exclusion, and provides the less-motivated part of the population with at least some useful work. However, it looks better than it is because in the OECD accounting system the wages paid by the government sector are considered contributions to GDP even if these wages could not have been earned in the private sector. Like the Franco-German way, the Scandinavian way is financially problematic, to say the least, as the high government share of GDP of the Scandinavian countries proves. It neglects the forces of international factor-price convergence in a way similar to that of France and Germany, because it forces artificially augmented wage demands on the private economy. Moreover, it probably misallocates the available labor force, because the government hardly knows better than the market where scarce human labor can be made to work most efficiently.

This leaves the American way, as exemplified by the Earned Income Tax Credit. Although American social standards do not satisfy European objectives, Europe could copy the incentive structures of the American welfare system, first introduced by President Clinton in the 1990s, but could make it more generous to fit European social preferences—something that has been discussed in Germany under the rubric of "an activating social welfare state." The advantage of this approach is that it decouples income distribution from wage distribution, satisfying social objectives while employment and growth stay high and the financial burden on the state remains limited.

This chapter makes the case for implementing reforms that liberalize the labor market as in Britain and go in the American direction concerning the incentive structure of the government welfare program (although Britain's working family tax credit should not be forgotten in this regard). Using the German economy as an example, it describes how these could be implemented without violating Europe's social standards and without costing more tax money than is absorbed by the present welfare state. These reforms are also advisable for other countries that have similar wage-replacement systems, including France, Austria, Belgium, the Netherlands, and Luxembourg. Moreover, these reforms may be advisable for the Scandinavian countries, because they bring about the efficiency gains of having a high employment level in the private economy while satisfying Europe's social objectives.

The reform proposals focus on implementing a better incentive structure in the labor market and making the wage distribution more flexible. This chapter suggests a number of policy measures that complement the move to an activating welfare state and help marry efficiency and equity objectives in an arguably better way than has so far been the case in Europe. Although the policy recommendations have been tailored to the German case, these are highly relevant to many European countries and even to the new emerging economies in Asia and elsewhere that have to set up their social systems from scratch.

The German Case

Arguably, Germany's labor market is one of the most defective in Europe. While most German firms seem to adjust well to the forces of globalization, expand worldwide and make good profits, German workers suffer from mass unemployment that has grown at an exceptional rate for the past 35 years. Germany's firms stay competitive, but Germany's workers do not. In fact, German firms stay competitive only because they find ways to do business by eschewing non-competitive German workers.

But human labor remains the fundamental source of a country's wealth and prosperity. If the domestic labor market no longer functions, soon nothing will function in Germany. Thus, economic reforms must focus on conditions in the labor market. The effects on the labor market of population growth, immigration, and the government's redistribution activities must be taken into account in this program of reforms.

High labor costs and aspirations to a high standard of living are Germany's most important problems. Except for national taxes, labor costs are the only relevant costs for location decisions in international business competition. In order to prevail in this now global competition, one can be more expensive only to the extent to which one is superior. Whether German workers are superior to those of other countries is doubtful. In any case, however, they are more expensive. Germany's manufacturing industry had the highest hourly labor costs in the world in the 1980s and the 1990s and was only recently overtaken by Denmark's. Unskilled labor, in particular, is extremely expensive in Germany, and the country's wage spread is extremely narrow by international standards. That Germany has the highest rate of unemployment among unskilled workers and that it has the second-lowest net investment share among all OECD countries are obviously due to Germany's high labor costs for industrial workers. In turn, Germany's high labor costs are due in part to the German labor unions' unrestrained cartel policy. Equipped with the right to make binding sector-wide wage agreements, unions extracted as much as they could for the employed workers at the expense of the unemployed, whose number has grown steadily. The rest of the explanation can be found in the welfare state's attempts to cushion the consequences of unemployment by offering increasingly generous wage-replacement benefits, including unemployment compensation, social assistance, and early retirement. These once well-intended measures have been counterproductive, because they operate like competitive counter-bids in the labor market, creating high minimum wage demands that the private sector has been unable to satisfy in an increasing number of cases. In the global economic environment, low-wage competitors from all over the world harass German companies in their product markets. The welfare state, as a high-wage competitor, harasses them on the domestic labor market. German jobs are being gradually squeezed out by this double competitive bind.

Unemployment has risen in West Germany according to a linear trend for 35 years, and there is no end in sight. There is, however, no way for the country to survive an extension of this trend for another 35 years. The German economic model, underpinned by a generous welfare state, has come to its historical and logical end.

German firms have successfully tried to escape from the high wages by buying robots instead of people. Their owners have used their capital for a rapid expansion of capital-intensive export industries or sent it abroad via the financial system, creating a huge export volume and a large current-account surplus. Many German firms have reacted to the country's high labor costs by moving part of their production to other countries. In most cases the structural change has been smooth, but in many cases it has involved bankruptcy. The number of bankruptcies reached a postwar record in 2005.

In spite of record unemployment, high wages for unskilled work produced by the wage competition of the welfare state have attracted many immigrants to Germany. But these same high wages have prevented German businesses from providing additional jobs. That is why there has been migration into unemployment, albeit in an indirect manner. While the foreign immigrants took the low-paid jobs, the German workers preferred to rest in the easy chairs provided by the welfare state. The downward adjustment of wages that would have been necessary to create new jobs for the immigrants was impossible because of the replacement incomes offered by the welfare state. Germany has not yet found a way to integrate immigrants into its economy in a meaningful way by creating additional jobs for them instead of providing them with the existing jobs of the domestic workers. EU eastern enlargement and the still-enormous wage differences between Eastern and Western Europe will likely induce additional immigration into Germany's overly rigid labor market.

Despite immigration, Germany's population is shrinking and aging as fewer and fewer families are started and fewer and fewer children are born. In Germany, the age group that tends to set up firms and conduct innovative research is shrinking rapidly, and as a result fewer and fewer new competitive jobs are created. At the same time, pension claims are mounting, and in 30 years these will be difficult to meet for lack of jobs and for lack of employable people.

After a temporary lull resulting from Gerhard Schröder's tax cuts, the public sector's share in GDP may again rise faster than aggregate output, as a result of increasing unemployment and an aging population. Such an event would require a further increase in tax rates, and indeed the new German coalition government under Angela Merkel enacted quite a number of tax increases since it came to power in 2005; the largest of these increases is in the value-added tax (three percentage points). Today, the value added produced by Germany's industrial workers is already subject to the highest marginal tax burden among comparable advanced countries. Many Germans escape the high taxes by moonlighting or by withdrawing from working life, while young people lose interest in obtaining education and other training because there are no discernible rewards for these efforts.

Germany must be liberated from the vicious circle in which it has been caught for more than 30 years. Germans should not stand idly by while their country falls behind and becomes a land in which retirement homes and holiday parks prosper, financed by a dwindling stock of private wealth and evaporating public resources.

Germany must at last come to terms with the laws of the market and give up its idealistic illusions regarding the potential of the welfare state. The "crash test" of the market economy that the Social Democrats proclaimed in the 1970s has failed, unequivocally. Even Willy Brandt, former German chancellor and president of the Socialist International from 1976 to 1992, would agree with this assessment, were he still alive to render an opinion. During the 1970s, a period that seemed to affirm the country's successful postwar rebuilding, all of Germany was too naive regarding economic issues. Politicians and the elite neglected the laws of economics and underestimated the harm the development of the welfare state did to the economy. The mistakes they made turned out to be even more destructive as the winds of global change became stronger in the 1980s, when the Asian Tigers appeared in the markets, and turned into a storm in the 1990s, when the formerly communist countries freed themselves from the fetters of central planning.

Germany needs a system in which the natural incentives for people to create wealth and security for themselves come to the fore once again. In the past few decades, these incentives were massively distorted by state intervention, with the result that the dynamism of the postwar period was lost. A program that is consistently aligned with the demands of the global market economy, that relies on the self-healing forces of the domestic economy, and that induces people to once again take greater responsibility for the consequences of their own actions without sacrificing Germany's social objectives will succeed in laying a firm foundation for the country's recovery. The necessary reforms may be painful in individual cases and will not have immediately realized effects, as these changes are a long-term structural solution, not a short-term cyclical response to current economic conditions. A truly effective turnaround will take time. But it will be successful, generating more growth and more employment while preserving Germany's social standards in the sense of maintaining the living standard of the poor. The laws of economics work slowly, but when invoked they work persistently and powerfully.

The six items below summarize the political demands that follow from this book's analysis of Germany's economic problems. They do not exhaust the roster of necessary reforms, but they encompass the most important ones, at least with respect to economic considerations. There is another program with regard to East Germany, which is especially urgent but not really different since it builds on the recommendations for West Germany. Therefore, this is a "6 + 1" program.

Item 1: A U-turn in Collective Bargaining

Working Longer Hours

In order for German workers to regain their international competitiveness, hourly wages must decline. By how much is unclear in view of the rapidly changing global economic environment. A good beginning point of reference is a comparison with the Netherlands, which 25 years ago had problems similar to Germany's and solved them by means of long-term wage moderation, initiated with the 1982 Wassenaar Agreement. If the German wage differential relative to the Dutch that accumulated from 1982 to 2005 is to be offset, Germany's employer contributions to pension and unemployment insurance will have to be assumed by the employees, or wage increases will have to lag one percent behind productivity gains for 11 years.

Happily, the same objective may be achieved more quickly and more simply just by lengthening weekly working hours without imposing the wage offset. If Germans worked 13 percent longer at the same wage, the wage gap with the Netherlands, which has accumulated since the employment-generating Wassenaar agreement of 1982, could be closed. Statutory weekly working hours would have to be raised from 38 to 43 (the number at which they stood 25 years ago). Germans would still be working fewer hours than the British or the Irish, and about the same as the Italians. Evidently a 43-hour working week is still compatible with "la dolce vita."

An increase in working hours permits a better utilization of firms' capital stock. The increase is similar to labor and capital augmenting technological progress and triggers a similar growth surge. Raising the productivity of every single worker by extending individual work time, given his or her labor costs, also induces firms, in a second step, to create additional jobs.

Agreeing on longer working hours is the responsibility of the bargaining parties and not the state. But the German government can encourage the bargaining parties to make a favorable compromise. If they fail to react, the government can threaten to eliminate some holidays instead. The Wassenaar Agreement between the Dutch bargaining parties was brought about by the Dutch government's threat to impose legal limits upon wage increases.

In this respect the German government should not be too cautious. Germany unambiguously finds itself in a serious state of emergency that does not permit any regard for particular interests. The long-term economic welfare of the nation must be placed above short-term political calculations.

Investment Wage Instead of Cash Wage, Co-Ownership Instead of Co-Determination

Additional wage reductions could be agreed to in exchange for workers' co-ownership in their firms. This would require longer-term collective wage agreements. If co-ownership were available only to those people now employed as compensation for wage moderation, whereas newly hired employees were excluded, a positive employment effect would result without present workers suffering any disadvantages. Such agreements would correct the historical mistake made by the unions in the 1960s when they decided in favor of co-determination and against investment wages.

Investment wage models have already been successfully implemented in thousands of German firms. These include such well-known companies as Bertelsmann, BMW, Altana, and Otto (Germany's biggest mail-order company), but also many unincorporated small firms. The know-how of co-ownership in large and small firms is amply available in Germany, and the practice could easily be extended to other companies.

Once again, agreeing on co-ownership is up to the bargaining parties. However, the state could promote such agreements by improving the legal framework for protecting employees and subjecting investment wages only to ex-post or cash-flow taxation.

Item 2: Less Power to the Unions!

More Firm-Level Bargaining

German unions have used bargaining autonomy to implement wage cartels with respect to employers and indirectly also with respect to consumers. By raising wages beyond the level that would balance supply and demand, unions have created more unemployment than otherwise would have resulted. This excessive unemployment rate is the very proof that a cartel policy succeeds in bringing about higher wages than those the market would establish by itself if left alone.

Bargaining autonomy must not be understood as cartel power. It should be interpreted in such a way that it is compatible with firm-level competition in labor and product markets. Companies should be put into a position to under-bid the prices and wages of their competitors, if necessary, without their competitors' or a unions' being able to prevent this action.

The bargaining partners should therefore be obliged by law to include effective opening clauses in their agreements that would enable a firm's workforce to deviate from the pattern bargaining contract by way of a voluntary firm-level agreement with management. The opening clauses must include the possibility of such measures as an extension of working time and/or a wage cut that prima facie are unfavorable to employees, but allow employees to safeguard their jobs. A two-thirds majority of the workforce should suffice for deviating from union-mandated wage agreements. This rule would not change the system of pay setting in normal cases and would not require firms to negotiate future wage increases, but it would permit backdoor adjustments should these be necessary. Opening clauses would strengthen bargaining autonomy by granting a firm's employees more say in pay setting.

In view of the high number of bankruptcies among German companies, firm-level opening clauses are an urgently required emergency measure to avoid an even bigger disaster. Thousands of company bankruptcies could still be prevented if legislation were passed quickly to grant employees the right to help their firms by agreeing to voluntary wage moderation.

Free Choice of Dismissal Protection

Statutory protection against dismissal is one of the unions' most effective weapons in the bargaining game. It forces private business to continue hiring labor even when it has become too expensive, and it shares responsibility for the unions' aggressive wage policy, which led to high unemployment. Dismissal protection has not created secure jobs for German workers; rather, it has reduced job security by inducing excessive wage demands by unions thus increasing unemployment. Nothing creates more job security than a high employment rate and a well-functioning labor market.

Not only should statutory protection against dismissal be abolished for small firms, as it has been; it should be abolished for all firms, regardless of size. Employers and employees should be permitted to sign work contracts according to their own preferences, be these contracts for a limited time, for an unlimited time, or with full dismissal protection with the wage rates varying inversely with the degree of protection. The state should not restrict individual freedom of choice. In practice, contracts for an unlimited time without dismissal protection will prevail in the majority of cases. Each party must then remain content with the ongoing employment relationship, and if one party is no longer content it will have the right to end this relationship in line with the contract. After all, an employment contract is not a lifelong marital agreement.

Abolishing enforced dismissal protection will encourage German unions to practice wage moderation, which will then induce firms to create more jobs. In addition, it will encourage firms to risk hiring more people even at the prevailing wage rates, as they will be able to react more flexibly to unexpected changes in their business conditions. Finally, doing away with legal dismissal protection will strengthen work incentives, as employees will fear getting fired for laziness. As German wage costs are too high relative to labor productivity, abolishing statutory dismissal protection is a contribution to regaining competitiveness. Allowing more freedom in the choice of labor contracts will save very many jobs in Germany. Job security will rise.

Of course, the reform must be implemented with care. Initially, it is advisable to abolish only the statutory dismissal protection of newly hired employees in order to prevent a breach in the system, as otherwise pent-up dismissals could be implemented all at once with adverse short-term economic consequences. By limiting dismissal protection to newly hired employees, natural employee turnover will allow a gradual transformation of the economy. Statutory dismissal protection should not be abolished only for private-sector employees. As a rule, civil servants do not need such protection either. Surely, their enthusiasm for work can also be boosted.

Item 3: Less Money for Staying Out of the Game, More Money for Participating

Activating Social Assistance

As was mentioned in the introduction to this chapter, of central importance for the recovery of the German labor market are steps that lead from wage replacements to wage supplements. Wage replacements in the form of unemployment compensation, social assistance, and early retirement are the main reasons for the malfunctioning German labor market. By providing wage-replacement income, the state becomes a competitor to private business in the labor market. If a person does not work, he receives income from the state, and if he does work, state income support is halted. A person will, therefore, demand that a potential employer pay at least as much in wages as the state pays for doing nothing. An employer who wants to avoid losses, on the other hand, will not hire anybody who costs more than they produce. Thus, all those who are unable to produce more than the wage-replacement income provided by the government will remain unemployed.

The generous wage-replacement system has been responsible for the fact that immigration to Germany during the past 30 years has essentially resulted in indirect migration into unemployment. Domestic workers, who were able to rely on the state's wage-replacement benefits, preferred being pushed into unemployment over entering into low-wage competition with immigrants for scarce jobs. As a consequence, wages did not fall, jobs remained scarce, and the immigrants simply replaced domestic workers in the same jobs.

The biggest problem was among the unskilled workers, as social assistance pushed their wages above the market-clearing level the most. In past decades Germany had more immigration even in relative terms than other big countries, and now it also has far higher unemployment among unskilled workers. It brought millions of people into the country and then prevented wage adjustment to foster their employment by providing wage-replacement benefits. Wage-replacement benefits were expanded in the 1970s and the 1980s primarily to solve social problems at the margins of a well-functioning market economy, but since then the wage demands these policies produced have caused mass unemployment. A policy that was meant to help the poorer strata of the population has, in fact, deprived them of the right to be integrated into the working society. German politicians seem to be gradually realizing that this was the wrong approach. The Schröder government rightly shortened to 12 months the period when unemployment compensation is paid and merged the second-tier unemployment system with social assistance, but this was far from enough. Social assistance is much too high to be compatible with a functioning labor market for unskilled workers. Social assistance puts an absolute floor on the wage scale that prevents the necessary wage dispersion and upsets the entire wage structure in the low-wage range.

Despite some easing of the rules on additional earnings, the effective marginal tax burden on recipients of social assistance (Unemployment Compensation II) resulting from transfer withdrawal when an income is earned is still in the range of 80–90 percent, and in some income ranges even 100 percent and more.

The Ifo Institute has developed an alternative to wage replacement called Activating Social Assistance. With Activating Social Assistance, the benefit levels for employable persons who are not gainfully employed are reduced by about one-third. The funds saved are redistributed to low-wage earners who take a paying job. For incomes up to 500 euros per month no social assistance is withdrawn, in contrast to today's system. On the contrary, the state even supplements self-earned income up to 200 euros at a rate of 20 percent. Above an earned income of 500 euros per month, more generous additional earnings are possible without social assistance being withdrawn at today's excessive rate.

Persons who cannot find a job may be employed by their local community's loan employment program at a wage rate equal to today's social-assistance rate. The local community then leases their labor to private businesses at the highest possible fee they can get, which however may be close to zero in particular cases. As long as the communities collect at least some money, this scheme is better for them than paying the social assistance without receiving anything in exchange. Moreover, people do work and make a contribution to GDP that otherwise would not have been available.

Local businesses will benefit from this measure, as Activating Social Assistance is a program for integrating moonlighting workers into their firms. First, these businesses will have more customers, as the recipients of social assistance will no longer have time to offer their services in the underground economy. Second, the persons concerned will be available as affordable labor to the local firms, either directly by way of subsidized employment or indirectly by way of loan employment.

The Activating Social Assistance program will create many jobs by making labor cheaper, so that an increasing number of the potential jobs that employers have in mind become profitable for them. Labor employed directly in the private sector will become cheap because the abolishment of the transfer withdrawal rate will reduce people's reservation wages to the natural level determined by the lost black-market income. Labor offered by the local communities and the loan agencies will become even cheaper because the required pay will be decoupled from individual reservation wages. At a sufficiently low wage rate, it will be possible to find demand for nearly all the loan labor offered.

The effect of the reform will extend beyond the group of employable social-assistance recipients directly affected, as the entire range from low to medium wage rates will be lowered. The economy as a whole will therefore experience an increase in employment that will be accompanied by an increase in aggregate supply and demand, boosting economic growth. According to conservative estimates by the Ifo Institute, not yet taking this secondary employment effect into account, the long-term increase in jobs to be expected as a result of abolishing unemployment assistance and introducing the Activating Social Assistance program will amount to about 3.2 million.

Despite lower wages for unskilled workers, past recipients of social assistance will be better off than before. The sum of self-earned wages and supplemental social assistance will yield a higher income than such a person receives today in the form of social assistance. And the state will be no worse off. The program is constructed in such a way that the government will save about 8 billion euros per year in the short run and 21 billion euros per year in the long run relative to the current system of unemployment assistance.

With Activating Social Assistance, a more rational welfare state may be constructed than the one that exists today. The help that the new system will provide is best described as a change from government help to self-reliance. In the existing system, a person receives maximum state assistance only if he or she does not work. With Activating Social Assistance, maximum state assistance will be provided only for those who work. Everyone will be required to work according to his ability to receive an adequate income, and if one does not earn enough from one's job one will receive supplemental support from the state.

With this reform, Germany would no longer be the leader in unemployment among unskilled workers. The reform would also put an end to indirect immigration into unemployment, which results from the fact that wage-replacement incomes push up the wages of the unskilled, attracting more immigrants to a shrinking labor market, from which they crowd out the nationals. As the Activating Social Assistance program would clear the labor market, immigration no longer would crowd Germans out of employment. In view of the additional immigration that can be expected to follow liberalization of labor migration after EU eastern enlargement, there is no alternative to implementing this reform. The Activating Social Assistance program will help Germany to extract benefits from immigration and to summon the strength for new economic growth.

Work during Early Retirement

Besides the current system of unemployment compensation, Germany's early-retirement programs also have the effect of rewarding idleness at the expense of fostering productive labor-force participation. Those who take advantage of part-time retirement are able to raise their hourly wage rate by 60 percent, and those who retire before reaching age 65 need not fear any actuarially adjusted pension reduction. Someone who retires early receives, at present value, a higher pension payments from the state until death than someone who retires later, but the proviso is that the recipient leaves the labor market permanently, and may not continue working even part-time.

Early retirement also raises wage claims on the employer and increases unemployment. By reducing low-wage competition among workers—competition that would lead to wage moderation and job creation—it creates the conditions under which it appears to be a useful policy measure for managing unemployment.

If jobs are to be created, paid idleness must not be rewarded and working for relatively low wages must not be punished. This maxim must also be considered in the overhaul of the current pension system.

In the future, early retirement should be granted only with actuarially fair pension reductions that are also fair to employers and the state and therefore do not cost extra money. In exchange, those who decide to retire early despite the pension reductions should have the right to continue working while receiving their pensions, albeit under new labor contracts, without being able to transfer dismissal protection from their previous jobs. As has been the case in Japan and Italy, a second labor market with low wages will develop in which people who have ended their primary careers will still be active. At low wages, economic activity will arise that will contribute to Germany's aggregate income and wealth.

Item 4: Turning Off the Immigration Magnet

Delayed Integration and the Home-Country Principle

In addition to high wages for unskilled workers, artificially pushed up by the wage-replacement incomes offered by the government, Germany's direct redistribution of income to immigrants attracts more of them than are needed. The German welfare system functions as a magnet because the state pays immigrants, who have below-average productivity and earn below-average wages, a migration premium. The state demands fewer taxes and contributions from the immigrants than it returns to them in the form of public services, including the freely available infrastructure and similar in-kind services. According to calculations by the Ifo Institute using the German socio-economic panel, in 1997 the migration premium amounted to almost 2,400 euros per year for immigrants who had been in Germany less than 10 years. For a family of five, this corresponds to an advantage of 118,000 euros in 10 years.

Such migration premiums should not be offered. Every EU citizen who wants to migrate to another EU country should be allowed to do so. Immigration from the new EU accession countries in Eastern Europe ought not to be restricted, but no gifts should be distributed that distort the decision to migrate relative to the incentives that the market alone would have provided. Only undistorted migration is advantageous to all countries concerned. That is why migrants should be fully integrated into the host country's social welfare system only after a waiting period. To be sure, immediately after their arrival they should participate in those welfare benefits that are financed out of their own contributions, and they should also have access to most state services. But tax-financed benefits not paid for by the immigrants should temporarily be restricted to such an extent that immigration does not become a net fiscal burden for the host government. Housing allowances, free access to social housing, allowances for children that remained abroad, and similar benefits are among the things that could be taken off the list to make sure that immigrants receive only the benefits for which they pay. Full integration should be granted only after a waiting period that is long enough to ensure that the immigrant's fiscal status is balanced.

Inactive immigrants from other EU countries should not be included in the welfare system of the host country. They should direct their claims against the country of origin, which has satisfied the EU's entry standards. Welfare recipients should be free to consume their benefits in the EU country of their choice, but this cannot mean that that the host country should provide these benefits.

No European Social Union

In this context, a warning is warranted against a European social union as defined in the new EU draft constitution that failed to pass the French and Dutch referendums, and in the Directive on Free Movement that became binding on May 1, 2006. According to the directive, non-working EU citizens may choose to reside in any member country, and, after a waiting period of 5 years, during which they must support themselves, they may claim social assistance and other benefits just as local residents may. Active EU citizens who are employed or self-employed are even included after only a year, at which time they have the right to permanent support in the host country.

A European social union based on such rules will not work. German social assistance is a multiple of the net wage rate of an industrial worker in Eastern European EU countries and is even much higher than the net wage paid in some regions of Portugal, Spain, and Greece. Expanding the inclusion rights of migrants will result in a strengthening of migration flows and will aggravate the problems of the German welfare state and the German labor market.

A European social union will have problematic consequences not only for Germany but for all Western European-type welfare states. The European welfare states will be forced to enter a competition of deterrence aimed at rerouting migration around their nation in order to control costs. Every country will want to be a bit less generous than the neighboring ones; however, as each country reduces its benefits, the European welfare state will gradually erode.

In this situation, calls for harmonizing welfare standards at the EU level will become louder, as it will be hoped that leveling benefits will prevent a race to the bottom. Such a harmonization of welfare standards would be in line with the draft constitution. However, in view of the differences in economic performance among Europe's individual countries and regions, harmonizing social-assistance rates would be fatal. Harmonized social replacement incomes, which are still acceptable to the rich countries, would determine wage floors in the poorer countries and regions that the latter could not cope with, and would ruin their economies. As was noted in chapter 8, there would not be two but twenty Mezzogiorni in Europe. The richer countries would then be asked to pay more in order to finance unemployment in the poorer countries. The German unification experience would be repeated at the pan-European level. In order to prevent this, the European social union cannot be constructed as laid out in the Directive on Free Movement and in the draft constitution. Real economic convergence of the European states would have to advance much further to avoid the devastating consequences of welfare harmonization. Any attempt to speed up real EU economic convergence via a legislated social union would end in a labor-market disaster. For this reason, the corresponding sections of the draft constitution should be changed in such a way that the individual states have the right to differentiate between the local population and the immigrant population in regard to their welfare benefits. Doing without a social union is an essential precondition for a uniform internal market with free labor mobility and for a prosperous Europe in which living standards will eventually converge.

Item 5: A Leaner Tax System

Less Government and Less Taxation

Since the social-liberal coalition took office in Germany (more than 35 years ago), the government share of gross domestic product, which was less than 40 percent in the early 1970s, has risen substantially. At present it is 47 percent, and a further increase is in sight because of various tax increases recently enacted. Related to net domestic product or the sum of all incomes earned in Germany, the government share has already reached 55 percent. That is more than is compatible with a well-functioning market economy. The taxes and fiscal charges that finance public-sector spending hamper private-sector activity and deter people from pursuing productive undertakings, because avoiding a larger tax burden becomes the paramount aim. This incentive can trigger deleterious changes in the behavior of international and national investors, savers, and workers, and useful economic activity is lost.

The explanation for the large government share of GDP is not that Germany has an unusual amount of public-sector employees relative to other nations. Indeed, the opposite is the case. Germany even ranks behind the United States in government employment share, and it does not apply the Scandinavian accounting trick of boosting GDP with an excessive government wage bill. The education sector is not to blame, either. Germany spends proportionately less on education than most other OECD countries. Rather, the government share is so high because Germany has extremely high welfare expenditures. Besides interfering with the labor market and distorting migration flows, the benefits provided by the German welfare state cost a lot of money.

The welfare state tends to reinforce itself. An estimated 41 percent of German voters receive their income primarily in the form of pensions or other social benefits. Thus, there is already a large group of voters that tends to oppose any change to the status quo. The expected increase in the future share of retirees will further raise the proportion of voters who receive state benefits. The chances for fundamental reforms in Germany may therefore be waning. Only if and when the beneficiaries of the state realize that the disincentives present in an excessively generous welfare state will ultimately pull everyone down will a political turnaround in Germany be possible.

Relative to other European countries, Germany's average burden of tax and social security contributions is not excessive. However, the marginal tax rates are extremely high. The value added of an average manufacturing worker bears a marginal tax burden of about two-thirds. No other European government deducts so much from the workers' paychecks when they increase their income by additional effort or additional training. A reduction in income taxes, especially a flattening of the progressive tax rates, is urgently needed.

At the same time, capital income should be taxed less, as a capital income tax causes massive evasive reactions by international investors. These evasive reactions are at the expense of German workers, whose high wages are essentially made possible by the large capital stock available to them, which generates a high measured labor productivity. In addition, taxes on capital income clearly violate the postulate of horizontal equity, because those who intend to consume their wealth later are forced to sacrifice a higher percentage of their consumption than those who prefer to consume their income immediately.

A Dual Income Tax

An income tax system incorporating horizontal equity in a very simple form and providing an incentive to keep mobile capital in Germany could look like this: There would be only four tax rates (0 percent, 15 percent, 25 percent, and 35 percent) and four tax brackets for jointly assessed source income from labor and similar sources. Capital income, including the implicit return on capital contained in firm profits, which is not source income, is excluded from the general assessment and is taxed at 20 percent. With lower taxation of the explicit and implicit returns on capital, this proposal imitates the dual income taxation practiced in the Scandinavian countries.

Profits of corporations and unincorporated firms exceeding the pure return to capital are uniformly taxed at 35 percent, of which 10 percentage points go to the local communities as the trade tax, the essential function of which is to give local communities an incentive to provide urban space for businesses. The German "half earnings procedure" for distributed profits is retained, albeit at reduced rates.

The fiscal offset for these measures may be sought in a radical reduction of subsidies that do not have any place in a market economy, beginning with subsidies to the agriculture and coal mining industries. In addition, the welfare state must be reduced, for it consumes gigantic sums and, as has been explained throughout this book, imposes many disincentives on the willingness of transfer recipients to offer their labor in the market. The aim must be to reduce the size of the government budget and to strengthen private-sector activities.

Item 6: More Children, More Retirement Income, More Progress

Learning from France

The most difficult and most important long-term policy problem facing Germany is the extremely low number of births relative to other countries. In fact, Germany has fewer newborn children relative to its population size than any other developed country. A big demographic crisis is therefore inescapable. Ever since the Nazis abused population policy, the topic has been taboo in Germany. But it is too important to be ignored any longer. Like any other country, Germany needs children in order to maintain its society, to preserve its social security system from ruin, and in general to safeguard its future.

For policy ideas on raising its birth rate, Germany can look to France. France's population had declined relative to Germany's in the nineteenth century, but since losing the 1870–71 Franco-Prussian War France has succeeded in raising its birth rate with the help of state incentives.

In contrast to Germany, France has an excellent system of all-day kindergartens and elementary schools that helps working women decide in favor of having children. It also provides great financial incentives for having a second and a third child. Those incentives exceed Germany's even for lower-income families, and they increase net family income for each additional child more than is the case in Germany.

Of special note is France's "family splitting" policy of income taxation, a device that assesses children, similar to the spouse in the German tax system, jointly with the income earners. Family splitting reduces the tax progression considerably and provides incentives—especially to middle-income families—to decide in favor of having several children.

The Child-Funded Pension Scheme

Because of the demographic crisis, retirement pension insurance should be fundamentally redesigned. In today's pay-as-you-go system, retirement pension insurance can be seen as an obligation that ensures that children support their parents in old age. At the same time, it can be seen as insurance against childlessness, as those who cannot have children of their own are put in a position to be supported by other people's children. Socializing part of the children's pension contributions is the rational decision of a society that wants to protect its members from the economic consequences of individual childlessness.

Yet socializing the children's contributions eliminates the link between individuals' child-raising efforts and their pensions. For a comfortable living standard in old age, it suffices if other people raise children. Having children of one's own is not necessary. One's pension claims do not depend on one's children; they depend only on one's contributions to financing the pensions of one's parents' generation. As a consequence, the natural economic motivation for having children to get old-age support from them has been completely eliminated from the minds of young people. This has contributed to the drastic decline of German birth rates since the introduction of retirement pension insurance under Bismarck. Pension insurance itself is among the factors that have caused to the demographic crisis from which it suffers today.

Full insurance against childlessness, as offered by the pension system, has not stood the test of time. It should be replaced by partially funded pension insurance that will still insure an individual against the consequences of childlessness to some extent but will leave part of these consequences to those who decide not to have children. Everyone's responsibility for the decision whether to have children should be strengthened.

To put this idea into concrete terms, one could react to the impending 50 percent reduction in the number of contributors relative to the number of retirees by introducing a retirement pension system based on three pillars.

The first pillar is the existing statutory retirement pension system. It should be preserved as a basic insurance scheme, but the state should not keep pumping ever more money into it. The contribution rate is fixed, and so is the percentage of federal subsidy in excess of non-insurance benefits. Because of demographics, pensions will rise more slowly than they would under present law.

The second pillar is a new child-funded pension system for parents. It will be granted independently of whether these parents have worked, and it will be available to civil servants, to the self-employed, and to non-working spouses. A supplemental pension will be paid per child up to a maximum of three children. The size of the pension per child will depend on how long one cared for the child. This second pillar will be financed by a general contribution of all people who are employed including the self-employed. The pension is designed in such a way that the average earner with three children receives the same amount of retirement pension from it and the first pillar that he would have received according to present law.

The third pillar consists of a wealth-funded pension for the childless. Young people entering the labor market must save part of their income in order to fund a pension that comes in addition to the first pillar so that today's protection level is maintained during the pension crisis expected by the mid 2030s despite the dwindling of the statutory pay-as-you-go pension. When the first child is born, one-third of the accumulated savings is released and one-third of the current savings obligation is waived, and similarly with the second child and the third. The missing wealth-funded pension is successively replaced by the child-funded pension according to the second pillar. This new retirement pension system is equitable, as the working generation must bear two burdens as it has throughout human history. It must, first, support its parents by paying contributions to pension insurance. Second, it must make provisions for its own old age. It does so by either raising children (i.e., forming human capital) or by saving and forming financial or real capital, or by some combination of the two.

The new system will safeguard pensions despite the demographic crisis. Furthermore, it will restore some of the natural economic motives for having children, which the state has destroyed by fully socializing the children's contributions. If Germans start having more children, there will be higher pensions as well as more economic progress and growth. The country will once again have a future,

Item 6 + 1: New Dynamism in East Germany

The policy recommendations of the first six items also apply to East Germany. But the question "Can Germany be saved?" is even more urgent there than in West Germany, and as a consequence the need to act is also greater there. Since 1997 East Germany's economy has been growing more slowly than West

Germany's, even though West Germany's growth rate was the second-lowest in Europe during the period 1995–2005. The ratio of East German to West German aggregate labor productivity has been stuck at 60 percent since 1996. Per capita investment in machinery and equipment is substantially lower in East Germany than in West Germany, although it should be higher if East Germany is ever to catch up with West Germany. The number of employees subject to social security has been declining by 2 percent per annum during recent years.

It is no contradiction that East Germany's standard of living has already reached 90 percent of West Germany's in real terms. This fact is due mainly to West-to-East transfers via social security, the federal states' fiscal equalization scheme, and the federal budget. More than 15 years after unification, East Germany's absorption of goods and services by private households, investors, and the state still exceeds East Germany's production by half. One in three euros spent in East Germany originates in West Germany. Of this euro, 75 cents is a gift and 25 cents is a loan. Even from an historic perspective, it is hardly possible to find another region in the world that is as dependent on outside transfers in percentage terms and where the excess of purchasing power over production has taken on such gigantic magnitudes. East Germany has become a transfer economy that could not survive without the funds from West Germany. As 47 percent of East German voters receive their main income from the state in the form of social benefits, there is a great inclination to continue this state of affairs.

The historical reason for the obvious failure of German unification is found in the fact that wages in East Germany rose more quickly than productivity. And this fact is itself due to long-binding collective bargaining agreements, forged in 1991 and since renegotiated, in which West German competitors represented East German employers and West German unions represented East German workers. Another reason for the failure of German unification is the social union that imposed the West German wage-replacement system on the East German labor market, building up wage claims that the market was unable to satisfy. People wanted too much too fast, and as a result the 14-year lead that East Germany had over its formerly communist partners that only recently joined the European Union was wasted. Now East Germany has to catch up to the dynamism of its fellow formerly communist nations, amid a much harsher international macroeconomic climate.

Activating Social Assistance as Protection against Formerly Communist Friends
General unemployment in the East German Länder, at about 20 percent, is as bad as unemployment among West Germany's unskilled workers. And the

causes are similar. Although East Germany's formal skill level is high, and there are hardly any unskilled workers there, labor productivity is still very low because of substantial deficiencies of other soft and hard factors, ranging from geographic location to the infrastructure to the social acceptance of entrepreneurship. Because of low productivity, wages that have been equalized at a high level are a problem shared by the unskilled workers in West Germany and the skilled workers in East Germany, as dissimilar as these two employee groups may be in other respects.

While East German aggregate productivity is about 60 percent of the West German level, wage costs per hour stand at about 73 percent. This mismatch is the problem.

At present, the high East German wages are due primarily to the wage-replacement benefits of the welfare state. Collective bargaining agreements are playing a smaller and smaller role as more and more firms leave the employers' organizations. With social assistance as the basis of their wage claims, East Germans keep waiting in vain for the establishment of firms that are willing to pay more. Their excessive demands cement a lamentably low level of industrial employment—a rate comparable to that in the Italian Mezzogiorno.

Politicians cannot set wages, but they can determine the framework that permits market forces to work. To eliminate the high-wage competition posed by the welfare state, the Activating Social Assistance program, as described above, must be introduced by the East German Länder unilaterally if the Western Länder object to a nationwide solution. Today's social assistance blocks the road to lower wages, with which one could fend off the competition by the new EU countries in Eastern Europe. The funds that today flow to East Germany in the form of unemployment benefits and social assistance may continue to flow, but in the future these will be needed for co-financing wage incomes instead of paying for idleness. If the state opened its pockets for those who earn low wage incomes and kept them closed for those who could work but do not, the East German labor market would start recovering. Reservation wages, and with them actual wages, would decline, and as a result employers would offer more jobs in Germany. Rather than move production to Krakow, Posen, or Pilsen, they would invest in Zwickau, Chemnitz, or Magdeburg.

There is no realistic alternative to this reform if East Germany is to withstand the competition from other formerly communist countries that have been members of the European Union since May 1, 2004. Poland and the Czech Republic, East Germany's immediate neighbors, are attracting investors with wages that are only small fractions of East German wages and even much lower than German social-assistance rates. One need not be an economist to see that East Germany has no chance of coping with EU eastern enlargement in economic terms if the social-assistance system and the wage floor it creates are left unchanged.

It must be emphasized that the Activating Social Assistance program is designed in such a way that recipients of social assistance will be no worse off financially than they are today and, as a rule, will enjoy even higher incomes. At the present level of social assistance, they will at least be able to find jobs with the state, which will lease their labor to the highest bidder in the private sector. They will do better, however, if, provided with a wage supplement, they look for a job in the private sector, where they will earn as much in a half-day job, despite the wage reduction, as in a full-time job with the state. The poorer population groups in East Germany will do markedly better financially than they would in the absence of the reform.

Co-ownership in Exchange for Wages

East Germany needs investment wage schemes. Lower wages in exchange for co-ownership granted to those employees covered by the collective bargaining agreement will cushion the necessary wage reduction in East Germany. Besides strengthening the competitiveness of East German firms, this will correct the fundamental economic mistakes made by the unification policy that did not give the new citizens shares in the old state enterprises but instead promised them high wages. In view of the high social transfers that came with the high wages, the mix was more than fair to the new citizens, yet it was inefficient. Lower wages were needed in order to stimulate investment, and asset ownership by East Germans was needed to help them safeguard their future and establish their own businesses. Sharing in the productive assets in exchange for reduced wages would allow some ex-post correction of past economic mistakes.

Furthermore, ownership participation by the citizens of East Germany would fulfill the mandate of Article 25, Section 6 of the Unification Agreement, which provides for the distribution of securitized shares in the former socialized assets to the former citizens of the GDR. After all, this mandate has a constitutional status, because the Unification Agreement itself has this status.

This is the reform agenda that Germany really needs. It goes far beyond Gerhard Schröder's Agenda 2010, as necessary as that was. As the election results of 2005 showed, however, the Germans are not yet convinced that they should go further. Although Angela Merkel had adopted a significant share of the proposals of this book in her party platform before the election (and had given the author a chance to help formulate that platform), her near-failure in the elections has changed the balance of power in her party and perhaps even changed the balance of priorities in her mind. Merkel seems to have forgotten her courageous campaign, and there are influential party members who even want to step back from the Agenda 2010 in the direction of a renewed expansion of the old welfare state based on replacement incomes, because this promises to win more votes in the upcoming Länder elections. The opportunism is breathtaking. If Germany does not want to condemn its children to suffer as guinea pigs of history, it must act now. The necessary reforms are time consuming, but Germany has no time. The rest of the world is not waiting, industrial sectors that go astray will never come back, and the German Baby Boomers who are now about 40 years old will soon lose their energy. There is no alternative for Germany, and none for the rest of Europe.

Epilogue: Reason or Experience

The patient is sick, so the physician diagnoses the disease and recommends a therapy. But the patient distrusts the diagnosis because he does not like the prescribed therapy. He turns to homeopaths and quacks instead, but he remains unconvinced. Perhaps the doctor is right after all. The patient knows he has to start treatment or risk becoming even sicker. He suspects that if he waits too long no amount of therapy is going to cure him; his disease will have progressed too far by then. But doubts remain, and it is hard to make a decision.

Germany is this patient. The economist is the physician. This book is the medical report based on mainstream economic analysis. It lacks the mysticism of the quack and the mystique of the homeopath. Economic medicine is unglamorous, and the treatment is not fun. It will be painful. Yet the physician is convinced of his therapy and foresees good chances for healing. He hopes that other physicians reading his report will share his opinion. But he does not know whether the patient will understand the diagnosis and accept the therapy. Time will tell.

In the physician's opinion, the patient can choose between reason and experience, between rational action and experiencing the increasing hardship of delay. The physician hopes for timely action, as the patient is dear to him.

This is not the first time I find myself in this position. In the summer of 1991, my wife Gerlinde and I published a book titled *Kaltstart*, which in 1992 came out in English under the title *Jumpstart*. The book dealt with the economic unification of Germany. In it we criticized the privatization policy of the Treuhandanstalt, and we spoke of "bankruptcy procedures with a social compensation plan." We smiled at the high-tech pipe dream in which East Germany was to overtake West Germany, and we warned against the policy of wage equalization, denouncing it as a death knell for employment in the manufacturing sector.

Our pleas for a change in direction were met with widespread incomprehension. I do not know whose private interests we compromised at the time.

I only know that I was threatened with career derailment if I did not desist from my criticism. This only reinforced my resolve. The threats never materialized, but perhaps that was because our book did not have any political effect. I sometimes had the feeling that, as our ideas gained popularity, politicians became doubly determined to stay their predetermined course, even in the face of mounting failure.

As an economist, I have never been able to understand the superficial, half-baked arguments of the many otherwise upstanding politicians who try desperately to make patent nonsense appear at least partially plausible. And it was frightening to watch how fast a social consensus formed around quasi-arguments that lacked economic foundations. Germans value a consensual society that rallies around its political leaders, all too often even when the leaders are wrong.

Unfortunately, Gerlinde and I made the right diagnosis then. Instead of a self-sustained upswing, there was only a temporary recovery in East Germany. The patient had been given stimulants meant to be temporary remedies until he could stand on his own two feet. Today he cannot do without the drip.

It is possible to keep the East German states on the drip, but only if the rest of the country is healthy enough to provide the refill. The trouble will come when Germany as a whole starts ailing, because no one is going to be willing to nurse the entire country back to health. Germany does not have a big brother.

Germany has no alternative to a course of painful economic reforms that ignores the romanticism of the welfare state and looks reality in the eye. It is my hope that this book will strengthen the German people's resolve for change and will give them the courage to bet on the market economy this time.

Notes

Chapter 1

1. Statistisches Bundesamt, Fachserie 18, Volkswirtschaftliche Gesamtrechnungen, Reihe S. 15, Revidierte Ergebnisse 1950 bis 1990, 1991.

2. Cologne Institute for Economic Research, 2002 (on request).

3. Statistisches Bundesamt, Fachserie 18, Volkswirtschaftliche Gesamtrechnungen, Reihe S. 15, Revidierte Ergebnisse 1950 bis 1990, 1991; Reihe S. 21, Revidierte Ergebnisse 1970 bis 2001, 2002; Reihe 1.4, Inlandsproduktsberechnung, Detaillierte Jahresergebnisse 2005, 2006.

4. Statistisches Bundesamt, Fachserie 18, Volkswirtschaftliche Gesamtrechnungen, Reihe 1.2, Inlandsproduktsberechnung, Vierteljahresergebnisse, 2. Vierteljahr 2006.

5. Deutsche Bundesbank, Kapitalverflechtung mit dem Ausland, Sonderveröffentlichung 10, 2006.

6. Statistisches Bundesamt, Fachserie 18, Volkswirtschaftliche Gesamtrechnungen, Reihe S. 15, Revidierte Ergebnisse 1950 bis 1990, 1991; Arbeitskreis Volkswirtschaftliche Gesamtrechnungen der Länder, 2002.

7. Sachverständigenrat zur Begutachtung der gesamtwirtschaftlichen Entwicklung, Jahresgutachten 2005/06, table 16.

8. H.-U. Bach, C. Gaggermeier, A. Kettner, S. Klinger, T. Rothe, E. Spitznagel, and S. Wanger, Der Arbeitsmarkt in den Jahren 2005 und 2006, IAB Kurzbericht no. 23, 2005, p. 6.

9. Social assistance including in-kind benefits, unemployment benefits, early-retirement benefits ("Altersteilzeit" pensions and pensions to people below 65 because of unemployment, to miners, and to women) Sources: Statistisches Bundesamt, Fachserie 18, Reihe 1.4, Detaillierte Jahresergebnisse 2005, table 3.4.4.7, Bundesagentur für Arbeit, Amtliche Nachrichten der Bundesagentur für Arbeit, Januar 2006, table VI/1; Verband Deutscher Rentenversicherungsträger, VDR Statistik Rentenbestand am 31. Dezember 2004.

10. In April 2006, the Ifo business climate indicator climbed to its highest level since 1991.

11. See chapter 5.

12. The difference in the growth rates is so small that the ranking could easily be changed with the foreseeable revisions of official statistics. Moreover, Italian statistics are chronically false due to the enormous size of the black economy there.

13. Until 1806 the empire had the official name Holy Roman Empire of German Nation. The last emperor was Francis II.

14. See A. Maddison, *Monitoring the World Economy 1820–1992* (OECD, 1995).

15. See ibid.

16. J. Williamson, *Regional Inequality and the Process of National Development* (University of Chicago Press, 1965), pp. 68–70.

17. See D. Card and R. Freeman, What Have Two Decades of British Economic Reform Delivered? NBER Working Paper 8801, 2002.

18. OECD, Economic Outlook no. 71, 2000.

19. See C. Beatty and S. Fothergill, The Diversion from 'Unemployment' to 'Sickness' across British Regions and Districts, mimeo, Centre for Regional Economic and Social Research, Sheffield Hallam University, 2005.

20. For conversion to real values one would need absolute purchasing-power parities, which are not available in official statistics because the composition of the market baskets of different countries is very different and therefore there is no meaningful basis for comparison. Existing relative purchasing-power parities are applicable to growth comparisons, but not to comparisons of levels (as they do not require uniform market baskets). Figure 1.3 contains such a real growth comparison.

21. Gross national income is the new name for what formerly was called gross national product.

22. OECD, Economic Outlook no. 72, 2002, appendix table 26.

23. Copernicus was German-Polish.

24. See http://www.nobel.se. The respective first five places are as follows. Physics: Germany 10, France 7, UK 6, US 2, Netherlands 2. Chemistry: Germany 14, UK 5, France 4, Sweden 3, US 2. Medicine: Germany 6, UK 5, France 4, Denmark 3, Netherlands 2. Literature: Germany 5, France 5, Norway 3, UK 3, Sweden 3.

25. Siemens was knighted in 1888 for his inventions; after that he was called Werner von Siemens. The dynamo motor, the first usable electrical motor, was far more powerful than earlier electrical motors based on natural magnets. In 1879 Siemens used the dynamo motor in the construction of the first electrical locomotive. In contrast to the steam engine, the motor was also economical in smaller units and supplied tradesmen and small producers with a cheap power source. In the second half of the nineteenth century, probably no invention accelerated the development of German industry as much as the dynamo motor.

26. Ohain and Braun were among the prominent German scientists who, as part of the US armed forces' Operation Overcast, were captured toward the end of World War II and transported to the US. Both US and Russian occupying forces transported to their countries thousands of scientists who would later play important roles in developing their respective aerospace and military capacities.

27. "Die Luft der Freiheit weht" is a German translation of "Videtis illam spirare libertatis auram," which is credited to the German religious reformer Ulrich von Hutten. David Starr Jordan, the first president of Stanford University, chose the German version as Stanford's mission statement. On the history of the motto, see "Die Luft der Freiheit weht—On and Off," a speech given by Stanford University president Gerhard Casper on October 5, 1995 (available at http://www.stanford.edu). The motto was contested during World War I, and Jordan, who as pacifist was in contact with the German anti-war activist Bertha Freifrau von Suttner and turned against the war against Germany, was put under considerable political pressure. Nonetheless, the motto was retained between the wars, especially as a sign of opposition to Hitler, and it remains Stanford's motto today.

28. See the Nobel Foundation's website (http://www.nobel.se).

29. Knowledge and Skills for Life. First Results from the OECD Program for International Student Assessment (PISA) 2000 (OECD, 2001). See also PISA 2000 (Max-Planck-Institut für Bildungsforschung, 2001).

30. European Economic Advisory Group at CESifo, Report on the European Economy 2003, Ifo Institute for Economic Research, Munich, 2003.

Chapter 2

1. A. Toynbee, A Study of History, volumes 1–10, London, 1934–1954.

2. World Bank, World Development Indicators (database), May 2006.

3. Deutscher Industrie- und Handelskammertag, Produktionsverlagerung als Element der Globalisierungsstrategie von Unternehmen, Results of a Business Survey (Berlin, May 2003), p. 10; Deutsche Bundesbank, Kapitalverflechtung mit dem Ausland, Statistische Sonderveröffentlichung 10 (April 2006), pp. 12, 48.

4. Deutscher Industrie- und Handelskammertag, Produktionsverlagerung als Element der Globalisierungsstrategie von Unternehmen.

5. See Institut für Mittelstandsforschung, Unternehmensgrößenstatistik 2001/2002—Daten und Fakten (http://www.ifm-bonn.org, June 2003), p. 112f. See also Ifo calculations. Note that 80% of all private jobs corresponds to two-thirds of total jobs, including those in the public sector.

6. Institut der deutschen Wirtschaft, IW-Trends, Dokumentation 4, 2002.

7. See Deutsche Bundesbank, Kapitalverflechtung mit dem Ausland, p. 18.

8. Total direct investment in the Czech Republic, Estonia, Latvia, Lithuania, Hungary, Poland, Slovenia, and Slovakia, end of 2003 by source: Germany 29.2 billion euros; US 8.1 billion euros; France 9.8 billion euros; UK 8.7 billion euros. See Eurostat database, EU direct investment positions by country, May 18, 2006.

9. Istvan Csillag, Hungarian Economics Minister, in a speech on the event of the tenth anniversary of the establishment of the German-Hungarian Chamber of Commerce on May 15, 2003, quoted in W. Klein, "Für deutsche Investoren hat der Standort an Attraktivität verloren," *Handelsblatt*, May 29, 2003. (*Handelsblatt* is a commercial newspaper.)

10. For more extensive discussions of this theme, see the transcript of my 2003 Deutschlandradio program "Deutsche Rede. Der kranke Mann Europas: Diagnose und Therapie eines Kathedersozialisten," Deutschlandradio Berlin (available at http://www.Ifo.de). See also H.-W. Sinn, *Die Basar-Ökonomie. Deutschland: Exportweltmeister oder Schlusslicht?* (Econ, 2004), H.-W. Sinn, "The Pathological Export Boom and the Bazaar Effect: How to Solve the German Puzzle?" *The World Economy* 29, 2006: 1157–1175.

11. F. Dudenhöffer, "Wie viel Deutschland steckt im Porsche?" *Ifo Schnelldienst* 58, no. 24, 2005: 3–5.

12. See Sinn, *Die Basar-Ökonomie*, p. 95.

13. See R. Hild, "Produktion, Wertschöpfung und Beschäftigung im Verarbeitenden Gewerbe," *Ifo Schnelldienst* 57, no. 7, 2004, p. 11.

14. The calculations do not considered that intermediate inputs supplied by domestic sectors contain foreign inputs and vice versa that foreign intermediate inputs contain domestic inputs.

15. See OECD STAN Database for Industrial Analysis, January18, 2006.

16. Ifo Institute calculations based on Statistisches Bundesamt, Fachserie 18, Volkswirtschaftliche Gesamtrechnungen, Reihe 1.4 Inlandsproduktsberechnung, Detaillierte Jahresergebnisse 2005, 2006; Institut für Arbeitsmarkt- und Berufsforschung, IAB Kurzbericht 10, 2005.

17. P. Bofinger, "Wir sind besser, als wir glauben. Wohlstand für alle," Pearson Studium, Munich, 2004; R. Hickel, "Deutschland ist noch zu retten," *Frankfurter Rundschau* 274, November 23, 2004, p. 7.

18. Source: http://www.rrz.uni-hamburg.de.

19. Statistisches Bundesamt, Volkswirtschaftliche Gesamtrechnungen. Input-Output-Rechnung. Importabhängigkeit der deutschen Exporte 1991, 1995, 2000 und 2002, Wiesbaden 2004.

20. See Sinn, *Die Basar-Ökonomie*, p. 112.

21. See Sinn, *Die Basar-Ökonomie*, p. 115.

22. Bofinger, "Wir sind besser"; Hickel, "Deutschland ist noch zu retten."

23. For detailed analyses, see Sinn, *Die Basar-Ökonomie* and "The Pathological Export Boom." The argument is based on a short remark by Srinivasan in a comment on Krugman and could formally be traced back with the Heckscher-Ohlin models of trade with fixed wages as provided by Brecher and Davis. See R. Brecher, "Minimum Wage Rates and the Pure Theory of International Trade," *Quarterly Journal of Economics* 88, 1974: 98–116; D. Davis, "Does European

Unemployment Prop Up American Wages? National Labor Markets and Global Trade," *American Economic Review* 88, 1998: 478–494. See also P. Krugman, "Growing World Trade: Causes and Consequence," *Brookings Papers on Economic Activity* 1, 1995: 327–377; T. Srinivasan, Comments and Discussion on 'Growing World Trade: Causes and Consequence,'" *Brookings Papers on Economic Activity* 1, 1995: 368–373.

24. See Statistisches Bundesamt, Fachserie 18, Volkswirtschaftliche Gesamtrechnungen, Reihe 1.4, Inlandsproduktsberechnung, Detaillierte Jahresergebnisse 2005 as of August 2005. In Deutsche Bundesbank, Zahlungsbilanzstatistik, March 2006, p. 7, a figure of 93 billion is shown for the same quantity. This is due to slightly different measuring conventions.

25. Bofinger, "*Wir sind besser*"; Hickel, "Deutschland ist noch zu retten"; G. Horn and S. Behncke, "Deutschland ist keine Basarökonomie," *DIW Wochenbericht* 71, no. 40, September 30, 2004, p. 588; G. Horn, "Deutschland ist keine Basarökonomie," *Handelsblatt* 192, October 4, 2004, p. 9, A. Müller, *Die Reformlüge: 40 Denkfehler, Mythen und Legenden, mit denen Politik und Wirtschaft Deutschland ruinieren* (Knaur-Taschenbuch-Verlag, 2005).

26. On the influence of German reunification on the current account, see H.-W. Sinn, "International implications of German unification," in *The Economics of Globalization*, ed. A. Razin and E. Sadka (Cambridge University Press, 1999).

27. Aggregate savings of the private sector exceed this sum by the dissaving of the government sector, which was 57 billion euros in 2005. See Statistisches Bundesamt, Fachserie 18, Volkswirtschaftliche Gesamtrechnungen, Reihe 1.4, p. 191.

28. EC Commission, "The Economics of 1992," *European Economy*, no. 35, 1988; P. Cecchini, *The European Challenge 1992* (Wildwood House, 1988).

29. For a detailed analysis of this phenomenon and its welfare implications, see H.-W. Sinn and R. Koll, "The Euro, Interest Rates and European Economic Growth," *CESifo Forum* 1, no. 3, 2000: 30–31.

30. Surely the euro will increase European welfare in a "first-best" world where other distortions are absent and only the distortions in the capital market are removed. A full welfare analysis would, however, have to address the second-best problem of the euro being introduced in a system of inflexible labor markets. Suppose, for example, only Germany has rigid wages and unemployment while wages in the rest of Europe are determined by supply and demand. In this case the establishment of a common EU capital market through the introduction of the euro could be harmful. As the capital market equates foreign social and private returns with the German private return. which is below the German social return, it drives too much capital out of the country. With a sufficiently large labor market distortion to start with, German welfare would be declining, and it could even decline more than welfare in the rest of Europe is rising. While this case is only one of many theoretical possibilities, it demonstrates how difficult a sound welfare judgment would be in a more realistic second-best scenario.

31. In addition, Malta and Cyprus joined the EU at that time.

32. S. Bhalla, *Imagine There's No Country: Poverty, Inequality and Growth in the Era of Globalization* (Institute of International Economics, 2002; S. Bhalla, "Poor Results and Poorer Policy: A Comparative Analysis of Estimates of Global Inequality and Poverty," *CESifo Economic Studies* 50, 2004: 85–132.

33. F. von Hayek, "The Use of Knowledge in Society," *American Economic Review* 35, 1945: 519–530.

34. Maddison, *Monitoring the World Economy 1820–1992*, p. 39; Statistisches Bundesamt, Fachserie 18, Volkswirtschaftliche Gesamtrechnungen, Reihe 1.1, 4. Quartal 2002, February 2003.

35. See K. Borchardt, "Globalisierung in historischer Perspektive," *Sitzungsberichte der Bayerischen Akademie der Wissenschaften*, no. 2, 2001.

36. It is not easy to delineate the border between the higher-skilled winners and the lower-skilled losers. According to an econometric study by Geishecker and Görg, university graduates win, whereas people with less than higher secondary education belong to the losers. Even workers who finish an apprenticeship already belong to the losers from globalization. See I. Geishecker and H. Görg, Winners and Losers: Fragmentation, Trade and Wages Revisited, Discussion Paper 385, German Institute for Economic Research, 2004.

37. H.-W. Sinn, C. Holzner, W. Meister, W. Ochel, and M. Werding, "Aktivierende Sozialhilfe— Ein Weg zu mehr Beschäftigung und Wachstum," *Ifo Schnelldienst* 55, no. 9, 2002.

38. Sources: Working time per employed person 1982 to 1990: OECD, *Economic Outlook*; 1991 to 2002; H.-U. Bach, S. Koch, E. Magvas, L. Pusse, T. Rothe, and E. Spitznagel, "Der Arbeitsmarkt in der Bundesrepublik Deutschland in den Jahren 2003 und 2004," *Mitteilungen aus der Arbeitsmarkt- und Berufsforschung*, no. 1, 2003; gross domestic product, wage, and salary earners, workers, wages and salaries 1982 to 1990: Statistisches Bundesamt, Fachserie 18, Volkswirtschaftliche Gesamtrechnungen, Reihe S. 21, Revidierte Ergebnisse 1970 bis 2001, 2002; 1991 to 2002: Arbeitskreis Volkswirtschaftliche Gesamtrechnung der Länder, database July 2003. Division of Berlin according to own calculations.

39. The most popular of these is Peter Bofinger, who holds the union slot on the German Council of Economic Advisors.

40. In 2004, Germany purchased 57.1 billion euros' worth of tourist services abroad and the US 52.8 billion euros' worth. See Deutsche Bundesbank, Zahlungsbilanzstatistik, August 2005, p. 20; Deutsche Bundesbank, Devisenkursstatistik, Juli 2005, p. 6; Bureau of Economic Analysis, US International Trade in Goods and Services, Annual Revision for 2004, Tables from news release.

41. Here total employment is being presented including public-sector employment in order to make the employment effects independent of the effect of the large volume of privatizations occurring in the countries.

42. US Census Bureau, Statistical Abstract of the United States: 2001, table 4; Statistical Abstract of the United States: 2006, table 4; Statistisches Bundesamt, Fachserie 1, Reihe 1.2, Wanderungen 2002 and 2004; http://statline.cbs.nl, May 10, 2006.

43. OECD, Economic Outlook no. 67, June 2000, p. 266, and Main Economic Indicators, April 2005, p. 17. The unemployment figures for the US and the Netherlands are standardized rates. Such rates are not available for West Germany after reunification. In 1982, the standardized rate for West Germany was 5.7% (i.e., one percentage point below the rate shown in German statistics). See Bundesanstalt für Arbeit, Arbeitsstatistik 1997—Jahreszahlen.

44. The percentage employment gain resulting from the reaction of business to 1% wage restraint is called the elasticity of labor demand. Meant is not the comparison over time, but rather the comparison of various scenarios at a given future point in time. The following estimates of the elasticity of labor demand can be found in the literature: −0.85 (Bauer and Zimmermann) for the area of unskilled workers in Germany; −0.96 (Franz and König) for the manufacturing industry in Germany; −1.85 (Burgess) for the manufacturing industry in Great Britain; −1.92 (Nickell and Symons) for industry in the US; −0.60 (Riphahn, Thalmaier, and Zimmermann) for the low-wage sector in Germany; −2.04 (Schneider et al.) for part-time workers in Germany with a monthly income of less than 325 euros; −1.14 (Schneider et al.) for the low-wage sector in Germany with a monthly income of 325–910 euros. Sources: T. Bauer and K. Zimmermann, "Integrating the East: The Labor Market Effects of Immigration," in *Europe's Economy Looks East*, ed. S. Black (Cambridge University Press, 1997); W. Franz and H. König, "The Nature and Causes of Unemployment in the Federal Republic of Germany since the 1970s: An Empirical Investigation," *Empirica* 53, 1986: 219–244; S. Burgess, "Employment Adjustment in UK Manufacturing," *Economic Journal* 98, 1988: 81–103; S. Nickell and J. Symons, "The Real Wage–Employment Relationship in the United States," *Journal of Labor Economics* 8, 1990: 1–15; R. Riphahn, A. Thalmaier, and K. Zimmermann, Schaffung von Arbeitsplätzen für gering Qualifizierte, IZA, 1999; H. Schneider, K. Zimmermann, H. Bonin, K. Brenke, J. Haisken-DeNew, and W. Kempe, Beschäftigungspotenziale einer dualen Förderstrategie im Niedriglohnbereich, Gutachten im Auftrag des Ministeriums für Arbeit und Soziales, Qualifikation und Technik des Landes Nordrhein-Westfalen, mimeo, Forschungsinstitut zur Zukunft der Arbeit, Bonn, 2002.

Chapter 3

1. In 1863, Ferdinand Lassalle founded the Allgemeiner deutscher Arbeiterverein (General German Labor Society). In the same year, August Bebel founded the Vereinstag deutscher Arbeitervereine (Society of German Labor Societies), which later became the Sozialdemokratische

Arbeiterpartei (Social Democratic Labor Party). Whereas Lassalle was in conflict with the unions with his iron law of wages, Bebel especially identified himself with the union movement. He actively promoted the foundation of socialist labor unions in order to create an alternative to the middle-class unions, which were not affected by Bismarck's Laws against the Socialists.

2. The edict of October 9, 1807 abolished inherited subservience and (from 1810) farm subservience.

3. Peonage implied mutual obligations between the laird and the serf. The laird had to protect the serf; the serf had to tithe in exchange. A serf had more liberties than a slave, but he did not have the right to leave the territory or to marry without the consent of the laird.

4. See R. Gömmel, *Realeinkommen in Deutschland. Ein internationaler Vergleich (1810–1914)* (self-published, 1979), p. 12. Historians still dispute, however, the exact time path of real wages. According to the GDR historian Jürgen Kuczynski, the real wage of the 1820s was not reached again until 60 years later. See J. Kuczynski, *Die Geschichte der Lage der Arbeiter unter dem Kapitalismus, Part I: Die Geschichte der Lage der Arbeiter in Deutschland von 1789 bis zur Gegenwart, Volume 3: Darstellung der Lage der Arbeiter in Deutschland von 1871 bis 1900* (Akademie-Verlag, Berlin, 1953), p. 303.

5. See K. Marx, *Das Kapital, Kritik der politischen Ökonomie*, volume 3, book III; K. Marx and F. Engels, *Werke*, volume 25 (Hamburg 1890) (here according to the new edition published by Dietz, p. 242ff.). On growth see W. Hoffmann, *Wachstum der deutschen Wirtschaft seit der Mitte des 19. Jahrhunderts* (Springer, 1965). On the interpretation of this phase of development in the framework of a growth theory multiple phases model see H.-W. Sinn, "Das Marxsche Gesetz des tendenziellen Falls der Profitrate," *Zeitschrift für die gesamte Staatswissenschaft* 131, 1975: 646–696.

6. See J. Williamson, *Regional Inequality and the Process of National Development* (University of Chicago Press, 1965), pp. 68–70.

7. The "socialists of the chair," most prominent among them Gustav Schmoller, Lujo Brentano, and Adolph Wagner, were professors of economics who in 1873 founded the Verein für Sozialpolitik. The Verein für Sozialpolitik later became the German Economic Association, covering all fields of economics. I chaired this association from 1996 to 2000.

8. In the literature, Bismarck's role is disputed, as there were also strong forces in industry supporting social security. See F. Tennstedt, "Bismarcks Arbeiterversicherung zwischen Absicherung der Arbeiterexistenz und Abwehr der Arbeiterbewegung. Anmerkungen zu den Voraussetzungen ihrer Entstehung," in *Bismarck und die soziale Frage im 19. Jahrhundert*, ed. H. Matthöfer et al. (Otto-von-Bismarck-Stiftung, 2001); G. Ritter, "Bismarck und die Entstehung der deutschen Sozialversicherung," *Pforzheimer Hefte* no. 8, 1998.

9. See *Der Spiegel*, no. 19, May 5, 2003, p. 44. The corresponding percentage of union members among Christian Democrats in the Bundestag is 4%, that among the Greens is 24%, that among the Free Democrats is 2%, and that among the Democratic Socialists is 50% (i.e., one of that party's two members of the Bundestag).

10. In addition, so-called efficiency-wage unemployment is possible, which acts as a disciplinary device in the labor market.

11. Bank of Israel, Annual Report 1999, Statistical Appendix (1969–1998); Main Economic Data (1999–2002), http://www.bankisrael.gov.il.

12. Calculations based on Statistisches Bundesamt, Lange Reihen zur Wirtschaftsentwicklung 1998, p. 150; Statistisches Bundesamt, Fachserie 16, Löhne und Gehälter, Reihe 2.1 Arbeiterverdienste im Produzierenden Gewerbe, January 1996, p. 10; Statistisches Bundesamt, Statistisches Jahrbuch 2005, Table 21.3.

13. The Industrial Constitution Law (§ 77, Section 3) states that firm-level agreements between the employee council and the employer may not extend to topics that are, as a rule, decided by collective bargaining, unless the collective agreement contains a corresponding clause that explicitly permits such agreements. Not even in firms that do not belong to the employers' association may the employee council negotiate wages and working times. The negotiation would have to take place with the individual employee. The Collective Agreements Law (§ 4, Section 3) defines the so-called favorability principle, which states that an individual firm may only deviate from a

collective agreement when so doing is to the employee's advantage, which, as a rule, means higher wages or shorter working hours. The Collective Agreements Law (§ 5) says that the Federal Minister of Labor may, under certain conditions, declare a collective agreement as generally binding. It then applies even to firms that are not members of the employers' association.

14. Press release, labor court, city of Marburg, August 7, 1996.

15. Monopolkommission, Hauptgutachten 1992/1993; *Mehr Wettbewerb auf allen Märkten* (Nomos, 1994), p. 376.

16. It is essential that the Industrial Constitution Law clarifies in this case that deviations from a collective agreement are only allowed in the case of voluntary agreements on the firm level. In the case of a true co-determination right with binding firm-level agreements a conciliation board would have to be asked that might decide against the employer or against the employee council. Such a solution would be extremely complicated. In technical terms, the necessary legal adjustments could be achieved by completely deleting § 77, Section 3 of the Industrial Constitution Law. At the same time § 4, Section 3 of the Collective Agreements Law should be amended to allow firm-level agreements on wages and working conditions that deviate from the collective agreement. The right of the labor minister to declare an agreement collectively binding for firms that are not members of the employers' association (§ 5 Industrial Constitution Law) could be deleted.

17. See H.-W. Sinn, "Wieder 42 Stunden arbeiten," *Frankfurter Allgemeine Zeitung*, July 23, 2003; H.-W. Sinn, "Warum wir länger arbeiten müssen," *Welt am Sonntag*, November 14, 2004. English translations: "Working Longer" and "Why Extending Working Hours Will Create More Jobs," Ifo Viewpoints 47 (2003) and 59 (2004), available at www.cesifo.de. See also "Longer Working Hours—The Beginning of a New Trend?" in Report on the European Economy 2005 (Ifo Institute for Economic Research, 2005).

18. Unlike profit sharing, investment wages give access to profit income only after the accumulation of the corresponding ownership rights.

19. See Sachverständigenrat zur Begutachtung der gesamtwirtschaftlichen Entwicklung, Gleicher Rang für den Geldwert, Jahresgutachten 1972/73, section 501ff.; W. Krelle, J. Schunck, and J. Siebke, *Überbetriebliche Ertragsbeteiligung der Arbeitnehmer: mit einer Untersuchung über die Vermögensstruktur der Bundesrepublik Deutschland* (Mohr-Siebeck, 1968).

20. Deutsche Bundesbank, time-series database (http://www.bundesbank.de), May 11, 2006.

21. Thus, more than 500 firms that practice various forms of workers' capital participation and/or cooperation models have joined the study group "Partnership in Business." See http://www.agpev.de.

22. This confirms the results of Calmfors and Driffill, according to which semi-decentralized unions perform a more aggressive wage policy than either perfectly centralized and perfectly decentralized unions. See L. Calmfors and J. Driffill, "Bargaining Structure, Corporatism and Macroeconomic Performance," *Economic Policy* 6, 1988: 14–61.

23. See J. Agell and H. Bennmarker, Wage Policy and Endogenous Wage Rigidity: A Representative View from the Inside, CESifo Working Paper 751, 2002, p. 9. I thank Jan Herin, Chief Economist of the Swedish Employers' Association, for information.

Chapter 4

1. They also remain uninsured because of the phenomenon of adverse selection: If the insurer cannot differentiate his premia between good and bad risks for lack of information, but the insured know their risk type, the good risks will be hesitant to buy insurance or will not buy any. If there are many risk classes, the market may be left only with the very poor risks, although the good risks are interested in insurance protection and willing to pay premia that suffice to compensate the insurance companies for assuming their risks. Besides the already-mentioned late point in time for a contract, adverse selection is a second respectable reason for state insurance protection or at least compulsory insurance.

2. Moderne Dienstleistungen am Arbeitsmarkt. Vorschläge der Kommission zum Abbau der Arbeitslosigkeit und zur Umstrukturierung der Bundesanstalt für Arbeit, Kommissionsbericht unter dem Vorsitz von P. Hartz im Auftrag der deutschen Bundesregierung, Berlin, August 16, 2002.

3. In May 2003, 960,000 East Germans were receiving unemployment assistance, the second-tier unemployment benefit. That was neraly as many as in West Germany (1.07 million), although the West German population is four times as large. See http://www.pub.arbeitsamt.de.

4. There were 1,792 additional recipients below the age of 15.

5. Average monthly per capita expenditures for current support to the cost of living of recipients outside of institutions rose from 123 deutschmarks in 1970 to 485 deutschmarks (a factor of 3.94) in 2000. The average monthly net income of an employee rose from 892 deutschmarks to 2,687 deutschmarks (a factor of 3.01). See Statistisches Bundesamt, Fachserie K, Reihe 1 1970; Fachserie 13, Reihe 2, 2000; Fachserie 18, Reihe S. 21. These numbers sound small in absolute terms. Note, however, that average social assistance includes the supplementary payments to those working at low wages. In 2000, full social assistance for a West German family with two children was 2,907 deutschmarks ($1,373) per month, about 8% more than the average net wage income per employee, and amounted to about 76% of the net income per household (including child allowances) of an average fully employed West German married wage recipient with two children, which was about 3,829 deutschmarks ($1,808).

6. The number includes 303.000 asylum seekers who also received social assistance. See Statistisches Bundesamt, Fachserie 13, Reihe 2, Sozialhilfe 2000, pp. 130 and 134.

7. Unemployment Benefit II: 5.247 million. Other recipients of social assistance (Sozialgeld-Empänger): 1.876 million. See Bundesagentur für Arbeit, Der Arbeits- und Ausbildungsmarkt in Deutschland, Monatsbericht, May 2006, p. 5.

8. Sachverständigenrat zur Begutachtung der gesamtwirtschaftlichen Entwicklung, Jahresgutachten 2000/2001: Chancen auf einen höheren Wachstumspfad, Wiesbaden 2000, pp. 92–94.

9. This has also been observed by E. Prasad ("The Unbearable Stability of the German Wage Structure. Evidence and Interpretation," *IMF Staff Papers* 51, no. 2, 2004: 354–385). Prasad correctly attributes the stability of the wage distribution to institutional factors, in particular the unions. Arguably, however, the wage-replacement policy of the welfare state is the deeper reason, for it explains non-union as well as union wages.

10. See A. Reinberg and M. Hummel, Höhere Bildung schützt auch in der Krise vor Arbeitslosigkeit, IAB Kurzbericht no. 9, 2005.

11. According to the only data documented by the Federal Statistics Office, the share of the unskilled in the total labor force has increased from 15.7% in 1991 (or 15.8% in 1993, respectively) to 16.9% in 2002. Statistisches Bundesamt, "Ergebnisse des Mikrozensus," on request, August 2003.

12. See the section on "Immigration into Unemployment" in chapter 8.

13. Knowledge and Skills for Life, First Results from PISA 2000 (OECD, 2001); Summary of Central Findings, Program for International Student Assessment (Max-Planck-Institut für Bildungsforschung, 2001), p. 21.

14. L. Wößmann and M. West, "Class-Size Effects in School Systems around the World: Evidence from Between-Grade Variation in TIMSS," *European Economic Review* 50, no. 3, 2006: 695–736.

15. The calculations were done in discrete gross income steps of 50 euros.

16. However, there is also a successive reduction of the housing allowance between an income of 2,100 and an income of 2,550 euros. The marginal tax rate is more than 20 percentage points higher there than implied by taxes and social security contributions alone.

17. Exact presentations for alternative family types, also as of 2005, may be found in H.-W. Sinn, C. Holzner, W. Meister, W. Ochel, and M. Werding, *Redesigning the Welfare State: Germany's Current Agenda for an Activating Social Assistance* (Elgar, 2006).

18. First and Second Law for Modern Services in the Labor Market, BGB1, part I, no. 87, December 30, 2002, pp. 4607–4636.

19. See Bundesagentur für Arbeit, Arbeitsmarkt in Zahlen, Beschäftigung in Deutschland, Monatszahlen, March 2006, tables 1 and 28; Bundesagentur für Arbeit, Amtliche Nachrichten der Bundesagentur für Arbeit, January 2004, tables II/1 and II/9.

20. For a theoretical analysis of the crowding out effect in the presence of social replacement incomes, see H.-W. Sinn, "Migration and Social Replacement Incomes. How to Protect Low Income Workers in the Industrialized Countries against the Forces of Globalization and Market Integration," *International Tax and Public Finance* 12, 2005: 375–393.

21. For basic discussions along these lines, see the following: B. Haveman, *Starting Even* (Simon and Schuster, 1988); E. Phelps, "Economic Justice to the Working Poor through a Wage Subsidy," in *Aspects of Distribution of Wealth and Income*, ed. C. Papadimitriou (St. Martin's Press, 1994); E. Phelps, *Rewarding Work* (Harvard University Press, 1997); E. Phelps, "The Importance of Inclusion and the Power of Job Subsidies to Increase It," *OECD Economic Studies* 31, 2000: 85–113; R. Solow, *Work and Welfare* (Princeton University Press, 1988).

22. See Sinn et al., *Redesigning the Welfare State*, p. 142ff.

23. See H.-W. Sinn, C. Holzner, W. Meister, W. Ochel, and M. Werding, "Aktivierende Sozialhilfe—Ein Weg zu mehr Beschäftigung und Wachstum," *Ifo Schnelldienst* 55, no. 9, 2002; C. Holzner, W. Ochel, and M. Werding, Vom OFFENSIV-Gesetz zur "Aktivierenden Sozialhilfe, Ifo Research Report, 2003; Sinn et al., *Redesigning the Welfare State*. The Ifo model of Activating Social Assistance was published in May 2002 and has enjoyed recognition and attention ever since. The Scientific Council of the Ministry of Economics has adopted it, as has the German Council of Economic Experts. See Wissenschaftlicher Beirat beim Bundesministerium für Wirtschaft, Reform des Sozialstaats für mehr Beschäftigung im Bereich gering qualifizierter Arbeit, Report of June 29, 2002, Hamburg 2002; Sachverständigenrat, Jahresbericht 2002/03: Zwanzig Punkte für Beschäftigung und Wachstum, Wiesbaden 2002, esp. items 433–457. The states of Saxony, Bavaria, Schleswig-Holstein, and Hesse have argued for its implementation. The Hartz Commission had at least adopted the idea of loan employment in its August 2002 report. The Activating Social Assistance program had its biggest political success after its adoption, with minor modifications, by the state government of Hesse under the name of Hesse Model or Basic Livelihood Model and its introduction to the Bundesrat. The Ifo Institute had further specified its model in collaboration with the state chancellery of Hesse and helped prepare the proposal for a law. This proposal was accepted by a majority of the Bundesrat on September 26, 2003, and introduced to the mediation committee between Bundesrat and Bundestag in December 2003, where the Government wanted to have its Agenda 2010 accepted. The compromise found between the two chambers of parliament became law in 2005. For an alternative approach based on payments to firms rather than individuals see R. Schöb and J. Weimann, *Arbeit ist machbar* (Janos Stekovics, 2003).

24. See R. Blank, "Evaluating Welfare Reform in the United States," *Journal of Economic Literature* 40, 2002: 1105–1166.

25. See the overview of labor demand elasticity estimates available in the literature in note 45 to chapter 2.

26. This was determined in a cumbersome iterative calculation procedure that was a major factor in the design of the Activating Social Aid model. See Sinn et al., "Aktivierende Sozialhilfe."

27. See Sinn et al., *Redesigning the Welfare State*, p 167.

28. Horst Siebert is skeptical about the Activating Social Aid Program, because he finds it too voluminous relative to the small number of original recipients of social aid. However, he overlooks that the program saves money and that it will revitalize the whole labor market due to the reversal of the accordion effect: See H. Siebert, *Jenseits des Sozialen Marktes* (Deutsche Verlags-Anstalt 2005), chapter 4.

29. See Verband Deutscher Rentenversicherungsträger, Rentenversicherung in Zeitreihen, 2002, pp. 58–59 and 113.

30. Ibid., p. 51.

31. See Bundesagentur für Arbeit, Arbeitsmarkt in Zahlen. Aktuelle Daten, March 2002, table 6.1.1.

32. At present, unlimited additional earnings are only allowed after the regular retirement age of 65 is reached. Those who receive an old age pension before they reach this age may only earn 345 euros per month if they receive a full pension.

Chapter 5

1. See E. Streissler, "Deutschland, Deutschland über alles," *Wochenpresse* 14, April 1990: 48–53. See also G. Sinn and H.-W. Sinn, *Kaltstart* (Mohr-Siebeck, 1991), especially chapter V. (The English-language version of *Kaltstart*, titled *Jumpstart*, was published by The MIT Press in 1993.)

2. H.-W. Sinn, Schlingerkurs: Lohnpolitik und Investitionsförderung in den neuen Bundesländern," in *Die Wettbewerbsfähigkeit der ostdeutschen Wirtschaft*, ed. G. Gutmann (Duncker & Humblot, 1995).

3. Statistisches Bundesamt, Fachserie 14, Finanzen und Steuern, Reihe 6, Personal des öffentlichen Dienstes, pp. 114 and 120; Microcensus (wage and salary earners).

4. Ibid.

5. Concerning migration, see Institut für Arbeitsmarkt- und Berufsforschung, Daten zur kurzfristigen Entwicklung von Wirtschaft und Arbeitsmarkt, several issues; migration of persons of working age: Ifo Institute estimates. True migration is even somewhat higher than the figure cited, as the official statistics stopped differentiating between East Berlin and West Berlin in 2001.

6. See Statistisches Bundesamt, Fachserie 1, Gebiet und Bevölkerung, Reihe 1, and Fachserie 14, Finanzen und Steuern, Reihe 6, Personal des öffentlichen Dienstes; Working Group on National Income Accounting of the States; calculations and estimates of the Ifo Institute.

7. For this and the following statements on the Italian Mezzogiorno, see H.-W. Sinn and F. Westermann, "Two Mezzogiornos," *Rivista di diritto finanziario e scienza delle finanze* 60, 2001: 29–54.

8. Ibid., pp. 45ff.

9. The regions were not called "East Germany" at the time. "East Germany" referred to those areas that have been given to Poland and the USSR after the war—about one-third of German territory.

10. M. Kaser and E. Radice, eds., *The Economic History of Eastern Europe: 1919–1975*, volume 1 (Clarendon, 1985).

11. Arbeitskreis Volkswirtschaftliche Gesamtrechnungen der Länder, Länderergebnisse, Reihe 1, Band 1, May 2006, regional differentiation of Berlin, Ifo Institute estimates.

12. Ibid.

13. See Statistisches Bundesamt, Fachserie 1, Mikrozensus, Reihe 4.1.1, 2002; Istituto Nazionale di Statistica, Rapporto annuale sulla stuazione del paese, 2002; Statistisches Bundesamt, Fachserie 18, Volkswirtschaftliche Gesamtrechnungen, 2002. Unfortunately, the figures on the share of East German industry employment in total private-sector employment are ambiguous. Whereas a figure of 18% is derived on the basis of the national income accounts, the microcensus results presented in Fachserie 1, yield the higher figure of 20%.

14. See Arbeitskreis Volkswirtschaftliche Gesamtrechnungen der Länder, Länderergebnisse, Reihe 1, Band 1, May 2006.

15. See H.-U. Bach, S. Koch, E. Magvas, L. Pusse, T. Rothe, and E. Spitznagel, "Der Arbeitsmarkt in der Bundesrepublik Deutschland in den Jahren 2001 und 2002," *Mitteilungen aus der Arbeitsmarkt- und Berufsforschung*, no. 1, 2002, p. 36; "Der Arbeitsmarkt in der Bundesrepublik Deutschland in den Jahren 2003 und 2004," *Mitteilungen aus der Arbeitsmarkt- und Berufsforschung*, no. 1, 2003, p. 45.

16. Bundesagentur für Arbeit (http://www.pub.arbeitsamt.de), June 1, 2006; regional differentiation of Berlin: Ifo Institute estimates, and SVIMEZ Associazione per lo sviluppo dell'industria nel Mezzogiorno, Rapporto 2005 sull'economia del Mezzogiorno, chapter 8, table 5.

17. Bundesagentur für Arbeit, Arbeitsmarkt in Zahlen, Arbeitslosenquoten Monats/Jahreszahlen 2005.

18. Calculated by the Ifo Institute. West Germany including West Berlin and East Germany including East Berlin. Income includes wages, welfare transfers, income of the self-employed and

income on financial assets. See also W. Nierhaus, "Höhere Rentenanpassung in Ostdeutschland erforderlich?" *Ifo Schnelldienst* 52, no. 19, 1999: 20–24; W. Nierhaus, W. Meister, O.-E. Kuntze, and J.-E. Sturm, "Prognose 2002/2003: Chancen für einen neuen Aufschwung," *Ifo Schnelldienst* 55, no. 15, 2002: 19–44, here p. 38.

19. Eurostat, press release no. 10, January 30, 2003.

20. Bundesministerium für Arbeit und Soziales, Rentenversicherungsbericht 2005, February 2006, p. 106, http://www.bmas.bund.de, and Ifo Institute calculations.

21. Ibid., p. 58. For a fair comparison one should also include company pensions, the supplementary benefits of the public service, and other occupational benefits that are additionally received by about one-third of the retirees in the West. Furthermore, account must be taken of the fact that nearly 10% of the Western retirees receive civil service pensions that are higher than the average pension paid by the public pension insurance system. Adding all sources available in the West, then in 1999 East German public pensions were 92% in nominal terms and exactly 100% in real terms of average West German public and private pensions. Note, however, that in certain, smaller volume, today, 16 years after reunification, company pensions and supplementary benefits are also paid in East Germany in addition to the pensions of the public pension insurance fund so that in real terms East German pensions exceed West German pensions from all sources. While the size of this excess is not known, it can be stated with certainty that the pensions in the East no longer lag those in the West.

22. See K. Behring, "Infrastruktureller Nachholbedarf der neuen Bundesländer," *Ifo Schnelldienst* 54, no. 9, 2001: 21–29.

23. See "Cross-Border-Leasing" at http://de.wikipedia.org; T. Moerschen and A. Schrinner, "Steuersparmodelle werden für Kommunen zur Falle," *Handelsblatt* 32, February 15, 2005, p. 3.

24. See Statistisches Bundesamt, May 2006 (http://www.destatis.de) and Ifo Institute calculations.

25. According to research by Burda and Busch, 601.3 billion euros in public net transfers went to East Germany from 1991 to 1999, and according to figure 5.4 these transfers amounted to 97 billion euros in 2005. See M. Burda and U. Busch, "West-Ost-Transfers im Gefolge der deutschen Vereinigung," *Konjunkturpolitik* 47, no. 1, 2001: 1–38.

26. See Deutscher Bundestag, Sitzungsberichte, 11. Wahlperiode, 220. Sitzung, Bonn, November 22, 1990, p. 18900.

27. P. Clough, *Helmut Kohl. Ein Porträt der Macht* (dtv, 1998), p. 247.

28. Arbeitskreis Steuerschätzung, Lübbenau 2003.

29. Statistisches Bundesamt, http://www.destatis.de, May 31, 2006; regional differentiation of Berlin: Ifo Institute estimates.

30. See chapter 2 of Sinn and Sinn, *Jumpstart*.

31. R. Barro and X. Sala-i-Martin, *Economic Growth*, second edition (MIT Press, 2004).

32. See H.-W. Sinn and W. Ochel, "Social Union, Convergence and Migration," *Journal of Common Market Studies* 41, 2003: 869–896.

33. Statistisches Bundesamt, Fachserie 1, Bevölkerung, Reihe 1.2, Wanderungsstatistik, several issues.

34. Deutsche Bundesbank, Kapitalverflechtung mit dem Ausland, Statistische Sonderveröffentlichung 10, April 2006, and Deutsche Bundesbank database, June 2, 2006.

35. Concerning "green card" permits granted in the period of August 2000–December 2004, see Bundesagentur für Arbeit, on request; concerning unemployed IT specialists in January 2005, see Bundesagentur für Arbeit database, June 2, 2006.

36. Concerning sector employment, see Statistisches Bundesamt, Fachserie 4, Produzierendes Gewerbe, Reihe 4.1.1, Beschäftigung und Umsatz der Betriebe des Bergbaus und der Gewinnung von Steinen und Erden, 2005, table 1.1. The figure cited refers to production of office machines, computers, electrics with together 6.08 million employees.

37. Institut für Arbeitsmarkt- und Berufsforschung, Die Entwicklung der Flächentarifbindung 1995–2001: Ergebnisse aus dem Betriebspanel (http://www.iab.de).

38. H.-W. Sinn, "Volkswirtschaftliche Probleme der deutschen Vereinigung," Nordrhein-Westfälische Akademie der Wissenschaften, Vorträge no. 421, 1996, p. 15.

39. Press release no. 21, October 27, 2003.

40. See Gasunie, The History of Natural Gas in the Netherlands (http://www.gasunie.nl).

41. The notion stems from an article: "The Dutch Disease," *The Economist*, November 28, 1977: 82–83. For a first attempt to model the phenomenon theoretically, see W. Corden and J. Neary, "Booming Sector and De-Industrialisation in a Small Open Economy," *Economic Journal* 92, 1982: 825–848.

42. See htttp://www.pub.arbeitsamt.de.

43. A. Boss, Sozialhilfe, Lohnabstand und Mindestarbeitslosigkeit, Working Paper 1075, Institute for World Economics, Kiel, 2001, p. 15. See also table 8.2.

44. "According to Article 10, section 6 of the Treaty of May 18, 1990, possibilities are to be determined that, at a later point in time, give the savers a securitized share claim to the people's assets in exchange for the amount reduced by the 2:1conversion."—§ 25, Section 6, Reunification Treaty. The Treuhand has never tried to seriously execute this task of constitutional rank and has refused it by arguing that the poor sales revenue from the cash sale of East German firms showed that there was nothing to distribute. This argument is not appropriate, however, because a securitized claim can also be distributed if no shares are sold, and because one would have found investors interested in joint ventures if the securitized share claims had been combined with a wage moratorium until the end of the privatization activities.

45. Sinn and Sinn, *Jumpstart*.

46. See Statistisches Bundesamt, Fachserie 5, Bautätigkeit und Wohnungen, Heft 5, Eigentumsverhältnisse und Rückübertragungsansprüche, Wiesbaden, 1997.

47. Expertenkommission Wohnungspolitik, *Wohnungspolitik für die neuen Länder* (Mohr-Siebeck, 1995).

Chapter 6

1. T. Hobbes, *Leviathan* (London, 1651).

2. For scholarly discussions of this view of the state, and for a friendlier view, see J. Buchanan and R. Musgrave, *Public Finance and Public Choice—Two Contrasting Visions of the State* (MIT Press, 2000).

3. See "Jahresbericht 2006—Fakten und Zahlen zur maritimen Abhängigkeit der Bundesrepublik Deutschland" (available from www.marine.de), p. 2–17.

4. See C. Pauly, "Hollywood statt Babelsberg," *Der Spiegel*, no. 42, October 15, 2001: 144ff. Pauly writes: "More than 700 million DM are invested by people to support the domestic movie industry and to lower their own tax burden. Most of the money flowed to Hollywood. . . . Hardly ever have taxes been so misdirected. Thus, according to a report to the owners, the Film Fund no. 117 used funds of the German Treasury to finance among other things 93.18% of the movie *Eight Millimeters*, 87.49% of the movie *Crazy in Alabama*, and 32.18% of *Stuart Little*, the movie hit with the little mouse. The German movie industry hardly benefited from the funds at all."

5. This is true independent of how and whether the debt is repaid. Even if the repayment is always negative because a part of the interest payments on the existing debt is paid out of new borrowing, as is the case in Germany today, the present value of the remaining and now especially fast growing tax burden to service the remainder of the interest payments is identical to the original debt. Only if the interest burden is completely met by net borrowing, will there be no future tax burden and the calculation is no longer valid. In this case, however, because the interest burden of an economy exceeds its growth rate in the long run, the public debt grows faster than GDP. The result is national bankruptcy.

6. Statistisches Bundesamt, Fachserie 18, Volkswirtschaftliche Gesamtrechnungen, Reihe 1.4, Inlandsproduktsberechnung, detaillierte Jahresergebnisse 2005, February 2006.

7. The 2005 NDP for Sweden and Switzerland was estimated on the basis of the 2004 share of NDP in GDP.

8. A. Baring, "Bürger auf die Barrikaden! Deutschland auf dem Weg zu einer westlichen DDR," *Frankfurter Allgemeine Zeitung*, November 19, 2002.

9. OECD, Economic Outlook no. 79, Paris 2006 and OECD, National Accounts Statistics, volume I, Vol 2006 release 02, Paris 2006. The OECD figure refers to those 26 of the 30 OECD countries for which data were available. The data for Hungary, Poland, Mexico, and Turkey are missing in this average.

10. Not even all public expenditures of that time are included in the public-sector accounts. The funds that the Treuhand borrowed and used to subsidize East German business, were kept in an off-budget special account. Only the accumulated debt of the Treuhand, which amounted to 104 billion euros by the time it was wound up, was changed into official public debt in 1995 and has been included in the debt/GDP ratio since that date. (The local community debt of 14.9 billion euros was similarly transferred to the federal government this year.) If the debt-financed expenditures of the Treuhand are added to the public expenditures, then the government share of GDP is higher by one percentage point in the period from 1991 to 1995 than shown in the graph.

11. Spring forecast of EU Commission, 2006.

12. According to the website of the Federal Statistical Office (http://www.destatis.de, June 6, 2006), there were 2.224 million civil servants (in the narrower sense) in 2005, and total employment amounted to 36.566 million persons during the same year.

13. Data from Statistisches Bundesamt, Statistisches Jahrbuch 2005, pp. 640, 599 and passim.

14. This share is calculated as government employment over total dependent employment. The numbers are forecasts by the OECD (Economic Outlook no. 78, 2005).

15. The low number for Germany is due in part to the privatization of railroads, postal services, and telecommunications, which to some extent is not a real privatization as the government still holds substantial fractions of the shares, if not the majority. However, even if the reported figures are corrected for this effect, the German share of government employees increases only from 12% to 15% which still is low by international standards. Even in that case it would be lower than the (uncorrected) US share.

16. See Education at a Glance, OECD Indicators 2002 (OECD, 2002), p. 170.

17. Until recently this error was carried even into the OECD statistics on the government share of GDP, which was lower there than in the statistics of the German Federal Statistics Office. The OECD corrected its government share of GDP correspondingly, and it is likely to correct the welfare spending ratio soon.

18. See Bundesministerium für Gesundheit und Soziales, Sozialbericht 2005.

19. Ibid., p. 195.

20. Bundeswahlleiter, press release, January 30, 2002.

21. Figures on unemployment assistance and unemployment compensation for March 2003 are from the Federal Employment Office (http://www.pub.arbeitsamt.de); recipients of social assistance at the end of 2001 according to a press release of the Federal Statistical Office dated August 21, 2002 (http://www.destatis.de); retirees 2002: Verband Deutscher Rentenversicherungsträger, VDR Statistik, Rentenbestand 2002, table 13; accident insurance (2000) and housing allowance recipients (end 1999) from Bundesministerium für Gesundheit und Soziales, Sozialbericht 2001; pensioners 2001: http://www.destatis.de; BAföG recipients 2001: http://www.destatis.de.

22. See G. Tullock, "The Welfare Costs of Tariffs, Monopolies and Theft," *Western Economic Journal* 5, 1967: 224–232; G. Tullock, "Efficient Rent Seeking," in *Toward a Theory of the RentSeeking Society*, ed. J. Buchanan, R. Tollison, and G. Tullock (Texas A&M University Press, 1980).

23. See Tullock, "The Welfare Costs of Tariffs, Monopolies and Theft."

24. Neunzehnter Subventionsbericht der Bundesregierung, Berlin 2003, p. 27.

25. A. Boss and A. Rosenschon, "Subventionen in Deutschland: Quantifizierung und finanzpolitische Bewertung," Kieler Diskussionsbeiträge no. 392/393, Institute for World Economics, Kiel 2002.

26. See Agricultural Policies in OECD Countries—Monitoring and Evaluation 2005 (OECD, 2005), p. 34. For Japan the study reports a corresponding subsidy share of 56% and for Switzerland one of 68%, but for the US only one of 18%.

27. OECD, PSE/CSE Support Estimate Data Base 1986—2002, calculated by DG AGRI. In addition, author's calculations on the basis of: Association of South German Sugar Beet Producers, June 20, 2003; Food and Agricultural Organization of the United Nations (FAO), http://www.fao.org, March 2003 prices, June 20, 2003; EU Commission, Agricultural Markets no. 1/2003, March 2003 prices, http://europa.eu.

28. Because the calculations are extremely time consuming as the complicated details of each country's tax and social security laws must be regarded, it has not been possible to date for the Ifo Institute to analyze more than the countries covered here.

29. See F. Schneider, "Nur noch leicht sinkende Schattenwirtschaft in Deutschland im Gegensatz zu anderen OECD-Ländern im Jahr 2006: Fluch oder Segen?" (http://www.economics.uni-linz.ac.at, June 2006).

30. The calculations refer to the worker's value added, not to gross income. Gross income is a value lying between a worker's value added and the net income that he receives. This value lacks any economic meaning and is therefore not used in international comparisons. Calculations showing the total tax burden as a percentage of gross income would be incorrect as they would yield a smaller percentage burden for a country with a small employer share and a high employee share of taxes than for another country, even if the total burden of taxes and contributions, value added, and net income were identical.

31. *iwd* (newsletter of Institut der deutschen Wirtschaft) 29, no. 22, 2003.

32. At a rally in Berlin during the conflict of a collective bargaining agreement for the public sector employees, Frank Bsirske came out in favor of a reintroduction of the wealth tax and named several rich citizens who would be affected (ZDF: heute-journal, December 11, 2002; short video: http://www.zdf.de, June 23, 2003).

33. In the Scandinavian countries, the lower tax is also levied on the share of imputed interest in business profits. See the discussion of the dual income tax later in this chapter.

34. See P. Musgrave, *United States Taxation of Foreign Investment Income: Issues and Arguments* (Harvard University Press, 1969).

35. This is a topic of great significance in the context of the German tax reform of 2000. Strangely enough, this reform resulted in a huge tax relief on past investment, eliminating the corporate tax revenue quasi overnight. The corporate tax revenue declined from 24 billion euros in 2000 to −400 million euros in 2001. Profits retained and taxed since 1977, the last big German tax reform, ex post enjoyed the huge tax cut due to unforeseen implications of a new system of dividend taxation.

36. Although taxes on dividends are a burden on returns on investment, they do not reduce the incentive to re-invest retained earnings for the simple reason that they can be postponed by not paying out the dividends and investing them in the firm. The initial tax savings in the investment phase and the later taxation of the distributed returns just offset each other. For this reason, taxes on dividends belong to the most neutral taxes available to the tax system. Mere calculations of average tax burdens hide the fact that divident taxes impose no burden on marginal investment financed with retained earning. However, taxes on dividends also are distortionary insofar as they discriminate against new foundations and new issues of shares.

37. See Sachverständigenrat zur Begutachtung der gesamtwirtschaftlichen Lage, *Staatsfinanzen konsolidieren—Steuersystem reformieren, Jahresgutachten 2003/04* (Poeschel, 2003); "Reform der Einkommens- und Unternehmensbesteuerung durch die Duale Einkommensteuer," published April 3, 2006; H.-W. Sinn, *Ist Deutschland noch zu retten?* (Econ, 2003), pp. 323–329; D. Radulescu and M. Stimmelmayr, "Implementing a Dual Income Tax in Germany: Effects on Investment and Welfare," *Ifo working papers* 20, 2005; P. Sörensen, "Dual Income Taxation: Why and How?" *FinanzArchiv* 61, 2005: 559–568.

38. H.-W. Sinn, W. Leibfritz, and A. Weichenrieder, "Ifo Vorschlag zur Steuerreform," *Ifo Schnelldienst* 52, no. 18: 3–18.

39. As has already been mentioned in the text, this dual income tax was proposed in the first printing of the German edition of this book, published in early October of 2003. Shortly before that, it was proposed by the German Council of Economic Advisors. See *Staatsfinanzen konsolidieren—Steuersystem reformieren, Jahresgutachten 2003/2004* (Poeschel, 2003), pp. 333–360.

Chapter 7

1. United Nations Population Division, World Population Prospects: The 2004 Revision, middle projection.

2. Here and in the following, the nationalities normally include the foreigners living in the respective countries. It should become obvious from the context when, in contrast, the formal nationality is meant.

3. See chapter 8 for details.

4. Statistisches Bundesamt, Bevölkerung Deutschlands bis 2050, 10. koordinierte Bevölkerungsvorausberechnung, Wiesbaden, 2003. The projection of the population excluding immigrants is the author's own, based on variants 4 and 5 of the Statistical Office. The other numbers are cited from the report of the Statistical Office, always using the mid variant of immigration for the assumed life expectancy.

5. Federal Statistical Office, upon request.

6. The fertility rate of a given calendar year is defined as one-hundredth of the number of children 100 woman would bear from age 15 to age 49 if the frequency of births during their life cycle followed the exact pattern observable for women of various ages *in this calendar year*.

7. See World Bank, World Development Indicators Database, April 2004.

8. To be precise, Germany ranked third in terms of the fertility rate among the 16 OECD countries for which birth data were available for the mid nineteenth century. See A. Maddison, *Dynamic Forces in Capitalist Development: A Long-Run Comparative View* (Oxford University Press, 1991), p. 241.

9. An official survey conducted in 2000 showed the fifteen largest ancestries of the US population as follows: German 15.2%; Irish 10.8%, African American 8.8%, English 8.7%, American 7.2%, Mexican 6.5%, Italian 5.6%, Polish 3.2%, French 3.0%, American Indian 2.8%, Scottish 1.7%, Dutch 1.6%, Norwegian 1.6%, Scotch-Irish 1.5%, Swedish 1.4%, Austrian 0.3%, and Swiss 0.3%. See U.S. Census Bureau, Ancestry: 2000, June 2004, p. 3.

10. To understand why population growth implies a pyramid, think of women who in 1875 were 20 years old because they were born in 1855. Owing to the high population growth, there were about 200,000 fewer newborn baby girls in 1855 than in 1875. This implies that in 1875 the cohort of these 20-year-old women was about 200,000 smaller than the cohort of children born in 1875.

11. See Statistisches Bundesamt, Leben in Deutschland. Haushalte, Familien und Gesundheit –Ergebnisse des Mikrozensus 2005, Wiesbaden, 2006, pp. 9 and 74.

12. See F. Weinert, "Wissen und Denken—Über die unterschätzte Bedeutung des Gedächtnisses für das menschliche Denken," in *Jahrbuch der Bayerischen Akademie der Wissenschaften* (C. H. Beck, 1997), p. 98; J. Guilford, *The Nature of Human Intelligence* (McGraw-Hill, 1967); H. Lehmann, *Age and Achievement* (Princeton University Press, 1953).

13. See J. Brüderl, P. Preisendörfer, and R. Ziegler, *Der Erfolg neugegründeter Betriebe* (Duncker & Humblot, 1996).

14. German Patent Office, Munich, 2002.

15. H.-W. Sinn and S. Übelmesser, "Pensions and the Path to Gerontocracy in Germany," *European Journal of Political Economy* 19, 2002: 153–158.

16. Decisions of the Constitutional Court, ruling of February 28, 1980, volume 53, p. 257. See also the ruling of July 16, 1985, ibid., volume 69, p. 272ff. and p. 301.

17. Calculated according to a method proposed by H. Adrian in a mimeo titled Die demographische Entwicklung in Deutschland und Europa mit ihren katastrophalen Auswirkungen auf Wirtschaft und Gesellschaft. Vergleich Deutschland, Europe, Japan, USA, Welt, Problematik und Lösungswege (University of Mainz, 2003).

18. Statistisches Bundesamt, Bevölkerung Deutschlands bis 2050, variants 4 and 5, pp. 41–42.

19. The CESifo pension model was also used for the report of the Scientific Advisory Council at the Ministry of Economics ("Grundlegende Reform der gesetzlichen Rentenversicherung," Bonn, 1998), which laid the foundations for the pension reform under Walter Riester, the German Minister of Labor, which introduced subsidized private savings as a second pillar of the German pension system.

20. See M. Werding, "Kinderrente und Vorsorgepflicht," Ifo Schnelldienst 59, no. 7, 2006: 44–53.

21. The federal subsidy was raised in two steps. The April 1998 Gesetz zur Finanzierung eines zusätzlichen Bundeszuschusses zur gesetzlichen Rentenversicherung provided that the 1% increase in the VAT was to be used to fund the federal subsidy. Then, the Rentenkorrekturgesetz of December 1998 provided that the revenue of the "eco-tax" was also to be allocated to the federal subsidy.

22. The calculations are based on the most recent population projection of the Federal Statistical Office, based on the assumption of a medium rise in life expectancy and the "medium" assumption regarding annual net immigration of 200,000 persons.

23. R. Koll, Die Entwicklung der Staatsquote in Deutschland bis 2050, mimeo, Ifo Institute for Economic Research, 2001.

24. See M. Miegel, "Perspektiven der sozialen Sicherung: über die fehlende Nachhaltigkeit des Umlageverfahrens," in Freiheit und Fortschritt: die Suche nach einem gemeinsamen Nenner (Zurich Verlag, 2001); M. Miegel and S. Wahl, Solidarische Grundsicherung—private Vorsorge: der Weg aus der Rentenkrise (Olzog-Verlag, 1999).

25. United Nations Department of Economic and Social Affairs, Population Division, Replacement Migration: Is It a Solution to Declining and Aging Populations? (2001), p. 42.

26. Statistisches Bundesamt, Bevölkerung Deutschlands bis 2050.

27. Wissenschaftlicher Beirat beim Bundesministerium für Wirtschaft, Grundlegende Reformen der gesetzlichen Rentenversicherung, Report of February 21, 1998. See also H.-W. Sinn, "Die Krise der Gesetzlichen Rentenversicherung und Wege zu ihrer Lösung," in Jahrbuch der Bayerischen Akademie der Wissenschaften (C. H. Beck, 1999). At the request of the Economics Ministry, the Center for Economic Studies had seconded a staff member, Jakob von Weizsäcker, to integrate the CES results into the draft of the ministry.

28. G. Mackenroth, "Die Reform der Sozialpolitik durch einen deutschen Sozialplan," in Verhandlungen auf der Sondertagung des Vereins für Socialpolitik, ed. G. Albrecht (Duncker & Humblot, 1952).

29. See H.-W. Sinn, "A General Comment on the Old Age Pension Problem: A Funded System for Those Who Caused the Crisis" (Comment on M. Persson), in Redesigning Social Security, ed. H. Siebert (Mohr-Siebeck, 1998). For formal proofs of the various present-value equivalencies, see H.-W. Sinn, "Pension Reform and Demographic Crisis: Why a Funded System Is Needed and Why It Is Not Needed," International Tax and Public Finance 7, 2000: 389–410. For a repetition of these proofs and related literature, see A. Lindbeck and M. Persson, "The Gains from Pension Reform," Journal of Economic Literature 41, 2003: 74–112.

30. See H.-W. Sinn, "The Value of Children and Immigrants in a Pay-as-You-Go Pension System," Ifo Studien 47, no. 1, 2001: 77–94, here p. 91.

31. See H.-W. Sinn and M. Werding, "Zuwanderung nach der EU-Osterweiterung: Wo liegen die Probleme?" Ifo Schnelldienst 54, no. 8, 2001: 18–27.

32. A. Auerbach and P. Oreopoulos, "Analyzing the Fiscal Impact of U.S. Immigration," American Economic Review 89, Papers and Proceedings 1999: 176–180.

33. UN Department of Economic and Social Affairs, Population Division, Replacement Migration: Is It a Solution to Declining and Aging Populations? (scenario VI, p. 42).

34. Calculations by the author, based on those done by H. Adrian. (See figure 7.7.)

35. For a formal discussion of these two motives, see H.-W. Sinn, "The Pay-as-You-Go Pension System as a Fertility Insurance and Enforcement Device," *Journal of Public Economics* 88, 2004: 1335–1357.

36. I. Ehrlich and J.-G. Chong, "Social Security and the Real Economy: An Inquiry into Some Neglected Issues," *American Economic Review* 88, 1998: 151–157; I. Ehrlich and J. Kim, Social Security, Demographic Trends, and Economic Growth: Theory and Evidence from the International Experience, working paper, SUNY Buffalo, 2001.

37. See A. Cigno and F. Rosati, "Jointly Determined Saving and Fertility Behaviour: Theory, and Estimates for Germany, Italy, UK and USA," *European Economic Review* 40, 1996: 1561–1589. See also A. Cigno and F. Rosati, "Rise and Fall of the Japanese Saving Rate: The Role of Social Security and Intra-Family Transfers," *Japan and the World Economy* 9, 1997: 81–92.

38. See A. Cigno, L. Casolaro, and F. Rosati, "The Impact of Social Security on Saving and Fertility in Germany," *Finanzarchiv* 59, 2003: 189–211.

39. See W. Schreiber, "Zur Reform der gesetzlichen Rentenversicherung," *Zeitschrift für Sozialreform* 1956: 2–4; O. von Nell-Breuning, *Soziale Sicherheit? Zu Grundfragen der Sozialordnung aus christlicher Verantwortung* (Herder, 1979), pp. 59, 60, 84, and 87.

40. The assumptions were: Start of employment subject to social security contributions at age 20; growth of annual wages during the working life according to an average wage profile derived from micro data; average probability of disability from age 54, definitive retirement at age 65; average wage income of all insured rises by 1.5% p.a. in real terms; the real bond rate is 4%; and the contribution rate to social security amounts to 20%. See Sinn, "The Value of Children and Immigrants," pp. 77–94. The figure for 2003 was derived from the rate of increase of gross wages and salaries per employee.

41. See M. Werding and H. Hofmann, Die fiskalische Bilanz eines Kindes im deutschen Steuer- und Sozialsystem, Ifo Institute, 2005, p. 55; K. Biedenkopf, H. Bertram, M. Käßmann, P. Kirchhof, E. Niejahr, H.-W. Sinn, and F. Willekens, Starke Familie. Bericht der Kommission "Familie und demographischer Wandel," Robert Bosch Foundation, 2005, p. 94.

42. Werding and Hofmann, Die fiskalische Bilanz, pp. 84–86; Biedenkopf et al., Starke Familie, p. 100f.

43. Germany: Federal Statistical Office, on request. France: INSEE, press release no. 882, January 2003, p. 2f.

44. See Maddison, *Dynamic Forces in Capitalist Development*, p. 226ff.

45. See H.-W. Sinn, "Das demographische Defizit," *Ifo Schnelldienst* 56, no. 5, 2003: 20–36.

46. Ibid.

47. Carl Schurz (1829–1906) was arrested during Germany's 1848 revolution, was able to flee, emigrated to America with his wife Margarethe (née Meyer), was an advisor to Abraham Lincoln, and served as a general in the Civil War. He had many functions in the new American government. Among other things, he was secretary of the interior under President Rutherford B. Hayes, a function in which he could influence the spread of kindergartens that his wife had founded in Watertown, Wisconsin in 1856. The kindergarten in Watertown, which taught in German, existed until World War I.

48. In 1999, average hourly wages of women reached 81% of men's wages in Germany and 88% in France. See Eurostat press release no. 27, March 5, 2003, p. 3.

49. See K. Vogel, "Berücksichtigung von Unterhaltspflichten im Einkommensteuerrecht," *Deutsches Steuerrecht* 1977: 31ff., esp. 41.

50. See H. Birg, "Strategische Optionen der Familien- und Migrationspolitik in Deutschland und Europa," in *Demographie und Wohlstand*, ed. C. Leipert (Leske und Budrich, 2003).

51. See W. Meister and W. Ochel, "Steuerliche Förderung von Familien im internationalen Vergleich," *Ifo Schnelldienst* 56, no. 5, 2003: 65–67.

52. See also E.-J. Borchert, *Die Berücksichtigung familiärer Kindererziehung im Recht der gesetzlichen Rentenversicherung* (Duncker & Humblot, 1981); E.-J. Borchert, *Innenweltzerstörung. Sozialreform in die Katastrophe* (S. Fischer, 1989); J. Resch and W. Knipping, "Die Auswirkungen des in der Bundesrepublik Deutschland bestehenden gesetzlichen Alterssicherungssystems auf die

wirtschaftliche Situation der Familie," *Jahrbuch für Sozialwissenschaft* 33, 1982, pp. 92–122; H. Schmidt, U. Frank, and I. Müller-Rohr, "Kritische Bemerkungen zum System des Kinderlastenausgleichs—zugleich ein Vorschlag zur Neugestaltung der gesetzlichen Rentenversicherung," *FinanzArchiv* N.F. 43, 1985: 28–66; R. Dinkel, *Die Auswirkungen eines Geburten- und Bevölkerungsrückgangs auf Entwicklung und Ausgestaltung von gesetzlicher Alterssicherung und Familienlastenausgleich* (Duncker & Humblot, 1984); M. Werding, *Zur Rekonstruktion des Generationenvertrages. Ökonomische Zusammenhänge zwischen Kindererziehung, sozialer Alterssicherung und Familienlastenausgleich* (Mohr-Siebeck, 1998).

53. An objection to the scaling of pay-as-you-go pensions to the number of children refers to the circumstance that some of the children do not become contributors to the statutory pension insurance system, but as civil servants, self-employed or non-working pay no contributions. It is considered unfair that those whose children do not contribute to the pension system still receive a higher pay-as-you-go pension. (See F. Ruland, "Volle Rente für Kinderlose," *Financial Times Deutschland*, January 20, 2003.) This problem is of limited quantitative importance, though. Given today's conditions, a newborn will become a contributor to pension insurance with a probability of two-thirds. One could therefore also justify a system in which two-thirds of the claims to pay-as-you-go pensions are made conditional on the existence of children and only one-third is made available as a base for all, including the childless. In similar form, this was also ascertained by the Federal Constitutional Court in its so-called mother-pension opinion of July 7, 1992. The argument that the size of the pension cannot be made to depend on the number of pensioners' children, because some of the children do not become contributors, was pushed aside as trivial. See BVerfGE 87, 37. In a sentence dated April 3, 2001 (1 BvR 1629/94) the Supreme Court declared equal contribution rates for people with and without children for the new nursery insurance unconstitutional.

54. Considerations arise to align the pension claims to the "quality" of the human capital investment, for example to the income and the contributions of one's own children, in order to give incentives in this way for a good education of one's own children. Such a differentiation of the proposal would, however, mean a probable overloading. It could be objected to by the argument that the differences in the incomes of the children due to the parents' efforts are minimal in a state with a public school system. These differences are likely to result primarily from inherited differences in intelligence or capability. Insurance of the parents against such differences seems appropriate.

Chapter 8

1. Institut der deutschen Wirtschaft, Deutschland in Zahlen 2003, p. 72.

2. The comparison is based on current exchange rates and not on purchasing-power parities, because for competitiveness it is the actual labor costs that are important. An entrepreneur who is thinking about producing his products in the Czech Republic instead of Germany is not interested in the question of what the Czechs can buy for their wages. Purchasing-power parities are relevant for migration processes to the extent that the immigrants spend their money in the host country rather than in the home country. Wage differences in terms of purchasing-power parities are always smaller than differences at current exchange rates, because a country with low wages also has low prices for local services. This effect tends to reduce the differences in real terms, but does not change, as a rule, the ranking.

3. See Sinn and W. Ochel, "Social Union, Convergence and Migration." Sigma convergence is the reduction in the standard deviation of wages or per capita incomes.

4. Barro and Sala-i-Martin, *Economic Growth*.

5. See Statistisches Bundesamt, Leben in Deutschland. Haushalte, Familien und Gesundheit–Ergebnisse des Mikrozensus 2005, 2006, pp. 9 and 74. Subdivided by nationality and country of birth, persons with migration background consist of foreigners (first-generation immigrants and second- and third-generation immigrants born in Germany) and Germans with migration background (e.g., ethnic Germans from the former Soviet Union, naturalized immigrants, and non-immigrants with migration background, including naturalized non-immigrants, children of immi-

grated ethnic Germans, children of immigrated or German-born naturalized foreign parents, children of foreign parents who, in addition, received German citizenship by birth (*ius soli*), and children with unilateral migration background, only one parent of whom is an immigrant or a German-born naturalized citizen).

6. At the time of German unification, there were about 2 million ethnic Germans in the Soviet Union and about 230,000 in Transylvania (Romania). The ethnic Germans in the Soviet Union are the descendants of the inhabitants of the German Wolga Republic, dissolved by Stalin in 1941, who had been brought there by Catherine the Great in the 1760s. The Germans in Transylvania had emigrated from Austria and Germany (Siebenbürger Sachsen) in the period 1141–1161 and later in the eighteenth century (Banater Schwaben).

7. For hourly wages in Germany, Spain, and Portugal in 1985, see Statistisches Bundesamt, Statistisches Jahrbuch für das Ausland 2001, p. 141; Ifo Institute calculations. See also H.-W. Sinn, "EU Enlargement and the Future of the Welfare State," *Scottish Journal of Political Economy* 49, 2002: 104–115, here p. 107.

8. Average gross monthly earnings in manufacturing in 2003: 2001 gross monthly earnings in the accession countries from table 13.2 in the Statistisches Jahrbuch für das Ausland were extended to 2003 with the help of the data on monthly earnings in manufacturing in the ILO database. The gross monthly earnings of the accession countries are weighted by the number of inhabitants. Conversion into euros was done with the average annual euro reference rates of the European Central Bank. West Germany: Statistisches Bundesamt, Fachserie 16, Reihe 2.3, 2003.

9. See H.-W. Sinn, G. Flaig, M. Werding, S. Munz, N. Düll, and H. Hofmann, "EU Enlargement and Labour Mobility: Consequences for Labour Markets and Redistribution by the State in Germany," CESifo Research Report no. 2, 2003.

10. Handwerkskammer für München und Oberbayern, June 9, 2006. In upper Bavaria the number of tile setters increased from 708 in 2003 to 2324 in 2005. All data refer to the end of the year.

11. Sinn et al., "EU Enlargement and Labour Mobility." See also T. Boeri et al., The Impact of Eastern Enlargement on Employment and Labour Market in the EU Member States, Final Report, European Integration Consortium, Berlin, 2002; H.-W. Sinn and M. Werding, "Zuwanderung nach der EU Osterweiterung: Wo liegen die Probleme?" *Ifo Schnelldienst* 54, no. 8, 2001: 18–27; K. Bade, Legal and Illegal Immigration into Europe: Experiences and Challenges, Netherlands Institute for Advanced Studies in the Humanities and Social Sciences, Wassenaar, 2003.

12. See Trends in International Migration SOPEMI (OECD, 2000), p. 66.

13. See p. 45 of EU Enlargement. Achievements and Challenges (EU Commission, 2003): "According to expert calculations, potential migration will tend to be small."

14. US population: Economic Report of the President 2003. US migration: US Bureau of the Census, Annual Geographical Mobility Rates by Type of Movement, 1947–2001. Unemployment in Israel: Bank of Israel, Annual Report 1999, Statistical Appendix. Israeli population: Central Bureau of Statistics Israel, Selected Data, Population.

15. See Bundesagentur für Arbeit, Der Arbeits- und Ausbildungsstellenmarkt in Deutschland, December 2004.

16. See H.-W. Sinn, "Migration and Social Replacement Incomes. How to Protect Low Income Workers in the Industrialized Countries against the Forces of Globalization and Market Integration," *International Tax and Public Finance* 12, 2005: 375–393.

17. For the metaphor of a welfare magnet, see G. Borjas, "The Welfare Magnet," *National Review*, March 11, 1996: 48–50. For an introduction to the theory of welfare migration and further references to the literature, see chapter 3 of H.-W. Sinn, *The New Systems Competition* (Blackwell, 2003).

18. The last migrant is a person for whom the migration cost net of the wage increase from replacing the wage of his home country with the wage of the host country just equals the gift he receives from the state. As the migration cost net of the wage increase, which reflects an increase in the joint GDP, equals the welfare loss that results from the migration of an extra migrant, the gift from the state equals this welfare loss in a migration equilibrium. If there were a little less migration, the taxpayer would be better off, while the migrants would not be harmed.

19. To be more precise, the "marginal congestion costs" of using impure public goods should be included. Assuming that the local communities and provinces that provide these goods are of optimal size (long-run minimum average cost), one can show, using a theorem of Mohring and Harwitz, that the marginal congestion cost equals the average fiscal cost of providing the goods. See H. Mohring and M. Harwitz, *Highway Benefits. An Analytical Framework* (Northwestern University Press, 1962).

20. See Sinn, "The Value of Children"; H.-W. Sinn, "EU Enlargement, Migration and the New Constitution," *CESifo Economic Studies* 50, 2004: 685–707; A. Razin and E. Sadka, "Net Fiscal Burden as a Measure of Migration's Economic Impact on the Welfare of the Native-Born Population," *CESifo Economic Studies* 50, 2004: 709–716.

21. See the section on Activating Social Assistance in chapter 4.

22. According to a poll conducted by the market research institute Forsa for the German news magazine *Stern* (May 10, 2006), Germans continue to support the project for a European constitution in principle. Of those polled, 61% were of the opinion that the EU needed a unitary constitution.

23. R. Kanitz and P. Steinberg, "Grenzenloses Gemeinschaftsrecht? Die Rechtsprechung des EuGH zu Grundfreiheiten, Unionsbürgerschaft und Grundrechten als Kompetenzproblem," *Europarecht* 6, 2003: 1013–1036. See also S. Damm, "Bürgergleichheit in Europa—Zur wechselbezüglichen Entwicklung von Unionsbürgerschaft und europarechtlichem Gleichheitsschutz," in *Europa der Bürger? Nach der Euro-Einführung und vor der EU-Erweiterung—Zwischenbilanz und Perspektiven,* ed. R. Scholz (Hanns Martin Schleyer-Stiftung, 2002).

24. See in particular article 39 of the EU Treaty, articles 10–12 of Regulation (EEC), no. 1612/68, and articles 43 and 49 of the EU Treaty.

25. European Court of Justice, Rec. 1998, p. I-07637, Case C-274/96, esp. Rz. 14ff.

26. See the Directive of the European Parliament and the Council regarding the right of EU citizens and their families to move and reside freely in the territory of the Member States, passed by the European Parliament on March 10, 2004: Directive 2004/38/EG of April 29, 2004 (Official Journal L158, p. 77ff.).

27. There is a legal ambiguity hereto the definition of resources. On the one hand, the directive specifies that subsistence may not be a fixed amount but must be determined according to the individual's circumstances (article 8.4). It says that no person seeking entry may be discriminated against on the basis of insufficient assets (preamble 31). German communities normally do not control whether these requirements are met but satisfy themselves with mere declarations of the immigrants.

28. The purchasing-power parities considered here are from http://www.oecd.org (June 8, 2006).

29. Pensions at a Glance (OECD, 2005), p. 163.

30. See Sinn, *The New Systems Competition*, and references cited therein.

31. See M. Thum, EU Enlargement, Fiscal Competition and Network Migration, working paper, TU Dresden, 2000.

32. See Wissenschaftlicher Beirat beim Bundesministerium der Finanzen, Freizügigkeit und soziale Sicherung in Europa, report 2001 (http://www.bundesfinanzministerium.de); Sinn et al., "EU Enlargement and Labour Mobility."

Chapter 9

1. Presidency Conclusions, Lisbon European Council, March 23 and 24, 2000, p. 2.

2. Sources: http://www.imf.org, http://devdata.worldbank.org, http://epp.eurostat.ec.europa.eu, Ifo Institute calculations.

Index